Information Access and Library User Needs in Developing Countries

Mohammed Nasser Al-Suqri
Sultan Qaboos University, Oman

Linda L. Lillard
Clarion University, USA

Naifa Eid Al-Saleem
Sultan Qaboos University, Oman

A volume in the Advances in Library and
Information Science (ALIS) Book Series

An Imprint of IGI Global

Managing Director:	Lindsay Johnston
Editorial Director:	Joel Gamon
Production Manager:	Jennifer Yoder
Publishing Systems Analyst:	Adrienne Freeland
Development Editor:	Myla Merkel
Acquisitions Editor:	Kayla Wolfe
Typesetter:	Erin O'Dea
Cover Design:	Jason Mull

Published in the United States of America by
Information Science Reference (an imprint of IGI Global)
701 E. Chocolate Avenue
Hershey PA 17033
Tel: 717-533-8845
Fax: 717-533-8661
E-mail: cust@igi-global.com
Web site: http://www.igi-global.com

Library of Congress Cataloging-in-Publication Data

Information access and library user needs in developing countries / Mohammed Nasser Al-Suqri, Linda L. Lillard, and Naifa Eid Al-Saleem, editors.
     pages cm
  Includes bibliographical references and index.
  Summary: "This book highlights the struggles that developing countries face in terms of information gaps and information-seeking user behavior, providing ways in which users in developing countries can benefit from properly implementing LIS services"--Provided by publisher.
  ISBN 978-1-4666-4353-6 (hardcover) -- ISBN 978-1-4666-4354-3 (ebook) -- ISBN 978-1-4666-4355-0 (print & perpetual access) 1. Library science--Developing countries. 2. Information science--Developing countries. 3. Information behavior--Developing countries. 4. Information services--Developing countries. 5. Electronic information resources--Developing countries. 6. Digital divide--Developing countries. 7. Libraries--Developing countries. 8. Library education--Developing countries. I. Al-Suqri, Mohammed Nasser, 1973- II. Lillard, Linda L., 1951- III. Al-Saleem, Naifa Eid, 1971-
  Z665.2.D44I54 2014
  020.9172'4--dc23
                                                2013011320

This book is published in the IGI Global book series Advances in Library and Information Science (ISSN: 2326-4136; eISSN: 2326-4144)

British Cataloguing in Publication Data
A Cataloguing in Publication record for this book is available from the British Library.

All work contributed to this book is new, previously-unpublished material. The views expressed in this book are those of the authors, but not necessarily of the publisher.

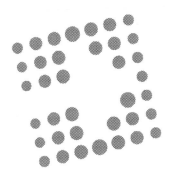

Advances in Library and Information Science (ALIS) Book Series

ISSN: 2326-4136
EISSN: 2326-4144

MISSION

The **Advances in Library and Information Science (ALIS) Book Series** is comprised of high quality, research-oriented publications on the continuing developments and trends affecting the public, school, and academic fields, as well as specialized libraries and librarians globally. These discussions on professional and organizational considerations in library and information resource development and management assist in showcasing the latest methodologies and tools in the field.

The **ALIS Book Series** aims to expand the body of library science literature by covering a wide range of topics affecting the profession and field at large. The series also seeks to provide readers with an essential resource for uncovering the latest research in library and information science management, development, and technologies.

COVERAGE

- Academic libraries in the digital age
- Blogging in libraries
- Cataloging and classification
- Collection development
- Community outreach
- Digital literacy
- Ethical practices in libraries
- Green libraries
- Librarian education
- Mobile library services
- Remote access technologies
- University libraries in developing countries

IGI Global is currently accepting manuscripts for publication within this series. To submit a proposal for a volume in this series, please contact our Acquisition Editors at Acquisitions@igi-global.com or visit: http://www.igi-global.com/publish/.

Titles in this Series

For a list of additional titles in this series, please visit: www.igi-global.com

Information Access and Library User Needs in Developing Countries
Mohammed Nasser AI-Suqri (Sultan Qaboos University, Oman) Linda L. Lillard (Clarion University, USA) and
Naifa Eid AI-Saleem (Sultan Qaboos University, Oman)
Information Science Reference • copyright 2014 • 358pp • H/C (ISBN: 9781466643536) • US $175.00 (our price)

Advancing Library Education Technological Innovation and Instructional Design
Ari Sigal (Catawba Valley Community College, USA)
Information Science Reference • copyright 2013 • 339pp • H/C (ISBN: 9781466636880) • US $175.00 (our price)

Library Reference Services and Information Literacy Models for Academic Institutions
Rosanne M. Cordell (Northern Illinois University, USA)
Information Science Reference • copyright 2013 • 355pp • H/C (ISBN: 9781466642416) • US $175.00 (our price)

Challenges of Academic Library Management in Developing Countries
S. Thanuskodi (Annamalai University, India)
Information Science Reference • copyright 2013 • 348pp • H/C (ISBN: 9781466640702) • US $175.00 (our price)

Robots in Academic Libraries Advancements in Library Automation
Edward Iglesias (Central Connecticut State University, USA)
Information Science Reference • copyright 2013 • 260pp • H/C (ISBN: 9781466639386) • US $175.00 (our price)

Recent Developments in the Design, Construction, and Evaluation of Digital Libraries Case Studies
Colleen Cool (Graduate School of Library and Information Studies, Queens College, USA) and Kwong Bor Ng
(Queens College, CUNY, USA)
Information Science Reference • copyright 2013 • 275pp • H/C (ISBN: 9781466629912) • US $175.00 (our price)

Design, Development, and Management of Resources for Digital Library Services
Tariq Ashraf (University of Delhi, India) and Puja Anand Gulati (University of Delhi, India)
Information Science Reference • copyright 2013 • 438pp • H/C (ISBN: 9781466625006) • US $175.00 (our price)

Public Law Librarianship Objectives, Challenges, and Solutions
Laurie Selwyn (Law Librarian [Ret.], USA) and Virginia Eldridge (Grayson County, Texas Law Library, USA)
Information Science Reference • copyright 2013 • 341pp • H/C (ISBN: 9781466621848) • US $175.00 (our price)

IGI GLOBAL
DISSEMINATOR of KNOWLEDGE

www.igi-global.com

701 E. Chocolate Ave., Hershey, PA 17033
Order online at www.igi-global.com or call 717-533-8845 x100
To place a standing order for titles released in this series, contact: cust@igi-global.com
Mon-Fri 8:00 am - 5:00 pm (est) or fax 24 hours a day 717-533-8661

Editorial Advisory Board

Table of Contents

Detailed Table of Contents

Chapter 1

This chapter examines the changing nature of the information environment and its implications for Library and Information Science (LIS), with a focus on developing countries in general and the Arab Gulf states in particular. Drawing on key findings from previous LIS literature, it explores what is needed to ensure the future viability of the profession in the GCC region so that it can help underpin social and economic development in these states. Examples of successful practice in LIS innovation from other parts of the developing world are included to demonstrate some possible approaches and the chapter concludes by summarizing some key points for consideration by LIS education specialists, library managers, and policymakers in the Gulf States.

Chapter 2

In both developed and developing countries culture, tradition and technology are key issues that affect the dialogue relating to how the three elements can be integrated in socio-economic development programs. This chapter examines the extent to culture and technology has an influence in the integration of technology in socio-economic development in Africa. It also inquires about the extent to which technology influences culture and traditions in developed countries. Furthermore, it scrutinizes the degree to which culture and traditions are receptive to the integration of technology within the socio-economic fabric of the society. The chapter concludes that school libraries should develop a curriculum that is relevant to the information needs of the community, especially those in rural areas. It is imperative to engage communities in developing programs that help to elevate communities without compromising on fundamental and internationally recognized standards. If local conditions are taken into cognizance programs to integrate culture, tradition and technology will be successful.

The chapter tries to highlight the influence of social networking and library 2.0 in providing access to information and knowledge sharing in Africa. It further discusses the panorama at which the information environment is changing from traditional to electronic, where access to information and knowledge stands to benefit all. The chapter, however, exhibits that in most developing worlds today the electronic information environment is gradually spreading and obviously will take time to be fully integrated into the systems, especially in Africa. The chapter provides a highlight on the value, usefulness, access to information, and knowledge sharing, which has become a necessary component for human existence and development. The premise is that librarians' role is to facilitate this effective management and promote access to information and knowledge sharing through the influence of social networking and library 2.0; this in turn will strengthen and empower the African people to be among global players in the knowledge-based economy. The emergence of Web 2.0 principles and technologies that has given rise to social networking and library 2.0 offer libraries and information centers many opportunities for sharing information and knowledge among people regardless of distance or geographical areas. This reaches out beyond the walls of the library and Websites of any library or institutions. These developments make it possible for people to share knowledge and information online, borrow locally, and buy or sell on a global scale as appropriate to their needs and circumstances.

Chapter 4

There has been an enormous increase for information written in different languages by users from various backgrounds and disciplines. This chapter proposes a research design to examine multilingual information users' information behaviors when using a Cross Language Information Retrieval (CLIR) system. Development of a true CLIR is absolutely necessary so that the system would allow users to access information written in the user's languages of choice. Kuhlthau's Information Search Process (ISP) model was borrowed as a theoretical framework. Of particular concern are those users who want information represented by a language different than the users' original query or for those users who would like to retrieve additional information written in a second and/or third language or in a language which cannot be understood by them. This research is expected to yield a revised or new ISP model applicable to CLIR environments. It is expected that this study will also increase our understanding of CLIR users. The expected CLIR users include many of non-English speakers, especially users in developing countries who need this kind of CLIR system due to lack of materials in their own language. It is possible that the results of this research could inform CLIR system designers. The chapter is composed of purpose of study, literature review, theory, research questions, methodology, and discussion section. In the literature review section, pertinent research studies from information seeking behavior, cross language information retrieval, and general relevance studies are presented. Kuhlthau's ISP model is introduced in detail in the theory section. A possible application of Kuhlthau's ISP Model to the CLIR environment is presented in a table format. Research questions are developed from the literature reviews and Kuhlthau's model. Each research question, premises/assumptions, and its correspondent methodology are proposed in the methodology section. Limitations are discussed in the discussion section.

Most current models of information seeking behavior (ISB) do not explicitly address the effects of the environmental context on ISB. Wilson (1996) identified several intervening variables, but these have not been systematically considered. This chapter explores the use of the Katz, Levin and Hamilton (1963) model of diffusion of innovations to provide a framework for examining the various elements of an environmental context. In particular, this model provides the means to account for the cultural, social, communicative, and actor components of ISB. The model is described and its use as a supplementing analytic framework in ISB is examined, paying particular attention to its use in research in developing nations.

Chapter 6

This chapter explores the relationship between the Ellis Model of Information Seeking Behavior and the scientific community of Venezuela. The research employs a qualitative method to investigate the main information seeking activities of a scientific community in the periphery in the context of dependency theory. The following elements of the Ellis model are supported by the data gathered and analysis: starting, browsing, chaining, filtering, extracting, and information management.

This chapter focuses on multidisciplinary research about needs and the behavior of real and potential information users. The research is carried out in a university context to address social issues as well as to find solutions appropriate to the Uruguayan context, which is rather different from the one in developed countries. The chapter focuses on the discussion of the research results, on the developed electronic information resources, and on the impact on the target population and social mediators. The chapter also focuses on the multidisciplinary work experience, which carries out the research group through meetings and workshops with social actors and decision makers on social policies. This research constitutes a step forward in the development of information and communication sciences as well as to improve the information domain in Uruguay.

In today's knowledge and technology driven society, most scholarly information is increasingly being produced and distributed in digital formats. Yet, in Sub-Saharan Africa, academic libraries have been very slow at joining this digital movement, and hence stand the risk of losing their relevance, particularly with regard to locally generated intellectual material. To better serve the knowledge and information seeking needs of their patrons, librarians need to reinvent services. The challenges are discussed as well as prescriptions of workable strategies that librarians, information scientists, and other stakeholders can adopt to overcome these barriers. Such strategies mostly involve appropriately leveraging the existing Information and Communication Technology (ICT) tools and resources to make library resources more accessible. Consequently, digitizing indigenous intellectual resources may keep libraries from perishing and respond to user needs and information seeking habits in Sub-Saharan Africa.

"Entrepreneurial spirit has been described as the most important economic development stimulus in recent decades" (Chalhoub, 2011, p. 67). In the early 1990s it was estimated that small to medium sized enterprises SMEs employed 22% of the adult population in developing countries and the role of SMEs is viewed as increasingly important in developing countries because of their capacity to create jobs (Okello-Obura, Minishi-Majanja, Cleote, & Ikoja-Odongo, 2007, p. 369). According to Lingelback, de la Viña and Asel (2005), even though entrepreneurship has been linked to wealth and poverty in developing countries and has played an important role in growth and poverty alleviation, it is the least studied significant economic and social phenomenon in the world today. Examining how the information needs and information seeking behavior of entrepreneurs from developing countries may differ from entrepreneurs in developed countries is important as it has been suggested that "entrepreneurship in developing countries is distinctive from that practice in developed countries and that understanding these distinctions is critical to private sector development in developing countries" (Lingelback, de la Vina, & Asel, 2005, p. 2). A review of the studies produced thus serves as a beginning for designing information packages and information services that can benefit a global population. Consequently, this chapter targets the information needs and information seeking behavior of entrepreneurs revealed in studies associated with SMEs in both developed and developing countries and offers conclusions and recommendations for meeting the information needs of this population.

Developing countries must overcome the obstacles to information access so that they can join the global networks of the developed world and become part of the "information age." Studies on the information-seeking behavior and information needs of library users in developing countries are limited. This chapter examines the information-seeking behavior of social science faculty in developing nations in an attempt to explain the barriers to information access for these specialized scholars. Information users in developing countries face different challenges than users in developed nations so it is essential to understand the various obstacles that must be overcome by library and information users in developing nations. Comparisons are made to the information-seeking behaviors and information use of social science faculty in developed nations. Patterns of information-seeking behavior in social science faculty are examined and also compared to existing and proposed models of such behavior.

Thomas Scheiding, Cardinal Stritch University, USA
Borchuluun Yadamsuren, University of Missouri, USA
Gantulga Lkhagva, Mongolian Libraries Consortium, Mongolia

In developing countries, one of the many challenges faced by researchers is increased pressure to conduct research, but inadequate resources provided to do their work. Perhaps nowhere is the inadequacy of research resources more apparent than in the area of access to scholarly research. In this chapter, using survey data, usage statistics, and interviews of researchers, librarians, and research administrators, we describe the information seeking behavior of scholars in Mongolia and how this behavior intersects with the resources made available by research administrators and librarians. Much of the existing research on scholarly communication in developing countries has focused on whether access to scholars should be donated or provided free of charge without restriction. In Mongolia, the issue isn't so much whether access to scholarly communication should be donated or not, but rather whether the scholarly communication system meets researcher needs, is adapted to constraints within the country, and reduces communication dependency. What we find is that the scholarly communication system in Mongolia fails to completely meet researcher needs and makes the country dependent on the scholarly communication products provided by outsiders.

Chapter 12

James M. Nyce, Ball State University, USA
Gail E. Bader, Ball State University, USA
Cheryl Klimaszewski, Bryn Mawr College, USA

This chapter looks at the experiences older adults have using computers and the Internet in the context of one e-inclusion effort in Romania. Biblionet – Global Libraries Romania is a project that provides computers to public libraries throughout that country. One of Biblionet's first public access computer centers located outside of a public library opened at a pensioners' club in the city of Zalau. Local librarians who have taken Biblionet-sponsored "train the trainer" courses have adapted instructional methods for older users. Ethnographic research at the pensioners' club has uncovered a variety of experiences around new technology, especially in how computer use is both informed by and extended kin or family work. The project is discussed in the context of NGO-led development initiatives to illustrate the importance of including the wider ICT development landscape (and methods) when studying users, ICTs, and information use.

Mohammed Nasser Al-Suqri, Sultan Qaboos University, Oman

Many researchers in the area of information seeking behavior have highlighted the importance of context in influencing information-seeking behavior. However, few have elaborated on how contextual factors influence information-seeking in practice. This chapter explores the impact of disciplinary traditions of non-western, developing country external environments on patterns of information seeking and retrieval. Conditions that influence information seeking behaviors of social science scholars in non-western, developing countries impact research traditions, publication patterns, and subsequent formats are examined. This chapter draws on existing literature to examine the impact of contextual factors on information seeking by social science scholars as well as, on relevant findings based on research with other categories of researchers. The chapter concludes that there is substantial evidence from previous research to indicate the importance of contextual factors in influencing the information-seeking behavior of social scientists. Some of these factors are related to the nature of social science as a domain of study, while others are related to researcher's external environment, including constraints on the availability of particular types of information.

Naifa Eid Al-Saleem, Sultan Qaboos University, Oman

There has been a great deal of research conducted to investigate the information-seeking behavior of difference group of users. A search of current literature, however, reveals few studies dealing with information-seeking strategies of undergraduates in the electronic era. This chapter presents the results of a preliminary study of information-seeking among 675 undergraduates at Sultan Qaboos University (SQU). The study was designed to 1) explore undergraduates' information-seeking behavior with e-resources; 2) identify the role of faculty members and librarians in assisting undergraduates to attain search skills; and 3) discover the differences between undergraduates in terms of their age, gender, academic year, and college. The study results indicated that only 3% of undergraduates use the electronic services and databases subscribed to by the SQU main library. In addition, the results showed that 57.7% of the undergraduate students at SQU used the Google search engine for their initial search. There is a statistical difference between undergraduate students in terms of their age and use of e-resources. Finally, this study found the role of faculty members and librarians in assisting undergraduates to learn search strategies is almost absent.

Foreword

This book is a collection of papers by 23 authors focusing on various aspects of information needs and information-seeking behavior of users in developing countries. In the preface, Mohammed Nasser Al-Suqri, Linda L. Lillard, and Naifa Eid Saleem, the editors of the book, highlight a major need for this book. Their main concern is that there is a lack of research on information needs and information seeking behaviors of users in the non-Western world.

Although there is a substantial body of research on the information needs and information-seeking behavior of users and a number of established theories and models, most of the studies have been conducted and theories and models developed in the English-speaking developed countries. The editors of this book question the applicability of these models and theories in the developing world and believe that they do not reflect the nuances of cultural context and different ways of thinking and behaving. However, the importance of contextual factors in information behavior has been highlighted by several authors, including the characteristics of the information seeker and the nature of their environment. This suggests that local conditions might have a significant impact on information behavior, and information needs and information seeking-behavior may be different in the developed and developing world.

The editors of this book are concerned that library and information professionals in the developing countries lack a robust evidence base for designing products and services that fit real user needs and face difficulties in determining how to prioritize their already limited resources to maximize their value and return on investment. Users in developing countries face particular barriers and constraints in information seeking that are not generally experienced in more developed countries. In addition, there is also a need for research into the challenges and opportunities offered by the new digital and social media within the developing country context. Thus, a paucity of empirical studies focusing on infomation behavior influences negatively the development of high quality library and information services that are crucial for professional and personal development as well as for economic and social development, and effective participation of developing countries in the global economy.

Therefore this book is of an utmost importance for offering a variety of perspectives and examples of research in the developing country context. The book brings together research on the information needs and information seeking behaviors of various groups of users in developing countries, and the ways in which the library and information professionals in these countries are adapting to the changing information environment. Twenty three authors attempt to provide a comprehensive overview of key issues relating to information needs and information seeking behavior in developing countries and challenges that library and information professionals need to address in order to play an effective role in designing and delivering of library and information services and facilitating and supporting personal and professional as well as socio-economic development. The book also provides practical guidance and information to inform the design and delivery of library and information science curricula as well as library products and services.

The book contains 14 chapters, each covering a different issue or perspective of information needs and information seeking behavior in developing countries, or discussing the challenges being faced by library and information professionals and how they are being addressed. A variety of countries and regions are covered in this book; for example, the Arab Gulf states, various African countries, Venezuela, Uruguay, Mongolia, and Romania.

The editors provide a good overview of the chapters of this book in the Preface. The topics discussed in this book include the changing nature of the information environment and its implications for library and information science in developing countries in general and the Arab Gulf states in particular; the ways in which library and information science schools in developing countries can contribute towards promoting the integration of culture, tradition, and technology to support socio-economic development; the influence of social networking and Library 2.0 in providing access to information and knowledge sharing in Africa; an examination of multilingual information users' information behaviors when using a Cross Language Information Retrieval system in the framework of Kuhlthau's Information Search Process model; an examination of various elements of an environmental context using the Katz, Levin, and Hamilton model of diffusion of innovations; the applicability of the Ellis Model of Information Seeking Behavior to the scientific community of Venezuela; the needs and behaviors of real and potential information users in Uruguay; the importance of digitization in improving access to Indigenous Intellectual Resources in Sub-Saharan Africa; a comparison of information needs and information seeking behavior of entrepreneurs in developing and developed countries; the information-seeking behavior of social science faculty in developing nations; an examination of information seeking behavior in Mongolian scholarly communities; the information behavior of older adults in Romania; contextual factors influencing information seeking behavior of social scientists and the impact of disciplinary traditions in non-western environments on patterns of information seeking and retrieval, and the information needs and information-seeking behavior of undergraduate students in Oman.

The book reflects different perspectives and research approaches as well as research styles and therefore offers good food for thought about the challenges and opportunities in developing countries. This book is a good reading material to library and information science professionals as well as to students of library and information science interested in various aspects of information needs and information-seeking behavior of users in developing countries. However, the primary target audiences for the book are library and information science professionals in developing countries.

Sirje Virkus
Institute of Information Studies, Tallinn University, Estonia

Sirje Virkus *is a Professor of Information Science at the Institute of Information Studies (IIS) at Tallinn University. She has worked at TLU since 1985; she has been the head of the Department of Information Studies and vice dean of the Faculty of Social Sciences. She is a coordinator of the Erasmus Mundus Master programme "Digital Library Learning" (DILL) (2007-2013) at TLU and teaches information and knowledge management within this programme. Since October 2012 she is a head of the Centre for Information and Knowledge Management. She has an extensive experience working with educational innovation and research in the higher education sector in Estonia. She has been taking part in more than 30 national and international* *projects, aiming at methodological research, e-learning, course development and networking. Her research interests are focused on the development of information-related competencies, ICT innovation in education and internationalisation. She received her PhD from Manchester Metropolitan University ("Development of Information-related Competencies in European Higher Open and Distance Learning: An Exploration of Contextual Factors"). She has written more than 150 research publications and is a frequent speaker at international conferences. She belongs to the editorial board of several international journals (e.g.* Information Research; Education for Information; Library Review; Nordic Journal of Information Literacy in Higher Education; Qualitative and Quantitative Methods in Libraries: QQML; Journal of the Bangladesh Association of Young Researchers: JBAYR) *and book series* Knowledge & Information: Studies in Information Science. *She has been involved as a member of expert teams in evaluating higher education in Greece and Croatia. She is a member of the Board of the European Association of Distance Teaching Universities (EADTU). In 2012 she was elected as an Erasmus Ambassador in honor of the 25th anniversary of the Erasmus programme by the European Commission.*

Preface

In recent years, the field of Library and Information Science (LIS) has been rapidly expanding in the non-Western world to meet the increasing demands for information among users in these developing regions. The role of information provision in economic and social development is often overlooked, yet access to high quality information is an important facilitator of progress, supporting the work of governments, industry, the education sector, and all other areas of activity within developing societies.

This is especially important in the current economic climate: according to a recent United Nations report, the global economy continues to struggle some four years after the financial crisis, and the outlook for the foreseeable future is not encouraging. Developing countries have not been directly affected as severely as the Western world by the crisis, but the knock-on effects of the global problems are severely hindering economic and social progress in many of these countries, reducing the speed of poverty reduction, and severely constraining much needed investments in health, education, and other critical areas (UN, 2013).

Though there are wide variations in levels of social and economic development in the non-Western world, most developing countries have relatively low levels of education and literacy, high unemployment rates, and often an over-reliance on a small number of main economic sectors. It has recently been reported that among developing countries as a whole, 200 million people aged 15 to 24 have not even completed primary school education and the youth unemployment rate is as high as 1 in 8 (UNESCO, 2102).

In these countries, Library and Information Science (LIS) can potentially make a significant contribution to economic growth, poverty alleviation, improving literacy and education levels, and reducing inequalities by providing governments, businesses, and the general population with the information resources they need and helping to ensure they have the ability to understand and apply it in their work or daily lives. Information is important to help ensure that activities, policies, and resource allocation are well-informed by evidence about what works in practice, and to generate human capital in the form of skilled and educated people able to contribute to the development of their countries.

However, the LIS profession in the non-Western world is itself struggling with challenges that must be overcome if it is able to effectively fulfill this central role of supporting economic and social development. For one thing, the problems of severely limited financial resources and weak technological infrastructure hinder the development of LIS products and services in many developing countries. These are longstanding problems; however, there are now also heavy demands on the LIS profession to adapt to a rapidly changing information environment in which digital resources are largely replacing physical information materials and the Internet and Web 2.0 technologies are becoming the main tools of information seekers. Libraries in developing countries are well behind their counterparts in the Western world in this trend: by 2005 it was already being reported that up to 70% of information in developed countries had been converted to digital format compared with only around 2.5% in some developing countries such as India, with the lag being attributed to problems such as limited funding, low literacy levels which have reduced the demand for digital resources, and a lack of skilled library personnel who could lead digitization initiatives (Kaur & Singh, 2005).

The new information environment offers significant opportunities for improving information access to information within developing country populations, but also imposes extensive new demands on the LIS profession. For example, there is a pressing need to develop new types of skills and knowledge, such as IT and information security skills, as well as the ability to evaluate the quality of online resources and educate users to navigate the Internet effectively and determine which sources of information are most reliable. Addressing these is difficult when resources remain severely limited, yet it is important to do so to serve the expanding needs of library users in these countries and ensure that socio-economic progress is supported by high quality information which can be readily accessed.

To exacerbate the difficulties facing the LIS profession in developing countries, however, research-based knowledge about the information needs and seeking behaviors of library users in the non-Western world is very limited, and the applicability of formal theories and models of information seeking in this setting is largely unknown. The academic field of LIS is grounded in a series of models and theories (Ellis, 1989; 1991; Kuhlthau, 1991; Dervlin, 1992; Wilson, 1996) which were almost exclusively based on the experiences of information seekers in English-speaking developed countries, and reflect their cultures and ways of thinking and behaving. These do not necessarily apply in the same way to library users in the developing world, where cultures, thought patterns, and behaviors are often very different.

What this means in practice is that, unlike many of their counterparts in the developed world, LIS specialists in developing countries often lack a robust evidence base for use in designing products and services targeted to the needs of users, and face difficulties in determining how to prioritize their already limited resources to maximize their value and return on investment.

This is the context in which the need for this book has become increasingly evident. As a small body of research on information seeking in developing countries gradually emerges, it is becoming clear that LIS specialists across the non-Western world face similar challenges and opportunities, which to some extent at least are unique to the developing country context. Until now, however, there has been little attempt to bring together research and theoretical perspectives relating to the needs and behaviors of information seekers in developing countries, and the ways in which the LIS profession in these countries is adapting to the changing information environment. This ground-breaking book, based on the contributions of experts and specialists in LIS and related fields from around the globe, addresses these information gaps and the types of questions and issues that are pertinent to an understanding of the role of LIS in socio-economic development.

Collectively, the chapters provide a comprehensive overview of key issues relating to information seeking in developing countries and the challenges that the LIS profession needs to address in order to play an effective role in facilitating and supporting socio-economic development. They also provide extensive research-based information on current patterns of information seeking among various groups in developing countries, as well as examples of best practice in LIS within these countries and proposed theoretical approaches and models to help support the transformation of LIS in the developing country context as it adapts to the new information environment.

The wealth of information and wide variety of perspectives presented in this book mean that it is likely to appeal to diverse audiences, as well as becoming a key source of reference for years to come. The book will provide readers with an enhanced understanding of information needs and information seeking behavior in the developing regions of the world and the challenges and opportunities facing the LIS profession in this context, as well as practical information and guidance to help inform the design and delivery of library and information services.

The primary target audiences for the book are those working or studying within the field of Library and Information Science (LIS) in developing countries, including LIS academics and researchers, heads of university departments and faculties, LIS students, and library and information service managers. More generally, the book helps to fill a significant gap in the literature relating to LIS in developing countries, and as such is likely to appeal to the international community of LIS academics and practitioners wishing to broaden their understanding and knowledge of user needs and seeking behavior, especially now that that many LIS products and services are delivered via the Internet across international boundaries.

The book is also likely to be of interest and relevance to prospective funders as well as commercial providers of LIS facilities, products and services, providing useful background information to help support resource allocation and product design.

The book contains 14 chapters, each covering a different issue or perspective relating to the information needs and information seeking behavior of users in developing countries, or discussing the challenges being faced by LIS specialists in these countries and how they are being addressed. A variety of developing countries and regions are the focus of different chapters of the book, specifically the Arab Gulf states, various African countries, Venezuela, Uruguay, Mongolia, and Romania. Some chapters focus on the issues and challenges faced by the LIS community in developing countries more generally. To provide a little more information and help guide readers to the parts of the book in which they have the most interest, the chapter content is summarized here.

In the first chapter of the book, Mohammed Nasser Al-Suqri examines the changing nature of the information environment and its implications for Library and Information Science (LIS), focusing on developing countries in general and the Arab Gulf states in particular. Drawing on key findings from a review of LIS literature, the author considers in this chapter what is needed to ensure the future viability of the profession in the GCC region so that it can help underpin social and economic development in these states. Examples of successful practice in LIS innovation from other parts of the developing world are included to demonstrate some possible approaches, and the chapter concludes with a summary of key points for consideration by LIS education specialists, library managers, and policymakers in the Gulf States.

Next, Collence Takaingenhamo Chisita and Ismail Abdullahi look at the ways in which LIS schools in developing countries can contribute towards promoting the integration of culture, tradition, and technology to support socio-economic development. In Chapter 2 of the book, they examine the extent to which culture and technology have an influence in the integration of technology in socio-economic development in Africa, as well as exploring how technology influences culture and traditions in developed countries and the degree to which culture and traditions are receptive to the integration of technology within the socio-economic fabric of society. Since the development of any society is hinged upon the effective and efficient utilization of information and knowledge, the chapter examines the extent to which the LIS

Curriculum addresses issues relating to the integration of technology and how this integration affects education and training, research, and development. Abdullahi and Chisita highlight how LIS schools in developing countries are grappling with issues relating to the integration of culture, tradition, and technology, and examine their readiness to do so, focusing in particular on the merits and demerits of integrating technology in Africa.

Africa remains the focus in Chapter 3, which examines the influence of social networking and Library 2.0 in providing access to information and knowledge sharing in this continent. Manir Abdullahi Kamba examines the transition from a traditional to an electronic information environment and highlights the ways in which these technologies provide libraries and information centers with new opportunities for sharing information and knowledge among people regardless of distance or geographical location. The chapter highlights the importance of access to information and knowledge sharing in Africa's socio-economic development and stresses the importance of managing this effectively to benefit all, while observing that as in other developing regions, it takes time for the changes to be fully integrated into systems. Kamba argues that the developments will help strengthen and empower the African people to be global players in the knowledge-based economy and provide opportunities for their development more generally.

The non-availability of research materials in their own language is one of the problems facing many information seekers in developing countries. In many academic fields including the social sciences, the vast majority of research has been published only in English, often presenting difficulties for scholars in non-English speaking countries. Now, technology is providing opportunities to retrieve information resources in different languages, as discussed in Chapter 4 by YooJin Ha. Drawing on a review of relevant literature, this author observes that there has been an enormous increase in demand for information written in different languages by library users from various backgrounds and disciplines, especially in developing countries. She proposes a research design to examine multilingual information users' information behaviors when using a Cross Language Information Retrieval (CLIR) system, using as a theoretical framework Kuhlthau's Information Search Process (ISP) model. Development of a CLIR is argued to be essential to enable users to access information in their languages of choice; for example, when this is different to the language of their original query or when users wish to retrieve additional information written in a second and/or third language or one which they cannot understand. YooJin Ha concludes that the research presented in this chapter is expected to yield a revised or new ISP model applicable to CLIR environments, provide increased understanding of CLIR users, and inform CLIR system design.

Information seeking behavior in developing countries may be influenced or constrained by factors unique to the developing country environment in which it takes place, which must be identified and understood so that initiatives and measures can be adopted to improve the effectiveness of information seeking. For example, the types of factors influencing information seeking in developing countries may include levels of literacy and education, available technology, restrictions on data access imposed by governments, or cultural traits. However, as Rebecca L. Miller notes in Chapter 5, most current models of information seeking behavior (ISB) do not explicitly address the effects of the environmental context on ISB. She observes that, though Wilson (1996) identified several intervening variables in information seeking, even these have not been systematically considered since the formulation of his model. In this chapter, Miller proposes the use of the Katz, Levin, and Hamilton (1963) model of diffusion of innovations to provide a framework for examining the various elements of an environmental context. The proposed new model provides, in particular, the means to account for the cultural, social, communicative, and actor components of ISB. The model is described and its use as a supplementary analytic framework in ISB is examined, paying particular attention to its potential use in LIS research in developing nations.

Chapter 6 continues the focus on models of information seeking and their applicability to library users in developing countries, in this case within South America. Ellis' (1987; 1989) six-stage model of information-seeking is one of the main conceptual models underpinning the international field of Library and Information Science and still forms the framework for much research in this area. In this chapter of the book, Simon Aristeguieta-Trillos presents the findings of a qualitative research study which explored the applicability of the Ellis Model of Information Seeking Behavior to the scientific community of Venezuela. The research investigated the main information seeking activities of this peripheral country scientific community in the context of dependency theory, and generated evidence for the applicability of the starting, browsing, chaining, filtering, extracting, and information management elements of Ellis' model in this setting. This provides at least some evidence that established models of information-seeking can be useful to LIS professionals in the developing world, at least as a general framework within which environmental factors can be considered.

The following chapter has a more practical focus, but is also based on empirical research with scholars in South America. Martha Sabelli et al. present the findings of a multidisciplinary study which examined the needs and behaviors of real and potential information users in Uruguay. The research was conducted for the purpose of developing electronic information resources to promote the social inclusion of vulnerable communities in Uruguay, and was carried out in a university context to address social issues as well as to find solutions appropriate to the Uruguayan context. The authors discuss their multidisciplinary research methods and the study results, as well as the electronic information resources developed, and their impact on the target population and social mediators. The findings are likely to be of particular interest to LIS practitioners in developing countries as they digitize their library collections and develop electronic tools and resources for the purpose of improving information access, especially among disadvantaged populations.

Continuing on a similar theme, Stephen Asunka explores in Chapter 8 the importance of digitization as a means of improving access to Indigenous Intellectual Resources in Sub-Saharan Africa. In today's knowledge and technology driven society, he observes, most scholarly information is increasingly being produced and distributed in digital formats. Yet, in Sub-Saharan Africa, academic libraries have been very slow at joining this digital movement, and hence stand the risk of losing their relevance, particularly with regard to locally generated intellectual material. As a contribution to efforts being made towards the reinvention of these libraries so they can better meet the knowledge and information seeking needs of their patrons, this article first discusses the challenges that these libraries have to contend with, and prescribes some workable strategies that librarians, information scientists, and other stakeholders within the sub-continent can adopt to overcome these barriers. Such strategies, it is argued, mostly involve appropriately leveraging the existing Information and Communication Technology (ICT) tools and resources to make library resources more accessible, and also working towards a better understanding of user needs and information seeking habits so they can be better served.

Entrepreneurs in small to medium sized enterprises (SMEs) are the focus of a chapter by Dr. Linda Lillard, which is based on a review of relevant literature conducted for the purpose of comparing the information needs and information seeking behavior of these entrepreneurs in developing and developed countries. Entrepreneurial spirit is observed to be an important stimulus to economic development stimulus, with SMEs employing 22% of the adult population in developing countries and having a significant job creation capacity, yet the author notes that this is one of the least studied economic and social phenomena. Entrepreneurship in developing countries is found to be distinctive from that practiced in developed countries, and the chapter offers valuable recommendations for meeting the information needs of this population, as well as more general information for use in designing information packages and information services to benefit entrepreneurs globally. Given the important role of entrepreneurs in economic development, it is especially important for the LIS community in developing countries to understand and address the information needs of this group, as well as raising awareness among entrepreneurs of the products and services available through libraries that are relevant to their work and can help drive business growth.

Chapter 10 has a more general focus, and returns to the problem of the limited research available on the information-seeking behavior and information needs of library users in developing countries. In this chapter, Lisa Block notes that since information users in developing countries face different types of challenges to users in developed nations, it is essential to understand the various obstacles that must be overcome by library and information users in developing nations. In order to address this research need, Block reports on a study which examined the information-seeking behavior of social science faculty in developing nations, in an attempt to explain the barriers to information access for this specialist group. In the chapter, patterns of information-seeking behavior among social science faculty are examined and comparisons made with the information-seeking behaviors and information use of social science faculty in developed nations, and also with existing and proposed models of information-seeking behavior.

Shifting the focus to Asia in Chapter 11, Scheiding, Yadamsuren, and Lkhagva examine information seeking behavior in Mongolian scholarly communities. The inadequacy of information resources and limited access to scholarly research, often experienced by researchers in developing countries, was found to be a particular problem in Mongolia. However, the researchers note that while much of the existing LIS research in developing countries has focused on whether access to information should be donated or provided free of charge without restriction, in Mongolia the most important issues are whether the scholarly communication system meets researcher needs, is adapted to constraints within the country, and reduces communication dependency. Using survey data, usage statistics, and interviews with researchers, librarians, and research administrators, the authors examine the information seeking behavior of scholars in Mongolia and how this behavior intersects with the resources made available by research administrators and librarians. They conclude that the current system is not meeting researcher needs and that the country is currently dependent on scholarly communication products provided by outsiders.

Within developing countries, there are many sub-groups within the population with different information seeking needs and behaviors, and it is important to ensure that LIS products and services are effectively tailored to these different groups. Addressing this issue, chapter 12 of the book focuses on a specific group of library users in Romania: older adults. Nyce, Bader, and Klimaszewski examine the experiences among this group of using computers and the Internet in the context of the Biblionet-Global Libraries Romania project, which provides computers to public libraries throughout the country. One of Biblionet's first public access computer centers located outside of a public library opened at a pensioners' club in the city of Zalau, and Local librarians who had taken Biblionet-sponsored "train the trainer" courses adapted instructional methods for older users. The authors report on their ethnographic research at the pensioners' club uncovered a variety of experiences around new technology, especially in relation to how computer use is informed by and extended kin or family work. The project is discussed in the context of NGO-led development initiatives to illustrate the importance of including the wider ICT development landscape when studying users, ICTs, and information use.

In chapter 13, Mohammed Nasser Al-Suqri draws on a review of literature to examine contextual factors influencing information seeking behavior of social scientists and explores the impact of disciplinary traditions in non-western environments on patterns of information seeking and retrieval. Research traditions and publication patterns and formats and their impacts on the information seeking behaviors of social science scholars in developing countries are explored in the chapter. Existing literature is reviewed to examine the impact of contextual factors on information seeking by social science scholars and other categories of researchers. The author concludes on the basis of his literature review that there is substantial evidence from previous research to demonstrate the importance of contextual factors in influencing the information-seeking behavior of social scientists, which are relevant to the development of LIS in developing countries. While some of these factors are related to the nature of social science as a domain of study, others are specifically related to the developing country environment, including constraints on the availability of particular types of information.

As noted earlier, LIS practitioners in developing countries are under pressure to keep up with changes in the information environment in order to serve their users effectively, but often face constraints on the ability to do so due to the nature of the developing country environment. In chapter 14, Naifa Eid Saleem presents the findings of a descriptive study which investigated the information needs and information-seeking behavior of undergraduate students at Sultan Qaboos University in Oman, an example of a developing country. The study was designed to explore how undergraduate students define their needs and seek for the required information; identify the role of faculty members and librarians in assisting undergraduate students to attain search skills; and discover the differences in information-seeking behavior by factors such as age, gender, academic year, and college. Results of the study indicated that only 3& of undergraduates use the electronic services and databases subscribed to by the SQU libraries. The study also found a statistical difference between undergraduate students in terms of their age and the use of e-resources, indicating that as students mature, their use of e-resources increases. In addition, the results showed that 57.7% of the undergraduate students at SQU use a Google search engine for their initial search. The study also found that the role of faculty members and librarians in assisting undergraduates to learn search strategies is almost absent.

As observed by many of the authors in this volume, relatively little has been published in the past about the information needs and seeking behaviors in developing countries. This is a major problem for the ongoing development of Library and Information Science (LIS) in the non-Western world, since the profession lacks a robust evidence base for the development of products and services to meet user needs. Moreover, there has been a pressing need for research into the challenges and opportunities offered by the new digital, Internet, and social media-based information environment within the developing country context, to enhance understanding of how the LIS community needs to adapt to this environment, and to provide examples of the best practice that can be adopted. This is essential so that the community can effectively fulfill its increasingly important role of providing good access to up-to-date, accurate information to underpin all areas of social and economic development.

This book represents a major step forward in helping to address these issues and information gaps and provides a diverse range of research-based evidence, theoretical contributions, and practical recommendations likely to be of value to LIS practitioners, academic researchers, students, and other groups. More generally, the book represents a significant contribution to the evolving body of knowledge and theory about information seeking behavior and information needs, which has in the past been dominated by research conducted in the Western, developed world. This will help the worldwide LIS community play an increasingly central role in the information-focused global economy. The book also provides practical guidance and information to inform the design and delivery of LIS academic program curricula as well as LIS products and services. We are sure that it will be a welcome addition to the LIS literature, thanks to the many eminent, knowledgeable, and highly skilled individuals who have taken the time to contribute their work to the volume.

Mohammed Nasser Al-Suqri
Sultan Qaboos University, Oman

Linda L. Lillard
Clarion University, USA

Naifa Eid Al-Saleem
Sultan Qaboos University, Oman

REFERENCES

Kaur, P., & Singh, S. (2005). Transformation of traditional libraries into digital libraries: A study in the Indian context. *Herald of Library Science, 44*(1/2), 33–39.

UN. (2013). *World Economic Situation and Prospects 2013: Global Outlook* (pre-release). Retrieved on January 2, 2013, from http://www.un.org/en/development/desa/policy/wesp/wesp_current/2013Chap1_embargo.pdf

UNESCO. (2012). *Education for All Global Monitoring Report*. Retrieved on January 2, 2013, from http://www.unesco.org/new/en/education/themes/leading-the-international-agenda/efareport/

Acknowledgment

No work ever is completed without support, and this manuscript is no exception. The first special thanks and sincere gratitude go to the publisher (IGI Global) for giving us the opportunity to work on this book.

We would like also to express our sincere thanks to the members of the Editorial Advisory Board and reviewers for generously providing support in this book. We are very grateful for their helpful comments.

Our sincere thanks and deepest gratitude go to all contributors who have taken time out of their busy schedules to contribute to this publication.

Finally, an honorable mention goes to our families for their understanding, patience, and support for us in completing this important manuscript. Without their help we would face many difficulties while doing this.

Mohammed Nasser Al-Suqri
Sultan Qaboos University, Oman

Linda L. Lillard
Clarion University, USA

Naifa Eid Al-Saleem
Sultan Qaboos University, Oman

Chapter 1
The Changing Nature of Information Behavior and the Information Environment:
Challenges for LIS in the Arab Gulf States

Mohammed Nasser Al-Suqri
Sultan Qaboos University, Oman

ABSTRACT

This chapter examines the changing nature of the information environment and its implications for Library and Information Science (LIS), with a focus on developing countries in general and the Arab Gulf states in particular. Drawing on key findings from previous LIS literature, it explores what is needed to ensure the future viability of the profession in the GCC region so that it can help underpin social and economic development in these states. Examples of successful practice in LIS innovation from other parts of the developing world are included to demonstrate some possible approaches and the chapter concludes by summarizing some key points for consideration by LIS education specialists, library managers, and policymakers in the Gulf States.

INTRODUCTION

It might be said that Library and Information Science in the Gulf Cooperation Council (GCC) countries has arrived at a crossroads. From this time forward, the profession could either play an increasingly important and central role in the ongoing development of these states, or find itself unable to adapt sufficiently to the changing information environment and have its roles gradually appropriated by other specialist groups.

The demand for information in the GCC states has been rapidly expanding in recent decades as their economies develop and diversify, presenting LIS specialists with an opportunity to play a key role in economic and social development by delivering the information services and products required by all categories of users in the personal, academic, business, and government sectors. To date, the field of LIS has been growing steadily within these countries along with an expansion in educational participation and literacy rates;

DOI: 10.4018/978-1-4666-4353-6.ch001

reflecting this growth there are now numerous LIS programs in universities across the region (Rehman, 2008). However, LIS in the Gulf States has experienced the types of challenges and problems typical of LIS in other developing countries, such as inadequate technological infrastructure, a lack of reliable information about user characteristics and needs, a paucity of materials in Arabic and low levels of networking and collaboration.

In recent years, the information environment and the nature of information seeking has been dramatically changing, driven by technological developments and the impact of new Web technologies. In common with their counterparts around the world, LIS specialists in the Arab Gulf states must adapt to these changes and become more innovative in their approach to meeting user needs. This is proving a major challenge for the LIS profession even in the developed world; in developing countries such as the GCC states there is the added difficulty of overcoming other longstanding issues and problems, in order to strengthen LIS and enable it to cope with the demands on it. Technological developments help to provide solutions as well as challenges, however; facilitating the types of best practice initiatives that have helped strengthen and enhance the role of LIS in other developing countries and regions.

This chapter examines the changing nature of the information environment and its implications for LIS, with a focus on developing countries in general and the Arab Gulf states in particular. Drawing on key findings from previous LIS literature, it explores what is needed to ensure the future viability of the profession in the GCC region so that it can help underpin social and economic development in these states. Examples of successful practice in LIS innovation from other parts of the developing world are included to demonstrate some possible approaches and recommendations are made for future research directions to provide a firmer evidence base for the future development of LIS in the Gulf States.

BACKGROUND

In 1981, the six Arab Gulf countries of Saudi Arabia--Kuwait, Bahrain, Qatar, Oman, and the UAE--formed the Gulf Co-operation Council, with the objective of facilitating "coordination, integration and inter-connection between them in all fields" (The Cooperation Council for The Arab States of the Gulf, 1981). Collectively, these countries cover around 3 million sq. kilometers and have a total population of about 30 million, 27 million of whom live in the largest of the GCC states, Saudi Arabia. (Al-Mulhim, 2012) These oil rich countries have experienced rapid development since the Gulf oil boom of the early 1970s and have encouraged high levels of labor in-migration to meet the demands of their growing economies. There is high population growth across the region from natural increase as well as immigration: the total population has been forecast to increase to 53 million in 2020, with the majority under 25 years of age (Economist Intelligence Unit, 2009).

The oil reserves on which these countries have built their economies are projected to run out in the near future, and policymakers are now turning their attention to the pressing need to diversify economies to reduce their dependency on oil (Business Monitor International, 2010). Already, between 60 and 70% of GDP in the UAE and Bahrain is accounted for by sectors other than the oil industry (Samba Financial Group, 2011).

In particular, the GCC governments have been placing a heavy emphasis on developing the information sector and on a transformation to "digital societies", as reflected in Oman's Five Year Development Plan (2011-2015) (Anonymous, 2010) and in the UAE's economic development policy. Resulting initiatives such as Dubai Internet City, Dubai Silicon Oasis, and other information industry-focused developments have attracted many high-tech and media companies from around the world into the region (Walters, Kadragic, & Walters, 2006).

Despite their economic success, the GCC countries are experiencing high levels of unemployment among nationals, due largely to a mismatch between local demand and supply of labor. Many private sector jobs are low-paid and unattractive to the affluent local population who prefer to seek jobs in the already saturated public service. They also often lack the skills and knowledge required by private sector employers for higher quality positions. In response, the governments of these countries have been implementing reforms to the labor market and education systems in an attempt to decrease dependence on expatriate workers and increase the employability of the indigenous workforce (Economist Intelligence Unit, 2009; Samba Financial Group, 2011).

Within this regional context, Library and Information Science has grown steadily as a field of research and study, educating and training specialists to deliver library and information services to the academic and business communities as well as the general population. In 2008 there were reported to be ten LIS programs within Universities in the region, including six in Saudi Arabia, two in Kuwait, one in Qatar and one in Oman (Rehman, 2008). This growth has mirrored the recent expansion of university education in general in the Gulf: in Saudi Arabia, for example, the number of public universities increased from 15 in 2004 to 32 at the time of writing (Anonymous, 2012, April 29), with at least the same number of private universities and colleges, while the UAE is home to the largest number of branch campuses of overseas universities (Anonymous, 2012, May 13). Despite this, and though education participation levels generally have increased substantially in all GCC countries in recent years, levels of tertiary education participation remain relatively low. A recent study reported, for example, that in the UAE there is a need to double the number of Emiratis entering tertiary education to achieve par with developed countries (Davids, 2011). It can be expected, therefore, that future policies might be targeted at increasing higher education participation levels as well as providing Emiratis with more vocational skills.

All this indicates that there will be a continuing high demand for library and information services within the GCC region to meet the needs of expanding education sectors and the increasingly diverse economies with their growing emphasis on information and communications. However, changes in the information environment and in information-seeking behavior may challenge the ability of LIS in the Gulf States to successfully meet these demands. These changes are considered in the following sections.

OPPORTUNITIES AND CHALLENGES: THE KEY THEMES

The New Information Environment

Until recently, a shift from print-based resources to digital resources (e-books and e-journals) as well as other Internet-based information services was the main technology-driven change affecting the LIS sector (Thomas, Satpathi & Satpathi, 2010). With the evolution of the technology often referred to as Web 2.0, users are now directly involved to a much greater extent than ever before in the creation of information resources rather than just being passive recipients. They do so by participating in various social media sites and forums, or posting material on blogs or other interactive websites, practices which have been readily adopted by the academic as well as the business community around the world and are reportedly driving new forms of scholarly collaboration. The term Library 2.0 has sometimes been used to define the impact of Web 2.0 on LIS, in which interactive technologies are increasingly being adopted to enhance library services and electronic collections.

Today's information environment is, above all, user-centered and increasing mobile. Rapid advances in information and communications technology in recent years have resulted in a decline in demand for print-based resources and physical library facilities: many information seekers typically now use Google Internet searches via desktop computers, laptops or – increasingly – their hand-held Personal Digital Assistant (PDA), while education resource and database providers are focusing largely on the design of materials for use via mobile devices (Sun, Chen, Tseng & Tsai, 2011).

It is often said that we are now in a further stage of Internet evolution known as Web 3.0, a more intelligent version sometimes referred to as the semantic or data driven web. This identifies information-seekers' needs based on their browsing patterns and history and generates search results and other content based on this personalized understanding of needs. A further aspect of Web 3.0 is the introduction of cloud-based technology which enables users to access their own or other information from any device.

Changing Roles and Requirements

These changes in the information environment and nature of information seeking are resulting in major shifts in the relationship between information seekers and libraries which effectively require a major paradigm change in this field and the adoption of new roles and responsibilities for LIS specialists.

According to one definition, the roles of information professionals encompass "collecting, evaluating, organizing and providing access to information" (Koltay, 2007, para. 7). In the new information environment, these are still central to the work of many LIS professionals, but the ways in which they are carried out and the skill requirements needed to do so have become very different. Moreover, the physical library – once the main repository of information, is rapidly becoming more typically just the holder of a small archive of print materials and the home of technological hardware and software, as well as the expertise of librarians, to provide access to and guide the use of electronic and online resources. Beyond this, LIS professionals also have a role to play, in collaboration with academic faculty and researchers, in the production and dissemination of locally generated information resources via the Web (Chiware, 2010). The new reliance on technology and the Internet for information-seeking, however, requires that LIS specialists develop new technical knowledge and skills in order to develop and implement and maintain electronic resources and digital collections. These include, for example, expertise in ICT, multimedia design, electronic data storage and archiving and information security, as well as expert knowledge of issues relating to privacy, intellectual property rights and so on (Al-Suqri & Afzal, 2007; Fatuyi & Al-Suqri, 2009).

Clearly many of the newly required skills overlap with those of other professional groups, especially ICT professionals, and terms such as "hybrid librarians" and "blended librarians" have been used in the literature to describe this overlapping of roles (Corrall, 2010). In some respects this can be seen as a threat to the LIS profession, especially in the Gulf States where there are rapidly growing numbers of ICT professionals with at least some of the skills now required of information professionals. However, the traditional information professional role of guiding users to high quality, relevant information resources remains important, arguably much more so in the new information environment and this is what LIS specialists in the Gulf, as in other countries, must focus on. Users need to develop not only the technical ability to effectively use computers and the Internet to locate relevant information, but also an understanding of how to differentiate between high and low quality information and a willingness to do so. The ready availability of information via Google and other search engines has resulted in what one author refers to as the law of "least effort" having a major influence on information-seeking behavior (Ameen, 2011) and there is a need to counteract this trend among users.

In collaboration with academic researchers and other experts, therefore, the LIS profession in the Gulf States, as elsewhere, has a responsibility both to ensure the quality of resources to which users are directed, and to educate and train users in best practice on-line research techniques. In other developing countries, the lack of such training has been documented as being a major barrier to the use of digital information resources by academics, policy makers and government officials alike (Ameen, 2011), with likely adverse effects on the development of a robust evidence base for research and policy development.

Following the provision of initial training, a major role of information professionals is to use their own technical expertise and expert knowledge of relevant digital resources and databases, to provide users with guidance and assistance in their information searches. Since much information seeking now likely takes place online from users' own workplaces or homes rather than in the library environment, this guidance may increasingly involve less face to face interaction and more virtual communication using video conferencing, on-line help facilities, instant messaging or other tools (Thomas, Satpathi & Satpathi, 2010). This will require information professionals to develop not only relevant technical knowledge but also different types of inter-personal and communication skills. In the technical realm, they will need to understand and utilize the potential of Web 3.0 technologies to improve the quality of their services to users, and ensure that users understand its limitations as well as its benefits for enhancing the outcomes of their own searches.

Overall, this means that LIS programs must adopt a new approach to ongoing development and modification of their curricula, and introduce a new focus on life-long learning and continuing

professional development for working practitioners (Thomas, Satpathi & Satpathi, 2010). Incorporating a new focus on business and leadership skills in LIS curricula is also necessary to ensure the future viability of the profession. Business acumen and expertise are necessary to identify and assess the costs and benefits of commercially available resource databases and the tools for accessing these (Chiware, 2010), and for developing proposals for funding purchases and developing other initiatives and services for users. More generally, library managers may have to argue the case for continued funding as mobile technology becomes increasingly dominant in information-seeking (Ameen, 2011; Sun, Chen, Tseng & Tsai, 2011) and learn to market their services to users as never before.

Solutions and Recommendations

So what are the prospects for LIS in the Arab Gulf states to rise to the challenges and exploit the opportunities offered by the new information economy, thus ensuring its continued viability and importance in these countries? It is difficult to provide an accurate assessment, since very little research has been conducted into LIS in the Gulf States. The information that is available, however, suggests that there are still significant weaknesses, mirroring those of LIS in other developing regions (Khan & Bhatti, 2012), which must be overcome in order to provide a strong foundation for future growth and adaptation of the profession. For example, a review of previous LIS conducted by Al-Suqri (2010) reported evidence of shortcomings in resources, expertise and facilities resulting from limited funding, poor technological infrastructure and the limited availability of printed resources in Arabic, which has reduced demand for library resources and services among local populations and stunted growth of the library sector. Moreover, there are still relatively low levels of literacy and technology literacy in this region, despite rapid improvements in these, which hamper the demand for library and information services and hinder progress in new technology adoption.

Until recently, the problem of limited bandwidth severely limited the use of online information resources by information seekers in the Gulf States, a situation which mirrored that in other parts of the developing world and could be largely attributed to the "digital divide" between these regions and the developed western world. Advances in digital libraries and resource collections were very modest and within the GCC region the use of e-books was been limited and local efforts to produce them largely restricted to the conversion of print texts to PDF files without interactive features (Sawahel, 2010, December 12). Considerable advances have been made however in converting Arabic language resources into digital format for Internet dissemination in recent years, which has helped facilitate research and study into local issues. LIS in the GCC states has also benefited from the open content movement, in which much government-sponsored research from around the world is increasingly being made readily accessible to libraries via the Internet. This has vastly extended access to high quality information resources without the need to purchase print copies or subscribe to expensive databases.

One implication of Web 3.0 and cloud technologies is that some of the investment and effort involved in creating local digital libraries can now potentially be avoided, though LIS specialists still have a role in converting locally generated research and information products into digital format to make them more widely accessible via the Internet and the "cloud". The developments in mobile computing also offer benefits in terms of extending the reach of library services to remote populations, such as those in rural areas of the Arab Gulf region.

Most importantly, the prevailing policy focus and heavy investment in development of the technological infrastructure of these countries provides a positive and encouraging environment for the development of new services and expertise within LIS to meet the evolving needs of information seekers in these economies. By 2008, efforts to improve technological infrastructure had resulted in Internet penetration levels for the Gulf countries that were considerably higher than the world average of 21.9%, including 49.8% in the UAE (Whitaker, 2009), and it has recently been reported that the Arab states of the Gulf are demonstrating the greatest improvement of all regions in terms of digital readiness (Sawahel, 2010, December 12). A positive development which is likely to drive demand for library services based on new technologies is the establishment of a number of E-universities by GCC member states, often in collaboration with leading overseas universities. These include Bahrain's Asian e-University, the UAE's Hamdan Bin Mohamed e-University, Kuwait's Arab Open University and the Arab Gulf Virtual University, established to provide a hub of knowledge sharing and best practice promotion for universities in the Gulf region (Sawahel, 2011, April 3). However, there is still a need to educate and encourage students to use the Internet as an academic search tool, and to develop the skills and abilities to do so effectively: among students in Oman, for example, research has revealed low levels of skills in searching, retrieving and evaluating information via the Internet and a general reluctance to use this source to update their specialist knowledge (Bouazza & Al-Mahrooqi, 2010).

While technology facilitates strengthening and adaption of the LIS profession as well as driving the need for such changes, other issues are more organizational or human resource related. First, reflecting findings from other developing countries, there is evidence from the Arab region that graduates of Departments of Library and Information Science have deficiencies in the types of skills and expertise that are required by employers, both in libraries and more non-traditional LIS employment contexts such as private sector organizations (Jabr, 2010; Rehman & Marouf, 2007).

In particular, studies (e.g. Ameen, 2011) have highlighted a lack of adequate senior faculty and people with the skills and qualities to take on leadership roles in the LIS sector in developing countries. These inadequacies hinder not only the development and delivery of high-quality, relevant LIS education but also have a serious negative impact on the adoption of new technologies, innovative approaches to service delivery and the ability to secure funding for these. A related problem is a low level of continuous professional development or employer-sponsored training (Ameen, 2011), which not only prevents the acquisition of new ICT skills and knowledge about the information environment but also hinders the development of leadership abilities. This suggests that curriculum review and continual improvement should be a priority for the profession, including programs for updating and extending the skills and knowledge of those already in employment. This might follow the example of Japan, where a management program is now being offered to early and mid-career LIS specialists, delivered flexibly online using open courseware tools and resources and covering topics such as library governance, facility planning and public services (Mizoue, Matsumoto, Nakayama, Ishii & Joho, 2010).

In Europe and North America, and in some parts of the developing world, regional collaboration and the development of consortia of LIS schools have emerged as strategies contributing to the growth and sustainability of this field, and are generating innovative ways of addressing resource limitations, the impact of technological change, and other challenges facing the profession (e.g. see Abdullahi, Kajberg, & Virkus, 2007; Lin, 2004; Virkus, 2007). Forms of collaboration range from informal networks of professionals to highly structured international associations such as the International Federation of Library Associations (IFLA) and consortia developed for a specific purpose such as shared access to resource databases. More than 200 such organizations worldwide are now listed on the International Coalition of Library Consortia's Web site (Sheshadri, Shivalingaiah & Manjunatha, 2011).

The benefits of these initiatives include the ability to pool knowledge and expertise, make optimum use of available resources, minimize costs and avoid duplication of effort (Kigongo-Bukenya & Musoke, 2011; Ocholla 2007), benefits which are of particular importance to developing countries given the high cost of access to electronic journals and other digital resources. They also offer the opportunity for library staff to learn about best global practices in LIS and to benchmark their own institutions against international standards (Sheshadri, Shivalingaiah & Manjunatha, 2011). Networks and consortia also provide vastly enhanced access to information resources for their users. Some of the leading developing country examples of consortia development for resource sharing are provided by the Indian sub-continent: India's UGC-Infonet Digital Library Consortium provides all universities and colleges in India with access to an extensive range of e-resources for teaching and research including shared subscription to all major academic journals (Bhatt, 2010). Similarly, Pakistan's HEC Digital Library provides researchers in around 250 universities and non-profit organizations across the country with access to more than 150 million items available through the British Library Document Delivery Service in addition to 10,000 or more e-books readily available through open access (Ameen, 2011). In general, academic libraries in the developing world appear to be more advanced than the public library sector in their innovation and adaption to the new information environment. In India however, the successful DELNET network links more than 1597 public libraries across India and in seven nearby countries, and is based on a self-sustainable funding model which might be considered by adoption by the Gulf States (Kaul, 2010).

In the Arab Gulf states in contrast there is little evidence of collaboration or other forms of networking, though there are limited signs that things are improving. In 2001 research into LIS faculty in GCC library schools reported that faculty were not generally involved in professional associations and that there was little evidence of any organized activity across the region; even more worryingly the authors noted that "indifference of almost all the faculty members to these activities poses some serious questions about their sense of professional activism (Al-Ansari, Rehman, & Yousef, 2001). Formal associations appear to be limited to the Arabian Gulf Chapter of the Special Libraries Association, which holds annual conferences in the region, as well as participation in the International Federation of Library Association's Asia and Oceana regional section, and there is little evidence of ongoing collaboration or networking within or outside the region (Al-Suqri, 2010; Al-Suqri, Al Saleem, & Gharieb, 2012).

The prospects and potential for increased collaboration are healthy however. Many of the pre-conditions for collaboration in LIS are already in place within these countries due to their similar historical, linguistic, political and cultural characteristics (Al-Ansari, Rehman, & Yousef, 2001, Al-Suqri, Al Saleem, & Gharieb, 2012) and there has been a good record of regional co-operation in social, economic and business matters, reflected in the formation and activities of the Gulf Co-operation Council. This trend is continuing - at a recent summit, GCC country leaders held discussions about the establishment of a regional alliance, and a special task force was commissioned to study this possibility. Moreover, within the LIS profession itself, studies have revealed a growing receptivity to increased

collaboration between schools. For example, a qualitative research by Al-Suqri, Al Saleem and Gharieb (2012) has revealed that though little formal collaboration has taken place to date, Heads of LIS Departments in the GCC states are well aware of the many potential benefits as well as the types of barriers that must be overcome to achieve these. Another study reported that eighty percent of LIS professionals in UAE surveyed agreed that there is a strong need to establish a consortium of libraries within the country. The vast majority (95.8%) saw the main function of this to be shared access to online resources at reduced rates, but 86% thought that the functions of such a consortium should extend beyond resource sharing to other areas of co-operation. Encouragingly, 91% indicated a belief that their employing authorities would support moves to develop this form of collaboration (Sheshadri, Shivalingaiah & Manjunatha, 2011).

Perhaps even more importantly, the LIS profession in the GCC region needs to adopt more innovative and creative approaches to marketing its services and making itself indispensable to users. Training in marketing of LIS should be offered as a core component part of LIS curricula, as has already been introduced within Pakistan LIS schools (Ameen, 2011). Outcomes of this in Pakistan have included the increasingly innovative use of library space for different types of learning activities to encourage user visits. Singapore offers leading examples of the ways that LIS specialists are exploiting up-to-date technologies and social media to promote their services to users in ways that are aligned with their new information-seeking behaviors. Nanyang Technological University library staff have created a library toolbar within the e-learning platform used daily by all faculty and students, with links to library resources and services. The library also took on a leading role in coordinating the development of all blogs for the University community, providing advice, guidance and templates for use by students and staff as well as direction to relevant content for inclusion (Choy, 2011).

Finally, though not documented specifically in relation to the GCC countries, it is possible that factors identified in other parts of the developing world may also hinder progress in LIS in the Gulf region, requiring awareness of the risks and the development of strategies and measures to overcome these. Some of the most significant are documented by Alimohammadi and Jamali (2011). They observed, for example, that state-run universities are often relatively inflexible with regard to curriculum development or adaptation, due to their funding arrangements and typical bureaucratic budget processes. These authors also highlighted the risks of lack of accreditation of LIS programs, in the absence of national or regional Library Associations which have this role. Accreditation, it is argued, is an important quality control mechanism and its absence often results in a "mushrooming" of programs, many of which are low quality, and which graduate large numbers of students who are not well prepared to enter the labor market and typically become unemployed. Additionally, Alimohammadi and Jamali (2011) observe that LIS departments are most often located within arts and humanities faculties, which typically do not have the extensive IT facilities and expertise that are becoming crucial to effective library and information service delivery. Furthermore, the LIS sector in developing countries is often subject to inconsistent policies and objectives, which may even involve withdrawal of funding for particular initiatives, due to changes within political or administrative structures Though there are no straightforward or easy solutions to these types of issues, LIS departments in the Gulf region would be advised to incorporate consideration of these in their forward planning and business strategy development, and seek opportunities to collaborate both formally

and informally with their peers throughout the region in addressing such issues as accreditation and curriculum development.

FUTURE RESEARCH DIRECTIONS

As mentioned earlier, there has been relatively little research into LIS in the Arab Gulf states or the nature of information-seeking in these societies. Furthermore, since LIS originated as an academic field of study in the Western developed world, most established theories and models of information seeking do not readily transfer to the developing country context, where specific types of constraints and challenges are common in information seeking and in the provision of library services. This means that there is a limited theoretical or empirical evidence base on which to formulate future LIS strategies and initiatives in this region.

This chapter has considered wider developments in the information environment and the nature of information seeking, and has considered the future prospects of LIS in the Arab Gulf States in the light of these. Examples from the literature of collaborative and other approaches for meeting the new challenges are cited as possible models for LIS specialists in the Gulf to consider. However, it is recommended that LIS researchers, especially those within the region, conduct primary research to generate information about the characteristics and needs of all categories of information seekers in the Arab Gulf States, especially those in growing business sectors who represent potential new "customers" for library and information services. Such research might investigate, for example, levels of information literacy and IT ability, as well as requirements for specific types of information content or resources. This is crucial to underpin the development of appropriate LIS skills, services and new initiatives that will contribute positively to social and economic development in these developing countries. Additionally, research is urgently needed into the skill requirements of employers of LIS program graduates, to ensure that curricula are designed to deliver these and improve the employability and value of LIS specialists.

The chapter has provided just a few examples of best practice in the adaption of LIS in developing countries to the new information environment. More extensive reviews of literature in this area would be beneficial to the profession, to identify a range of potential models and initiatives that might be adopted, especially in the area of collaboration and consortia, and to consider their pros and cons and suitability to the Arab Gulf region. Likewise, research into LIS education programs from around the world will be beneficial in informing efforts to redesign curricula to better reflect the new information environment and changing demands on LIS specialists.

CONCLUSION

This chapter has highlighted the opportunities as well as the challenges being faced by LIS specialists in the Arab Gulf States. These developing countries are experiencing rapid economic and social progress and a diversification of their economies, suggesting that there is likely to be a high and continuing demand for information services to support this growth. LIS in the region has traditionally suffered from the types of weaknesses and limitations common in the developing world, such as poor technological infrastructure, which have to some extent hindered progress in this field. Moreover, networking and collaboration across the region has been almost non-existent. Now, LIS specialists are faced with the new challenges of re-aligning their roles and services with the rapidly changing information resulting

from technological developments and the ongoing evolution of the Internet and web technologies. Given the existing state of published information and knowledge about LIS and information seekers in the Arab Gulf States, it has only been possible to consider the issues in general terms, and make inferences from the limited available information on LIS in the Arab Gulf. On balance, the conclusion is that there are good prospects for successfully meeting these challenges and securing a central role for LIS in the ongoing development of these societies. However, this can only be achieved if LIS schools are prepared to invest a great deal of time and effort into reforming the profession, to work collaboratively across the region, and adopt new ways of thinking about how to market and promote LIS in innovative ways to the whole community of users.

REFERENCES

Abdullahi, I., Kajberg, L., & Virkus, S. (2007). Internationalization of LIS education in Europe and North America. *New Library World*, *108*(1/2), 7–24. doi:10.1108/03074800710722144.

Al-Ansari, H., Rehman, S., & Yousef, N. (2001). Faculty in the library schools of the Gulf Co-operation Council member nations: an evaluation. *Libri*, *51*(3), 173–181. doi:10.1515/LIBR.2001.173.

Al-Mulhim, A. (2012, June 1). Gulf states and an era of cooperation. *ArabNews.com*. Retrieved July 16, 2012 from http://www.arabnews.com/gulf-states-and-era-cooperation

Al-Suqri, M. N. (2010). Collaboration in library and information science education in the Gulf Co-operation Council (GCC): current status, challenges and future trends. *The Emporia State Research Studies*, *46*(2), 48–53.

Al-Suqri, M. N., & Afzal, W. (2007). Digital age: challenges for libraries. *Information. Social Justice (San Francisco, Calif.)*, *1*(1), 43–48.

Al-Suqri, M. N., Al-Saleem, N. E., & Gharib, M. E. (2012). Understanding the Prospects and Potential for Improved Regional LIS Collaboration in the Developing World: An Empirical Study of LIS Departments in the GCC States. World Library and Information Congress 2012, 78th IFLA General Conference and Assembly: Libraries Now! - Inspiring, Surprising, Empowering. Helsinki, 11-17 August 2012, Helsinki, Finland.

Alimohammadi, D., & Jamali, H. R. (2011). Common problems of Library and Information Science education in Asian developing countries: a review article. *International Journal of Information Science and Management*, *9*(2), 79–92.

Ameen, K. (2011). Changing scenario of librarianship in Pakistan: managing with the challenges and opportunities. *Library Management*, *32*(3), 171–182. doi:10.1108/01435121111112880.

American Library Association. (1989). *American Library Association Presidential Commission on Information Literacy. Final report*. Chicago, Ill.: American Library Association.

Anonymous (2010, October 29). Spanish investors encouraged to tap into Oman market. Asia Pulse.

Anonymous. (2012, April 29). Saudi Arabia to launch $21 billion education projects. *Albawaba. com*. Retrieved on July 15, 2012 from http://www. albawaba.com/business/saudi-arabia-university-education-projects-422936.

Anonymous. (2012, May 13). UAE hosts highest number of international branch campuses worldwide. *UAEInteract.com*. Retrieved on July 15, 2012 from http://www.uaeinteract.com/docs/UAE_hosts_highest_number_of_International_Branch_Campuses_worldwide/49461.htm

Bhatt, R. K. (2010). Use of UGC-Infonet Digital Library Consortium resources by research scholars and faculty members of the University of Delhi in History and Political Science: A study. *Library Management*, *31*(4/5), 319–343. doi:10.1108/01435121011046371.

Bouazza, A., & Al-Mahrooqi, H. (2010). Use of the Internet by Arts and Social Science students as a source of information: the case of the Sultanate of Oman. *Digest of Middle East Studies*, *18*(2), 72–84. doi:10.1111/j.1949-3606.2009.tb01106.x.

Business Monitor International. (2010). *Oman infrastructure report: Q3 2010*. Business Monitor International.

Chiware, E. R. T. (2010). Positioning the technological university library in higher education and human resources development in Africa. *Library Management*, *31*(6), 391–403. doi:10.1108/01435121011066153.

Choy, F. C. (2011). From library stacks to library-in-a-pocket: will users be around? *Library Management*, *32*(1/2), 62–72. doi:10.1108/01435121111102584.

Cooperation Council for The Arab States of the Gulf. (1981). *The Charter*. Retrieved from http://www.gcc-sg.org/eng/indexfc7a.html?action=Sec-Show&ID=1

Corrall, S. (2010). Educating the academic librarian as a blended professional: a review and case study. *Library Management*, *31*(8/9), 567–593. doi:10.1108/01435121011093360.

Davids, G. (2011, February 5). Gulf states lag world in university participation rates. *Arabianbusiness.com*. Retrieved on July 12, 2012 from http://www.arabianbusiness.com/gulf-states-lag-world-in-university-participation-rates-378740.html

Economist Intelligence Unit. (2009). *The GCC in 2020: the Gulf and its people.* The Economist Intelligence Unit Limited. Sponsored by the Qatar Financial Center Authority.

Fatuyi, E. O. A., & Al-Suqri, M. N. (2009). Information security and privacy in digital libraries. In Theng, L., Foo, S., Goh, D., & Na, J. C. (Eds.), *Handbook of research on digital libraries: Design, development, and impact.* Singapore: IGI Global.

Jabr, N. H. (2010). Measuring Omani information professionals' competencies: From the professionals' perspectives. *The Electronic Library, 28*(2), 263–275. doi:10.1108/02640471011033620.

Kaul, S. (2010). DELNET – the functional resource sharing library network: a success story from India. *Interlending & Document Supply, 38*(2), 93–101.

Khan, S. A., & Bhatti, R. (2012). A review of problems and challenges of library professionals in developing countries including Pakistan. *Library Philosophy and Practice (e-journal).* Paper 757. Retrieved on July 18, 2012 from http://digitalcommons.unl.edu/libphilprac/757

Kigongo-Bukenya, I., & Musoke, M. (2011). *LIS Education and training in developing countries: developments and challenges with special reference to Southern Sudan and Uganda.* Paper delivered at the Satellite Pre-Conference of SIG LIS Education in Developing Countries, IFLA Puerto Rico, 11th -12th August 2011. Retrieved on February 11, 2012 from http://edlib.b.uib.no/files/2011/08/IFLA_2011_pre_conf_paper_with_KB.pdf

Koltay, T. (2007). A new direction for library and information science: the communication aspect of information literacy. *Information Research, 12*(4) paper colise06. Retrieved on July 16, 2012 from http://InformationR.net/ir/12-4/colise06.html

Lin, C. P. (2004). *The challenges and opportunities of regional co-operation in LIS education in East Asia.* World Library and Information Congress: 70th IFLA General Conference and Council 22-27 August 2004, Buenos Aires, Argentina. Retrieved on February 9, 2012 from http://archive.ifla.org/IV/ifla70/papers/065e-Lin.pdf

Mizoue, C., Matsumoto, M., Nakayama, S., Ishii, H., & Joho, H. (2010). Ideas for the International Collaboration in the LIS Education and Research at Tsukuba. In *Proceedings of the Workshop on Global Collaboration of Information Schools (WIS 2010),* JCDL/ICADL 2010, Queensland, Australia.

Ocholla, D. (2007). The current status and challenges of collaboration in library and information studies (LIS) education and training in Africa. *New Library World, 109*(9/10), 466–479. doi:10.1108/03074800810910496.

Rehman, S. (2008). Quality assurance and LIS education in the Gulf Cooperation Council (GCC) countries. *New Library World, 109*(7/8), 366–382. doi:10.1108/03074800810888186.

Rehman, S., & Marouf, L. (2007). MLIS program at Kuwait University: Perceptions and reflections. *Library Review, 57*(1), 13–24. doi:10.1108/00242530810845026.

Samba Financial Group. (2011). *The GCC: prospering in uncertain times. Samba Report Series.* Riyadh: Samba Financial Group.

Sawahel, W. (2010, December 12). Arab States: e-books still at an early stage. *University World News* Retrieved on July 16, 2012 from http://www.universityworldnews.com/article.php?story=20101210215454146

Sawahel, W. (2011, April 3). Gulf States: virtual universities on the rise. *University World News* Retrieved on July 16, 2012 from http://www.universityworldnews.com/article.php?story=20110401190727550http://www.universityworld

Sheshadri, K. N., Shivalingaiah, D., & Manjunatha, K. (2011) *Library consortia in United Arab Emirates: an opinion survey.* Paper presented at the Asia-Pacific Conference On Library & Information Education & Practice 2011 (A-LIEP2011): Issues, Challenges and Opportunities, 22-24 June 2011, Pullman Putrajaya Lakeside, Malaysia.

Sun, Hao-Chang, Chen, Kuan-nien, Tseng, C., Tsai, Wen-Hui. (2011). Role changing for librarians in the new information technology era. *New Library World*, *112*(7/8), 321–333. doi:10.1108/03074801111150459.

Thomas, V. K., Satpathi, C., & Satpathi, J. N. (2010). Emerging challenges in academic librarianship and role of library associations in professional updating. *Library Management*, *31*(8/9), 594–609. doi:10.1108/01435121011093379.

Virkus, S. (2007). Collaboration in LIS education in Europe: Challenges and opportunities. Proceedings of the World Library and Information Congress: 73rd IFLA General Conference and Council. Libraries for the future: Progress, Development and Partnerships, 19-23 August 2007, Durban, South Africa.

Walters, T. N., Kadragic, A., & Walters, L. M. (2006). Miracle or mirage: is development sustainable in the United Arab Emirates? *Middle East Review of International Affairs*, *10*(3), 79.

Whitaker, B. (2009). *What's really wrong with the Middle East*. London: Saqi Books.

ADDITIONAL READING

Al-Gharbi, K., & Ashrafi, R. (2010). Factors contribute to slow Internet adoption in Omani private sector. Communications of the IBIMA (2010), 1-10. Retrieved from http://www.ibimapublishing.com/journals/CIBIMA/2010/698412/698412.pdf.

Ameen, K. (2011). Changing scenario of librarianship in Pakistan: managing with the challenges and opportunities. *Library Management*, *32*(3), 171–182. doi:10.1108/01435121111112880.

Benejelloun, S. (2007). *Digital Libraries as Development Catalysts in the Arab World*. Paper submitted for the Digital Library for the Maghreb Workshop held in Rabat, Morocco, January 25-27, 2007 Retrieved on July 10, 2010 from http://citeseerx.ist.psu.edu/viewdoc/summary?doi=10.1.1.93.5317.

Bhatt, R. K. (2010). Use of UGC-Infonet Digital Library Consortium resources by research scholars and faculty members of the University of Delhi in History and Political Science: A study. *Library Management*, *31*(4/5), 319–343. doi:10.1108/01435121011046371.

Bhattacharya, P. (2004). Advances in digital library initiatives: a developing country perspective. *The International Information & Library Review*, *36*, 165–175. doi:10.1016/j.iilr.2003.10.008.

Chand, S., & Dheer, L. (2009). *Training: A technique for empowerment of LIS professionals*. Paper presented at the International Conference on Academic Libraries (ICAL-2009), 5th to 8th October, 2009, Delhi, India.

Chaparrio-Univazo, S. (2005). Some issues on LIS education and collaboration in Latin America. Retrieved on February 10, 2012 from http://www.docstoc.com/docs/43933689/Some-issues-on-LIS-Education-and-collaboration-in-Latin

Chaudhry, A. S. (2007). Collaboration in LIS education in South-east Asia. *New Library World*, *108*(1/2), 25–31. doi:10.1108/03074800710722153.

Cottingham, M. (2008). *The Evolution of Virtual Universities*. In IGL Global. Virtual Communities. Retrieved from http://www.igi-global.com/chapter/encyclopedia-networked-virtual-organizations/17659

Economist Intelligence Unit. (2009). *The GCC in 2020: the Gulf and its people.* The Economist Intelligence Unit Limited. Sponsored by the Qatar Financial Center Authority.

Elaiess, R. (2009) *General guidelines for designing bilingual low cost digital library services suitable for special library users in developing countries and the Arabic speaking world.* Paper presented at the World Library and Information Congress: 75th IFLA General Conference and Council, 23-27 August 2009, Milan, Italy. Retrieved on July 10, 2010 from www.ifla.org/files/hq/papers/ifla75/175-elaiess-en.pdf.

Fan, F. (2006). Collaboration and resource sharing among LIS schools in China. In C. Khoo, D. Singh, & A.S. Chaudhry (Eds.), *Proceedings of the Asia-Pacific Conference on Library & Information Education & Practice 2006 (A-LIEP 2006),* Singapore, 3-6 April 2006 (pp. 284-287). Singapore: School of Communication & Information, Nanyang Technological University

Kaur, P., & Singh, S. (2005). Transformation of traditional libraries into digital libraries: A study in the Indian context. *Herald of Library Science, 44*(1/2), 33–39.

Khoo, C., Majid, S., & Chaudhry, A. S. (2003). Developing an Accreditation System for LIS Professional Education Programs in Southeast Asia: Issues and Perspectives. *Malaysian Journal of Library & Information Science, 8*(2), 131–149.

Kigongo-Bukenya, I., & Musoke, M. (2011). *LIS Education and training in developing countries: developments and challenges with special reference to Southern Sudan and Uganda.* Paper delivered at the Satellite Pre-Conference of SIG LIS Education in Developing Countries, IFLA Puerto Rico, 11th -12th August 2011. Retrieved on February 11, 2012 from http://edlib.b.uib.no/files/2011/08/IFLA_2011_pre_conf_paper_with_KB.pdf

Lin, C. P., & Wang, M. L. (2006). *Regional LIS education cooperation in Asia, a continuing effort.* Paper presented at the World Library and Information Congress: 72nd IFLA General Conference and Council 20-24 August 2006, Seoul, Korea. Retrieved on February 9, 2012 from http://www.ifla.org/IV/ifla72/index.htm

Mahesh, G., & Mittal, R. (2008). Digital libraries in India: a review. *Libri, 58*(1), 1–62. doi:10.1515/libr.2008.002.

Mahmood, K. (2009). *LIS Curriculum Review Using Focus Group Interviews of Employers.* Paper presented at Asia-Pacific Conference on Library & Information Education & Practice, 2009. Retrieved from http://a-liep.kc.tsukuba.ac.jp/proceedings/Papers/a1.pdf.

Maness, J. (2006). Library 2.0 theory: Web 2.0 and its Implications for libraries. *Webology 3*(2), Article 25. Retrieved on July 15, 2012 from http://www.webology.org/2006/v3n2/a25.html

Mizoue, C., Matsumoto, M., Nakayama, S., Ishii, H., & Joho, H. (2010). Ideas for the International Collaboration in the LIS Education and Research at Tsukuba. In *Proceedings of the Workshop on Global Collaboration of Information Schools (WIS 2010),* JCDL/ICADL 2010, Queensland, Australia.

Robinson, L., & Glosiene, A. (2007). Continuing professional development for library and information science: case study of a network of training centers. *Aslib Proceedings, 59*(4/5), 462–474. doi:10.1108/00012530710817645.

Singh, S.P. & Pinki (2009). *New skills for LIS professionals in technology-intensive environment.* Paper presented at the International Conference on Academic Libraries (ICAL-2009), 5th to 8th October, 2009, Delhi, India.

Sonnenwald, D. H., Lassi, M., Olson, N., Ponti, M., & Axelsson, A. S. (2009). Exploring new ways of working using virtual research environments in library and information science. *Library Hi Tech*, *27*(2), 191–204. doi:10.1108/07378830910968155.

Sun, Hao-Chang, Chen, Kuan-nien, Tseng, C., Tsai, Wen-Hui. (2011). Role changing for librarians in the new information technology era. *New Library World*, *112*(7/8), 321–333. doi:10.1108/03074801111150459.

Tella, A., & Issa, A. O. (2011). *Library and Information Science in developing countries: contemporary issues*. IGI Global. doi:10.4018/978-1-61350-335-5.

Wei, W. & O'Neill Johnson (2004). Leadership and Management Principles in Libraries in Developing Countries. New York, NY: Haworth Information Press.

Wijetunge, P. (2009). A critical evaluation of the curriculum development strategy of the LIS education programs in Sri Lanka. *Library Review*, *58*(9), 670–684. doi:10.1108/00242530910997955.

KEY TERMS AND DEFINITIONS

Arab Gulf States: Oman, Saudi Arabia, Kuwait, Bahrain, Qatar and the UAE.

Cloud-Based Technology: Technology that enables users to access their own or other information from any device.

Developing Countries: A term generally used to refer to countries with relatively low living standards, under-developed industrial base and low Human Development Index compared with other countries.

Information Seeking: The behavior and thought processes of individuals involved in searching for information and resources to meet their needs.

Library and Information Science (LIS): Though there is no formal definition of LIS, the term is usually used to refer to the academic field which developed when schools of librarianship began to add "information science" to their names, to reflect the increasing use of information technology in the latter half of the 20th century.

New Information Environment: All data and resources available in digital format via computers and the Internet.

The Cooperation Council for the Arab States of the Gulf (GCC): A political and economic alliance of the Arab Gulf States, formed in 1981.

Web 2.0: A stage of development of the World Wide Web in which users are directly involved to a much greater extent than ever before in the creation of information resources rather than just being passive recipients, through their participation and contributions to social media sites, forums, blogs etc.

Web 3.0: The most recent stage of development of the World Wide Web, sometimes referred to as the semantic or data driven web. This identifies information-seekers' needs based on their browsing patterns and history and generates search results and other content based on this personalized understanding of needs.

Chapter 2

Culture, Tradition and Technology:
The Role of Library and Information Science Schools as Integrative Forces

Collence Takaingenhamo Chisita
Harare Polytechnic University School of Library Information Sciences, Zimbabwe

Ismail Abdullahi
North Carolina Central University, USA

ABSTRACT

In both developed and developing countries culture, tradition and technology are key issues that affect the dialogue relating to how the three elements can be integrated in socio-economic development programs. This chapter examines the extent to culture and technology has an influence in the integration of technology in socio-economic development in Africa. It also inquires about the extent to which technology influences culture and traditions in developed countries. Furthermore, it scrutinizes the degree to which culture and traditions are receptive to the integration of technology within the socio-economic fabric of the society. The chapter concludes that school libraries should develop a curriculum that is relevant to the information needs of the community, especially those in rural areas. It is imperative to engage communities in developing programs that help to elevate communities without compromising on fundamental and internationally recognized standards. If local conditions are taken into cognizance programs to integrate culture, tradition and technology will be successful.

INTRODUCTION

The Library and Information Sector is dynamic due to rapid advancements in technology and this inevitably stimulates the growing need to adapt services to meet new demands; this is achieved through continuous professional training and the ability to channel expertise into innovative ways of working. Libraries are a pivotal part of stable and viable societies because of their ability to provide access to social learning spaces whereby people can access information and knowledge.

DOI: 10.4018/978-1-4666-4353-6.ch002

However, the rapid advances in technology due to Information and Communication Technologies are forcing librarians to become more innovative as they grapple with the drive to integrate culture and technology to meet the information demand of the new millennium. In Africa, culture and tradition has an impact on the integration of new technology because many projects have faltered because of a failure to merge the differences between interests of designers of technology and those of the recipients. However, culture is not the only factor because there are other social, economic, political, geographical, and educational variables of equal importance. UNESCO (1998) noted that today's children are entering a dynamic world whereby there is rapid change in science, technology, politics, economics, and socio-cultural life, and this presents challenges for libraries and educational institutions in preparing the young for the future.

Every human society – whatever its level of technical evolution – devotes considerable attention to transmitting its cultural heritage to the young. This trans-generational transmission of culture has helped to cement human solidarity and to ensure the continued survival of societies over the ages. (Obanyi, 2005)

CULTURE AND TRADITION AND DIGESTION OF TECHNOLOGY

Palvia et al. (1992, p. 4) note that culture, economic stability, and social priorities influence the extent to which a country or any organization adapts new technology. The Fontana Dictionary of Modern Thought (2000) defines culture as the social heritage of a community comprising the total body of material artifacts and non–material collective mental and spiritual artifacts knowingly and unconsciously created by people in their ongoing activities and transmitted from one culture to another. Culture is changed through internal or external factors; for example, innovation and diffusion have transformed the world into what it is today. The adaptation of technology is dependent upon a number of cultural factors; for example, power differences, individualism versus collectivism gender and sex, attitude towards time, and monochronism versus polychronism. Hall (1976) noted that generally, people in the developing world have a polychronistic culture since there is relatively general conformity in doing a number of things as long as this does not undermine interpersonal relations; for example, multitasking through ICTs. The concept of collectivism goes well with interactive social media like Web 2.0, online chats, and blogging, which promotes collaborations.

Rogers (1995) highlights the extent to which people resist particular innovations and culture is viewed as one of the barriers that any innovation must cross before it is accepted. The greatest of these barriers is organizational culture, mental promptness and psychological resilience of the members which determine how individuals decide what is valuable and what is not. In organizations like libraries there are those old guards or laggards or idea killers who are skeptical of any new innovation from idea generators and feel threatened and are comfortable to preserve and perpetuate the status quo even at the expense of quality service delivery. Kumar (1999) notes laggards represent tradition and a source of stability because they bring positive results through their dissonant acts. The integration of culture, tradition and technology in adapting library technology has been premised on maintaining equilibrium between stability and change, resulting in consensus between those who want change and promote new innovations and those against change as both interact with each other. Culture determines the technology that people will build and accept. "…any culture is a set of techniques for adjusting both to the external environment and other men…cultures produce needs as well as provide a means for fulfilling them" Shoremi (1999).

TECHNOLOGY AND CULTURE

Postman (1997a) is of the view that culture pays a price for technology; for example, it changes our behaviors, our thinking, and the way we work. The author further notes that technology has a serious ecological impact because of its propensity to radically alter everything. Kumar (1999) notes that the printing press and modern ICTs have indeed radicalized society by giving birth to new ways of thinking, doing work, and patterns of human interaction; for example, Gutenberg's printing press fostered the notion of individuality and destroyed the social cohesion of the feudal era, while ICTs have made it possible for people to collaborate and create and exchange content. Postman (1997a) argues that it is dangerous to put technology on a higher pedestal because a high enthusiasm with technology can develop into some form of idolatry or megalomania. African librarians are struggling to keep up with technology because of higher costs versus dwindling budget. With each passing year there is a danger of sliding into a state of technological dependency as technology begets more technology; for example, the dynamic nature of ICTs.

Postman (1997a) talks of the concept of "technocracy" which refers to a society in which tools play a critical role in the thought world of cultures. The technocratic society is characterized by traditions, social mores, myth, politics rituals and religion will have to fight for space in the techno-centered world. In the second half of the twentieth century writers predicted that that real power was shifting from elected representatives to the technical experts resulting in a new form of governance referred to as technocracy. However even though in industrialized societies the role of experts or technocrats in science and research is more pronounced but it has not yet totally replaced political order which is a product of the superstructure. Postman (1998b) notes that in the age of vast technological change it is of utmost stupidity for librarians to sheepishly shape their lives with dogged tenacity to fit the requirements of technology instead of those of culture. Kumar (1999) also concurs with Postman (1998b) in that both believes that the leaders of the next phase of the new brave world will not be products of the computer industry, but rather people who will understand and appreciate that this new world is not about technology.

Roberts and Rowley (2009) highlight the fact that that the adaptation of an innovation involves complexities which require proper planning and stakeholders' engagement. Christensen and Overdorf (2000), quoted in Roberts and Rowley (2009), distinguish between sustaining innovations and disruptive innovations with the former refereeing to those innovations that improve existing products and services; for example, the use of ICTs in libraries, while the latter refer to the development of completely new processes, services, and procedures and products. Generally, for an innovation to succeed it must be in sync with local circumstances and have local support. Carr (2003, p. 81) posits that technology has the immense potential to move learning institutions to learner centered environments. However, this transformation can only happen if technology is viewed as a "catalyst rather than a panacea," according to Gandolfo (1998, p. 29). Rowley (2004, p. 52) reiterate the same sentiment: "technology is certainly no longer seen as a panacea to all problems but can nevertheless provide creative possibilities with new opportunities driving change or providing solutions to challenging problems."

ACADEMIC LIBRARIES AND INTEGRATION OF NEW TECHNOLOGIES

Bush (1945) foresaw a future whereby technology would be used to manage storage, and retrieval of information with relatively high speed and flexibility thus adding value to the information needs of scholars. This has become a reality with storage capacity now measured in Megabytes, Gigabytes, and Zetabytes. The modern ICTs driven world is a realization of Bush's (1945) dream of the electronic library that is a product of rapid technological advancements. Ocholla (2008) notes that Africa libraries still find themselves lagging behind the age of rapid technological advancement with the only exception being Academic libraries in Higher and Tertiary Education because of the mandatory requirement to establish libraries as a requirement and maintain them for accreditation. In Africa, modern library and Information science technology is more pronounced in private university libraries and those belonging to the state, special libraries belonging to non-governmental organizations, and elite and up market public schools and less prominent in underprivileged schools and public libraries.

The adaptation of modern library technology such as proprietary Millennium INNOPAC and other free open source software packages, provide integrative library services including access to the Networked Digital Library of Theses and Dissertations (NDLTD). The repository consists of digital collections that capture and preserve the intellectual output the institution. Modern technology helps to enhance academic visibility, provides easier access and sharing of resources with institutions in the global virtual learning and research community.

Roseburg (1997) conducted a study on the status of academic libraries in Africa and noted that libraries were affected by; underfunding, minimal collection development, dependence on foreign or external funding, less utilization of ICT's and connectivity problems. Zimbabwe University Library Consortium (ZULC) has responded to the challenges of the digital environmental through creating a consortium to increase the capacity to effectively exploit online local and global information resources from full texts and bibliographic databases from numerous publishers.

Academic libraries have no option other than to develop through embracing and exploiting new technologies to improve services. Walsh (2011) states that academic libraries have responded positively to changes in curricular and pedagogy

by successfully grappling with the challenges of developing spaces and services that support the organization's learning objectives. The author further notes that the information environment is becoming more complex as technologies change and this implies that librarians have to be fully integrated into the learning and teaching in order to add value to learning. The migration of library resources online will help to liberate librarian's professional enabling time for other activities, for example, providing assistance to institutions in the teaching and learning exercises through information literacy, research skills training, specialist information advice and working with ICT's Department or units to develop new flexible online facilities.

The incorporation of information skills development or information literacy and digital literacy as a core part of the curriculum is a progressive step towards enhancing the status of librarians, especially those in higher and tertiary education.

Web and Prowis (2004) highlight how librarians are now able to play a Socratic midwifery role using the armory of information literacy to positively contribute to the educational and training life of higher and tertiary education and the promotion of independent learning. This marks a paradigmatic shift and a break from paradigm paralysis whereby the academic library community were viewed as playing the backside armchairish role of mere information providers. In an academic setting, the library and librarians are important and strategically positioned because they are critical in defining the future of the institution. The recognition of librarians as academic staff as critical contributors to the curricular and pedagogy can also bring in conflict as traditional academicians might not be prepared to fully accept *fait accompli* of librarians as educators but rather as support staff. This calls for a paradigm shift amongst policy makers to appreciate the pedagogical aspect of Library and Information Science. Education, (e.g., information literacy programs) in universities is anchored on a triumvirate of content, pedagogy, and classroom practice that can provide a model for the collaboration needed to fulfill the transformative power of technology, according to Car (2003, p. 83).

DIGITAL AND INFORMATION DIVIDE: SEPARATE DEVELOPMENT

The global information order is characterized by the digital and information divide as reflected by socio-economic and technological challenges developing countries are encountering in the drive to realize the dream of becoming digital. Kumar (1999) notes that Bush in 1939 predicted that information technology would ultimately replace the librarian and the library through the establishment of "scholar's workstations" but even now in the new millennium librarians are still indispensable and obituaries written by pundits have proved to be false. Licklider (1966) also launched a war on libraries by re-emphasized similar point by advocating for the replacement of the library because of the advent of new multimedia or digital technology. However, Sherman (2007) notes that despite the professed obsoleteness of libraries in the digital age they still remain relevant and exceptional because the process of digitization still has a long way to go to ensure that everything is online, some online material require subscriptions, the complementary relationship of the internet and libraries, the ability of physical libraries to adapt to technological change and the digital divide between developed and developing countries. Machlup's (1972) prediction that the there would be an exponential rise in the production of information that would surpass the quality and quantity available prior to the dawn of the information age has come to fruition with the dawn of the new knowledge driven 21st millennium. This justifies the changing nature of the LIS nomenclature, for example, digital librarians, information navigators, cyber-librarian among other trendy titles.

The convergence of the information age and the new capacity to communicate irrespective of space and time has created new possibilities and challenges for information professionals. The opportunity exists to harness this force and use it positively, consciously, and with design, in order to contribute to meeting defined learning needs. It is a challenge for developing countries to fully and effectively integrate traditions and modern technology with regards to library development. The integration of modern technology is achievable through mutually symbiotic and generous public and private sector partnerships to create financial reserves to support software research and development, hardware, and revamping of Library and Information Science Schools. The other alternative for developing countries is to exploit international co-operation and assistance, indoor to bridge the technological lacunae. Husing and Selhofer (2002) argue that development on the basis of information and knowledge will only be possible through the adaptation of ICTs.

Hawkins (1998) notes that in industrialized countries, education is highly equipped with the modern technologies than any other areas of social and economic activity, unlike in developing countries like Africa. Aqili and Moghaddam (2008) note that effective utilization of ICTs offer great potential to empower people in developing countries and underprivileged communities to overcome poverty, address the most critical social problems, promote social cohesion, and contribute to the global information economy.

Deschamps (2001) defines the digital divide as the growing gap between developed and developing countries with regards to access to information, knowledge and ideas, and works of information through technology. It also refers to the incongruity between people who have access to and resources to use new information and communication tools and those who lack such access according to Webopedia (2007). The Digital divide is dependent upon access to information and knowledge through the use of modern ICTs.

Omekwu (2006) notes that developing countries should formulate and implement information technology policies to facilitate the development of information technology infrastructure and Zimbabwe, Uganda, Ethiopia, Tanzania, Botswana, Zambia, Tanzania, Nigeria, Ghana, Tunisia, and South Africa are among many that have such policies. The digital divide can be traced to the end of the second half of the 20th century when the Internet began to be used resulting in digital lacunae. Norris (2001) in his analysis of the digital divide, distinguished three hierarchical levels: namely the macro, meso, and macro level. These levels are critical because they affect the role of libraries in integrating tradition and technology in developing countries; for example, the macro-level deals with distribution of technological and economic resources, while the meso level deals with role of political institutions while the micro level deals with individual resources and motivation.

Mchombu (1991) states that a country's level of economic development strongly determines that country's pattern of information system; for example, in developing countries the levels of technology in libraries is still very low as compared to developed countries because of poverty. The author further notes that in the drive to integrate modern technology, African libraries should borrow technology that enhances oral traditions. Serageldin (2008) echoes similar sentiments: "There is one thing developing countries cannot do without: home-grown capacity for scientific research ... Increasingly, a nation's wealth will depend on the knowledge it accrues and how it applies it, rather than the resources it controls. The 'haves' and the 'have-nots' will be synonymous with the 'knows' and 'know-nots.' It is in this vein that the integration of culture, tradition, and technology is critical as Africa and African identities grapple with the culturally homogenized global community.

Michael Wise (1985) also reinforces the same point that African libraries or librarians should consider the oral traditions as a complement to the print and electronic media. There is a need to borrow what is relevant to local culture; for example,

the use of radio and television and Information Technology. Holliday (1993) speaking on models of curriculum innovation in English, lambasts the "center-periphery" model of development because of its failure to take full account of the social, cultural, and/or educational needs of the "recipients" of the innovation. The author speaks of the notion of "tissue rejection" which refers to the failure of the innovation to take root in the target context. This is applicable in information science whereby sometimes curricular and library technology is transferred from outside without due consideration of the socio-cultural milieu in which it will be used and it fails to take root because of disharmony in the process of integration. The former United Nations General Secretary Kofi Anani (2004) reiterated the critical role of local capacity in building science and technology: "in the world of the 21st century, critical issues related to science and technology confront every nation... Today, no nation that wants to shape informed policies and take effective action on such issues can be without its own independent capacity in science and technology."

Libraries and Librarians are strategically positioned to facilitate access to knowledge and information through the integration of culture and technology and building and providing quality collections, resource sharing, and other special services. Adeogun (2003, in Mphidi, 2004) notes that in a globalised world, there is nothing like library autarchy because with the exponential growth of knowledge and information there is need for interdependence: "...libraries need to establish effective resource sharing schemes. As a result of present proliferation of information, high costs of information resources and dwindling library budget; it is difficult for any library to provide all the information needs of its clients..." (Adeogun, 2003, in Mphidi, 2004).

It has been noted that in the modern technocentric organizational environments innovation and development of new ideas, devices, systems, processes, products or services. This implies that heads of library institutions and library schools need to be in touch with current technological and professional trends that affect all aspects of the organization's work. There is need to distinguish between innovations that improve library products and services, for example use of free open source software, incorporating oral traditions and disruptive innovations which can have a radical impact on the library's processes, procedures, and services.

LIBRARIES FACING TECHNOLOGY AND TECHNOCRACY

The theory of technological determinism argues that major changes in society are a result of changes in ideologies, tools, and technology resulting in seismic paradigm shifts; for example, the information society is a product of computers, according to Hickman (1990). The inherent capabilities of networked technology have presented libraries with opportunities to take their services to new levels. Libraries have been affected by general trends in computer technology. They also share the enormous challenges of integrating new skills and methods, facing new sources of competition, and adapting to the rapid pace of technological change. Hyman (2000, p. 97) is of the opinion that cooperation and collaboration provide libraries with essential tools for meeting the challenges of the future; for example, interlibrary lending provides members to access data on each other's holding through online databases.

The Information age history teaches us that significant developments and the meaningful and lasting solutions to library problems are dependent upon cooperative solutions, according to Wilson (2003). As technology presents libraries with many new challenges, it also provides collaborative tools to address these challenges. The use of social media like Web 2.0 technologies and applications has brought about a consequential and substantive change in the history of libraries through making the library's collection more in-teractive and fully accessible. It also has changed library services to enable it to focus more on the facilitation of information transfer and information literacy rather than providing controlled access to it. Researchers are also beginning to appreciate social media because of its usefulness in the cyclic nature of scientific research; for example, researchers can share ideas as they develop their thesis with others irrespective of space and time. The world over Libraries has adjusted to new technologies of shared online services whose growth is dependent upon increases in bandwidth and network reliability. The use of network communication, universally available e-mail, listservs, RSS news feeds, blogs, and wikis communication tools to focus the efforts of diverse groups is an essential feature of the existing advancement of library services through shared technology.

Ukoha (1998) notes that general survey of library education in developing countries reflects grandiose infrastructural inadequacy, lack of financial and material resources, information apartheid, and lack of coordination and communication amongst key players in the delivery of Library and Information Science Education. In this era of shortages of qualified teachers in universities, availability of Internet access for teachers and students would provide complementary information for their studies. Mphidi (2004) notes in the age of lifelong learning, public libraries need to shed off the elitist and anachronistic perception that people have by making a paradigmatic shift towards providing equal access to information for all through effective utilization of ICTs: "…libraries are for everyone, educated and uneducated, rich and poor. They are equalizers and democratic force in access to computers, the Internet, information, learning and training" (Mphidi, 2004).

DISCOVERY, CHANGE AND REINVENTION

Globally, there is a growing consensus in formal organization on the vitality of recognizing the value of historical, cultural, and social approaches in knowledge and knowledge organization. Information and communications technology have become powerful tools that are linking library schools in developing countries with library schools in the west, thus facilitating the ongoing revitalization of the educational system through resource sharing and collaboration. There is need to empower people with ICT tools, especially in underprivileged communities in order to bridge the divide; for example, the establishment of telecenters or ICT kiosks where people can share ideas. Alabi (2004) notes that the information society demands a workforce that can manipulate technology to increase productivity and creativity and this involves identifying reliable sources of information, effectively accessing these sources of information, synthesizing and communicating information to colleagues and associates to improve quality of life.

Kumar (1999) states that librarianship is a dynamic profession and that its survival will be dependent on how its members are able to "discover, change and reinvent" themselves in the globalised knowledge economies of the new millennium. It should be noted that the process permanent restitution is meant to find advantage in change, and finding new evolutionary niches in the shifting cutthroat information landscape because of the ubiquity of various media competing with libraries, for example, in the future mainstream media will migrate towards social media.

It is also useful for libraries to be able to revaluate and adjust their strategies, missions, functions and services as part of the reinvention so gain a competitive edge in a world where there are others competing to provide information. This calls for a complete change .The library organization has been compared to a biological system that adopts itself to changing times. Revolution of the library is dependent on the micro and macro-environment; for example, the psyches of those leading such institutions. Technology refers to applied scientific knowledge that adds value to the lives of people in a society; for example, in libraries the use of information and communication technology. Wilson (1992) defined information technology as the means by which science is used in the collection, storage, processing, and circulation of information. Shariful and Nazmul (2006) defined Information and communication technology as the use and application of computers, telecommunication, and microelectronics in the acquisition, storage, retrieval, transfer, and dissemination of information.

IMPACT OF TECHNOLOGY ON LIBRARIES

Mezey (2011) highlights the notion of an ambidextrous organization which has the ability to resolve the conflicting demands of efficiency and innovation. These polychromatic organizations are characterized by vibrant internal communication programs, active communities of practice, and a culture of continuous learning and benchmarking. Innovation in information technologies will also result in changes in use, work conditions, and people; for example, ICTs have radically altered the roles of information professionals and users, especially where library operations and procedures are digitised. Baldwin (1998, p. 11) states that technology continues to transform scholarships through use of the Internet for information sharing, information navigation and retrieval, collegial communication, and collaboration. It is also transforming service and outreach through applications to real world problems, unlimited access accessibility to resources, and breaking down of barriers between the tools of higher education and those of the community, according to Baldwin (1998, p. 12). ICTs have the potential to radically alter listing, accounting, serial control, circulation, book ordering and acquisitions, cataloguing, interlibrary cooperation, stock verification, management of information systems, and networking, among other operations.

Leavitt (1964) developed the "diamond model" which represents the dynamic relations among the structures of an organization, namely people, duties, and technology. This model implies that appropriation of technology by users of a library service will be easier if planning is guaranteed to facilitate changes in the internal environment so as to allow adjustments between technology and other organizational components. Technological acceptance sets the ground for real appropriation and makes it possible to intermediate librarians to be innovation and diffusion agents or *Avante garde* of modern technology. Libraries should be able to adjust to change as biological organisms but also to lead diffusion of change processes of information technologies in their institutions, according to Vreins (2005). Goldstein (1994) notes that the introduction of new technologies for information management creates opportunities for organizational transformation. Such tools aid in research and development in higher education and ultimate growth of institutions.

CHALLENGES OF THE DIGITAL REVOLUTION

Internationally, Libraries as cultural heritage institutions have integrated technology into all aspects of their strategies, management operations and services. These institutions face challenges of adapting appropriate technologies to enable them to migrate most of their holdings from the analogue format to digital format. Libraries in developed countries have been successful in utilizing modern technology to automate and digitize their services and products, but for those libraries in developing countries, it has not been easy to adapt to modern

technology. Analogue format includes paper and its variants, like vellum, papyrus, birch bark, or canvas, as well as surrogate forms like negatives, glass plates, microform, and microfiche. Analogue formats are characterized by fixation to a physical medium, bound to a sequential representation that is pre-determined by the author and degrades when copied. On the other hand, digital information can be linked to other material to create multimedia, stored and delivered in various ways, and one can produce copies without undermining the quality of the original. Digital libraries are said to soar ahead of traditional ones with regard to storage and retrieval. Currently it is quite daunting for print based libraries to manage storage space, but with digitization, large amounts of analogue content can easily be stored on a computer. It is also relatively easier to browse, search, index, or collate digital content than it is with analogue content that relies on manual technologies.

Baron (2011), speaking on behalf of the United Kingdom, called for development of a National Digital Library to conserve and preserve information that is currently publicly accessible, prevent the commoditization of information by private and profit oriented organizations like Google, and to enhance the role of the library in a techno-centric environment. The above statement is as important for developed as well as developing countries. The author further notes that the call for a National Digital Library should not be misinterpreted for a call to close down library buildings and dispose of physical books but rather the complimentary nature between print and digital libraries. This reflects the capacity of libraries in developing countries to successfully integrate tradition and technology. In Africa, where public libraries exist as physical places for community interaction, implies that the road towards digitization is marred by socio-economic and technological "briars and thorns.« While libraries in developed countries have adapted to modern information and communication technology easily, for those in developing countries, such progression is undermined by socio-economic and technological challenges.

ORAL TRADITIONS

In Africa, oral traditions are so strong and it is imperative for library and information science schools to incorporate such aspects in their curriculum. Vansina (1985) defined oral traditions as oral transmissions transmitted verbally from one generation to another. In Africa, knowledge was passed through from one generation to another orally; for example, griots, poets, spirit mediums, and the elders preserved cultural traditions, memories, and stories of the past through living libraries. A Kumar (1999) noted that oral traditions have shown greater resilience as they have managed to persist over time and space and are currently being manifested through digital technology. The author further notes that we should view oral, print, and digital technologies not as alternatives to each other, but rather as unity and continuum that has helped in shaping public knowledge and sustaining the collective memories of communities and organizations.

The incorporation of oral traditions in the contemporary LIS curriculum provides a productive ground to integrate culture, tradition, and technology through combining indigenous and modern knowledge systems. Ochoola(2011) states that traditional African access, transfer, and use systems are anchored on oral traditions and indigenous knowledge. This includes intangible heritage in the form of the art of conversation; for example, proverbs, folktales, myths, legends, dirges and mirges, and other socio-cultural capital like drama and dance, which has helped to sustain the lives of the struggling people of the world.

The United Nations for the safeguarding of Intangible Cultural Heritage (2003) calls for the protection of oral traditions, performing arts, social practices, rituals and festive events and knowledge concerning nature and the universe and know-how on handicrafts. Libraries, archives, and related institutions as part of superstructure are better positioned to help in the realization of such a noble objective through integrating culture, tradition, and technology in the provision of information services.

Polanski (2007) notes that African filmmakers have blended traditional forms of storytelling with modern technologies, creating a new social/political medium through which African identities are both formed and given voice. The author further notes that the filmmaker's ability to utilize technology to capture and record an event or moment which can be shown and re-shown, becomes the new guardian of tradition, and this reflects the recovery of the oral storyteller through the medium of the film. Libraries can also utilize modern technology to repackage oral traditions; for example, the use of podcasts, radio, and video recorders to capture human narratives that are relevant to the local culture. Nyana (2009) concurs with Nawe (1993) as they both advocate for a paradigm shift in library school education and philosophy to a technology driven afrocentric paradigm: "…adaptation is required in the creation of information structures and methodologies that would encompass Africa's traditional knowledge and modern knowledge resources…"

CONCLUSION

Fergusson and Metz (2003, p. 110) notes that organizational cultures, discernments, and typecasts and vicissitude of history and personalities and complexities to operational realities discourage some institutions from embracing integration. The authors further argue that it is achievable to integrate two cultures with such a predilection for misinterpretation and to forge them in humane fashion into something colossal than either would be capable of disjointedly. Overall, the integration of the triumvirate of culture, tradition, and technology is critical for the development of library services that will be relevant to local needs of the developing countries. However if this integration is to take place there is need to overcome paradigmatic paralysis and heightened sensitivity to psychological, cultural and political nuances. Indeed technology can be used as a catalyst and not a remedy in the drive towards technology driven library services in developing countries

REFERENCES

Alabi. (2004, April 30). Evolving Role of ICT's in Teaching, Research and Publishing. *Nigerian Tribune.*

Anderson, J. D. (2003). *Analysing the role of knowledge organization in scholarly communication: An inquiry into intellectual foundation of knowledge organization.* Retrieved on July 3, 2011, from http://arizona.openrepository.com/arizona/bitstream/10150/105100/1/jackandersen-phd.pdf.

Annan, K. (2004). Science for all Nations. *Science Magazine, 303,* 925. PMID:14963291.

Aqili, S. V., & Moghaddam, A. I. (2008). *Bridging the digital divide: The role of Librarians and Information Professionals in the third millennium.* Retrieved on April, 27, 2011, from http://www.emeraldinsight.com/0264-0473.htm.

Baldwin, R. C. (1998). *Technology's impact on faculty life and work. The Impact of Faculty Life and Work: New Directions in Teaching and Learning.* San Fransisco, CA: Jossey-Bass.

Baron, S. (2011, March). Why we need a UK National Digital Library. *Update.*

Bush, V. (1945). As We May Think. *The Atlantic Monthly* (Vol. 176, No. 1). Retrieved on August 26, 2004, from http://www.theatlantic.com/unbound/flashbks/computer/bushf.htm

Carr, J. A. (2003). Exploring cultural challenges to the integration of technology. In *Leadership, Higher Education and The Information Age: A new Era for Information Technology Libraries.* London: Neal Schuman.

Haddad, W. D., & Draxler, A. (2002). *Technologies for Education: Potentials, Parameters, and Prospects.* Paris: United Nations, Educational, Scientific and Cultural Organization.

Hall, E. T. (1976). *Beyond Culture.* Garden City, NY: Anchor Press/Doubleday.

Hassan, H., & Ditsa, G. (1999). The Impact of Culture on the Adoption of IT: An Interpretive Study. *Journal of Global Information Management, 7*(1), 26–37.

Hawkins, R. J. (1998). Ten Lessons for ICT and Education in the Developing World. In *World Bank Development Indicators* (pp. 38–43). New York: World Bank.

Hickman, L. A. (1990). *Technology as a human affair.* New York: McGraw-Hill.

Holliday, A. (1992). Tissue rejection and informal orders in ELT projects: Collecting the right information. *Applied Linguistics, 13*(4), 403–424. doi:10.1093/applin/13.4.403.

Hyman, K. (2000). Struggling in a one-stop shopping world, or people want what they want. In Laughlin, S. (Ed.), *Library Networks in the New Millenium: Top Ten trends.* Chicago, IL: Association of Specialized and Cooperative Libraries.

Machlup, F. (1972). *The production and distribution of knowledge in the United States.* Princeton, NJ: Princeton University.

Maness, J. (2006). Library 2.0 Theory: Web 2.0 and Its Implications for Libraries. *Webology, 3*(2).

Mchombu, K. J. (1991). Which way African Librarianship? *IFLA Journal, 17*(1), 43–50. doi:10.1177/034003529101700108.

Mezey, M. (2011, March). The challenges of creating ambidextrous organizations. *Update.*

Mphidi, H. (2004). *Digital divide or digital exclusion? The role of Librarians in bridging the digital divide.* Paper presented at LISA 7th Annual conference. Pholokwane, South Africa. Retrieved on April 27, 2012, from http://www.liasa.org.za/conference/conferences2004/papers/LIASA-conference

Nawe, J. (1993). The realities of adaptation of western librarianship to African situation. *Journal of Libraries. Archives and Information Science,* 2(9), 1–9.

Occholla, D. (2009). Are African Libraries active participants in today's Knowledge and Information Society? *South African Journal of Library and Information Science,* 75(1), 20–27.

Ocholla, D. (2010). *Is African Information ethic unique?* Retrieved on April 30, 2011, from http://www.lis.uzulu.ac.za/2011/Ocholla%20Prolissa%202011%20information%20ethics%20Feb%2018.pdf

Peplinski, C. (2007). *Oral Traditions and Weapons of Resistance: The Modern Africa Filmmaker as Griot.* Retrieved on April 4, 2011, from http://ccms.ukzn.ac.za/index.php?option=com_content&task=view&id=382&Itemid=48

Postman, N. (1997a). Science and the story that we need. Retrieved on April 4, 2011, from http://www.firstthings.com/ftissues/ft9701/articles/postman.html

Postman, N. (1998b). Five things we need to know about technological change. Retrieved on April 14, 2011, from http://itrs.scu.edu/tshanks/pages/Comm12/12Postman

Rogers, E. M. (1995). *Diffusion of innovations.* New York: Free Press.

Serageldin, I. (2008). Joining the Fast Lane. *Nature, 456,* 18–20. doi:10.1038/twas08.18a PMID:18987709.

Shariful, I. M., & Nazmul, I. M. (2006). Information and Communication Technology (ICT) for Librarianship. *Asian Journal of Information Technology, 5*(8), 809–817.

Ukoha, O. (n.d.). *Igwe Harnessing Information Technology for the 21st Century: Library Education in Nigeria.* Retrieved April 15, 2011, from http://www.webpages.uidaho.edu/~mbolin/igwe.htm

UNESCO. (1998). Harnessing Information Technology for Development in Africa. Retrieved on April 5, 2011, from http://www.unesco.org/education/educprog/Iwf/doc/IAI.html

Vreins, D. (2005). Information and Communication Technology: Tools for competitive inteligence. Encyclopedia of Information Science and Technology, 3, 1-6.

Wilson, B. (1992). *Information Technology: The Basics.* London: MacmiIlan.

Wise, M. (1985). *Aspects of African Librarianship: A collection of writings.* London: Mansell.

ADDITIONAL READING

Al-Jaghoub, S., & Westrup, C. (2008). Reassessing social inclusion and digital divides. *Journal of Information. Communication & Ethics in Society, 7,* 2–3.

Appadurai, A. (1997). *Modernity at Large: Cultural Dimensions of Globalization.* Minneapolis, MN: University of Minnesota Press.

Armand, M. (2000). *Networking the World, 1794-2000.* Minneapolis, MN: University of Minnesota Press.

Bauman, Z. (1998). *Modernity and the Holocaust*. Ithaca, NY: Cornell University Press.

Beck, U. (1999). *What is Globalization?* Cambridge, UK: Polity Press.

Beck, U. (2000). *The Brave New world of work*. Cambridge, UK: Cambridge University Press.

Berger, P., & Luckmann, T. (1966). *The Social Construction of Reality: Garden City*. New York: Anchor Books.

Bernama. (2011). *National Broadband Penetration Rate Reaches 81 percent*. Retrieved on April 12, 2012, from http://blis2.bernama.com/getArticle.do?id=96956&cid=2

Beynon, J., & Dunkerley, D. (2000). *Globalization: The Reader*. London: Athlone Press.

Bourdieu, P. (1977). *Outline of a Theory of Practice*. London: Cambridge University Press. doi:10.1017/CBO9780511812507.

Bureau of Labour Statistics. (2011). *Occupational outlook handbook*. Washington, DC: U.S. Department of Labour. Retrieved on May 15, 2012, from www.bls.gov/oco/

Cushman, M., & Klecun, E. (2006). How (can) nonusers engage with technology: Bringing in the digitally excluded? *IFIP International Federation for Information Processing, 208*, 347–364. doi:10.1007/0-387-34588-4_23.

Cushman, M., & McLean, R. (2008). Exclusion, inclusion and changing the face of information systems research. *Information Technology & People, 21*(3), 213–221. doi:10.1108/09593840810895993.

Edzan, N. N. (2008). Information literacy development in Malaysia: A review. *Libri, 58*, 265–280. doi:10.1515/libr.2008.027.

Giddens, A. (2006). *Sociology*. Cambridge, UK: Polity Press.

Hashim, R. (2008). *Political issues in ICT implementation in local government*. In *Proceedings of the 4th International Conference on E-Government*. Melbourne, Australia: EJEG.

Held, D., & McGrew, A. (2000). *The Global Transformations Reader: An introduction to the globalization Debate*. Malden, MA: Polity Press.

Jaeger, P. T., Bertot, J. C., Thompson, K. M., Katz, S. M., & Decoster, E. J. (2012). The intersection of Public Policy and Public Access: Digital divide, digital Literacy, digital inclusion, and public libraries. *Public Library Quarterly, 31*(1), 1–20. doi:10.1080/01616846.2012.654728.

Jitka, R. (2000). Demographic transition or demographic shock in recent population development in the Czech Republic? *University of Carolina, 1*, 89–102.

Kroeber, A. L. (1939). *Cultural and natural areas of native North America*. Oakland, CA: University of California Publications.

Lechner, F., & Boli, J. (2004). *The globalization reader*. Hoboken, NJ: Wiley-Blackwell, John & Sons.

Lesthaeghe, R. (1995). The second demographic transition in Western countries: An interpretation. In Mason, K. O., & Jensen, A.-M. (Eds.), *Gender and family change in industrialized countries*. Oxford, UK: Clarendon Press.

Lockwood, D. (1964). Social integration and system integration. In Zollschan, K., & Hirsch, W. (Eds.), *Explorations in Social Change*. London: Routledge and Kegan.

Postman, N. (1993). *Technopoly: The surrender of culture to technology*. New York: Vintage Books.

KEY TERMS AND DEFINITIONS

Culture: The sum total of peoples or institution's way of life reflected by material and, non-material aspects of life .It encompasses the patterns and symbolic structures that give such activities significance and meaning.

Curriculum Development: Systematic, continuous or ongoing activities that consist of conceptualizing, planning, implementing, field testing, and researching that are intended to generate innovative curricula or improve existing one.

Information Society: Society in which the quality of life and decision making is determined by access and effective use or utilization of information.

Integration: The process of combining into an integral whole. It is a situation of cohesion by consent rather than coercion resulting on entities combining into a workable whole.

Research and Development: Scientific Process of discovering new knowledge relating to products, services and processes and the application of new knowledge to create value added products, processes and services that fill market need .This knowledge is generated through basic and applied research.

Technology: Sum total of knowledge and skills available to humankind to apply in industry, commerce, science and art.

Tradition: A long established, inherited or cherished way of thinking.

Chapter 3

The Influence of Social Networking and Library 2.0 as a Gateway for Information Access and Knowledge Sharing in Africa

Manir Abdullahi Kamba
Bayero University-Kano, Nigeria

ABSTRACT

The chapter tries to highlight the influence of social networking and library 2.0 in providing access to information and knowledge sharing in Africa. It further discusses the panorama at which the information environment is changing from traditional to electronic, where access to information and knowledge stands to benefit all. The chapter, however, exhibits that in most developing worlds today the electronic information environment is gradually spreading and obviously will take time to be fully integrated into the systems, especially in Africa. The chapter provides a highlight on the value, usefulness, access to information, and knowledge sharing, which has become a necessary component for human existence and development. The premise is that librarians' role is to facilitate this effective management and promote access to information and knowledge sharing through the influence of social networking and library 2.0; this in turn will strengthen and empower the African people to be among global players in the knowledge-based economy. The emergence of Web 2.0 principles and technologies that has given rise to social networking and library 2.0 offer libraries and information centers many opportunities for sharing information and knowledge among people regardless of distance or geographical areas. This reaches out beyond the walls of the library and Websites of any library or institutions. These developments make it possible for people to share knowledge and information online, borrow locally, and buy or sell on a global scale as appropriate to their needs and circumstances.

DOI: 10.4018/978-1-4666-4353-6.ch003

INTRODUCTION

It is evident that the world has experienced transformations in information and knowledge development since time immemorial. These transformations cut across different civilizations and eras (i.e. from stone ages through the electronic/digital ages and information society of today). Allmand, Balantyne and Ngwira (2001) observed that in this new millennium the information world faces an era of great changes, which influence directly the way scientific information and knowledge are produced, processed by intermediaries, distributed and accessed. They noted that information and communication technology and especially the Internet have made a huge impact. It was therefore stated that information services, traditionally responsible for managing this information, are passing through a process of change. In this present time, information and knowledge are coordinated and transferred through the electronic information environment. This environment is a human centered and latest innovation of the development in information and communication technologies (ICTs). This environment could also be regarded as a creation of mind and a place of imagination. There are a number of factors that constitute this environment which include: computer, Internet, electronic resources, World Wide Web, social networking, and so forth. Electronic environment is one of the leading and rapidly growing information environments. This environment is sometimes called avatar or information resident, where different virtual activities take place.

The electronic environment is said to be a computer based communication channel and information and knowledge outfit that enables new ways of communication, collaboration, and coordination by the Internet in three dimensional environments by Voice Over Internet Protocol (VOIP) (Gajendara, Sun and Ye, 2010). In this type of environment, people interact, share with each other through e-mail, Yahoo Messenger, instant messaging, facebooking, online games, Lib 2.0,

blogs, Wikis, AJAX, RSS, Mashups, etc. All of these allow people to access, share, and transfer information and knowledge.

Access to information and knowledge sharing has become a necessary component for human existence and development. Over the years, information and knowledge experts have been trying to develop some framework or methodology upon which to effectively and precisely access and analyze relevant information. The information and knowledge arise in the technical, marketing, social, cultural, political, and legal activities of humankind. This information and knowledge is mostly created and delivered through various media, in both print and non-print, such as television, radio, newspaper, bulletin, pamphlets, electronic, and digital media. In today's information environments, access to and sharing of information and knowledge incorporates the use of computers and other electronic equipments for efficient communication of information among different user groups. These technologies apply scientific information to the end-users needs.

Information and knowledge has been identified as one of the basic resources required for the improvement of humankind. They are also said to be a resource that must be acquired and used in order to make an informed decision. Those who possess appropriate and timely information and apply knowledge appropriately will make a more rational decision than those without. The various information and knowledge users can be categorized as policy makers and planners, researchers, extension staff, educators and students, industrialists, services staff, rural people and farmers, and so forth. It was also observed that each of these sectors mentioned above contribute directly to the improvement and development of society, hence relevant information and knowledge provided to each category of these user populations will contribute positively to the development of any nation. Information and knowledge are potential ingredients for the advancement of any nation's political, economical, social, cultural, technological, educational, health and agricultural development. Without information and knowledge these sectors might degenerate into extinction. Information and knowledge provides the basis for scientific innovations in agriculture, health and education. Therefore, information and knowledge could be defined as all published or unpublished works on all aspects of human endeavors, as such access to and sharing it has become indispensable.

THE PANORAMA OF ELECTRONIC ENVIRONMENT

Electronic environment can be described as computer-related mechanisms through which information and knowledge is obtained and shared with relevant users. The development of electronic environment could be traced back to advent of the computer which gave a new direction to the information and communication technology industry. This is evident in the use of technologies such as electronic mail (e-mail), electronic commerce (e-commerce), and more recently mobile phone. According to Kerrigan, Lindsey and Novak (1994), communication technologies such as electronic mail (e-mail) and electronic conferencing provide scientists, administrators, and information staff with rapid and reliable communication, while increasing productivity and decreasing communication costs by reducing the physical means of communication channels. These are some of the benefits of electronic environment. In the same vein, while discussing electronic environment as tool for information access and knowledge sharing and transfer, Metcalfe and Gilmore (1990) observed that because of the remarkable pace of development within the short time that computers were introduced, electronic environment now impinges upon virtually every aspect of society, and has developed dramatically.

As people usually had little exposure to technical information through an electronic environment, it was natural for the information providers to take as their primary role the function of a linkage "between the producers of technology and the end-users of these innovations" to promote efficiency in information access and knowledge sharing. Access to information can only be meaningful if the users actually know how to use the complex electronic environment via information technologies (both hardware and software), and also to know when the information technology would be useful in discharging their duties adequately.

ACCESS TO INFORMATION AND KNOWLEDGE SHARING

The world today is going electronic and electronic information has many advantages over the traditional and conventional methods of using paper-based materials. A larger volume of information can be shared with the aid of information technology (which is electronic based), and it is faster and more efficient. Information and knowledge access, sharing, and communication can be made reliably possible with the electronic information technology, which overcomes the limitations of a distance barrier. However, in most developing worlds today the electronic information environment is gradually spreading and obviously will take time to be fully integrated into the systems, especially in Africa.

Today's information and knowledge users are expected to become active participants in the surrounding Knowledge Society, using complex communication networks for rapidly developing, accessing, sharing and exchanging information (Kankaanranta, 2005). Integrating ICT and network technologies in libraries, information centers, schools, institutions, organization, and so forth, will increase the opportunities for people to gain experience in the use of global information networks. It is obvious that the mode of information gathering of today has led to new ways of thinking about how people access and share out information and knowledge. The traditional view was one in which a user had a stable goal throughout the search process, searching for end information that met his goal. Therefore, it is important to note that information and knowledge is being gathered for a purpose and this purpose or goal is likely not only to have an influence upon how information is gathered, but also upon what and how it is being accessed, shared, and used.

Kidd (1994) provides an interesting example, suggesting that different types of tasks traditionally are carried out by different types of users, which may influence how information is handled, shared, or modified. For example, a communications worker may collect and classify information, enrich it, and pass it on. A clerical worker may collect and apply information (e.g. policies) and the information remains unchanged and the worker is not informed by it. In contrast, a knowledge worker processes, extracts information, and produces new concepts, ideas, and manipulations of the information. There are therefore opportunities for the development of tools that are better tuned to particular usages and purposes.

For people to become informed they need to develop methods by which they share the resulting information, knowledge, skills, and gathered information from such tasks with others. There is an assumption that information and knowledge from other people is of higher value and quality than, say, that found through a search engine, because it has already been judged in some way by someone else to be of use (Kanawati and Malek, 2000). However, literature indicated that information and knowledge does not have an inherent use or value across a general population. therefore, sharing it is different and easier between close work colleagues or those who have shared knowledge and purpose than between loosely coupled colleagues, novices and experts or those who wish to re-use information for other purposes, this statements is in line with the propositions made by Markus (2001), Paepcke (1996), and Wexelblat & Maes (1999).

Information and knowledge re-use should be a product of a shared work; therefore, a secondary knowledge miner will affect what a person needs from the information and knowledge. Consequently, a greater modification is being required when the re-user is not a shared work practitioner (Markus, 2001). This epitomizes Sellen and Harper's (2002) arguments that it often requires work to make information and knowledge sharable and that a certain amount of shared domain knowledge or history is needed to make sharing effective. Information and knowledge sharing between individuals is often observed within organizations or disciplines and it has been argued that information shared in this way preserves shared context and interpretations in a way that information shared through a central knowledge base, which is accessible to a wider audience (Bonifacio et al, 2002; Iamnitchi, Ripeanu, and Foster, 2002). The role of electronic information environment has mirrors this, and has been the design product of technologies specifically aiming at sharing of information and knowledge between different people.

Today, there are several technologies that are used for information and knowledge sharing in the electronic environment, one of the technological underpinnings of some of the ideas within both in terms of information seeking and in terms of sharing is the notion of Peer-to-Peer computing. Interest surrounding Peer-to-Peer systems has been stimulated by sites such as Napster which allowed and promoted the sharing of music files between individual users and what they kept in their own personal digital file systems. These new decentralized models of computing hold out the promise of opening up the world of information and knowledge sharing beyond pre-defined networks such as the Web, and reaching into the systems of individual users. While there is some dispute over the proper definition of Peer-to-Peer architectures, this vision is one in which the role of server-based networks is either minimized or bypassed altogether, allowing people to directly share resources (be they storage, cycles, or content) between people, or more accurately between people's individual PCs (Hayams and Sellen, 2003).

Another important technology for information and knowledge sharing is grid computing which describes the ability to share the processing power and storage capacity across institutional borders and across groups of individual computers. While other technologies are more clearly directed at the ability to share documents, multimedia or other kinds of content. One aspect of this that is interested is how this new vision is beginning to spark new ideas for ways in which people might share information and knowledge, and new ideas for tools to help people manage and access this information and knowledge. This includes the idea that, with an owner's permission, you might be able to look into and use files from your peer's PC. In support of these statements, Breidenbac (2001) noted that:

Most of the files in today's companies are on PCs, not servers, and peer-to-peer can let you see all these storage assets as one big distributed file space. A workgroup member might even be able to find the sketch of an idea you've just begun on your PDA (p. 26).

An alternative technology that is seen as "crucial" in information and knowledge sharing is the use of meta-data or "the Semantic Web." This is because, unlike the sharing of music files, which has a certain predictability and format (e.g., artist, song title, or album), the sharing of other documents or files is likely to require more complex ways of querying and searching. Turning from this point is the notion that the sharing of information and knowledge in electronic environment is a key goal to achieving an informed citizen. Whether or not the information and knowledge is gathered with sharing in mind, or with whom it is shared and how it is made sharable.

Information and knowledge sharing is most often with individuals or small groups, and this was done mainly through person-to person methods

(mostly via e-mail, or face to face, occasionally by fax or memo). With the advent of electronic information environment, information and knowledge sharing was with the larger organization or the public, this being done mainly via central repositories (the Web, intranet or central database or store). This suggested that the type or number of recipients, efficiency and effectiveness, and organizational policies or work practice, often dictated the methods of sharing to be used by individuals or organizations as the case may be.

The method to be used for information and knowledge sharing obviously and largely depends on "what" to be shared. For instance, e-mail is used for sharing virtual folders, while Web pages allowed digital text, images and attached files to be shared (email and shared folders showing a wider range of file types than the Web which tended to be PDF or program files). Moreover, post/fax, memos and shared shelves allowed hardcopy text or images to be shared among people or users. Face to face allowed both transient sharing of information and knowledge that was spoken or shown but not given to the recipient directly, but it could also allow physical information and knowledge to be retained by recipients whether that be by handing over a hardcopy printout or information on a CD.

SOCIAL NETWORKING AND LIBRARY 2.0 AS GATEWAY FOR INFORMATION ACCESS AND KNOWLEDGE SHARING

The existing information environment is fragmented with Google, Amazon, Wikipedia and several information retrieval tools that allow information and knowledge sharing, access, provision and storage for serving the needs of intended users. This development in the electronic information environment could raise the challenges before the library services. The emergence of Web 2.0 principles and technologies that gave rise to social networking and library 2.0 offer libraries and information centers many opportunities for sharing information and knowledge among people regardless of distance or geographical areas. This development also helps in reaching out beyond the walls of the library and web sites of the any library or institutions. This developments make it possible for people to share knowledge and information online, borrow locally, request from a far or sell as appropriate to their needs and circumstances.

The development of Web 2.0 technology has profound implications for information and knowledge sharing which provided numerous facilities on social system such as wikis, blogs, virtual worlds, podcasts, library 2.0, and media sharing. As a result of this development, a number of social networking software such as instant messaging, text chat, Weblogs, and social networking services are being used to share information and knowledge. The novelty of social networking and library 2.0 lies in their ability to address the possibilities and demands of sharing information and knowledge across dispersed groups and communities with diverse social prerequisites. The attitudes towards social networking and library 2.0 tools have changed rapidly and there have been a growing interest in using these interactive tools in accessing and sharing information and knowledge in various contexts. For example, blogs were first used as individual diaries with a description of an individual's political interest, but today as they are integrated into library activities, they become more as a collective tool where several people participate, generate, share, and accesses a wider information and knowledge. With these features, the blogs also allow users and readers to respond and comment on the information and knowledge shared (Ojala, 2005).

A clear benefit of social networking and library 2.0 is the fact they are technically not challenging; sharing information and knowledge is rewarding when the person knows their colleagues and peers will read about how the procedure works and con-tribute their own knowledge and information on the topic of their interest. Brady, (2005) and Ojala (2005) explained that the exchange of views leads to a more productive information and knowledge sharing environment. This brought about accessibility and public nature of social networking and library 2.0, which are motivating people to create, contribute, and enable them to share ideas accumulate information and knowledge, create networks, share, and manage it (Brady, 2005; Hasan & Pfaff, 2006).

The implication of social networking and library 2.0 lie also in the fact that they help people to collaborate electronically by merging fragmented information and knowledge content into sharable one. There are also important concern against the use of these interactive technologies, due to the risk of having misleading information and knowledge containing in one of the types of social networking tools like wikis such as quality assurance, reliability, and people tend to be more suspicious of the information and knowledge found or shared on the web (Schiltz, Truyen, & Coppens, 2007).

It is evident today that youth have become more addicted with social networking sites and the concept of library 2.0, especially those in the academic communities or university context. Discussing these tools in the context of librarianship, it is possible to discern that the subcategory of Web 2.0 (i.e., library 2.0) is introduced by Michael Casey in 2005 denoting a new concept of librarianship in the electronic information era. Library 2.0 comprises of user centered change in the context of information generation, storage, sharing, and provision; it highlights a library or information environment which encourages constant change and user participation in the creation of physical and virtual library services (Casey & Savastimuk, 2006; Widen-Wulff, Huvila, & Holmberg, 2008). Literature has indicated that libraries in most of the developed world and partly Asia have already adopted several components of Web 2.0 tools to extend their missions of service, sharing and providing access to information and knowledge. Blogs today are used in the libraries to market new materials, resources, events, and to share information and knowledge. Instant messaging is used as a means of providing virtual reference services. Social networking sites such as Facebook, Twitter, YouTube, MySpace, and so forth, are used by the libraries and librarians to interact with students, answer queries, and provide information about library and information services. Stephens and Collins (2008) stated that libraries are also using Rich Site Summary (RSS) services to offer users the ability to subscribe to catalogues and news from the library. All these features of social networking and library 2.0 could be signs of an implication or shift in sharing information and knowledge towards an open framework for information and knowledge access in the electronic environment.

Libraries in the world are increasingly enhancing their Websites by introducing Web 2.0 features. The incorporation of these features has allowed the Website to be more flexible and adaptable. With the adoption of these tools, librarians and users are better able to update the content of the Website instead of just relying on the website master. Casey (2007) envisioned that the next version of the library catalogue or OPAC will have to include many of the attributes that comprise the definition of Web 2.0. Key requirements include user participation, customization, maximum usability, and greatly enhanced discovery. This provides users with the navigational capability to link to alternative sources of information, based on attributes of the search results.

Several libraries today are using the wiki tool in the provision of information services. A wiki-like platform is usually created for the librarians to work collaboratively and concurrently on providing answers to the users' enquiries. This allows any staff to tap on the collective wisdom of the communities of subject librarians and provide quality answers to their queries. Besides using Wiki as a

collaboration tool, some libraries have used it to create research guides, for example, he Biz Wiki contains a variety of content, including information about reference books, Websites, research guides, how-to documents, and more (Casey, 2007). An advantage of using the wiki to create the research guide is the ability to add and edit content easily and anywhere to keep it updated. The wiki also allows the librarian to determine which content is used most and this can influence the type of content to focus on.

The use of messaging tools such as Twitter and SMS text messaging has enhanced library services via hand/mobile phones. The latter have also been incorporated into enquiry and reference services. Today, mobile phone usage (including SMS usage) is very high in the world. Current trends such as these suggest that SMS is an ideal way to reach out to a greater pool of potential users for reference enquiry services. Adding the advantages of portability of the mobile phones and ease in using SMS, it becomes clear that SMS provides an alternative and potentially ideal mode of posting reference enquiries for users on the move, or who may not have the luxury of visiting the library due to their schedules. Against this backdrop, URL links are also used to send information to the user's mobile phone. Upon opening up the URL link either through the mobile phone directly, or through a computer or PDA, the user would be able to view the full reply easily. This includes links to e-resources that are recommended to users asking the questions (Foo, Ng, & Soh, 2008).

Libraries are using the Web 2.0 platform as a channel for collection development. For example, the Flickr is used to expand the collection of a particular library. With respect to the implication of social networking sites on the information and knowledge sharing, the Website provides great opportunities for librarians to interact with their users as it places them in the digital social space of their users. The Websites can be used effectively for outreach and promotion. Librarians can get first hand information about the users through interacting with them. They can also understand the behavior of the users and design services to meet the needs of these users.

Libraries and information centers are also tapping into social video such as video blogging and YouTube to create a presence at these sites. These are being used as marketing tools. One library that makes use of video blogging is the Arlington Heights Memorial Library. Videos of programs and "What's new" segments and interviews were posted at the site. The podcast is now popularly used by libraries for book talk. Another prevalent use of the podcast is for storytelling. For example, the Denver Public Library offers podcasts of share nursery rhymes, fairy tales, and children stories as recorded by the librarians. Some libraries have also used podcast to provide library instructions and information literacy programs.

There are several examples of Web 2.0 applications in libraries today, especially in the developed world and in some parts of Asia. Based on this development, libraries of the developing countries need to decide on the application of Web 2.0 technologies that best suit their environment and their customers. In order to embrace this technology, a logical first step would be for the library staff to learn more about the various Web 2.0 technologies and best practices in libraries. There are already ready learning Web 2.0 courses available on the Web. Subsequently, new ideas to incorporating Web 2.0 technologies to provide new functions and services can emerge, evaluated and decided. Before embarking on adopting the technologies on a large scale, it is good practice and prudent to develop a prototype and build a proof of concept to test viability of the new function or service prior to a pilot and subsequent full implementation.

Library schools in developing countries also need to join this frenzy trend in order to have an equally important role to play in this new environment. They can also help to equip new generations of librarians with competencies and skills to adopting and use Web 2.0 technologies through curriculum development and other initiatives.

THE INFLUENCE OF SOCIAL NETWORKING AND LIBRARY 2.0 FOR AFRICA

Social networking and library 2.0 have revolutionized the way information and knowledge is created and the way users access, use, and contribute information. Libraries are increasingly adopting these technologies to design services that allow them to reach users in the virtual space that they could not reach before. This allows librarians to target a segment of users in the population who will never visit the library to use their services, no matter how hard they try. Foo & Ng (2008) stated that a large part of this population belongs to the generation that grew up with the Internet and they are often known as the digital natives. Rainie (2006) describes six realities of the digital natives as follows:

- Media and gadgets are common throughout everyday life.
- They enjoy media and carry on communications anywhere they wish with the new gadgets available to them.
- Internet is at the center of this change.
- Multitasking is the way of life.
- An ordinary citizen has a greater opportunity to be a publisher, moviemaker, artist, song creator, and storyteller.
- Everything will change even more in the coming years; we can expect more computing power, communication power, and storage power.

The digital natives would want to create, remix and share information and knowledge; they would expect to be able to access information whenever and wherever they are. They expect to be able to gather and share information and knowledge in multiple devices. There is also trust in the community they share the information and knowledge with. Coupled with the spread of affordable laptops or PCs, proliferation of handheld digital devices and affordable Internet access, social networking and library 2.0 tools would enable libraries to create new services for the non-users of libraries that were not possible before (Foo & Ng, 2008). The application of Web 2.0 and social networking technologies to libraries that resulted in the coining of the term "Library 2.0," Maness (2006) defined the term "Library 2.0" as "the application of interactive collaborative, and multimedia web-based technologies to web-based library services and collections." As the information environment changes, libraries must not only change with them, they must allow users to change the library. It should constantly seek new ways to allow communities to seek, find, and utilise information and knowledge. Thus, there is a necessity to understand the concept of Library 2.0, social networking, and the opportunities they create for libraries to provide content and services to their communities of users. Maness (2006) highlights that there is paradigm shift for librarianship as Library 2.0 demands libraries to focus less on secured inventory systems and more on collaborative discovery systems.

Increasingly, librarians will need to play a facilitation role to allow users to interact and create content for themselves. Library 2.0, where sharing is the norm, recognizes that the users utilize information and knowledge as a community rather than an individual. Librarians need to understand the wisdom of the clients and their changing roles. With Library 2.0 and social networking, the creation and delivery of content is not primarily done solely by the librarians. These technologies allow the user communities to participate in the creation of the content together with librarians. The appearance of blogs and wikis has enormous implications for libraries. Increasingly, blogs are becoming another form of publications and libraries need to look into ways to include them in their collection development and archival. Librarians will need to re-think the notions of being "authoritative" and "reliable."

Social networks such as MySpace, Facebook, and Ning have opened up new ways of users to connect to each other, engage in discussion, and share information and knowledge dynamically with other users. In the past year, there has been a sharp increase in the number of such sites with a huge number of users. Libraries can make use of these opportunities to be present in such spaces and make connections with their users to answer their questions. Maness (2006) suggests that the face of the library's Web-presence in the future may look very much like a social network interface. Tagging and social bookmarking have become common activities in Websites such as Flickr and Del.ious. us. Tagging and social bookmarking tools help librarians bridge the gap between the library's need to offer authoritative, well-organized information and their patrons' Web experience (Rethlefsen, 2007). Library 2.0 tools can allow the users to search both standardized and user tagged subjects, whichever makes most sense.

Thus, it could be said that the advent of the Internet, Web 2.0, and Library 2.0 in the last two decades through the digital era, have indeed posed a significance challenge for library and information science schools to keep pace with change and to ensure the education of information professionals be relevant and kept up to date and ensure maximum employability and effectiveness for the employers. It should be noted that competencies in the application of social networking and library 2.0 are very much relevant today. Especially in the context of Library 2.0, the emphasis perhaps must be shifted more towards the segments of "Tools & Technology" and "Strategic Thinking and Analytical Skills" to be kept up-to-date of IT tools (including Web 2.0 technologies) and the need to continue to create new ways to elicit information and knowledge (e.g., through social networking and collaborative OPACs) and value adding services, systems and products (e.g., through wiki-like collaborative and SMS reference services) (Hawamdeh & Foo, 2001).

This point to the new paradigms of information and knowledge sharing, collaborative workgroups, social networking, and so forth, all of which are now better supported by Web 2.0 technologies that are increasingly and rapidly embraced in Library 2.0. Such rapid changes in the information environment and the ever increasing demands on the information professional has placed a tall (and impossible) order on education and training, and significantly challenged library and information science schools education around the world to produce graduates who are relevant and can thrive in the Library 2.0 environment.

CONCLUSION

It is a well known fact that the implication of social networking and Library 2.0 are yet another gesture of rapid development driven by user-centered change that revolutionise and evolve libraries to deliver a new range of functions and services to meet the varying and new demands of its Web savvy users. Social networking and Library 2.0 encourages constant and purposeful change, engages users in the creation of physical and virtual products and services that are being constantly evaluated through feedback, contribution and conversations. Many libraries around the whole have embraced these changes quickly and we now witness a proliferation of new services and functionalities that were unheard of three years ago

Nonetheless, library schools in general have not kept pace with these changes–they have been slow to react and update their curriculum. There is a need for library schools to act promptly to ensure the gap is closed quickly so that their graduates remain relevant to industry. A number of ways to incorporate Web 2.0 and Library 2.0 education is proposed. We should expect to see a quick response by forward-looking library schools to review and adjust their program and integrate this aspect of education in the near future.

REFERENCES

Brady, M. (2005). *Blogging: Personal participation in the public knowledge-building on the web*. Colchester, UK: University of Essex.

Casey, M. E., & Savastinuk, L. C. (2006). Library 2.0: Service for the next generation library. *Library Journal, 131*(14), 40–42.

Foo, S., & Ng, J. (2008). Library 2.0, Libraries and Library School. Paper presented at Proceedings Of Library Association of Singapore Conference 2008. Singapore.

Gajendara, S., Sun, W., & Ye, Q. (2010). Second Life: A strong communication Tool in Social Networking and Business. *Information Technology Journal, 9*(3), 254–534.

Hasan, H., & Pfaff, C. C. (2006). The Wiki: An environment to revolutionize employees' interaction with corporate knowledge. In *Proceedings of OZCHI*. Sydney, Australia.

Kankaanranta, M. (2005). International Perspectives on the Pedagogically Innovative Uses of Technology. *Human Technology, 1*(2), 111–116.

Kerrigan, K., Lindsey, G., & Novak, K. (1994). Computer networking in International Agricultural Research Experience of the CGNET. New Information technologies in Agriculture. *Quarterly Bulletin of the International Association of Agricultural Information Specialists, XXXIX*(1&2), 182–193.

Metcalfe, J., & Gilmore, J. (1990). Information Technology in Agricultural development. In Speedy, A. (Ed.), *Development World Agriculture*. London: Grosvenor Press International.

Ojala, M. (2005). Blogging for knowledge sharing, management and dissemination. *Business Information Review, 22*(4), 269–276. doi:10.1177/0266382105060607.

Schiltz, M., Truyen, F., & Coppens, H. (2007). Cutting the trees of knowledge: Social software, information architecture and their epistemic consequences. *Thesis Eleven, 89*, 94-114.

Stephens, M., & Collins, M. (2007). Web 2.0, Library 2.0 and the Hyperlinked Library. *Serials Review, 33*(4), 253–256. doi:10.1016/j.serrev.2007.08.002.

Widen-Wuilff, G., Huvilla, I., & Holmberg, K. (2008). Library 2.0 as a new participatory context. In Pagani, M. (Ed.), *Encyclopedia of Multimedia Technology and Networking* (pp. 842–848). Hershey, PA: IGI Global. doi:10.4018/978-1-60566-014-1.ch115.

ADDITIONAL READING

Abram, S. (2005). Web 2.0 and Library 2.0, librarian 2.0. *Information Outlook, 9*(12), 44–46.

Adeyinka, A., Ajiboye, O. A., Emmanuel, A. O., & Wojuade, J. I. (2007). Stakeholders' Perceptions of The Impact of a Global System for Mobile Communication on Nigeria's Rural Economy: Implications for an Emerging Communication Industry. *The Journal of Community Informatics, 3*(4), 34–45.

Adomi, E. A. (2006). Mobile phone usage: Patterns of library and information science students at Delta State University, Abraka, Nigeria. *Electronic Journal of Academic and Special Librarianship, 7*(1), 1–11.

Aharony, N. (2008). *Web 2.0 in U.S. LIS schools: Are they missing the boat?* Retrieved on December 2, 2012, from http://www.ariadne.ac.uk/issue54/aharony/

Ahmed, A. (2007). Open access towards bridging the digital divide: Policies and strategies for developing countries. *Information Technology for Development, 13*(4), 337–361. doi:10.1002/itdj.20067.

Aker, J. (2008). *Does digital divide or provide? The impact of cell phones on grain markets in Niger.* BREAD Working Paper No. 177. Durham, NC: Bureau for Research and Economic Analysis of Development.

Anderson, P. (2007). All that glisters is not gold: Web 2.0 and the librarian. *Journal of Librarianship and Information Science, 39*(4), 195–198. doi:10.1177/0961000607083210.

Balogun, J. (2000). *Impact of GSM on Economy and Development.* Gwalada Abuja, Nigeria: Center for Culture and Technical Interchange between East and West.

Butagira, T. (2009). Uganda grapples with the pros and cons of increased access to mobile phones. *Business Daily Africa.* Retrieved on December 2, 2012, from http://www.businessdailyafrica.com/-/539552/805986/-/687oqn/-/index.html

Casey, M. (2006). *LibraryCrunch: Bringing you a Library 2.0 perspective.* Retrieved on December 2, 2012, from http://www.librarycrunch.com/

Casey, M. (2006). LibraryCrunch: Bringing you a library 2.0 perspective. Retrieved on December 2, 2012, from http://www.librarycrunch.com/

Casey, M. (2006a). Born in the biblioblogosphere. *LibraryCrunch.* Retrieved on December 2, 2012, from http://www.librarycrunch.com/2006/01/post_1.html

Casey, M. (2007). *Looking toward Catalog 2.0 in Library 2.0 and beyond: Innovative technologies and tomorrow's user.* London: Libraries Unlimited.

Castells, M. (2000). *The Rise of the Network Society.* Oxford, UK: Blackwell.

Clark, J. (2003). *Civil society, NGOs, and development in Ethiopia: A snapshot view.* Washington, DC: The World Bank.

Crawford, W. (2006). Library 2.0 and 'Library 2.0'. *Cites and Insights, 6,* 2. Retrieved on December 2, 2012, from http://cites.boisestate.edu/civ6i2.pdf

Cullnan, T. B. (2010). *Informing Development: Mobile Telephony, Governments, and Local Stakeholders in Africa.* Unpublished dissertation. Georgetown, MD: Georgetown University.

Denton, A. (2008). Policy priorities to connect Africa. In *Proceedings of the 1ˢᵗ International Conference on m4d Mobile Communication Technology for Development* (pp. 3-4). Karlstad, Sweden: Karlstad University.

Donner, J. (2008). *Research Approaches to Mobile Use in the Developing World: A Review of the Literature*. Paper presented at the International Conference on Mobile Communication and Asian Modernities. Hong Kong.

Foo, S. (2006). Developments in information science education at the School of Communication and Information, Nanyang Technological University, Singapore. In *Proceedings of 2006 Annual Symposium of Research Center for Knowledge Communities: New Directions for Information Science Education in the Networked Information Society.* Tsukuba, Japan: University of Tsukuba.

Foo, S., Chaudhry, A. S., Majid, S. M., & Logan, E. (2002). Academic libraries in transition: Challenges ahead. In *Proceedings of World Library Summit, Keynote address: Academic Library Seminar*. Singapore: National Library Board.

Foo, S., Ng, H., & Soh, A. (2008). Going virtual for enhance experience: A case study of National Library of Singapore. In *Proceedings of VALA 2008 14th Biennial Conference*. Melbourne, Australia. Retrieved on December 2, 2012, from http://www.valaconf.org.au/vala2008/papers2008/151_Foo_Keynote_Final.pdf

Granovetter, M. (1985). Economic Action and Social Structure: The Problem of Embeddedness. *American Journal of Sociology, 91*, 481–510. doi:10.1086/228311.

Habib, M. (2006). Conceptual model for academic library 2.0. *Michael Habib's weblog on library and information science*. Retrieved on December 2, 2012, from http://mchabib.blogspot.com/2006/06/conceptual-model-for-academic-library.html

Hale, M. (1991). Paradigmatic shift in library and information science. In McClure, C. R., & Hernon, P. (Eds.), *Library and Information Science Research: Perspectives and Strategies for Improvement*. Westport, CT: Praeger.

Hashim, R., & Becker, G. (2001). *Internet Malaysia*. Bangi, Malaysia: UKM.

Hawamdeh, S., & Foo, S. (2001). Information professionals in the information age: Vital skills and competencies. In *Proceedings of International Conference for Library and Information Science Educators in the Asia Pacific Region (ICLISE 2001)*. Kuala Lumpur, Malaysia.

International Telecommunications Union. (2003). *Mobile overtakes fixed: Implications for policy and regulation*. Geneva, Switzerland: ITU Publications.

International Telecommunications Union. (2009). *Information society statistical profiles 2009: Africa*. Geneva, Switzerland: ITU Publications.

Joseph, K. J. (2002). Harnessing ICT for Development: Need for a National Policy. *Information Technology in Developing Countries, 12*(3). Retrieved on December 2, 2012, from http://www.iimahd.ernet.in/egov/ifip/dec2002/article1.htm

Lawson, S. (2006). Library 2.0: rapid response to rapid change. *Colorado Libraries, 32*(2), 19–21.

LibraryThing. (n.d.). Retrieved on December 2, 2012, from http://www.librarything.com/

Litwin, R. (2006). The central problem of library 2.0: Privacy. *Library juice: On the intersection of libraries, politics, and culture*. Retrieved on December 2, 2012, from http://libraryjuicepress.com/blog/?p=68

Lochoee, H., Wakeford, N., & Pearson, I. (2003). A social history of the mobile phone with a view to its future. *British Telecom Technology Journal, 21*(3), 203–211.

Majumda, A., & Shukla, A. (2008). *Web 2.0: Implications on library*. Paper presented at International CALIBER-2008. Allahabad, India. Retrieved on December 2, 2012, from http://ir.inflibnet.ac.in/bitstream/handle/1944/1275/50.pdf?sequence=1

Maness, J. (2006). Library 2.0 Theory: Web 2.0 and Its Implications for Libraries. *Webology, 3*(2). Retrieved on December 2, 2012, from http://www.webology.ir/2006/v3n2/a25.html

Maness, J. M. (2006). *Library 2.0 Theory: Web 2.0 and its implication for libraries*. Retrieved on December 2, 2012, from http://www.webology.ir/2006/v3n2/a25.html

Manir, A. K. (2009). Access to information: The dilemma for rural community development in Africa. Paper presented at GLOBLICS, Dakar – Senegal. Retrieved on December 2, 2012, from https://smartech.gatech.edu/bitstream/handle/1853/36694/1238296264_MA.pdf

Miller, P. (2005). *Web 2.0: Building the New Library*. Retrieved on December 2, 2012, from http://www.ariadne.ac.uk/issue45/miller/

Miller, P. (2005a). *Do libraries matter?: The rise of library 2.0*. Retrieved on December 2, 2012, from http://www.talis.com/downloads/white_papers/DoLibrariesMatter.pdf

Miller, P. (2005b). Web 2.0: building the new library. *Ariadne, 45*. Retrieved on December 2, 2012, from http://www.ariadne.ac.uk/issue45/miller/

Miller, P. (2006a). Coming together around library 2.0: A focus for discussion and a call to arms. *D-Lib Magazine, 12*(4), 2006. Retrieved on December 2, 2012, from http://www.dlib.org/dlib/april06/miller/04miller.html

Miller, P. (2006b). *Library 2.0 - The challenge of distruptive innovation*. Retrieved on December 2, 2012, from http://www.talis.com/resources/documents/447_Library_2_prf1.pdf

O'Reilly, T. (2005). *Web 2.0: Compact definition*. Retrieved on December 2, 2012, from http://radar.oreilly.com/archives/2005/10/web-20-compact-definition.html

O'Reilly, T. (2005a). *What is Web 2.0?* Retrieved on December 2, 2012, from http://www.oreillynet.com/pub/a/oreilly/tim/news/2005/09/30/what-is-web-20.html#mememap

Rainie, L. (2006, October 27). *Digital Natives: How today's youth are different from their 'digital immigrant' elders and what they meant for libraries*. Presentation for Metro-New York Library/council. Retrieved on December 2, 2012, from http://www.pewInternet.org/PPF/r/71/presentation_display.asp

Rethlefsen, M. L. (2007). Tags help make libraries Del.icio,us: Social bookmarking and tagging. Retrieved on December 2, 2012, from http://www.libraryjournal.com/article/CA6476403.html

KEY TERMS AND DEFINITIONS

Access: This refers to path, ways, or means of approaching, communicating or means of making use of information.

Africa: This refers to one of the continents in the world and one of the developing countries in which access to information and knowledge is very low.

Gateway: This refers to the opportunity for having access to information and knowledge.

Information: This refers to a piece of data either on electronic or print format that people can access and share for their daily needs.

Knowledge: This refers to the condition of knowing facts, information, descriptions or skills acquire through learning process.

Library 2.0: This refers to a modified model of providing library services using modernized form of information service provision with the power of web 2.0 and other ICTs facilities.

Sharing: This refers to the in which information and knowledge are giving out for mutual benefit.

Social Networking: This refers to an online platform, site or portal that facilitates the building of social relations among people with common interest, activities, and backgrounds.

Chapter 4
A Proposal to Study of Cross Language Information Retrieval (CLIR) System Users' Information Seeking Behavior

YooJin Ha
Clarion University, USA

ABSTRACT

There has been an enormous increase for information written in different languages by users from various backgrounds and disciplines. This chapter proposes a research design to examine multilingual information users' information behaviors when using a Cross Language Information Retrieval (CLIR) system. Development of a true CLIR is absolutely necessary so that the system would allow users to access information written in the user's languages of choice. Kuhlthau's Information Search Process (ISP) model was borrowed as a theoretical framework. Of particular concern are those users who want information represented by a language different than the users' original query or for those users who would like to retrieve additional information written in a second and/or third language or in a language which cannot be understood by them. This research is expected to yield a revised or new ISP model applicable to CLIR environments. It is expected that this study will also increase our understanding of CLIR users. The expected CLIR users include many of non-English speakers, especially users in developing countries who need this kind of CLIR system due to lack of materials in their own language. It is possible that the results of this research could inform CLIR system designers. The chapter is composed of purpose of study, literature review, theory, research questions, methodology, and discussion section. In the literature review section, pertinent research studies from information seeking behavior, cross language information retrieval, and general relevance studies are presented. Kuhlthau's ISP model is introduced in detail in the theory section. A possible application of Kuhlthau's ISP Model to the CLIR environment is presented in a table format. Research questions are developed from the literature reviews and Kuhlthau's model. Each research question, premises/assumptions, and its correspondent methodology are proposed in the methodology section. Limitations are discussed in the discussion section.

DOI: 10.4018/978-1-4666-4353-6.ch004

INTRODUCTION

Ranganathan (1957) states in his 2nd and 3rd laws of library science: "Every reader his book" (p. 80) and "Every book its reader" (p. 80). He would be a proponent of an open access system, which can help readers to "make discoveries" (p. 258) using all information, no matter what their formats or languages. Since the Internet began expanding globally in the 1990s, accessing various types and formats of information on the Web has become a daily practice for many information users in the world. People now depend more on the Web, digital libraries, and other information retrieval systems to search for information.

In the current Web environment, however, only a limited amount of resources can actually be usable to certain user groups. Although this may be related to access to particular subject areas in the invisible Web, the biggest reason for limitation to information is due to language differences. One of these examples includes information users in developing countries where there is a lack of information access to the materials in their own language (Ugah, 2007; Uhegbu, 2002; Etim, 2001) so people would need translation help from one to another language–mostly English to their own language (Parry, 2011).

According to Cybermetrics Lab, roughly 63% of the world's top 400 institutional repositories have non-English content (cited on Lederman, Warnick, Hitson, & Johnson, 2010, p. 126). Also as of 2011, the World Internet Usage data shows that 73.2% of the world's online populations are non-English speakers and it is roughly three-fourths of all Internet users. English speakers are only 26.8%, which is about one-third of all Internet users.

As Chowdhury (2003) affirmed, multilingual information retrieval has become a major challenge to gaining access to the prolific information on the Web (p. 72). This challenge can be partitioned into several major components and this overview provides a structure for understanding the definition of and resolution for the symbolic representation of language differences between the query and the document and the environment in which the search occurs.

Global Environment

Examples of the challenges confronting access to the written record will now be highlighted with special attention to the bibliographic surrogate which stands as the gateway to more extensive data such as reports, books, and journal information. Technological developments of the Web, the effects of globalization, and the international emphasis in academic scholarship are three contributors to creating demand for ethnically diverse peoples to study, work, and collaborate together across borders and continents.

Accordingly, today's information needs articulated by potential users of the Web and library databases expand the need for access to resources written in languages not known to the individual conducting the search. It is also possible, even likely in many situations the pertinent information being sought might be in a language where the query is in a different character set from the information being retrieved. It might be further assumed that English is used as a standardized language and that most people in search environments might possess some knowledge of written or spoken English. This is, however, a tenuous assumption. For example, suppose there is a branch of a Japanese company located in Korea, where the common language will be either Japanese or Korean (or possibly English). Here the search queries could be expressed in one of several languages spanning different characters and alphabets. Yet, the relevant information in the data base could be in those languages or other languages.

Lack of User Study in Multilingual Information Environment

Matching or linking the query to the words associated with the documents in the database becomes problematic and, in some cases, impossible. Thus, the search will suffer or fail because relevant information cannot be retrieved. It is difficult enough to retrieve pertinent documents in a monolingual environment; moreover, in a multilingual situation where information is written in various languages, it can be a daunting experience. Additionally, if more than one language is used within a document or journal, then this can become a complex search process, difficult for those who are seeking information where the query and the surrogates do not correspond to each other. In effect, searching in a monolingual environment may differ not only in degree from a search in a cross-language information system but it may also differ in kind. Such environments can be so different that research knowledge of monolingual systems may not be applicable to cross-language information retrieval.

For the cross-language situation where users input their search questions in a different language than their result documents, it is obvious that there would be a strong need for effective and efficient systems that allow users to search document collections in multiple languages and retrieve relevant information that is useful to them, even when they have little or no linguistic competence in the target languages. There is, however, not yet an appropriate information retrieval system for multilingual or cross-language users; furthermore, the research in this area is recent but sparse. In order to provide users with access to the full array of resources, there is a concomitant need to assemble a body of research on individuals' Information Seeking Behavior (ISB) in cross-language retrieval systems. Such research will need to be sensitive to the differences across the user population and aware of differences across the languages employed in the searches as well cognizant of differences due to the topic matter being searched.

Representative users' studies in ISB include the work of Kuhlthau (1991, 1993a) who developed a model called the "Information Search Process (ISP)." This model presents the holistic process of how information users learn and recognize their information problems and finally work through a process to meet their evolving information needs.

This model accounts for how users engage in different information search processes depending on where the person is in each stage of the process. It also takes into consideration the circumstances involved when the user interacts with a specific retrieval system. Thus, it is known that this model is applicable to monolingual information retrieval environments and it is proposed here that it could be an appropriate theoretical framework to study users in a cross language information retrieval (CLIR) query/system environment. Furthermore, the model is adaptable to verify how users cope with differences in language, alphabet, and topics since the ISP model accounts the searcher's cognitive, affective, and physical changes.

In cross language information retrieval (CLIR) research, most of the studies have focused on the functionality of explicit retrieval characteristics such as its translation function or its recall and precision. Those studies did not focus on users and their expectations, frustrations, or perceived degree of success when using a CLIR with query/document incompatibility across languages. Additionally, users' relevance criteria are defined using a system emphasis without adequate attention to users' assessments of the results retrieved and the adequacy of the system that performs the retrieval.

Purpose of the Proposed Study

This study proposes a research design to examine multilingual information users' information behaviors when using a cross language information retrieval (CLIR) system. Useful for this design is the Information Search Process (ISP) model with its evaluation criteria of surrogates when searching multilingual resources in a working environment. Of particular concern are those users who want information represented by a language different than the users' original query or for those users who would like to retrieve additional information written in a second and/or third language or in a language which cannot be understood by them.

This research is expected to yield a revised or new ISP model applicable to CLIR environments. It is expected that this study will also increase our understanding of CLIR users. The expected CLIR users include many non-English speakers, especially users in developing countries. Al-Suqri (2011) claimed that there is still a lack of user studies in information seeking behavior in developing countries. Major researchers have conducted most of their user studies in Western countries, leaving information gaps to pursue in this area of study (p. 2). It is especially important to conduct user studies in developing countries.

It is possible that the results of this research could inform CLIR system designers. The implications for such multi-language information retrieval takes on greater importance when it is realized that new query systems span boundaries across different data bases and even across the web/Internet itself such as multilingual federate search (Lederman, Warnick, Hitson, & Johnson, 2010), MetaLib, and 360 search Fedrate . It becomes critical in some disciplines that searches not be limited to a specific language since a field advances regardless of one language (e.g., physics).

The following section will present pertinent research studies from information seeking behavior, cross language information retrieval (CLIR), and general relevance studies. In the next theory section, Kuhlthau's Information Search Process (ISP) model will be presented in order to link her ISP model to the situation encountered by CLIR users. Research questions will then be developed from the literature reviews and Kuhlthau's model. Following the theory will be a methodology section addressing the propositions raised by the problem definition given above. Specific information on a proposed actual study will conclude this paper with identification of variable candidates, sample selection considerations, and data analysis.

LITERATURE REVIEW

This literature review section will examine three different topical areas that are linked to each other under a common concept, the "users' point of view." First, pertinent literature about information seeking behavior is examined in general. It will give special attention to multilingual users' information search. Second, studies about user studies address within the notion of cross language information retrieval (CLIR) systems. Third, studies about users' relevance judgment in common monolingual information retrieval (IR) systems will be reviewed and discussed what would be needed to extend in terms of serving multilingual environments. Then, as a theoretical basis for this chapter, Kuhlthau's Information Search Process (ISP) model will be followed.

General Information Seeking Behavior (ISB)

Wilson (1999) defines the information seeking behavior as "those activities a person may engage in when identifying his or her own needs for information, searching for such information in any way, and using or transferring that information" (p. 249). There have been extensive users' studies under the name of "human information seeking behavior" in order to assess a pattern of information behavior in a certain environments, such as Belkin's "Anomalous States of Knowledge (ASK)" model (Belkin, 1980; Belkin & Oddy, 1982a; 1982b); Dervin's "Sense-making" approach (Dervin, 1983; 1992); Bates' berry-picking (Bates, 1989); Kuhlthau's "Information Search Process (ISP)" (Kuhlthau, 1983; 1988a; 1989b; 1993a); Taylor's "Information Use Environment (IUE)" model (Taylor, 1991); User-oriented information retrieval research focusing on human behaviors (social and cognitive situations), associated with a user's interaction retrieval system (Kuhlthau, 1993a; Kuhlthau, Spink, & Cool, 1992; Belkin & Vakkari, 1985; Vakkari, 2003).

Something as simple as a person using information becomes a complex layering of processes and changes as researchers explore the underlying structure in information seeking. An individual is assumed to have an information need which creates an internal motivation to behave in an information environment. Dervin (1983; 1992) addressed this need as a process of "sense-making" characterized by when an individual needs to resolve a problem. Kuhlthau (1993a) saw this instead as process people engaged in when assigned tasks required information. However, Belkin (1980) began his investigations of this process after the need had been expressed and saw it as an interaction between query and information source with a continuous modification of the need as new information informed the person and acted to modify the query.

Meanwhile, Pettigrew et al. (2001) attempted to define the sequence of the seeking process while Bates (1989) drew upon analogies to explain this process. Surprisingly, none of these researchers were able to predict which individuals would have internal and expressed needed in similar information environments. In short, two individuals could face the same situation (such as purchasing an automobile) and one has insatiable information needs to inform this decision while the other has few such needs. Nonetheless, those involved in studying information seeking, at least at the need state, admit that people do have such needs and that they follow particular processes to resolve that uncertain state. Further, these researchers would agree that the search process for an expressed need is ripe for exploration in order for information providers to offer better resources and services to help individuals make better, more informed decisions.

The need component is then followed by a search process and it is here that Kuhlthau offers her ISP model which shows how individuals sequence their information seeking into components which follow a predictable logic. Kuhlthau's ISP provides a more detailed explanation about users' search processes to encompass their motivations and thoughts as they progress during the conduct of a search. This value added information begins to complete the profiles developed by Belkin et al's (1980) "Anomalous Stage of Knowledge (ASK)" model where the focus was on the ever changing ambiguity of the query. Linking Belkin's

work to Kuhlthau's model provides an appropriate conceptual platform for studying CLIR. It is important here to note that Kuhlthau (1993a) argued that information seeking is "a learning process in which the choices along the way are dependent on personal constructs rather than on one universal predictable search for everyone" (p. 9).

Kuhlthau's ISP model also encompasses how users' emotions are altered during their process of searching information. Several studies have successfully used the Kuhlthau ISP model which will be employed here as a structural component of a CLIR model. After verified from Kuhlthau's ISP, many of ISB studies include also affective aspects of information seeking behavior, such as, feelings of anxiety (Jiao & Onwuegbuzie, 1997; Onwuegbuzie & Jiao, 1998); uncertainty (Shannon & Weaver, 1949; Kuhlthau, 1993a; 1999; Bates, 1986; Wilson et al., 2000; Kim, 2004; Yoon, 2002; Wilson, Ellis, & Ford, 2000; Wilson et al., 1999; 2002; Ingwersen, 1992), thought, feelings, and actions (Kuhlthau, 1993a; 1993b; Chung, 2004), frustration, preference, and satisfaction (Nahl & Tenopir, 1996; Dervin, 1999; Nahl, 2004).

ISB on the Web with Language Concern

There have been many studies that examine Web searching behavior using various methods in library research: query analysis (Beheshti, Large, & Tam, 2010; Spink & Jansen, 2004; Wang, Berry, & Yang, 2003; Rieh & Xie, 2001), laboratory experiments (Willson & Given, 2010; Kim, 2002; Wang, Hawk, & Tenopir, 2000), interviews in natural settings (Kim, 2004; Rieh, 2004) and participatory design to find librarians' preferences (Buck & Nichols, 2012). However, there have not been many studies involving how individuals search information across languages, especially those where the query and retrieved documents are in languages involving different alphabets.

It is estimated that the majority of Internet resources will be in Chinese, yet the research on how people seek information is mostly restricted to English. Little is known about how bilingual users make decisions about language selection when using multilingual information resources on the Internet: bilingual users' behaviors, perceptions, and preferences are beginning to be realized as being an important research focus to compare such entities as a choice of initial search strategies (direct address, subject directory, and search engines) (Rieh & Rieh, 2005); multilingual graduate students' information uses and needs (Dagli, 2005); a study to identify difficulties of individuals' experiences when accessing and using non-English information in current IR systems (Ha, 2008); a comparison study of Finnish and American Webpage usage by non-English/English speakers (Iivonen & White, 2001); language growth rate on the Web pages–the study found that in languages other than English were growing faster than English-language pages (Large & Moukdad, 2001).

The survey and experiment participants from Ha's study (2008) note the lack of non-English access via indexing terms, the lack of non-English records in major online databases which index journals, the lack of English translation of abstracts, and the lack of coherent and understandable access to non-Roman language materials. Also, the users of non-English information expect to have a system with cross language information retrieval functions providing clear access to full text non-English information. Importantly, having understandable bibliographic records are essential when individuals make decisions on their expected use of non-English documents.

Rieh and Rieh's study (2005) found that subjects who were Korean science and engineering scholars did not use Web search engines as multilingual tools. For their selection of search query, they chose a language that can represent their information need most accurately (pp. 255-260). There has been an assumption that multilingual users are still likely to submit their search queries in their first language since they cannot express their information need well enough (Ogden & Davis, 2000). The results of Rieh & Rieh's study indicated that users' choice of language is dependent upon types of tasks, rather than familiarity with the language. An early study by Petrelli et al. (2004) found that users chose the most appropriate language for their task, one that was not necessarily their native language. These studies are useful in mapping language construction of original queries, even though the studies employed limited sample sizes.

CLIR

Cross Language Information Retrieval (CLIR) is a retrieval system that operates with queries in one language to retrieve documents in other languages. It allows users to access information written in the user's languages of choice. CLIR has been studied from diverse research fields such as Information Retrieval (IR), Natural Language Processing (NLP), Machine Translation (MT), Linguistics, and Human-computer interaction (Oard et al., 1999). Until, recently, CLIR research has focused on physical system development, for example, development of translation technique for query translation or content (document) translation using various methods: Ontology, Machine translation lexicons, Bilingual dictionary and Corpora machine translation (Oard, 1997). Most studies have been done without considering actual users' use of the systems. Oard and Resnik (1999) argued that three disciplines, information retrieval, library science, and machine translation, should integrate their research in order to provide for a well-designed CLIR system (p. 364).

A critical issue for the CLIR research is how to define and study users who will use the systems. Lately, user studies have been proposed and implemented in CLIR research. The user studies in CLIR are now just beginning to examine particular CLIR systems in terms of users' needs, preferences, and behaviors (Ogden et al., 1999; Petrelli et al., 2004). It is recognized that users have diverse backgrounds, and it is implied they may have different information seeking behaviors due to culture, language, or learned styles. On the system side, designing a helpful interface is needed which can enhance formulating their queries to interact with the system (Resnik & Oard, 1999). Also designing a sensible and simple display of retrieval results (surrogates) will be required based on users' studies. These are important factors since these will affect users' relevance judgments—whether users will choose the specific document or not.

Petrelli et al. (2004) employed a case study method to observe and interview real users (10 subjects: business analysts, journalists, librarians, translators) at their work place. From these interviews, they identified a number of user requirements for CLIR systems. Users indicated that they want to search multiple languages simultaneously, to change query languages within the same search session, to support multilingual queries, to search by the most appropriate language they know for the task, which is not always their native language, and to filter results by language, genre, date, or other features (p. 928). They argued that designers of CLIR systems should examine cross-lingual information search tasks in real environments with real users to overcome the mismatch between user goals and system mechanisms.

In Information Retrieval (IR) system studies, many researchers assert that the users' intentions of pursuing information for a particular query and the users' interaction with the system as a query changes becomes a defining characteristic of the information search process (Belkin et al., 1980). So far, some researchers have explored a user interactive approach with a CLIR system: QUILT system, providing a display of the Spanish translation of English queries terms (Davis & Ogden, 1997); Arctos system, providing a browser-based interface with which to enter English queries. In the Arctos system, the user can interactively improve the query translation using links to on-line bilingual translation resources (

Ogden et al., 1999); Keizai system, which allows users to get Japanese and Korean Web data with displays of English summaries of the top ranking documents (Ogden & Davis, 2000); applying query expansion (Ballesteros & Croft, 1998); C*ST*RD is an interactive information access system using space visualization, which can make it possible to open a document or content as per users' selection. Hindi language for English speaker was also tested (Leuski et al., 2003).

CLIR system development is now actively studied based on users' needs although its current development stage still focuses on the physical system itself. However, because of its unique situation covering different languages, the system design should give equal attention to constructing algorithms and to defining user needs. Attention to each language's characteristics, representations, and specific needs should also be explored to particular intelligent interfaces. All these factors are essential or necessary prerequisites for structuring system components and features to make them more user-centered. Also, it is hoped that the system could produce more efficient representations of responses to users' queries within the framework of a culturally sensitive and helpful interface.

Relevance

Since information science's beginnings, information retrieval research has focused on how people seek information and how they judge its relevance. *Relevance* can be defined as how pertinent information is retrieved from a certain system which can serve users' particular needs. Relevance judgments occur as individuals evaluate surrogate language (such as index terms and abstracts) and how they evaluate and use the documents retrieved. System-centered approaches dominated early study of these phenomena and they used such metrics as precision and recall to assess the likelihood of retrieving relevant documents from a database. Later approaches were user-centered and included cognitive and interactive studies in IR to help explain users' relevance evaluations (Ingerwisen, 1982; Belkin & Vickery, 1985; Borgman, 1984; Dervin & Nilan, 1986; DeMay, 1977; Bates, 1986; Wilson, 1981). Here, relevance criteria were related to characteristics of the query and the individual.

Later, these concerns expanded to include recognition of important situational elements in the retrieval environment: the organization (social domain), the individual, and the cognitive complexities of a human working for an organization (Schamber et al., 1990; Schamber, 1991; Barry, 1994; Cosijn & Ingwersen, 2000). Schamber and Barry (1991) conducted similar research to find out end users' relevance criteria. Both used a small experiment making subjects conduct a search followed by an interview with each searcher. The interview transcription was analyzed using content analysis. The content categories were summarized into seven classes: information content of documents (accuracy, in-depth information etc), source of documents, physical entity, other information sources within the environment, users' situation, users' beliefs and preferences, and users' previous experiences or background.

Schamber (1991) also presented ten summary-level categories from her study: accuracy, currency, specificity, geographic proximity (since the subjects were from weather related work), reliability, accessibility, verifiability, clarity, dynamism, and presentation quality. Thus, as Cosijn and Ingwersen (2000) argued, the relevance judgments are representation of information objects and these results are from "manifestations of socio-cognitive relevance" (p. 546, 549). Hyldegård (2004) also argued it is important to consider users' social and collaborative dimension in their information seeking. It is because the system should support various user roles, needs and types of interactions during a problem solving process (p. 277).

CLIR system users will be in more complicated situations than monolingual information retrieval users, such as their information need, language uses, cultural differences, etc. There has not been much study about relevance in CLIR environment. Arnold et al. (1997) argued the operational evaluations should take into account the end-user's subjective measures of translation adequacy (such as intelligibility, accuracy), coverage of linguistic phenomena (such as via creation of standard test suits). Although it is not simple to satisfy every single user's need, especially users seeking information in a different language, the study of users' relevance judgment in CLIR is absolutely necessary.

To make a new and efficient CLIR system, a comprehensive user analysis including socio-cognitive concern should be considered. An advanced information retrieval system for multilingual users will require understanding: each different user's language abilities, the underlying cultural implications of the query, and each culture and language's characteristic itself as well as knowledge of documents (representations) and system. To offer a reasonable interface, when users process their information search, it should offer various options to approach and obtain the target queries or information. For example, this suggests that broader terms or common words are used within a particular language domain and that the system has the ability to offer synonyms with easy cross-referencing access. To process this, it is crucial to tap into users' analysis of queries within the users' culture and context; and, equally importantly, to have the system structure index terms extracted from documents of the system collection to create an interactive IR/CLIR environment. The terms should be created considering it's the users' perspectives based on their social and domain knowledge, so that the system can yield acceptable and understandable results to users.

THEORY

Kuhlthau developed the ISP model which is based on a series of empirical studies using qualitative research within a longitudinal design to investigate high school students' and college students' information seeking process (Kuhlthau, 1983; 1988a; 1988b; 1989b; 1991; 1993a; 2004). The model holds that people search for and use information differently depending on the stage of the process. That is, Kuhlthau sees information seeking as dynamic process. The movements during their information seeking processes are divided into six stages. Kuhlthau's ISP is initiated by "uncertainty" or a lack of understanding which will be changed gradually as the information seeker obtains information, reduces uncertainty, and resolves problems (Kuhlthau, 1991; 1993a).

Based on George Kelly's personal construct theory[1] (1955; 1963), Kuhlthau (1993) formulated the Information Search Process when people seek information. The processes are presented in six stages describing the user's thoughts, feelings and actions within each stage. The ISP model's six stages include: task initiation, topic selection, pre-focus exploration, focus formulation, data collection, and closure. At each stage, the "thoughts," "feelings," and "actions" are different as the person moves to the next stage reflecting how change occurs in the information seeking process. Kuhlthau also identifies four criteria that might affect information seekers' search processes to choose information: task, time, interest, and availability of the information (1993a, p. 39). These are critical criteria used to judge relevance when information seekers conduct their information search. Their relevance judgments also change as their thoughts, feelings, and actions change along with their information seeking. Table 2 presents Kuhlthau's ISP model by stages and its possible application to CLIR environment, which is a key framework for this chapter.

Kuhlthau (2005) emphasizes that information seeking is "not just finding and reproducing information" but it is "a process of seeking meaning" (p. 232). That is, throughout the whole process, information seekers are learning and constructing meaning. She found that individuals reported a sharp increase in uncertainty when they were in the exploration stage, which is after they attempted a search in their initiation stage. This affirms and in some ways verifies Serola and Vakkari's (2005) study, which is a comparison between early information seekers' expectations to obtain information and the end result of that search. They found that at the end of the task, the information seekers had learned more about their topic and could point out more easily other types of information as topical and useful than they might have expected when they began their search (p. 380).

The ISP model has been verified through her continued studies using multi-methods such as interviews, questionnaires, analyses of journals, search logs, written statements, and teachers' assessments. One of her studies conducted in-depth interviews with the same subjects, who initially participated when the subject was a high school student and later through the college years and then to his position as an information analyst. This longitudinal study used multiple interviews with the same subject over a 12-year period (1983 to 1995) which enabled Kuhlthau to obtain rich data collection to support her ISP model. It also enabled her to compare changes over time for the ISP model and how a user's perceptions change when seeking and using information.

Kuhlthau's (1993) model has been applied to many studies. Cheng's citation search (2004) found that from 1987 to September 2004 there were 398 citations to Kuhlthau's work. These citations spanned a number of research areas: information seeking research, system design and evaluation, reference services, and library education and bibliographic instruction (p. 24). Examples of applying Kuhlthau's ISP model for such research include: the information search process in the domain of IR (Vakkari, 2000, 2001; 2003); collaborative information behavior in a group-based educational setting (Hyldegård, 2004); and, assessments of the relationships among thoughts, feelings, and actions between

Table 1. Kuhlthau's ISP model and its possible application to CLIR environment

Kuhlthau's ISP Model	Possible Application to CLIR
1) Initiation stage: information seekers try to understand the task by connecting the problem to prior knowledge (thought). They become aware of their lack of knowledge. They feel uncertain and anxious about the approach they might take to seek information (feelings). They seek relevant information which might fit their needs (actions).	Users have a lack of understanding of the topic and how to formulate a search query in terms of language and translation/transliteration. They try to understand the overall information being sought (thought). They feel uncertain how to start the research (feelings). They might review the project and read old documents if there are any available, such as instruction sheet from teachers or company document files (actions).
2) Topic selection stage: users try to consider possible topics (thought) and feel little bit optimistic (feelings). The action might include consulting informal mediators or using reference collections (actions).	Users try to narrow down their broad thoughts to identify topics and seek related terminology which might be appropriate for the search (thought). They feel somewhat hopeful when they can narrow down the topic or ideas (feelings). They might consult with their friends, co-workers or librarians (actions).
3) Exploration stage: users investigate information on the general topic area (thoughts). They often encounter incompatible information. They feel confusion, frustration and doubt (feelings). Locating relevant information, reading, and taking notes might be typical of actions at this stage (actions).	Users try to investigate the possible topic area and attempt to find usable terms in their native languages and their target languages (thought). Since users can get various information about the topic area, they can feel confusion. They also realize that the terminology they used may not fit the project so they feel frustration and doubt (feeling). Users might experience difficulty because of inability to formulate their information need. This can be compounded by not being able to access information due to a lack of resources or problems seen to emanate from the CLIR systems. Users try to categorize the information they retrieved so far in order to restate their specific topic. Reading, searching, taking notes and classification of the documents will be assumed (actions).
4) Formulation stage: a focused perspective on the topic is formed (thought). They feel optimistic and have clarity about their search topic (feelings). After choosing topics, they try to develop search strategies to look for more related information and read notes for themes (actions).	Users expect to identify a focused topic (thought). They feel optimistic and positive about the project (feelings). Users verify the topic by searching various resources, such as CLIR systems or resources. They also consult informal mediators to verify their search, especially in its language use. They will find pertinent queries to meet the information systems which can provide information that they seek (actions).
5) Information collection stage: the users specify their needs and gather pertinent information (thought). They feel confident (feelings) and use library for information collection in physical forms or take detailed notes with bibliographic citations (actions).	Users get pertinent documents by searching with their specified terms (thought). They feel confident about getting relevant documents (feelings). They collect the resources and feel prepared to write the project report (action).
6) Presentation stage: the task is to complete the search. Users feel relief and confidence.	Task is completed.

earlier and later stages of information seeking. Multiple methodological approaches were used in these citing studies: quantitative methods (a survey questionnaire, maximum likelihood factor analysis, and canonical correlation analysis), qualitative methods (interviews and content analysis) (Cheng, 2004); and, longitudinal studies assessing students' information seeking processes (Yuan, 1999; Tang, 2005). Additionally, the methods included interviews, journal keeping, and so forth (Nahl, 1996; Hyldegård, 2006; Tang, 2005); system design and evaluation in of information

retrieval systems (Ellis, Allen, & Wilson, 1999); and, users' relevance judgments in its evaluation (Bates, 1989; Borgman, 1996).

Although Kuhlthau's ISP model has been applied to a number of research areas, no study was found which applied the ISP model to multilingual users of a CLIR system. A study combining ISP with CLIR could also include relevance evaluation in such an information environment. Difficulties in analyzing CLIR users' needs and their search processes are expected to emerge but the value of applying this model should outweigh such

Table 2. Premises and assumptions from the methods

Research Questions	Premises/Assumptions	Method
1. What are the stages which occur when a person seeks information using different languages?	Kuhlthau's six stages of learning may also emerge for users of CLIR systems	Observation/interview: questionnaires, journal records
2. What effect do the individual's cognitive, affective, and social characteristics have on information seeking in a CLIR environment?	In addition to Kuhlthau's discovery in thought, feelings and actions, it could be expected that these three factors make unique contributions to explaining CLIR behavior.	Observation/interview: questionnaires, journal records Experiment: talk-aloud protocol, audio tape, questionnaires
3. What are language choices and considerations occur when an individual constructs a query and evaluates the results of a search?	CLIR system users' search behaviors and their relevance criteria to use such systems will be identified. Expect to find different behaviors by users' language backgrounds and their experience in system use or topic knowledge.	Observation/interview, Experiment: search-log, questionnaires, search results
4. What would improve or facilitate searches in a CLIR environment?	Various suggestions in the CLIR system use would be expected, such as the person's preferences when using the online bilingual dictionary and the settings for content display etc.	Observation/interview, Experiment: questionnaires, search results
5. What implications do the findings of this study have for system design and access features?	[This is not directly tested; it is inferred from overall findings of users' preferences and behaviors.]	Inferred from overall findings.

considerations. Within a CLIR environment, it needs to be recognized that users are coping with language issues as well as query/document relationships. Language, the most representative artifact of human communication, embeds within it such notions as culture and such connections as community and society. An expanded ISP model would need to take into account such considerations and the CLIR environment may be an ideal situation to apply this layering of culture and society to the search process. Table 1 shows a possible application of Kuhlthau's ISP Model to CLIR environment.

RESEARCH QUESTIONS

The literature reviewed and the theory considered suggests five research questions related to CLIR system users' information seeking behavior:

1. What are the stages which occur when a person seeks information using different languages?

2. What effect do the individual's cognitive, affective, and social characteristics have on information seeking in a CLIR environment?

3. What language choices and considerations occur when an individual constructs a query and evaluates the results of a search?

4. What would improve or facilitate searches in a CLIR environment?

5. What implications do the findings of this study have for system design and access features?

METHODOLOGY

This study proposes multiple methodologies to explore how multilingual individuals seek information when constructing queries and using a CLIR system. Broadly, two separate studies will be suggested: 1. observations and interviews at subjects' work places using a realistic, non-controlled situation; and, 2. experiment with observations and interviews where users conduct searches with two retrieval systems. The observations/interview component will determine if all or part of the ISP model holds for multilingual users searching a CLIR system. For the second, experimental portion of this study, the search process will be mapped for each user as they use two different CLIR systems. The stages of the search process will be defined (as it may or may not fit the ISP model) and the changes to the query and changes to search tactics will be recorded. Additionally, using talk-aloud protocol, users will describe their approach and their expectations with each part of the search process. In both studies, any issue related to their language use in seeking information will be a key variable. Both qualitative and quantitative data analyses will be used from both designs.

Table 2 depicts each research question and its correspondent methodology. The methods will tap dimensions of more than one research question. For example, the questionnaire will address issues in all five of the research questions. It is envisioned that the questionnaire can be used to serve distinct purposes. For example, one part might be related to the search task and the other part to information about the person's expectations and assessments of query, search process, and search results. The detailed methodology and the study process part are omitted in this chapter due to space limitation.

DISCUSSION

It is important to determine if CLIR system users' information behaviors and their information search processes are similar to those using IR systems or if they differ substantially because of the language issues. The results from this study would be expected to shed light on CLIR system design which can be appropriate to real users' needs and difficulties. Most importantly, it is expected that a revised ISP model may emerge for the CLIR environment. It is also anticipated that this study might aid in understanding CLIR users as well as identify system characteristics important in

cross language searches. In this study observation, interviews, audio/video tapings, search log, and other instruments will be reviewed in order to confirm result with different methods. Such use of different methods can represent triangulation useful in identifying verifiable findings for the methods (Denzin, 1970; Lincoln & Guba, 1985).

This study would have some limitations. First, it would be extremely difficult to compare all of the world's different languages. The focus here would be selecting language groups that are difficult enough and represent different cultures as well as different alphabets and languages. It might be better if many languages were included and tested. However the benefit to generalization would probably result in a cost to precision. The next limitation would be sampling. If the sample was not randomly selected, then, the sample cannot be said to be representative of a larger population. This, then, decreases the generalization available from such a study and it limits validity beyond the sample. The more sample sizes would be desirable to give this study generalizability.

CONCLUSION

There has been an enormous increase for information written in different languages by users from various backgrounds and disciplines. Development of a true CLIR is absolutely necessary so that the system would allow users to access information written in the user's languages of choice. In this paper, a research design was suggested investigating CLIR systems users' information seeking behavior which is applied the ISP model to multilingual users of CLIR systems. A study combining ISP with CLIR also includes relevance evaluation in such an information environment. Kuhlthau's ISP model was borrowed as a theoretical framework. It is expected this will improve our knowledge of CLIR systems users' information requirements and the factors which might contribute to construction of adequate search queries and results. This research also has great potential to increase our understanding of users in developing countries who need this kind of CLIR system due to lack of materials in their language.

REFERENCES

Al-Suqri, M. N. (2011). Information-seeking behavior of social science scholars in developingcountries: A proposed model. *The International Information & Library Review, 43*(1), 1–14. doi:10.1016/j.iilr.2011.01.001.

Arnold, L., Sadler, L., Balkan, S. M., & Humphreys, R. L. (1997). *Machine Translation: An Introductory Guide*. London: Blackwell.

Ballesteros, L., & Croft, W. (1998). Resolving ambiguity for cross-language retrieval. *In Proceedings of SIGIR Conference*. Melbourne, Australia: ACM.

Barry, C. L. (1994). User-defined relevance criteria: An exploratory study. *Journal of the American Society for Information Science and Technology, 45*(3), 149–159. doi:10.1002/(SICI)1097-4571(199404)45:3<149::AID-ASI5>3.0.CO;2-J.

Bates, M. J. (1989). The design of browsing and berrypicking techniques for the online search interface. *Online Review, 13*(5), 407–424. doi:10.1108/eb024320.

Bates, M. J. (1991). The berry-picking search: User interface design. In Dillon, M. (Ed.), *Interfaces for information retrieval and online systems: The state of art* (pp. 55–61). New York: Greenwood Press.

Beheshti, J., Large, A., & Tam, M. (2010). Transaction logs and search patterns on a children's portal. *Canadian Journal of Information and Library Science, 34*(4), 391–402. doi:10.1353/ils.2010.0011.

Belkin, N. J. (1980). Anomalous states of knowledge as a basis for information retrieval. *Canadian. Journal of Information Science, 5*, 133–143.

Belkin, N. J., Oddy, R. N., & Brooks, H. (1982). ASK for Information retrieval Part I. *The Journal of Documentation, 38*(2), 61–72. doi:10.1108/eb026722.

Belkin, N. J., Oddy, R. N., & Brooks, H. (1982). ASK for Information retrieval Part II. *The Journal of Documentation, 38*(3), 145–164. doi:10.1108/eb026726.

Belkin, N. J., & Vickery, A. (1985). *Interaction in information system: A review of research from document retrieval to knowledge-based system*. London: The British Library.

Borgman, C. L. (1984). Psychological research in human-computer interaction. *Annual Review of Information Science & Technology, 19*, 33–64.

Borgman, C. L. (1996). Why are online catalogs still hard to use? *Journal of the American Society for Information Science American Society for Information Science, 47*, 493–503. doi:10.1002/(SICI)1097-4571(199607)47:7<493::AID-ASI3>3.0.CO;2-P.

Buck, S., & Nichols, J. (2012). Beyond the search box. *Reference and User Services Quarterly, 51*(3), 235–245. doi:10.5860/rusq.51n3.235.

Cheng, Y. (2004). *Thoughts, feelings, and actions: Quantitative comparisons of interactions and relationships among three factors in college students' information seeking*. Unpublished Doctoral Dissertation, Indiana University, Bloomington, IN.

Chowdhury, G. (2003). Natural language processing. [ARIST]. *Annual Review of Information Science & Technology, 37*, 51–89. doi:10.1002/aris.1440370103.

Cosijn, E., & Ingwersen, P. (2000). Dimensions of relevance. *Information Processing & Management, 36*, 533–550. doi:10.1016/S0306-4573(99)00072-2.

Dagli, A. (2005). *Culture and information needs in web-based learning: An instrumental case study of multilingual graduate students.* Unpublished Doctoral Dissertation, Florida State University, Tallahassee, FL.

Davis, M., & Ogden, W. (1997). QUILT: Implementing a Large-Scale Cross-Language Text Retrieval System. In *Proceedings of the 20th Annual International ACM SIGIR Conference on Research and Development in Information Retrieval* (pp. 92-98). Philadelphia, PA: ACM.

Dervin, B. (1983). *An overview of sense-making: Concepts, methods and results to date.* Paper presented at the International Communication Association Annual Meeting. Dallas, TX.

Dervin, B. (1992). From the mind's eye of the user: The sense-making qualitative-quantitative methodology. In Glazier, J. D., & Powell, R. R. (Eds.), *Qualitative research in information management* (pp. 61–84). Englewood, CO: Libraries Unlimited.

Dervin, B. (1999). On studying information seeking methodologically: The implications of connecting metatheory to method. *Information Processing & Management, 35*, 727–750. doi:10.1016/S0306-4573(99)00023-0.

Dervin, B., & Nilan, M. (1986). Information needs and uses. *Annual Review of Information Science & Technology, 21*, 3–33.

Ellis, D., Allen, D., & Wilson, T. (1999). Information science and information systems: Conjunct subjects disjunct disciplines. *Journal of the American Society for Information Science and Technology, 50*(12), 1095–1107. doi:10.1002/(SICI)1097-4571(1999)50:12<1095::AID-ASI9>3.0.CO;2-Z.

Etim, E. F. (2001). *Scientific and technological information utilization and industrial Development in Nigeria.* Uyo, Nigeria: Heinemann.

Foster, A. (2004). A nonlininer model of information-seeking behavior. *Journal of the American Society for Information Science and Technology, 55*(3), 228–237. doi:10.1002/asi.10359.

Ha, Y. (2008). *Accessing and using multilanguage information by users searching in different information retrieval systems.* Unpublished Doctoral Dissertation, Rutgers University, Newark, NJ.

Hyldegård, J. (2006). Collaborative information behavior – Exploring Kulthau's Information Search Process model in a group-based educational setting. *Information Processing & Management, 42*, 276–298. doi:10.1016/j.ipm.2004.06.013.

Iivonen, M., & White, M. D. (2001). The choice of initial Web search strategies: A comparison between Finnish and American searchers. *The Journal of Documentation, 57*, 465–491. doi:10.1108/EUM0000000007091.

Ingwersen, P. (1982). Search procedures in the library analyzed from the cognitive point of view. *The Journal of Documentation, 38*, 165–191. doi:10.1108/eb026727.

Jiao, Q. G., & Onwuegbuzie, A. J. (1997). Antecedents of library anxiety. *The Library Quarterly, 67*, 372–389. doi:10.1086/629972.

Kelly, G. A. (1963). *A theory of personality: The psychology of personal constructs.* New York: W.W. Norton.

Kim, K.-S. (2002). Information seeking on the Web: Effects of user and task variables. *Library & Information Science Research, 23*, 233–255. doi:10.1016/S0740-8188(01)00081-0.

Kim, Y.-W. (2004). *Typology of user of user uncertainty in Web-based information seeking: Insight into the information seeking context of scholarly researchers in the field of science.* Unpublished Doctoral Dissertation, Rutgers University, Newark, NJ.

Kuhlthau, C., Spink, A., & Cool, C. (1992). Exploration into stages in the information search process in online information retrieval. In *Proceedings of the ASIS Annual Meeting* (pp. 67-71).

Kuhlthau, C. C. (1983). *The Library Research Process: Case Studies and Interventions with high School Seniors in Advanced Placement English Classes Using Kelly's Theory of Constructs*. Doctoral dissertation, Rutgers University, Newark, NJ.

Kuhlthau, C. C. (1988a). Longitudinal case studies of the information search process of users in libraries. *Library & Information Science Research, 10*(3), 257–304.

Kuhlthau, C. C. (1988b). Perceptions of the information search process in libraries: A study of changes from high school through college. *Information Processing & Management, 24*(4), 419–428. doi:10.1016/0306-4573(88)90045-3.

Kuhlthau, C. C. (1988c). Developing a model of the library search process: Cognitive and affective aspects. *RQ, 28,* 232-242.

Kuhlthau, C. C. (1991). Inside the search process: Information seeking from the user's perspective. *Journal of the American Society for Information Science American Society for Information Science, 42*, 361–371. doi:10.1002/(SICI)1097-4571(199106)42:5<361::AID-ASI6>3.0.CO;2-#.

Kuhlthau, C. C. (1993a). *Seeking meaning: A process approach to library and information services*. Norwood, NJ: Ablex publishing corporation.

Kuhlthau, C. C. (1993b). A principle of uncertainty for information seeking. *The Journal of Documentation, 49*(4), 339–355. doi:10.1108/eb026918.

Kuhlthau, C. C. (1999a). The role of experience in the Information search Process of an early career information worker: Perceptions of uncertainty, complexity, construction, and sources. *Journal of the American Society for Information Science American Society for Information Science, 50*(5), 399–412. doi:10.1002/(SICI)1097-4571(1999)50:5<399::AID-ASI3>3.0.CO;2-L.

Kuhlthau, C. C. (1999b). Accommodating the user's information search process: Challenges for information retrieval system designers. *Bulletin of the American Society for Information Science,* (February/March): 12–16.

Kuhlthau, C. C. (2004). *Seeking meaning: A process approach to library and information services*. Westport, CT: Libraries Unlimited.

Kuhlthau, C. C. (2005). Kuhlthau's Information Search Process. In Fisher, K. E., Erdelez, S., & McKechnie, L. (Eds.), *Theories of Information Behavior*. Medford, NJ: Information Today Inc..

Large, A., & Moukdad, H. (2001). Multilingual access to web resources: An overview. *Program, 34*, 43–58. doi:10.1108/EUM0000000006938.

Lavrenko, V., Choquette, M., & Croft, W. B. (2002). Cross-lingual relevance models. In M. Beaulieu, R. Baeza-Yates, S.H. Myaeng, & K. Järvelin (Eds), *Proceedings of the 25th Annual International ACM-SIGIR Conference on Research and Development in Information Retrieval* (pp. 175–182). New York: ACM.

Lederman, A., Warnick, W., Hitson, B., & Johnson, L. (2010). Breaking down language barriers through multilingual federated search. *Information Services & Use, 30*(3/4), 125–132.

Leuski, A., Lin, C., Zhou, L., Germann, U., Och, F., & Hovy, E. (2003). Cross-lingual C*ST*RD: English access to Hindi information. *ACM Transactions on Asian Language Information Processing*, *2*(3), 245–269. doi:10.1145/979872.979877.

Lincoln, Y., & Guba, E. (1985). *Naturalistic inquiry*. New York: Sage.

Nahl, D. (2004). Measuring the affective information environment of web searchers. *Proceedings of the 67ᵗʰ ASIS&T Annual meeting*, (41), 191-197.

Nahl, D., & Tenopir, C. (1996). Affective and cognitive searching behavior of novice end-users of a full-text database. *Journal of the American Society for Information Science American Society for Information Science*, *47*, 276–286. doi:10.1002/(SICI)1097-4571(199604)47:4<276::AID-ASI3>3.0.CO;2-U.

Oard, D., & Resnik, P. (1999). Support for interactive document selection in cross language information retrieval. *Information Processing & Management*, *35*, 363–379. doi:10.1016/S0306-4573(98)00066-1.

Oard, D. W. (1997). Serving users in many languages: Cross-language information retrieval for digital libraries. *D-Lib Magazine*. Retrieved on April 12, 2011, from http://www.dlib.org/dlib/december97/oard/12oard.html

Ogden, D., Cowie, J., Davis, M., Ludovik, E., Molina-Salado, H., & Shin, H. (1999). G*etting information from documents you cannot read: An interactive cross-language text retrieval and Summarization System*. Joint ACM Digital Library/SIGIR Workshop on Multilingual Information Discovery and Access (MIDAS).

Ogden, D., Cowie, J., Davis, M., Ludovik, E., Nirenburg, S., Molina-Salgado, H., & Sharples, N. (1999). *Keizai: An interactive cross-language text retrieval system*. Paper presented at the Workshop on Machine Translation for Cross-language Information Retrieval, Machine Translation Summit VII. Sinagpore.

Ogden, D., & Davis, M. (2000). Improving Cross-Language Text Retrieval with Human Interactions. *Hawaii International Conference on System Sciences.* Maui, HI: IEEE.

Ogden, W. C., & Davis, M. W. (2000). Improving cross-language text retrieval with human interactions. In *Proceedings of the 33rd Hawaii International Conferences on System Sciences.* Maui, HI: IEEE. Retrieved July 1, 2012, from http://crl.nmsu.edu/Research/Projects/tipster/ursa/Papers/Hawaii.pdf

Onwuegbuzie, A. J., & Jiao, Q. G. (1998). The relationship between library anxiety and learning styles among graduate students: Implications for library instruction. *Library & Information Science Research*, *20*(3), 235–249. doi:10.1016/S0740-8188(98)90042-1.

Parry, K. (2011). Libraries in Uganda: Not just linguistic imperialism. *Libri: International Journal of Libraries & Information Services*, *61*(4), 328–337.

Petrelli, D., Beaulieu, M., Sanderson, M., Demetriou, G., Herring, P., & Hansen, P. (2004). Observing users, designing clarity: A case study on the user-centered design of a cross-language information retrieval system. *Journal of the American Society for Information Science and Technology*, *55*, 923–934. doi:10.1002/asi.20036.

Pettigrew, K., Fidel, R., & Bruce, H. (2001). Conceptual frameworks in information behavior. *Annual Review of Information Science & Technology*, *35*, 43–78.

Ranganathan, S. R. (1957). *The five laws of library science*. London: Blunt and Sons, Ltd..

Rieh, H. Y., & Rieh, S. Y. (2005). Web searching across languages: Preference and behavior of bilingual academic users in Korea. *Library & Information Science Research*, *27*(2), 249–263. doi:10.1016/j.lisr.2005.01.006.

Rieh, S. Y. (2004). On the Web at home: Information seeking and Web searching in the home environment. *Journal of the American Society for Information Science and Technology, 55,* 743–753. doi:10.1002/asi.20018.

Rieh, S. Y., & Xie, H. (2001). Patterns and sequences of multiple query reformulations in Web searching: A preliminary study. In E. Aversa, & C. Manley (Eds.), In *Proceedings of the 64th Annual Meeting of the American Society for Information Science and Technology, 38* (pp. 246–255). Medford, NJ: Information Today.

Saracevic, T. (1996). Relevance reconsidered. In P. Ingwersen, & N. Ple Pors (Eds.), *2ⁿᵈ International Conference on Conceptions of Library and Information Science* (pp. 201-218). Copenhagen, Denmark: Royal School of Librarianship.

Schamber, L. (1991). Users' criteria for evaluation in a multimedia environment. In J.-M. Griffiths (Eds.), In *Proceedings of the 54ᵗʰ Annual Meeting of the American Society for information Sciences* (pp. 126-133). Medford, NJ: Learned Information.

Schamber, L., Eisenberg, M., & Nilan, M. (1990). A re-examination of relevance: Toward a dynamic, situational definition. *Information Processing & Management,* (26): 755–776. doi:10.1016/0306-4573(90)90050-C.

Serola, S., & Vakkari, P. (2005). The anticipated and assessed contribution of information types in references retrieved for preparing a research proposal. *Journal of the American Society for Information Science American Society for Information Science, 55*(4), 373–381.

Shannon, C. E., & Weaver, W. (1949). *The mathematical theory of communication.* Urbana, IL: University of Illinois Press.

Spink, A., & Jansen, B. J. (2004). *Web search: Public searching of the Web.* Boston, MA: Kluwer Academic Publishers.

Spink, A., Ozmutlu, H. C., & Ozmutlu, S. (2002). Multitasking information seeking and searching processes. *Journal of the American Society for Information Science American Society for Information Science, 53*(8), 639–652. doi:10.1002/asi.10124.

Taylor, R. S. (1962). The process of asking questions. *American Documentation, 13*(4), 391–396. doi:10.1002/asi.5090130405.

Taylor, R. S. (1968). Questioning-negotiation and information seeking in libraries. *College & Research Libraries, 29,* 178–194.

Taylor, R. S. (1991). Information use environments. In Derwin, B., & Voigt, M. J. (Eds.), *Progress in Communication Sciences* (pp. 217–255). Norwood, NJ: Ablex.

Ugah, A. U. (2007). Obstacles to information access and use in developing countries. *Library Philosophy and Practice.* Retrieved June 23, 2011, from http://digitalcommons.unl.edu/libphilprac/160

Uhegbu, A. N. (2002). *The information user: Issues and themes.* Enugu, Nigeria: John Jacobs Classics.

Vakkari, P. (2000). Relevance and contributing information types of searched documents in task performance. In *Proceedings of SIGIR 2000 conference, Athens* (pp. 2-9). New York: ACM.

Vakkari, P. (2001). A theory of task-based information retrieval. *The Journal of Documentation, 57*(1), 44–60. doi:10.1108/EUM0000000007075.

Vakkari, P. (2003). Task-based information searching. *Annual Review of Information Science & Technology, 37,* 413–464. doi:10.1002/aris.1440370110.

Vakkari, P., Pennanen, M., & Serola, S. (2003). Changes of search terms and tactics while writing a research proposal: A longitudinal case study. *Information Processing & Management, 39*(3), 445–463. doi:10.1016/S0306-4573(02)00031-6.

Wang, P., Berry, M., & Yang, Y. (2003). Mining longitudinal Web queries: Trends and patterns. *Journal of the American Society for Information Science and Technology, 54,* 743–758. doi:10.1002/asi.10262.

Wang, P., Hawk, W. B., & Tenopir, C. (2000). Users' interaction with World Wide Web resources: An exploratory study using a holistic approach. *Information Processing & Management, 36,* 229–251. doi:10.1016/S0306-4573(99)00059-X.

Willson, R., & Given, L. M. (2010). The effect of spelling and retrieval system familiarity on search behavior in online public access catalogs: A mixed methods study. *Journal of the American Society for Information Science and Technology, 61*(12), 2461–2476. doi:10.1002/asi.21433.

Wilson, T. D., Ford, N. J., Ellis, D., Foster, A. E., & Spink, A. (2000, August). *Uncertainty and its correlates.* Paper presented at Information Seeking in Context. Gothenburg, Sweden.

Yoon, K. (2002). *Certainty, uncertainty and the role of topic and comment in interpersonal information seeking interactions.* Unpublished Doctoral Dissertation, Syracuse University, Syracuse, NY.

Yuan, W. (1997). End-user searching behavior in information retrieval: A longitudinal study. *Journal of the American Society for Information Science American Society for Information Science, 48*(3), 218–234. doi:10.1002/(SICI)1097-4571(199703)48:3<218::AID-ASI4>3.0.CO;2-#.

ADDITIONAL READING

Aihong, F. (2009). Creating a bilingual library information environment for foreign users. *The Electronic Library, 27*(2), 237–246. doi:10.1108/02640470910947584.

Al-Shammari, E. (2010). *Improving Arabic text processing via stemming with application to text mining and web retrieval.* Unpublished Doctoral Dissertation, George Mason University, Fairfax, VA.

Aliaga, B. P. (2011). *The navigation of non-English speaking elderly hispanic immigrants through the service system.* Unpublished Master's thesis, University of Toronto, Toronto, Canada.

Bassam, H. H. (2009). Towards enhancing retrieval effectiveness of search engines for diacritisized Arabic documents. *Information Retrieval, 12*(3), 300–323. doi:10.1007/s10791-008-9081-9.

Berendt, B., & Kralisch, A. (2009). A user-centric approach to identifying best deployment strategies for language tools: The impact of content and access language on web user behavior and attitudes. *Information Retrieval, 12*(3), 380–399. doi:10.1007/s10791-008-9086-4.

Case, D. (2007). *Looking for information: A survey of research on information seeking, needs, and behavior* (2nd ed.). Boston, MA: Academic Press.

Case, D. O. (2006). Information behavior. In B. Cronin (Ed.), Annual Review of Information Science and Technology, 40, 297-327.

Chakraborty, J. (2009). *A cross-cultural usability study on the internationalization of user interfaces based on an empirical five factor model.* Unpublished Doctoral dissertation, University of Maryland, Baltimore County, Baltimore, MD.

Dutta, R. (2009). Information needs and information-seeking behavior in developing countries: A review of the research. *The International Information & Library Review, 41*(1), 44–51. doi:10.1016/j.iilr.2008.12.001.

Fisher, K., Durrance, J., & Hinton, M. B. (2003). Information grounds and the use of need-based services by immigrants in Queens, New York: A context-based, outcome evaluation approach. *Journal of the American Society for Information Science and Technology*, *55*(8), 754–766. doi:10.1002/asi.20019.

Fisher, K. E., Erdelez, S., & McKechnie, L. (Eds.). (2005). *Theories of Information Behavior*. Medham, NJ: Information Today.

Foster, A., & Urquhart, C. (2012). Modelling nonlinear information behavior: Transferability and progression. *The Journal of Documentation*, *68*(6), 784–805. doi:10.1108/00220411211277046.

Garcia-cumbreras, M. Á., & Martinez-Santiago, F., & Urena0lopez, L.A. (2012). Architecture and evaluation of BRUJA, a multilingual question answering system. *Information Retrieval*, *15*(5), 413–432. doi:10.1007/s10791-011-9177-5.

Hirvonen, N., Huotari, M., Niemelä, R., & Korpelainen, R. (2012). Information behavior in stages of exercise behavior change. *Journal of the American Society for Information Science and Technology*, *63*(9), 1804–1819. doi:10.1002/asi.22704.

Hong, W. (2011). *A descriptive user study of bilingual information seekers searching for online information to complete four tasks*. Unpublished Doctoral dissertation, University of Pittsburgh, Pittsburgh, PA.

Hover, P. L., & Lu, J. (2009). Sentences like these: Multicultural information dynamics and international diversity of thought. *The International Information & Library Review*, *41*(3), 196–218. doi:10.1016/j.iilr.2009.07.002.

Islam, M. S., & Ahmed, S. M. Z. (2012). The information needs and information-seeking behavior of rural dwellers: A review of research. *International Federation of Library Associations and Institutions (IFLA). Journal*, *38*(2), 137–147.

Korobili, S., Malliari, A., & Zapounidou, S. (2011). Factors that Influence Information-Seeking Behavior: The case of Greek graduate students. *Journal of Academic Librarianship*, *37*(2), 155–165. doi:10.1016/j.acalib.2011.02.008.

Kostagiolas, P. A., Bairaktaris, K. D., & Niakas, D. D. (2010). An information behavior investigation of the community pharmacists in Greece for developing library and information services. *Health Information and Libraries Journal*, *27*(1), 46–56. doi:10.1111/j.1471-1842.2009.00846.x PMID:20402804.

Lazarinis, F., Vilares, J., Tait, J., & Efthimiadis, E. N. (2009). Current research issues and trends in non-english web searching. *Information Retrieval*, *12*(3), 230–250. doi:10.1007/s10791-009-9093-0.

Lewandowski, D., Drechsler, J., & Mach, S. (2012). Deriving query intents from web search engine queries. *Journal of the American Society for Information Science and Technology*, *63*(9), 1773–1788. doi:10.1002/asi.22706.

Marouf, L., & Anwar, M. A. (2010). Information-seeking behavior of the social sciences faculty at Kuwait University. *Library Review*, *59*(7), 532–547. doi:10.1108/00242531011065127.

Mutshewa, A., Grand, B., Totolo, A., Zulu, S., Sebina, P., & Jorosi, B. (2010). Information behaviors of non-users of libraries in Botswana. *African Journal of Library, Archives &. Information Science*, *20*(1), 1–10.

Nkomo, N., Ocholla, D., & Jacobs, D. (2011). Web information seeking behavior of students and staff in rural and urban based universities in South Africa: A comparison analysis. *Libri: International Journal of Libraries & Information Services*, *61*(4), 281–297.

Oladokun, O. (2010). Information seeking behavior of the off-campus students at the University of Botswana: A case of two satellite centers. *Journal of Library Administration*, *50*(7/8), 883–898. doi:10.1080/01930826.2010.488988.

Olsson, M. R. (2009). Re-thinking our concept of users. *Australian Academic & Research Libraries*, *40*(1), 22–35.

Petrelli, D., & Clough, P. (2012). Analysing user's queries for cross-language image retrieval from digital library collections. *The Electronic Library*, *30*(2), 197–219. doi:10.1108/02640471211221331.

KEY TERMS AND DEFINITIONS

Cross Language Information Retrieval System: A retrieval system that operates with queries in one language to retrieve documents in other languages. It allows users to access information written in the user's languages of choice.

Kuhlthau's Information Search Process (ISP) Model: This model presents the holistic process of how information users learn and recognize their information problems and finally work through a process to meet their evolving information needs.

Non-English Language Information Users: Information users whose native languages are not English or users who want to retrieve information written in non-English language.

Query: Search terms formulated by a user representing the users' information need. The terms may combine with operators.

Relevance: How pertinent information is retrieved from a certain system that can serve users' particular needs.

Relevance Judgment: Relevance judgments occur as individuals evaluate surrogate language (such as index terms and abstracts) and the documents retrieved.

User's Information Seeking Behavior: It is a study to investigate users' information needs and how they pursue the information need. This understanding helps to develop user-centered information system.

ENDNOTES

1. "The personal construct theory describes the affective experience of individuals involved in the process of constructing meaning from the information they encounter. New information is assimilated in a series of phases beginning with confusion which increases as inconsistencies and incompatibilities are confronted within the information itself and between it and the constructs presently held." (quoted from Kuhlthau, 1991; p. 362)

Chapter 5

Environmental Context of Information Seeking Behavior:
Applying a Diffusion Model to Account for Intervening Variables

Rebecca L. Miller
Realm Advising, LLC, USA

ABSTRACT

Most current models of information seeking behavior (ISB) do not explicitly address the effects of the environmental context on ISB. Wilson (1996) identified several intervening variables, but these have not been systematically considered. This chapter explores the use of the Katz, Levin and Hamilton (1963) model of diffusion of innovations to provide a framework for examining the various elements of an environmental context. In particular, this model provides the means to account for the cultural, social, communicative, and actor components of ISB. The model is described and its use as a supplementing analytic framework in ISB is examined, paying particular attention to its use in research in developing nations.

INTRODUCTION

Over the last 30 years, many models have emerged in the Library and Information Science field to explain information seeking behavior (ISB). These models have attempted to capture the processes used by individuals as they work out their information needs, and look for and select information to answer these needs. The most widely accepted and used models are from Wilson (1981; 1996), Dervin (1992; 1999), and Kuhlthau (1991; 1994),

but many others have contributed to the development of information seeking theory as well (see Fisher, Erdelez and McKechnie [2005] for a collection of current concepts and models). Information seeking behavior, and information behavior more generally, has continuously provided a rich terrain for research for the past 40 years, and interesting new avenues have recently opened up. Although the core models of ISB remain the fundamental basis for stimulating new research, as they captured quite well the process of seeking

DOI: 10.4018/978-1-4666-4353-6.ch005

information, there are still areas for refinement and further exploration. This chapter will address one such area: the environmental context and the role it plays in understanding ISB.

Examining the environmental context is important for understanding how it can affect the ways in which information needs arise and the actions undertaken to seek information. The term "environmental context" is used here to denote the web of social, cultural, technological and physio-psychological structures within which an individual exists. Most models of ISB at least mention the environmental context in passing, acknowledging that information seeking does not happen in a vacuum. Current ISB models have focused mostly on the emotional and mental effects of the search process, delving into the seeking individual's psychological response to information needs and the seeking process. Dervin's sense-making model, articulated by Dervin (1992; 1999) and discussed in depth in Dervin, Foreman-Wernet, and Lauterbach (2003), treats the cognitive gap experienced when an information need is recognized. Kuhltahu (1991; 1994) addressed the uncertainty and other emotional responses experienced when recognizing an information need and conducting the search process. A few other researchers have included mention of the larger context and environment within which an individual conducts the search (Ellis, 1989; Foster, 2004), but this area has not been of primary concern. Only Wilson (1981; 1996) has taken a more detailed look at possible contextual factors affecting ISB. The several that he identified were grouped as personal, social or role-related, and environmental. Even so, the discussion of these factors was not fully developed and an organizing structure other than broad categories was not proposed. These attempts to address the larger context within which ISB takes place are a good start, but more must be done to develop the consideration of such factors and their effects.

The overall picture of information seeking behavior is not complete without a thorough examination of the environmental context. Context provides the source of meaning for information behavior, enabling one to interpret the stimulus of information needs and the process of information seeking (Dervin, 1997). As Sonnenwald (1999) pointed out, contexts have boundaries, insiders, and outsiders, and characterizing a context requires multiple viewpoints. This chapter takes a very broad view of context; as mentioned above, environmental context as used in this chapter encompasses cultural, social, technological and physio-psychological structures and spaces. These all both enable and limit what is considered appropriate information needs, appropriate information to answer those needs, and appropriate methods of obtaining the information. They should be considered in every study on ISB in order to provide a more detailed and nuanced understanding of the behavior.

Examining the environmental context is especially important when attempting to transpose current ISB models to research carried out in the developing world. The major ISB models have been worked out in a context of the Western developed world, usually couched in academic settings. Given that the theorists developing these models were working within the same cultural and often social structures as their own, they did not need to articulate the effects of those aspects of context. The context they did not know was the internal, physio-psychological context of their participants, so perhaps this explains their focus on this area. Now that ISB studies have expanded into looking at information behavior in the developing world, the other aspects of environmental context become more salient. While it may be argued that information behavior *grosso modo* is the same for all humans, given that a perceived information need is a basic human experience, one's environmental context does play a significant role in pre-determining what that need may be, appropriate ways to seek information, as well as what is considered appropriate information to resolve the need. Therefore, expanding the ISB models to include a fuller appreciation of environmental context would contribute to a better understanding of ISB in any situation.

In an attempt to expand upon ISB models and offer a means for addressing environmental context, this chapter proposes the adoption and inclusion of a model from the discipline of communications, particularly the field of diffusion of innovations. ISB, as a part of more general human information behavior, is also tied to the larger notion of human communication (Wilson, 1999). As such, it is feasible to link to other theories of communication, such as diffusion. This chapter will make the argument that a diffusion model, particularly the model by Katz, Levin and Hamilton (1963), contributes to the development of current ISB models by providing a framework for considering the environmental context within which ISB occurs. Although not a widely known model of diffusion, the Katz, Levin and Hamilton model offers a means to account for the various facilitators and barriers (what Wilson [1996] termed "intervening variables") that affect ISB (as well as larger information behavior).

This chapter has four parts. The next section will look at how the major ISB models addressed the notion of environmental context in more depth. The third section makes the connection between ISB models, information behavior and communication to set the stage for the applicability of a model from diffusion. This section also discusses the choice of the Katz, Levin and Hamilton (1963) model over the better known model from Rogers (2003). The fourth section presents the Katz, Levin and Hamilton model and demonstrates how the intervening variables identified by Wilson (1996) can be accommodated by that model. Finally, the fifth section concludes the chapter by summarizing the applicability of the Katz, Levin and Hamilton

model and proposing ways that it might contribute to furthering the development of ISB models and the understanding of information behavior overall.

CONTEXT AS CONSIDERED IN MAJOR ISB MODELS

Most of the models of ISB do not explicitly address the context of the process, instead concerning themselves with examining the details of the process of seeking (and sometimes retrieving) information. The models also focus exclusively on the individual, generally separated from a larger context. A context may be mentioned in an ISB study to give the general demographic sketch of the individuals being studied, such as if the participants were students, professors, homeless, educated, rural or urban dwellers, age, gender, and so forth. These are useful details, particularly when it comes to attempting to replicate a study, but the broader context is more important for understanding intervening variables.

As discussed in the Introduction, only a few ISB models have included environmental contexts to some degree in their examination of the information seeking process. This section will briefly look at the work of Kuhlthau (1991; 1994), Dervin (1992; 1999) and Foster (2004) before dealing in more detail with Wilson (1996).

Kuhlthau

Kuhlthau (1991; 1994) addressed the psychological context in her model by including the feelings and thoughts experienced by an individual seeking information to solve a problem. Kuhlthau established a six-stage process generally followed in information seeking for a research paper, starting with task initiation and ranging through exploring and formulating a focus, actually conducting a search, and then search closure. Kuhlthau's primary contribution to ISB was to draw attention to the notion of uncertainty inherent in information needs, and the affective aspect of information seeking. Her model explicitly includes the emotional factors that are activated in each stage of the search process. These factors, as she explained, can facilitate or inhibit the information seeking process, depending on whether they are supportive (e.g., elation after deciding on a topic) or disruptive (e.g., doubt of ability to choose topic). By identifying the uncertainty found in conducting information seeking for an assigned research paper, she opened up the question of uncertainty in information seeking in general. Kuhlthau's model was a significant contribution to understanding the impact of emotional intervening variables and the affective context of ISB.

Dervin

Dervin's (1999; Dervin, Foreman-Wernet, & Lauterbach, 2003) theory of sense-making is usually included in any review of ISB, although her theory is on a grander scale of information behavior in general, reaching even into metatheory. Like Kuhlthau, her theory centers on the internal actions of a human being conducting the information seeking. Dervin, however, expanded the notion of human beings beyond the feelings and thoughts experienced during an active information seeking and retrieval experience to that of a confluence of "a body-mind-heart-spirit living in a time-space" (1999, p. 730) and in constant action to make sense of one's surroundings and experiences, giving order to chaos. She acknowledged that an individual comes from a given situation, with a history and past experience to draw upon when conducting information seeking, not operating in a vacuum. A more direct contribution to ISB model development though came from Dervin's focusing particularly on the cognitive "gap" one perceives when faced with an information need. This gap stops the individual's ongoing cognitive movement enough to require information be

sought to resolve the problem, and can retard or stimulate one's drive to seek information depending on how one perceives the intensity of the gap. This notion of a gap has driven significant work on the cognitive aspect of ISB and its influence as an intervening variable.

Foster

A more recent model that has considered the environmental context of ISB is Foster's (2004) model of a non-linear approach to ISB based on information seeking in interdisciplinary academic fields. He identified several external and internal "influences." The external influences he identified have more to do with access to information resources, including the limiting effect of the organizational climate and financing in universities to hinder procurement of interdisciplinary information resources. The internal influences are along the lines of the affective and cognitive limits identified by Kuhlthau and Dervin. Although Foster is one of the few to identify contextual elements affecting the ISB of a particular category of information seekers, he did not explore in detail how they might affect (either positively or negatively) the information seeking process.

Wilson

Of all the researchers in ISB, Wilson (1996) is the only one to have dealt in some detail with the environmental context, what he termed "intervening variables" to indicate they can work for or against information seeking. Wilson has long included consideration of the context of an information need, treating it as both the general circumstances that prompt information seeking and sources of barriers to that seeking. In an early model (1981), he recognized three general categories of context/barriers: environment, social role, and person. In the "environment" context he included work environment, socio-cultural environment, politico-economic environment, and physical environment. Contained within the "environment" context is the "social role" context, which included work role and performance level. The "person" context, including physiological, affective and cognitive barriers, is then couched within the "social role" context. The end result is a nested series of increasingly broader or narrower contexts.

In a later work, Wilson (1996) dealt more particularly with these intervening variables. Here he identified numerous factors that may act as "potential impediments between the recognition of a need to be informed and the activation of a search for information" (chapter 4, first paragraph). He still used the three categories from his earlier work--personal, social or role related, and environmental--to group the various factors he had collected during his review of ISB research in health that formed the basis of this work. However, in writing about these barriers, he expanded upon the original three categories and grouped factors as they related to personal characteristics, economic barriers, social/interpersonal barriers, environmental/institutional barriers, and information source characteristics.

Under the heading of "personal characteristics," Wilson collected intervening variables related to one's cognitive processing, emotions, and demographics such as age and gender. A primary cognitive barrier is cognitive dissonance, the notion that "conflicting cognitions make people uncomfortable" (section 4.1.1, para. 1). Reactions to cognitive dissonance vary, depending upon one's cognitive need: seek information to find cause to change extant perceptions, avoid information that conflicts with perceptions, seek information that supports only their perceptions, or avoid information altogether. Wilson noted that this difference in cognitive need "may be the ultimate driver of information behavior," depending on how one perceives the world (section 4.1.1, para. 3).

Also grouped with personal characteristics is one's education level. Wilson cited several ISB studies that showed one's educational level had a direct correlation with one's ability to seek and use information effectively. Of interesting note is the point that "personal perceptions of knowledge influence decision-making and behavior," such that when people feel knowledgeable about a topic they are less likely to seek information. Further, the perceived importance of a topic also biases perceived knowledge; "the more important a topic is to individuals, the more likely they will view themselves as knowledgeable about the subject" (section 4.1.1, para. 12). Therefore, perceived knowledge rather than actual knowledge may act as an important barrier to ISB.

Wilson described "economic barriers" in terms of direct economic costs and the value of time, based on research in consumer behavior in economics. Consumers search for information to assist in making purchasing choices, but research has shown that the amount of time a consumer will spend in searching is the chief consideration of how far a search will continue. Direct economic costs then concern the amount of resources expended in the search, and a key one is time as it can be measured in terms of dollars by wage calculation. Thus the expendable economic resources one has available in terms of money and time can act as barriers.

The "social/interpersonal" category collected barriers concerning one's interactions with others during information seeking. Wilson noted that "interpersonal problems are likely to arise whenever the information source is a person, or where interpersonal interaction is needed to gain access to other kinds of information sources" (section 4.1.3, para. 1). He also noted that established patterns for members of a social system can act as barriers. In particular, resistance to information can be held by individuals who benefit from the status quo, resulting in withholding information access or unduly influencing the perception of new information.

Under "environmental and situational" barriers Wilson grouped time, geography and national cultures. Time in this case meant actual time spent in contact with an information provider, not as an economic resource. Geography acts as an intervening variable in terms of whether an individual resided in an urban or rural area. In terms of national cultures, Wilson noted this can be a particular barrier when examining information transfer across cultures. He discussed Hofstede's (1991) cultural dimensions and put forward that "we might expect to find differences in information-seeking behavior and information use across cultures correlating with the five dimensions" (1996, section 4.1.4).

Finally, Wilson also identified "information source characteristics" that may act as barriers: access, credibility and communication channels. In terms of access, it is clear that if information is not easily accessible or its accessibility poses high costs, a seeker is likely not to pursue it. Information must also be considered credible if it is to be considered as a plausible solution to an information need. Wilson also included communication channels under the rubric of information source characteristics, even while acknowledging that it is not strictly a characteristic of a source. However, the characteristics of information may affect the channels used to communicate it. For example, interpersonal channels offer confidence in the message as long as there is confidence in the source, as well as specialized responses due to the ability to provide feedback.

Although researchers in ISB will readily acknowledge that ISB does not occur in a vacuum, they tend to avoid systematically examining the context in which it does occur. ISB studies will mention barriers or intervening variables when they act in a manner significant enough to warrant discussion, but rarely are they treated in any systematic manner. A few researchers have made significant contributions to understanding particular variables, such as Kuhlthau's (1991; 1994) work on affective aspects of uncertainty in the seeking process and Dervin's (1999) work on cognitive gaps as both stimulus and barrier to information seeking. Foster (2004) has most recently given some attention to the environmental context of ISB, but in a rather superficial manner.

Only Wilson (1981; 1996) has dealt with the question of a larger context in any significant manner, and even then did not do much more than identify variables. Perhaps the lack of consideration for the larger environmental context is due to a lack of organizing framework. If this is the case, then the framework proposed here, in terms of the Katz, Levin and Hamilton (1963) model of diffusion, should encourage the consideration of context.

AUGMENTING ISB WITH A DIFFUSION MODEL

As has been shown, consideration of the environmental context in which information seeking takes place has not been widely practiced in ISB model development. This may be because doing so opens up a wide array of issues to consider, reducing the simplicity that a model provides. However, there exists a model that can augment current ISB models and their future development by providing direct consideration of the context: the Katz, Levin and Hamilton (1963) model of diffusion of innovations. Although information seeking behavior and diffusion of innovations are two areas that are not typically linked together, their combination is logical in terms of the larger domain of communication theory.

Information seeking behavior, although situated in the library and information science domain, is a form of communicative behavior (Wilson, 1999). When individuals seek information that will help them solve a problem, they are enacting communicative processes. Although early models of ISB focused on the technical process of choosing information sources, later models have expanded to include the realm of wider information behavior. Recent research has taken a wider scope as well, examining other aspects of information behavior and how it affects the seeking process (Fisher, Erdelez, & McKechnie, 2005).

As a communicative process, diffusion of innovations can also be considered as information behavior. When a broader perspective is taken, diffusion can be considered less as a one-way process and more as a general communication behavior, with the focus on the proactive communication behavior of individuals. As Lajoie-Paquette (2005) described, "the essence of the diffusion process is the information exchange through which one individual communicates a new idea to others" (p. 119). Moving away from the traditional one-way action of diffusion and to a consideration of diffusion as the sharing of information among individuals–some of whom are likely proactively seeking information to make a decision about adopting an innovation–turns diffusion into a process associated with information behavior.

Thus, models of information seeking and of diffusion fit within the larger scope of information behavior and can work together to explain how people respond to an information need. Both theories share the same end point: the use of information to make a decision or solve a problem. Therefore, it makes logical sense that the two areas can be combined and inform each other. Lajoie-Paquette (2005) saw a clear connection, noting "possibilities for future information behavior research using diffusion theory research abound" (p. 121). One connection can be drawn by borrowing from a model of diffusion to provide a framework for understanding the environmental context within which an individual exists and how it can affect ISB.

Within the field of diffusion, the dominant model by far has been that of Rogers (2003). He offered a definition of diffusion in 1962: "the process by which (1) an *innovation* (2) is communicated through certain *channels* (3) over *time* (4) among the members of a *social system*" (p. 11, emphasis in the original). Although this model provides a concise means of capturing the diffusion process, it is overly simple concerning the context of diffusion. The notion of a "social system" is too broad to be of any good for in-depth analytical use (Miller, 2008). The term "social system," even as Rogers (1971) noted, subsumes several substantial components: a collection of individual people, a structure governing their interactions,

and a cultural perspective that guides behavior. By collapsing all these concepts into one term, Rogers eliminated the ability to examine the effects of each one on the diffusion process.

However, there is a little used diffusion model that does provide the ability to consider the components of a social system. At about the same time Rogers (1962) was articulating his first definition, Katz, Levin and Hamilton (1963) proposed an "accounting scheme" of the elements of diffusion:

The (1) acceptance, (2) over time, (3) of some specific item—an idea or practice, (4) by individuals, groups or other adopting units, linked (5) to specific channels of communication, (6) to a social structure, and (7) to a given system of values, or culture. (p. 240, emphasis in original)

Compared to the Rogers model, the Katz, Levin and Hamilton (KLH) model offers a set of definitional elements that provide a means to examine more finely grained aspects of diffusion (Miller, 2008).

It is unclear why Rogers' (2003) model became the field standard when the KLH model offered much better analytical capacity. Regardless, the more finely grained KLH model is better suited not only for providing structure for studying diffusion of innovations, but for identifying the various aspects of environmental context that can affect ISB. Thus, this chapter proposed borrowing the KLH model from the diffusion of innovations field to provide a framework for considering the various aspects of an environmental context that affects ISB.

THE KLH MODEL AS CLASSIFYING SYSTEM OF ENVIRONMENTAL CONTEXT

This section will present each element of the KLH model and briefly explore its role in the context of information seeking. The intervening variables identified by Wilson (1996) are integrated into the corresponding elements. Also, potential areas of consideration for ISB studies in the developing world are included. Although the KLH model ends with culture, this discussion will start with culture, because it affects all the other elements.

Culture

Encompassing all of the elements are the "shared attitudes and values" that make up a given culture (Katz, Levin & Hamilton, 1963, p. 249). Culture is notoriously difficult to define (Kroeber & Kluckhohn, 1952), but Keesing and Keesing (1971) argued that culture is an abstraction, made up of composites and generalizations, creating "ideational codes of a people with which they conceptualize their world and interact with one another" (p. 27). Although cultural bearings are difficult to access, they often become more evident when they are in contrast with another culture. Considering culture is particularly important when conducting ISB studies in the developing world, where an understanding of the culture will shed light on study findings, especially when such studies are conducted by an outsider.

Hofstede's (2001) five dimensions of culture provide a very useful measurement for describing and comparing national cultures. The Power Distance dimension considers inequality in a society, determined by how the less powerful members accept and expect unequal distribution of power. The Individualism dimension measures the strength of ties between individuals; individualist societies have loose ties and expect each person to look after himself whereas collectivist societies have tight ties and cohesive groups that protect members in exchange for loyalty. The Masculinity dimension measures the clarity of division of societal roles, particularly in terms of gender roles, with masculine societies valuing assertion and competition, while feminine societies value equality and compromise, traits which influence interaction between the two sexes as well as between supra/subordinates. The Uncertainty Avoidance dimension measures the ability to deal with uncertain

situations or ambiguity, and handle stress. Finally, the Long-term Orientation dimension addresses perspectives on time (long-term versus short-term) and emphasis on respecting tradition.

The culture within which one is embedded will have a subtle though profound effect on determining what appropriate information to seek is, how to seek it, and how to use it.

Wilson (1996) went into some detail on the dimensions of culture articulated by Hofstede (2001) and the effect they may have on ISB. For example, cultures with high power distance measures–meaning how acceptable society considers inequality based on prestige, wealth and power–may inhibit information exchange. Cultures with high collectivist measures may facilitate information sharing. Similarly, cultures with high uncertainy avoidance, that is, cultures that want to minimize uncertainty, are likely to foster ISB. Also, the masculinity dimension will influence what is considered appropriate ISB among the sexes as well as within hierarchies. Cultures with high long-term orientation will have an effect on the time taken to search for information as well as on the consideration of appropriateness of recent vs. old information.

Many developing nations, including those of the Middle East, have quite different cultural dimension measurements than the Western nations where ISB models have been developed. For example, many developing nations have high power distance and uncertainty avoidance measures, whereas Western nations have low power distance and uncertainty avoidance measures. Such differences in culture and the effects they have on ISB need to be considered when using Western-developed ISB models. Unfortunately, as Komlodi (2005) noted, culture has not often been considered in studies of information behavior.

Time

Time in diffusion studies is traditionally used to track the spread of an innovation, to establish the "S-curve" of the spread of an innovation throughout a population (Rogers, 2003). However, in terms of understanding information seeking behavior, time is closely related to culture in terms of determining when it is appropriate to seek information and how long is appropriate to wait for a response. Hofstede (2001) addressed perspectives on time in his Long-term Orientation dimension to account for a culture's tendency to take a long- or short-term perspective on history and actions. Hall (1984) addressed the cultural concept of time in terms of polychronic and monochronic: polychronic time is circular and deadlines are not important, whereas monochronic time is linear and time is not renewable. One's understanding and use of time is heavily influenced by one's culture.

Wilson (1996) included time twice in his intervening variables; once in terms of the economic value of time and later in terms of amount of time spent with an information source. Both considerations can be included under the umbrella of time in the KLH model. Understanding how time is considered by a culture can provide a better understanding of when it is appropriate to initiate information seeking behavior, how long it is appropriate for information seeking to endure, when answers are expected, and how often the search may be repeated. Most Western nations consider time as monochronic while many developing nations, including the Middle East, consider time as polychronic. Such perspectives can have a significant impact on ISB.

Social Structure

According to Katz, Levin, and Hamilton (1963), the social structure sets boundaries and proscribes the interpersonal channels of communication. Consequently, through boundaries and interpersonal relations, the statuses, roles and patterns of interaction between the actors in the system are established (p. 247). The social networks that simultaneously create and are created by the interaction between actors operate on many interrelated levels: individual, organizational, regional, national and even international. Understandings of hierarchy, power and informal relationships–contexts that affect ISB–are only possible through the greater lens of the overall social structure, itself informed by the cultural context.

The differences in cultural dimensions between developing nations and the West will also be demonstrated in the social structures constructed within different cultures, particularly in terms of power and hierarchy. Social structures will determine the appropriate routes of seeking information, including one's ability to access information based on one's position and the power and influence held. For example, some information is available only to the wealthy or to a particular gender. The established patterns of a social system that Wilson (1996) identified as part of social and interpersonal intervening variables can clearly map onto the social structure element.

Communication Channels

Katz, Levin, and Hamilton (1963) and Rogers (2003) both recognized two channels of communication: mass media and interpersonal. Mass media, such as TV, radio, or newspapers, disseminate information so that a message from one individual can reach an audience of many. On the other hand, interpersonal channels relay dialogue between individuals. A significant difference between the two channels is the availability and immediacy of interaction and feedback. Mass media do not allow for immediate interaction, whereas interpersonal communication does. Katz, Levin and Hamilton noted that "different media are appropriate for different tasks" (p. 246); mass media are better for creating awareness while interpersonal relations are better for persuading acceptance (Rogers, 2003).

Some particular aspects of sources of communication channels directly affect ISB. In terms of mass media, accessibility to sources is a critical component. This is measured by the availability of communication technology to access information in various formats; Internet penetration in the general populace, whether via individual access points or community providers; and the presence of libraries, with their collections of materials, trained professionals, and technology provision. Wilson (1996) included such considerations under his rubric of "information source characteristics." In terms of interpersonal channels, aspects such as the willingness of someone to provide information and the knowledge of the topic will have an effect on ISB. Wilson addressed this aspect under his "social and interpersonal" variables.

As with the other elements of this model, channels of communication can also be heavily influenced by culture. The appropriateness of use of certain channels is determined by culture, favoring certain channels over others, depending upon the appropriateness of interaction among people. Cultural influences notwithstanding, developing nations also must cope with simple issues of accessibility, due to the lack of widespread penetration and availability of technology.

Adopting Units

In the KLH model, adopting units referred to individuals or groups. ISB tends to focus only on the individual level, studying and aggregating the actions of individuals. Although the term "adopting units" may seem an incongruous term to denote the actors of information seeking, Chatman (1986) has made the argument that an individual doing the ISB is actually seeking information to adopt in order to make a decision. Accuracy of descriptive labels aside, the adopting units element draws attention to the individuals conducting the seeking.

Wilson's (1996) intervening variables of "personal characteristics," including cognitive dissonance, level of prior knowledge and simple demographics, would fall under the adopting units element. Information needs may be considered a basic human need. Any individual will encounter information needs, but the type of need will depend upon specific socio-economic and demographic

circumstances. Some may need information to fulfill basic needs, such as health care and housing; others who have those basic needs fulfilled will search for other information, such as for academic research. For many information seekers in the developing world, their restricted levels of economic and educational achievement will have a significant effect on the type of information sought and their ability to obtain it.

Item

Katz, Levin and Hamilton (1963) identified the item in diffusion as either an idea or a practice; that is, the ideational component of an innovation. Chatman (1986) made an argument that even "ordinary information" can be considered an item in the diffusion model: "it is conceivable that information which has not been part of one's awareness…can also be classified as new, and thus be considered an innovation" (p. 379). In the ISB process, the "item" is information.

None of the ISB models that address environmental context include the issue of the characteristics of information that may affect ISB. Although Wilson (1996) considers sources of information, he does not address the characteristics of information that may make it an intervening variable itself. The five characteristics of an innovation identified by Rogers (2003)–relative advantage, compatibility, trialability, observability, and complexity–can also describe information when it is considered an item. These may provide a guide for considering the qualities of the information being sought. The most important criterion, however, is whether or not the information answers the need, as determined by the individual doing the seeking.

Again, as with adopting units and social structure, culture plays a significant role in predetermining what appropriate information is. Some cultures may determine certain kinds of information as only appropriate for women or for men to seek. The type of information sought will also be affected by the applicability of it in one's particular environmental context; for example, advanced scientific articles on agricultural processes will not be sought by subsistence farmers.

Acceptance

The final element of the KLH model is whether or not an innovation is adopted. In terms of ISB, this translates to whether or not information found during the seeking behavior is accepted as a solution to the information need. An individual may choose not to accept information because it does not fit the problem. As Wilson (1996) noted, the "fact that a situation demands information to fill cognitive gaps, to support values and beliefs, or to influence affective states, and that sources of

information are available and accessible to the searcher is no guarantee that the information will be 'processed' (that is, incorporated into the users' framework of knowledge, beliefs or values) or used (that is, lead to changes in behavior, values or beliefs)" (chapter 6, section 6.1). Integrating information into one's understanding of the problem and using it to move forward in solving the problem is the desired outcome of ISB, that is, acceptance.

As such, the element of acceptance does not really pertain to the issue of classifying intervening variables in ISB. Still, it raises the question of whether or not the ISB was successful and should be included in any analysis of environmental context factors as an outcome measurement.

Table 1. KLH elements and questions to consider

KLH Element	Main Components	Questions to Consider
Culture	Acceptance of inequality Strength of ties between individuals in a society Division of social roles, hierarchy Acceptance of ambiguity, stress Short-term or long-term perspective on time; respect for tradition	What is considered appropriate information? How can a search be conducted? Who can do the searching for what kind of information? What are appropriate answers?
Time	Polychronic or monochronic	When is it appropriate to seek information? How long can an information search process take?
Social Structure	Social networks Hierarchy Power Formal and informal relationships	What is an appropriate route for seeking information? Who controls access to information?
Communication Channels	Mass media Interpersonal	How widely available is access to information through mass media (including the Internet)? How much do personal sources know and are willing to share?
Adopting Units	Actors of ISB Cognitive and affective components	What are the demographic characteristics of the seeker? How does the seeker act and react during the search process?
Item	Information as an item Characteristics of relative advantage, compatibility, trialability, observability and complexity	What information is being sought? Is it appropriate for the situation?
Acceptance	Incorporating information into one's knowledge base Answers to needs	Does the information answer the need?

CONCLUSION

In conclusion, the KLH model provides a useful framework for classifying and mapping the intervening variables from the environmental context–the cultural, social, technological and physio-psychological structures and spaces–within in which ISB takes place. Using the KLH model to classify intervening variables also draws the researcher's attention to them and brings awareness of their effects on ISB, which can then more richly inform the design and interpretation of ISB studies. Table 1 recaps the elements of the KLH model and suggests questions to consider in order to draw attention to possible intervening variables.

Borrowing the KLH model from the diffusion of innovations field and overlaying it onto ISB research calls out the need to address the various elements of environmental context that can contribute to a better understanding of ISB. This is especially important when ISB research is being conducted in developing nations that likely have significantly different cultural dimensions–and subsequently different environmental context–than the Western nations where the ISB models were developed. Applying the KLH model as a useful framework for identifying and examining intervening variables to ISB research will provide a more nuanced understanding of the information seeking process in any environmental context.

REFERENCES

Chatman, E. A. (1986). Diffusion theory: A review and test of a conceptual model in information diffusion. *Journal of the American Society for Information Science American Society for Information Science, 37*(6), 377–386.

Dervin, B. (1992). From the mind's eye of the user: The sense-making qualitative-quantitative methodology. In Glazier, J. D., & Powell, R. R. (Eds.), *Qualitative research in information management* (pp. 61–84). Englewood, CO: Libraries Unlimited.

Dervin, B. (1997). Given a context by any other name: Methodological tools for taming the unruly beast. In Vakkari, P., Savolainen, R., & Dervin, B. (Eds.), *Information seeking in context* (pp. 13–38). London: Taylor Graham.

Dervin, B. (1999). On studying information seeking methodologically: The implications of connecting metatheory to method. *Information Processing & Management, 35*(6), 727–750. doi:10.1016/S0306-4573(99)00023-0.

Dervin, B., Foreman-Wernet, L., & Lauterbach, E. (2003). *Sense-making methodology reader: Selected writings of Brenda Dervin*. New York: Hampton Press.

Ellis, D. (1989). A behavioral approach to information retrieval design. *The Journal of Documentation, 45*(3), 171–212. doi:10.1108/eb026843.

Fisher, K. E., Erdelez, S., & McKechnie, L. (2005). *Theories of information behavior*. Medford, NJ: Information Today.

Foster, A. (2004). A nonlinear model of information-seeking behavior. *Journal of the American Society for Information Science and Technology, 55*(3), 228–237. doi:10.1002/asi.10359.

Hall, E. T. (1984). *The dance of life: The other dimension of time*. Garden City, NY: Doubleday.

Hofstede, G. (1991). *Cultures and organizations: Software of the mind. Intercultural cooperation and its importance for survival*. London: McGraw-Hill.

Hofstede, G. (2001). *Culture's consequences: International differences in work-related values* (2nd ed.). Beverly Hills, CA: SAGE.

Katz, E., Levin, M. L., & Hamilton, H. (1963). Traditions of research on the diffusion of innovations. *American Sociological Review, 28*, 237–253. doi:10.2307/2090611.

Keesing, R. M., & Keesing, F. M. (1971). *New perspectives in cultural anthropology*. New York: Holt, Rinehart Winston.

Komlodi, A. (2005). Cultural models of Hofstede and Hall. In Fisher, K. E., Erdelez, S., & McKechnie, L. (Eds.), *Theories of information behavior* (pp. 108–112). Medford, NJ: Information Today.

Kroeber, A. L., & Kluckhohn, C. K. M. (1952). Culture: A critical review of concepts and definitions. Papers of the Peabody Museum of American Archaeology and Ethnology, vol. XLVII, no. 1. Cambridge: The Museum.

Kuhlthau, C. C. (1991). Inside the search process: Information seeking from the user's perspective. *Journal of the American Society for Information Science American Society for Information Science, 42*, 361–371. doi:10.1002/(SICI)1097-4571(199106)42:5<361::AID-ASI6>3.0.CO;2-#.

Kuhlthau, C. C. (1994). *Seeking meaning: A process approach to library and information services*. Norwood, NJ: Ablex Publishing.

Lajoie-Paquette, D. (2005). Diffusion theory. In Fisher, K. E., Erdelez, S., & McKechnie, L. (Eds.), *Theories of information behavior* (pp. 118–122). Medford, NJ: Information Today.

Miller, R. L. (2008). *The intercultural transfer of professional knowledge in international partnerships: A case study of the American Bulgarian Library Exchange*. Unpublished Doctoral Dissertation, Emporia State University, Emporia, KS.

Rogers, E. M. (1962). *Diffusion of innovations*. Glencoe, IL: Free Press.

Rogers, E. M. (2003). *Diffusion of innovations* (5th ed.). New York: Free Press.

Rogers, E. M., & Shoemaker, F. F. (1971). *Communication of innovations*. New York: Free Press.

Sonnenwald, D. H. (1999). Evolving perspectives of human information behavior: Contexts, situations, social networks and information horizons. In Wilson, T., & Allen, D. (Eds.), *Exploring the contexts of information behavior* (pp. 176–190). London: Taylor Graham.

Wilson, T. D. (1981). On user studies and information needs. *The Journal of Documentation, 37*(1), 3–15. doi:10.1108/eb026702.

Wilson, T. D. (1996). *Information behavior: An interdisciplinary perspective*. Sheffield, UK: University of Sheffield. Retrieved June 10, 2012, from http://informationr.net/tdw/publ/infbehav/cont.html

Wilson, T. D. (1999). Models in information behavior research. *The Journal of Documentation, 55*(3), 249–270. doi:10.1108/EUM0000000007145.

ADDITIONAL READING

Agada, J. (1999, January). Inner-city gatekeepers: An exploratory survey of their information use environment. *Journal of the American Society for Information Science American Society for Information Science, 50*(1), 74–85. doi:10.1002/(SICI)1097-4571(1999)50:1<74::AID-ASI9>3.0.CO;2-F.

Al-Suqri, M. N. (2011). Information-seeking behavior of social science scholars in developing countries: A proposed model. *The International Information & Library Review, 43*, 1–14. doi:10.1016/j.iilr.2011.01.001.

Ansari, S. M., Fiss, P. C., & Zajac, E. J. (2010, January). Made to fit: How practices vary as they diffuse. *Academy of Management Review, 35*(1), 67–92. doi:10.5465/AMR.2010.45577876.

Barnett, G. A., & Lee, M. (2002). Issues in intercultural communication research. In Gudykunst, W. B., & Mody, B. (Eds.), *Handbook of international and intercultural communication* (2nd ed., pp. 275–289). Thousand Oaks, CA: SAGE Publications.

Burt, R. S. (1999, November). The social capital of opinion leaders. *The Annals of the American Academy of Political and Social Science, 566*, 37–54. doi:10.1177/0002716299566001004.

Buttolph, D. (1992). A new look at adaptation. *Knowledge: Creation, Diffusion. Utilization, 13*(4), 460–470.

Case, D. O. (2002). *Looking for information: A survey of research in information seeking needs and behavior.* Amsterdam, The Netherlands: Academic Press.

Choi, H. J. (2009). Technology transfer issues and a new technology transfer model. *Journal of Technology Studies, 35*(1), 49–57.

Dutta, R. (2009). Information needs and information-seeking behavior in developing countries: A review of the research. *The International Information & Library Review, 41,* 44–51. doi:10.1016/j. iilr.2008.12.001.

Fahmy, E. I., & Rifaat, N. M. (2010). Middle East information literacy awareness and indigenous Arabic content challenges. *The International Information & Library Review, 42,* 111–123. doi:10.1016/j.iilr.2010.04.004.

Feller, I. (1979). Three coigns on diffusion research. *Science Communication, 1*(2), 293–312. doi:10.1177/107554707900100208.

Geertz, C. (1973). *The interpretation of cultures.* New York: Basic Books.

Hays, S. P. (1996). Patterns of reinvention. The nature of evolution during policy diffusion. *Policy Studies Journal: the Journal of the Policy Studies Organization, 24*(4), 551–566. doi:10.1111/j.1541-0072.1996.tb01646.x.

Hover, P., & Lu, J. (2009). "Sentences like these:" Multicultural information dynamics and international diversity of thought. *The International Information & Library Review, 41,* 196–218. doi:10.1016/j.iilr.2009.07.002.

Ikoja-Odongo, R., & Mostert, J. (2006). Information seeking behavior: A conceptual framework. *South African Journal of Libraries & Information Science, 72*(3), 145–158.

Martens, B. V. D., & Goodrum, A. A. (2006). The diffusion of theories: A functional approach. *Journal of the American Society for Information Science and Technology, 57*(3), 330–341. doi:10.1002/asi.20285.

Migir, S. O. (2006). Diffusion of ICTs and e-commerce adoption in manufacturing SMEs in Kenya. *South African Journal of Libraries and Information Science, 72*(1), 35–44.

Minishi-Majanja, M. K., & Kiplang'at, J. (2005). The diffusion of innovations theory as a theoretical framework in library and information science research. *South African Journal of Libraries and Information Science, 71*(3), 211–224.

Polanyi, M. (1966). *The tacit dimension.* Garden City, NY: Doubleday & Company, Inc..

Rogers, E. M., & Bhowmik, D. K. (1970-71). Homophily-heterophily: Relational concepts for communication research. *Public Opinion Quarterly, 34*(4), 523–538. doi:10.1086/267838.

Rogers, E. M., & Hart, W. B. (2002). The histories of intercultural, international, and development communication. In Gudykunst, W. B., & Mody, B. (Eds.), *Handbook of international and intercultural communication* (2nd ed., pp. 1–18). Thousand Oaks, CA: SAGE Publications.

Smith-Pfister, D., & Soliz, J. (2011). (Re)conceptualizing intercultural communication in a networked society. *Journal of International and Intercultural Communication, 4*(4), 246–251. doi:10.1080/17513057.2011.598043.

Ting-Toomey, S. (1999). *Communicating across cultures.* New York: Guilford Press.

Wejnert, B. (2002). Integrating models of diffusion of innovations: A conceptual framework. *Annual Review of Sociology, 28*(1), 297–326. doi:10.1146/annurev.soc.28.110601.141051.

Xia, J. (2012). Diffusionism and open access. *The Journal of Documentation, 68*(1), 72–99. doi:10.1108/00220411211200338.

Yi, Y. J., Stvilla, B., & Mon, L. (2012). Cultural influences on seeking quality health information: An exploratory study of the Korean community. *Library & Information Science Research, 34*(1), 45–51. doi:10.1016/j.lisr.2011.06.001.

KEY TERMS AND DEFINITIONS

Culture: An abstraction of attitudes, values and beliefs held in common by a group of people, which creates an ideational code that governs their behavior and perceptions of appropriateness.

Diffusion of Innovations: The purposeful and intentional sharing of information concerning a new product, process, or idea.

Environmental Context: The web of social, cultural, technological and physio-psychological structures within which an individual exists.

Information Need: The perceived gap of information that requires fulfillment in order to answer or aid in answering a problem or question.

Information Seeking Behavior: Processes used by individuals as they work out their information needs, and look for and select information to answer these needs.

Intervening Variable: Physical, virtual or environmental items or actions that facilitate or bar accessing information.

Social Network: The system of connections that creates and is created by the patterns of interactive, interpersonal connections between individuals, leading to establishment of hierarchies and power relationships.

Chapter 6

The Ellis Model of Information Seeking Behavior and the Peripheral Scientific Community

Simon Aristeguieta-Trillos
Clarion University of Pennsylvania, USA

ABSTRACT

This chapter explores the relationship between the Ellis Model of Information Seeking Behavior and the scientific community of Venezuela. The research employs a qualitative method to investigate the main information seeking activities of a scientific community in the periphery in the context of dependency theory. The following elements of the Ellis model are supported by the data gathered and analysis: starting, browsing, chaining, filtering, extracting, and information management.

INTRODUCTION

Access to scientific information is essential to the scientific endeavor, the process of creating scientific knowledge, and the scientific community. The primary channel for the communication of scientific information is the scholarly journal (McCain, 1989). Journals are composed of papers that are linked to each other by the use of citations, forming networks of knowledge (Price, 1965). There are other ways to communicate and disseminate scientific information, including personal communication, textbooks, conference attendance, conference proceedings, preprints, social media and digital content (Brown, 1999; Price, 1963; Tenopir, King, Edwards & Wu, 2009). However, accessing and examining current research published in refereed journals is paramount to scientific research (Kirsop, Arunachalam, & Chan 2007).

The accessibility of sources of scientific information is determined and mediated by the availability of funds and by the existence of an infrastructure capable of supporting access to

DOI: 10.4018/978-1-4666-4353-6.ch006

the information by the scientific community (Arunachalam, 2003). The rising price of scientific information is a concern in academic libraries around the world, because it is limiting the number of subscriptions that a library can afford to hold (Kirsop, Arunachalam, & Chan 2007; University of Illinois, 2009). Many academic libraries are canceling the subscriptions to individual journals and specialized databases and indexes. There has been a price increase in journals of 178.3% between 1990 and 2000. It is reported that a subscription to one scholarly journal may costs in an excess of US$20,000 a year. Many academic libraries have seen their budgets decrease by at least 3% from the 1980s to the present (Scientific Journals International, 2008). The increasing cost of scientific information is affecting universities and research institutions all over the world. Only those institutions with enough funds are able to maintain their collections of print and electronic subscriptions, and thereby continue to provide to the scientific community the desired level of access to current and reliable sources.

This situation, which has become increasingly problematic in the U.S. and Europe, has become critical in the case of countries in the periphery. "Periphery" refers to regions with monopolized, underdeveloped or developing economies. "Core" refers to highly developed regions with diversified economies (Cardozo, 1972; Valenzuela & Valenzuela, 1978). For nations in the periphery, access to scientific information is even more limited by a lack of funds, inadequate infrastructure, and in some cases, language difficulties (Kirsop & Chan, 2005; Kirsop, Arunachalam, & Chan 2007; May, 2006).

There is an asymmetrical trade relationship between nation in the core and those in the periphery. The periphery exports raw natural materials and agricultural products, while the core specializes in the production of manufactured goods (Cardozo, 1972; Peet, 1999; Valenzuela & Valenzuela, 1978),

which results in a cycle of continually increasing amounts of high tech products and informational services being offered to peripheral countries. Scientific information is a marketable good (Kingma, 2001) that is mainly produced and controlled in Europe and the U.S. For example, The *Journal Citation Report* (JCR) publishes usage and visibility indicators from 6,166 research and academic journals, and only 9.03% are published outside North America and Europe (Thomson, 2008a). This situation has placed peripheral countries at a disadvantage when they attempt to negotiate for access to sources with the oligopoly conglomerate providers of scientific information. Oligopoly refers to a group of suppliers that exercise market control by setting prices and establishing output quotas of goods and services (Kingma, 2001). The access to information sources acquired by the periphery is in most cases very limited, which in turn affects the access of relevant material by the scientific community. Kirsop, Arunachalam, & Chan (2007, Technology transfer/Capacity building, para. 1) point out that "any limitation on the selection of material available and barriers to access lead to reduced scientific progress and continuing dependence."

Many countries outside of North America and Western Europe lack the necessary information and communication technology (ICT) infrastructure to be part of the global communication network, and have not been able to enter the global information society (May, 2006). A robust ICT infrastructure is necessary to access and interact with digital content, social media, and the international community. Many scientists in the periphery feel left out and excluded from scientific communication and dissemination processes because they lack the proper ICTs; they are "technological deprived" (Arunachalam, 2003, p. 136). By the same token, library collections and services offered to the scientific community are limited by insufficient funding and staff. In some cases, the library staff lacks sufficient training and do not offer enough services to the community (Majid, Anwar, & Eisenschitz, 2000).

Language also limits the access to scientific information. In selecting journals for indexing for databases and other informational goods, the scholarly publisher Thomson favors English language journals (Thomson, 2008b). Vickery (2000) points out that even though English is the mother tongue of only 8% of the world, up to 46% of all scholarly journals are published in English. The language barrier affects science because it limits knowledge transfer and dissemination. On the one hand, scientists with limited English proficiency are forced to search, find, and use information written in their mother tongue, while on the other hand, English-speaking scientists have limited exposure to publications in other languages. Research published in the periphery has very little visibility (Arunachalam, 2003). Kirsop & Chan (2005) affirm that there is large gap in the "global knowledge pool" (p. 247) because there is a large portion of scientific research lost in the literature published in the periphery.

The study presented in this book chapter is part of a research carried out in Venezuela during the years 2009 and 2010. Venezuela is a country situated in the northern part of South America. Venezuela is a former Spanish colony that gained its independence in 1821. The official language is Spanish. It is a developing nation located in a peripheral region. Venezuela's economy is dependent on oil exports. Extracting, producing and exporting oil generate revenue for the Venezuelan state; oil revenues account for 90% of the nation's export earnings (CIA, 2009). Venezuela has an active scientific research community. The National Observatory of Science, Technology and Innovation (ONCTI, 2009) reports that in 2007, Venezuela had 5,222 scientists doing research in the following knowledge areas: biology, health, agriculture, environment, physics, chemistry,

math, engineering, earth science, and the social sciences (Aristeguieta-Trillos & Maura Sardo, 2006).

INFORMATION SEEKING BEHAVIOR

The Ellis Model

Ellis (1989) studied information seeking behaviors and patterns of social scientists from the University of Sheffield. The objective of the study was to gather information and recommendations to aid in the design of information retrieval systems. Data were collected through interviews, and analysis was done by inductively deriving concepts, categories and properties. Ellis & Haugan (1997) declare that many studies on information use are being investigated using a qualitative approach. Data collection is being done in small groups through observation and interviews. Information science researchers are attempting to generate models that explain information-seeking behavior in a wide array of situations and contexts.

In the 1989 study, Ellis developed a model of six information seeking activities that comprise a consistent pattern of information seeking behavior often exhibited by academic researchers: starting, chaining, browsing, differentiating, monitoring, and extracting. The first activity of the model, starting, involves the seeker's need to gather new ideas, form an impression of the subject area, and identify important existing studies on the topic. This activity normally centers on the individual's first search. It may also include sources the seeker was already aware of and had used before. The second activity, chaining, involves tracing the paths back and forth in the related literature that are created by following the citations for each article. The activity of browsing permits access to materials by authors, journals, conference proceedings, working papers, publishers' lists, cited works, subject terms, and broad or narrow subject headings. It is a more spontaneous, semi-directed way of looking and searching for literature in areas of particular interest. The fourth element, differentiating, implies a process of comparatively evaluating the quality, appropriateness, and relative utility of each of an array of materials that are related to the subject of interest by topic, methodology, or treatment. Differentiation is a way of filtering the results of a search. The fifth activity, monitoring, involves routinely searching specific sources and recently indexed articles, in order to keep up with new developments in a particular area of interest. The last activity, extracting, means systematically searching for material of interest in a particular database, journal collection or journal issue. Ellis & Haugan (1997) also studied information seeking patterns of engineers and other scientists in industry. The results refined and extended the original model by identifying eight activities: surveying, chaining, monitoring, browsing, distinguishing, filtering, extracting and ending.

Meho & Tibbo (2003) revised the Ellis (1989) model described above. The participants were social science faculty doing research on stateless nations. The rationale for participant selection was that this group of scholars had never been targeted before and they were diverse with regard to disciplines, institutions, countries and language. Participants were chosen from a pool of authors indexed in the Arts & Humanities Citation Index, Geobase, the Social Science Citation Index, and Sociological Abstracts. Sixty scientists were interviewed by e-mail. The data was coded twice. Information sources used by this group were found to be: their own personal collection of sources, fieldwork, and archives. Though the study confirmed the value of Ellis' original model, four more categories were added: accessing, networking, verifying, and information managing. Accessing is having the materials and sources of information on hand. Networking refers to sharing and interacting with colleagues, in the context of their research. Verifying was regarded

as crucial for this group because information had to be accurate, especially sensitive information. Information managing refers to the scientists' organizing the information they have found in order to facilitate using it for their research.

USER STUDIES

Five studies are examined here to illustrate information seeking behavior research. The first three studies: Grefsheim & Rankin (2007); Hemminger, Lu, Vaughan & Adams (2007), and Tenopir, King & Bush (2004), took place in the United States. The other two studies: Majid, Anwar & Eisenschitz (2000) and Schwartz (1995) were performed in Asia, one in Malaysia and one in India. Participants in the studies were from the health, basic, and agricultural sciences.

Grefsheim & Rankin (2007) surveyed 500 National Institutes of Health (NIH) scientists and administrators. The survey was administered by telephone. It was found that the information sources their respondents used were (in rank order according to the respondents' preference): journals, databases, books, conference proceedings, newsletters, technical reports, newspapers, statistics, lab manuals, standards, legal sources, study guides, patents, and market research. The overwhelming majority (84%) of the participants in the survey indicated that they prefer using electronic journals; only 5% of the participants prefer using printed journals. 11% of the participants responded that they like both formats.

In terms of information seeking behavior, it was found that the majority of the participants (91%) prefer to look for information themselves. Grefsheim & Rankin call them "self-sufficient information users" (p. 430). The NIH library website was mentioned as the main gateway for searching for information. The search engines Google and Yahoo were also mentioned. Participants reported spending an average of 9.3 hours a week in activities of searching, reviewing, and analyzing scientific information. However, there were three problems mentioned by the participants regarding information seeking: 1) "Not enough time to search for and gather information", 2) "Not knowing what is available", and 3) "Information is too hard to find" (p. 430). The authors of the study conclude that there needs to be a better synchronization between the services provided by the library and the scientists' work habits and information needs.

A 2007 study by Hemminger, Lu, Vaughan, and Adams, surveyed 902 scientists from the basic sciences and the medical science departments at the University of North Carolina. The Web based survey consisted of 28 questions. This study found that the most used information sources were: journals, Web pages, databases, personal communications, books, preprints, proceedings, and conferences. The journals *Science* and *Nature* were listed as the two sources used the most by basic and medical scientists.

Bibliographic and citation databases and general web searches were the two most frequently used tools for information searching. The study revealed a preference for electronic access and electronic retrieval of materials. This study also showed that the number of library visits made by these scientists was very small; 23% of those surveyed indicated that they visited the library fewer than two times in a period of twelve months. When asked why they visit the library, 23% of the participants answered that it was to make photocopies. A librarian's assistance was mentioned by only 7% of the participants. Infrequent library visits may be explained by the availability of electronic resources online (Hemminger et al., 2007), although this contrasts with the findings of the Majid, Anwar, & Eisenschitz (2000) study, that the proximity of a library accounts for its users' keeping current with scientific information.

Tenopir, King, & Bush (2004) studied medical doctors at the University of Tennessee Health Science Center (UTHSC). A critical incident technique approach was used to analyze information

seeking behaviors. In the study, the incident was defined as the most recent "reading"; the participant is then asked a series of questions about their reasons for reading, reading habits, and searching strategies. It was found that the respondents read an average of 322 journal articles per year. "Reading" is defined as "going beyond the table of contents, title, and abstract to the body of the article" (p. 236). Participants reported several reasons for reading articles: primary research, current awareness, teaching, writing, background research and consulting. Supporting primary research was the main reason given for reading journal articles. The preferred format for reading was the print journal. One explanation provided in the article is that this scientific community holds a significant number of personal subscriptions to scholarly journals. It is reported that this community averages 6.3 subscriptions per person, as compared to 3.8 for the University of Tennessee, Knoxville faculty (Tenopir et al., 2004).

Majid, Anwar & Eisenschitz (2000) surveyed 234 agricultural scientists from the University of Putra Malaysia (UPM), Malaysian Agricultural Research (MARDI), Palm Oil Research of Malaysia (PORIM), Rubber Research Institute of Malaysia (RRIM), and the Forest Research Institute of Malaysia (FRIM), about their information needs and information seeking behavior. It was found that scientists from UPM spent 9.3% of their time in searching and reading scientific literature. Participants from the other institutions were spending an average of 16% of their time in the same activities. Fifty-seven percent indicated that they are able to keep up to date on the scientific literature in their area of interest. A correlation was found between proximity to the library and keeping current with scientific information. Participants closer to libraries were able to keep current with the literature. Libraries proved to be very effective in providing access to current scientific information.

Forty-three percent of these respondents are unable to keep current with scientific information;

the reasons given for this were: being too busy with research, having to attend too many administrative meetings, being uncertain about where to look for information, needing information that is not available, and contending with deficient library collections and services.

The information sources that this study's respondents felt were most important for keeping current on scientific research were (in decreasing order of importance): journal articles, review articles, interaction with professional colleagues, conference abstracts and proceedings, professional meetings, sources of current contents, indexing and abstracting journals, research reports/patents/fact books, books, newsletters, bibliographies, and theses and dissertations.

Schwartz's (1995) study on physicians and biomedical scientists identified three issues that obstruct access to scientific information in India. They are as follows: 1) academic and hospital libraries do not maintain a core collection of journals, 2) national journals are not published in a consistent periodic schedule and are seldom indexed internationally, and 3) there is not a national indexing system.

Participants in the study were 49 medical doctors and PhD.s. Data were collected in six focus group sessions. Two head librarians carried out interviews. All participants belong to the All India Institute of Medical Science in New Delhi and the Tama Memorial Cancer Center in Bombay.

Participants partially met their information needs by consulting the Biological and Chemical Abstracts and the Current Contents databases. Participants reported that articles from international journals were very hard to find. Journals issues were passed from institution to institution in order to be photocopied for local use. MEDLINE was only available on CD-ROM and access to it was limited. Librarians were considered to be poorly trained by the scientists.

METHOD

A qualitative exploration was the preferable approach for conducting this study of the Venezuelan scientific community because the participants are the experts on the subject of the study. Each scientist's ideas, procedures, values and meanings are the result of each participant's individual biography, context and thinking. This approach aims to find the explanations of the phenomena targeted by the objectives of the study in the stories told by the participants (Gurwitsch, 1974; Powel, 1999; Punch, 2004).

The participants in the study were active members of the Venezuelan scientific community affiliated with the Research Incentive Program (PPI) with a "research" rank of level 3 or higher. This rank and level of scholarship and research is comparable to the associate professor rank in the North American academic context.

Participants in the study were recruited by convenience sampling (Corbin & Strauss, 2007) and snowball sampling (Lindlof & Taylor, 2002) techniques. The long interview technique was used to collect data. McCraken (1988) points out that any social science research is improved if one can understand the experiences of the participants. Interviews were transcribed and coded. Coding is the process of developing concepts from data. Haley (1996) defines analytic induction as a process that "consists of scanning…line by line for themes and categories" (p. 26). Thomas (2006) points out that "the outcome of an inductive analysis is the development of categories into a model or framework that summarizes the raw data and conveys key themes and processes" (p. 240). Important features of categories, according to Thomas (2006), are category labels; category descriptions; coded text that illustrates meanings and behaviors; links to other categories; and model or theoretical construct that is the end point of the inductive approach.

FINDINGS

Summary

As it was explained above the Ellis' (1989) information seeking behavior model initially identified six activities: starting, chaining, browsing, differentiating, monitoring and extracting. A later study on engineers and scientists in industry discovered eight activities: surveying, chaining, monitoring, browsing, distinguishing, filtering, extracting, and ending (Ellis & Haugan, 1997). Elements of the Ellis model on information seeking behavior are supported by the data collected in the study presented in this chapter.

The starting stage of search found in the study was mostly electronic searching, though searching printed sources was also identified in a minor scale, using the Internet (specifically Google Scholar, and international academic databases). These searches were focused on author, journal title, topics, and keywords. Searching by author and journal was found to be the most frequent searching pattern for Venezuela's scientists. Meneghini, Packer, & Nassi-Calo (2008) point out that Brazilian scientists cite well-known international scientists and high impact journals while avoiding citing other Brazilian scientists in an effort to increase the weight of their work. These findings might also explain the searching patterns of Venezuelan scientists; it might be perceived that citing renowned scientists and high impact journals increases the chances of getting published in those same journals.

Browsing was also mainly an electronically mediated activity. It was performed in the sources during the starting stage. Public access journal articles, references, and abstracts were the main types of documents reviewed in this stage. If preprints and conference proceedings were found at this stage, they were also browsed. However, Venezuela's scientists' information seeking is focused on finding established scientific knowledge. Therefore, preprints were less essential information sources for the scientific community under study.

Chaining references was only reported in the study when a national publication and author was cited by an international source, at which point the cited reference was traced and followed. (See the above comment on the Meneghini, Packer, & Nassi-Calo, 2008 study). The participants in the study also reported differentiating. One participant reported filtering results by year, source, authors and methodology. Participants also reported monitoring and extracting using the international databases available to them. Information management is reported and observed in two participants' offices; this finding coincides with the Meho & Tibbo (2003) study on social science faculty, which added four more categories to the Ellis model: accessing, networking, verifying, and information managing.

Initiating Search

Most of the searches done by the participants were electronic, either in the "open Internet" or in public or paid search engines and indexes, such as Google Scholar, Science Finder, and Web of Science, which were linked through the library's Website. This finding corresponds to other findings in the literature. Grefsheim & Rankin (2007) reported that 84% of the 500 scientists surveyed from the National Institute of Health prefer electronic searching. Hemminger, Lu, Vaughan, and Adams (2007) reported similar preferences among University of North Carolina scientists. All of the participants in the study had desktop computers at their offices and they were connected to the Internet. Few complained about the speed of the connection being extremely slow. Several participants mentioned that the changes brought about by the information and communication technologies (ICTs) are comparable to the invention of the printing press. They further established their innovative character by calling the Internet "revolutionary":

P1: ...I felt in love with information technologies. I believe that something similar might have happened when Gutenberg invented the printing press. Being able to access the net is a revolution...I still remember when I used the computer for the first time. I used the keyword and I thought that I had done something wrong and the computer was going to blow up...

However, participants still go to libraries to search and browse printed journals. Individual labs and research units have printed journals subscriptions for browsing and searching. However, for the most part, the action of initiating a search is an individual process that takes place in the researcher's office. Many times, the search is initiated at the researcher's office but browsing full-text articles is done at the library if the publication is only available in print. Another non-electronic search-initiating practice was to go to the library to browse the serial collection in search of important information:

P8: ...With the use of information technologies, it is easier to find information. Academic databases make it very easy to search for scientific information. When we don't have remote access to electronic sources, we go to the library and look journal by journal for the relevant topics.

For the most part, participants initiated searches using the author's name. They were aware of whom the leading scientists in the field were; therefore, initiating a search by an author's name is the preferred strategy. Search seems to depend heavily on their perceptions of who the big names are, as participant 7 pointed out in subsection 4.2.2.

Themes, topics, keywords and phrases were also identified as search fields.

Participants 6 preferred author search: ... *In most of the cases, I am interested in searching for authors.*

Participant 11 mentioned that information could be located in other ways; however, the participant also favored author search because it would retrieve recent and up-to-date research:

P11: You can locate information by phrases, authors and journals. You can also draw chemical compound structures. Sometimes I look for themes, but what interest me the most are authors. I know the researchers who work in my area or are close to it. Then, I just do a simple search by name and browse to the most recent works. In that manner, I can see the state of research in my area or discipline.

Participants 7 and 4 initiated searches by theme and topic, while Participant 4 explained that keywords were used to initiate a search:

P7: I look for themes, in my case pathogen organisms...then I am able to retrieve the references for the most recent work...

P4: When I search Web of Science, I search by topics...

P3: In most cases, I use keywords for searching; limiting the search to recent years... Yes, I combine keywords to retrieve what is relevant to me...

Browsing

Browsing is the second activity or behavior to be identified. Browsing was mainly an electronic activity that took place at the researchers' offices. Browsing of printed journals also occurred at the library and at the labs. Google Scholar was found to be the most popular open database for the participants. Other generic search engines were also used. For example, Google and Yahoo were used to search for relevant information sources. National and regional databases were reported to be irrelevant and of little use.

Internet

Searching and browsing the Internet was a common practice among the participants, as one participant put it "*...the Internet is a place to search and browse...*" After the search was performed, the retrieved information was browsed in order to find relevant sources. One of the participants defines browsing as: "*looking over*" or "*light reading*", while another terms it as "*window shopping.*" The type of informational items reported to be found on the Internet were: references, abstracts, open access journals, and links to the libraries' electronic journal collection.

P3: I do search by keywords in the Internet, and then print the references...Most of the time, I use Google Search. I also use Yahoo.

P6: ...I like to browse the Internet. I find references that are important for me. If I am lucky, I will be able to find the full text either on the Internet or in the library...

P9: I first search for abstracts on the Internet. I read the titles. I then read the abstracts. If the publication is in the library, there will be a link to the full text...

P7: I surf the Internet and search by title, journal, and author. Sometimes I can download the full text because I hit an open access full text journal. You don't need to be subscribed to those journals.

P8: The first thing I do is to read the abstract to find out if the publication is in my interest...

P13: ...I like to go to the Internet to see what I find...

Google Scholar

Google Scholar is the preferred tool for searching information sources on the Internet. It is an open access search engine of patent and scientific information managed by Google. Many participants initiated the search in Google Scholar instead of the subscription databases available to them through the library website. It was mentioned that citations or references are the only information items that can be retrieved from this database. Participants 4 and 5 stated:

P4: I always start each search in Google Scholar. It is being used around here a lot. It only cites the source. If our library has the publication then we are safe; if not, the process of getting the information is stopped and we don't have access.

P5: ...Google Scholar is great! However, it doesn't give you access to full-text...which is very frustrating..

Participant 3 stated that a search is initiated at the library first and then in Google Scholar.

P3: Now we have Google Scholar. It is a very good tool. When I don't find the information in the library, I use Google Scholar.

Regional Databases

There has been a sustained effort in the region to consolidate scientific, social science, and humanities information sources. This effort has materialized in several public access databases. There are, for example, Clase, Periodica, Latindex, LILACS and SciELO that index documents and offered, in some cases, access to full-text scientific articles. These databases were designed for the purpose of facilitating access to academic information for the regional and international scientific community. By the same token, these databases were intended to enhance visibility and impact of research in the region.

Participants were asked about how these regional databases were being used as sources of scientific information. It was discovered that the participants in the study either did not know of their existence, or found them to be irrelevant. They were only used if they were referenced in international publications. National publications and regional databases are not thought of as viable publication outlets (for information dissemination) or as information sources by the participants in this study. According to the participants, Venezuelan journals should be the training ground for aspiring scientists (graduate students) or just for publishing editorial and opinion pieces. In addition, regional databases were perceived as not indexing relevant research that could be used as references sources.

Participant 10 stated the following about national journals and regional databases: "...*Few national publications are relevant...if they are cited internationally I may take a look at it...*" Another participant said:

P3: *...I would only read and reference national publications if I find them cited in international journals. There is SciELO...I don't remember it well...with things from Latin America. I just use it when it is cited internationally.*

Other participants stated:

P2: *...[O]n full text or source references?...No, I don't know of any.*
P6: *I know of SciELO but I have never used it. I am not interested in reading or referencing regional publications.*
P7: *...Yes I know SciELO and LILACS. I am doing a review from the year 2000 to the present. I searched them, I could not find anything relevant...*
P2: *...SciELO is not important for me...*

International Databases

The advantages mentioned by the participants regarding electronic database search were the following: fast searching, easy browsing, not having to visit the library, and extensive record and information retrieval. Participants 4 and 7 stated:

P4: *Database searching is easier and faster that manually searching for information at the library. Searching and browsing printed journals takes more time. In the past, it was easier to miss some publications and research; today, when we search electronically, we recover more information and little published research is lost.*
P7: *It is very easy if we can search electronically for new molecular building methodologies in a database and not have to go to the library and browse journal by journal.*

The following quotes from Participants 1, 4, and 5 mentioned the use of international databases:

P1: *We use one that comes from the U.S.; it is part of the U.S. National Library of Medicine. It has millions of records and hundreds of publications on biomedical information. When I want to see something on research, it is where I go. I limit the search to the last ten years. For example: "keyword"; there you go, there are 562 papers in the last ten years.*
P4: *I search in a NASA database. It is on astrophysics and physics.*
P5: *...We are fortunate to have Science Finder... wish we had more databases available with links to full-text journal articles.*

Finally, Participant 12 made a distinction between access to scientific information in Venezuela and in the USA. Participant 12 stated:

P12: *...In the USA, they have more advanced and complete databases. There you can search information in detail. There, they are one or two steps ahead of us...libraries and* *professors have direct access to better collections, they have direct access from their computers...*

Reading Behavior and Information Management

Another behavior that was observed and discussed with the participants is how they read, organize and manage scientific information (references, abstracts, and papers). It was found that some participants read papers from the computer screen while others need to print them in order to use them. In one case, it was found that a participant had a very organized collection of scientific papers in print, that was classified using index cards and in another case reference management software. Other participants showed some degree of engaging information management activity.

Reading Abstracts

Reading abstracts was found to be a common practice among the participants of this research. This practice is used to go beyond the title and to get more information on the research published. It is also, in a context of limited access to full-text, a replacement for reading the full-text article. One participant mentioned that "Abstract reading substitutes for article reading," while another one stated that "…We read more abstracts than anything. It is easier to find the abstract than to find the complete full-text…"

Abstracts were also read to be informed and stay current in one's discipline. The participants said:

P3: I read the abstracts, and if I think they are important then, I will try to get the publication.

P10: I also read abstracts to find out in more detail about published research.

P11: I read the abstracts to keep me informed of what is happening in my area...

As noted above, reading abstract online replaces reading papers in the Venezuelan context, because abstracts are available online most of the time, while full-text papers have to be obtained following the strategies explained in section 4.4., unless they are part of the libraries' journal collection.

Reading Electronic Articles

Participants were found to start reading papers online or from a downloaded PDF file. However, once the paper caught the participants' interest, it was printed. Printing was limited by economic concerns, especially regarding the cost of ink. Participants 1 and 5 stated:

P1: It all depends. There are papers that I start reading in the computer because it is very expensive to print everything. I first read the abstract and if I am interested then I search for the full text. If I find it, I save it in the computer. In any case, I like to have it in PDF. Most of the time, I end up printing it because the information is vital for me.

P5: I see it and then I save it. Later, I will convert it to PDF to read it.

P12: I use the computer because I can copy and paste, zoom or minimize.

Printing

Once the paper catches the attention of the participant, the common practice is to print the PDF. The participants observe that printed-paper is easy to read and highlight and mark. The participants stated:

P10: I don't like to read from the computer. It is easier for me to read a print. I can read it from the computer screen; however, it is more fluid to read a printed copy.

P12: I still like to read from a printed copy, so I can highlight and cross out words and sentences with lines.

P3: It may be an age issue; the younger generation does everything on the computer, but not me, I have to print everything.

P7: Yes, I download and print a lot of things; the full text is read on printed paper.

P9: I download, print and then read.

P4: In my case, I print. I like to make marks on the paper.

Managing Information

As mentioned at the beginning of this section, activities related to organization of information were observed and discussed with the participants. Most of the time, there was not a visible pattern of information organization and management. There were papers all over the researchers' desk and in the offices' bookshelves. However, there were two participants who had a very impressive collection of printed papers in PDF format in their offices. One of the participants managed the paper collection using index cards. The index cards had the following elements: the full reference, notes, and a topically-coded homegrown classification system. Participant 3 stated:

P3: ...I have many boxes full of index cards. I like to keep track of what I read. I was fortunate to start managing and saving information from the beginning of my career. I also collected information on my specialized field ...

Participant 2 also has a very organized collection of papers on the office's shelf. In this case, however, management of the collection was made using the desktop computer, running reference management software. In the quote, the participant explains how the collection is managed:

P2: I print all the PDFs. I have a personal library where I keep all the papers. I also save them in the computer. I use a program

called Endnote, it runs under Windows. I do reference work after lunch. I have a whole stack of papers. I enter the information of two papers everyday. Then I put them in my personal library. I archived them there. I use my own classification scheme. To me is very important to find them later. To me, Endnote helps me to find them faster.

CONCLUSION

Information Seeking Behavior

The information seeking behavior of Venezuelan scientists is influenced by their need to find established scientific literature for the purpose of publishing research in international journals. The search strategy is focused on finding journal articles authored by well-known experts, and published in high impact journals. National and regional authors and journals are bypassed as irrelevant. The journal article is the document type preferred over others, such as preprints and conference proceedings. Meneghini, Packer & Nassi-Calò (2008) point out that Brazilian scientists "tend to produce reference lists containing a majority of prominent authors and prestigious journals, and avoid citations of their compatriots, as if this would give more weight to their publications" (p. 4). Though data collected in this study is not conclusive, it seems to indicate, as in the case of the Brazilian scientists, that the participants in the study perceive that having highly-cited references in their manuscripts increases the likelihood of getting published in international journals.

Some of the salient elements that identify information-seeking behavior of scientists in Venezuela were examined in light of the Ellis (1989) model. Ellis' (1989) model of information seeking behavior is derived from data collected at the University of Sheffield with the intent of aiding the design of information retrieval systems. The context and purpose of Ellis' study suggest a situation where information resources are readily available, while this study took place in a context where information sources are scarce. Nonetheless, Ellis' patterns of activity are identifiable in these data:

1. "Starting" is mostly an electronic activity occurring on the Internet (using Google Scholar and academic databases, for example), though library visits are also reported. The fields commonly used for electronic searching are author and source. As pointed out above, this searching strategy reflects the perceived necessity to find key authors who are the "big names" in their fields, and high impact international journals.

2. Browsing of abstracts, references, and journal articles are activities mainly done using electronic formats. Printed collections of journals held by libraries or individual labs are also browsed occasionally. References and citations are browsed with the intention of finding full-text journal articles. Participants report that abstracts and citations are more readily available than full-text articles; in the information resources open to them (e.g., Google Scholar and academic databases without links to full-text).

3. Chaining of citations is performed when a national source (author and/or journal) is cited by an international source. Participants reported that few national and regional publications are relevant information sources for their work unless they are cited in high visibility journals.

4. Filtering electronic searches according to publication year, source, author, and methodology, as well as monitoring journals and indexes for pertinent new research are activities reported by several participants, particularly those familiar with the use of information technologies.

5. Extracting information occurs if the resource is accessible from an open-access, full-text electronic database and/or a library collection (either electronic or print). If the resource

is not available in this way, finding a full-text version becomes a challenge. Four coping strategies are reported: seeking library-based provisional services (interlibrary loan and document delivery), purchasing the article online, purchasing a subscription to the publication, and contacting the first author for a courtesy copy. Contacting the author is the preferred extracting strategy, and it is also one of the main themes from which the model of scholarly communication in Venezuela emerges.

6. Information management is also identified in two participants' explanations. They each kept a well-organized personal collection of full-text scholarly articles in PDF format, obtained from both electronic and printed original sources.

REFERENCES

Aristeguieta-Trillos, S., & Maura Sardo, M. (2006). *A bibliometric study on scientific production in Venezuela from 1994 to 2003 based on Science Citation Index*. Retrieved on April 17, 2008, from http://www.congreso-info.cu/

Arunachalam, S. (2003). Information for research in developing countries: Information technology--A friend or foe? *The International Information & Library Review, 35,* 133–147. doi:10.1016/S1057-2317(03)00032-8.

Brown, C. M. (1999). Information Seeking Behavior of Scientists in the Electronic Information Age: Astronomers, Chemists, Mathematicians, and Physicists. *Journal of the American Society for Information Science American Society for Information Science, 50*(10), 929–943. doi:10.1002/(SICI)1097-4571(1999)50:10<929::AID-ASI8>3.0.CO;2-G.

Cardoso, F., H. (1972). Dependent Capitalist Development in Latin America. *New Left Review, 74*(I), 83–95.

Chan, L., Kirsop, B., & Arunachalam, S. (2005). Open access archiving: The fast track to building research capacity in developing countries. *Science and Development Network*. Retrieved on January 27, 2010, from http://www.scidev.net/ms/openaccess/

CIA. (2009). *South America: Venezuela.* Retrieved on June 15, 2009, from https://www.cia.gov/library/publications/the-world-factbook/geos/VE.html

Corbin, J. M., & Strauss, A. C. (2007). *Basics of qualitative research: Techniques and procedures for developing grounded theory*. Newbury Park, CA: Sage.

Ellis, D. (1989). A behavioral model for information retrieval system design. *Journal of Information Science, 15*, 237–247. doi:10.1177/016555158901500406.

Ellis, D., & Haugan, M. (1997). Modelling the information seeking patterns of engineers and research scientists in an industrial environment. *The Journal of Documentation, 53*, 384–403. doi:10.1108/EUM0000000007204.

Grefsheim, S. F., & Rankin, J. A. (2007). Information needs and information seeking in a biomedical research setting: a study of scientists and science administrators. *Journal of the Medical Library Association, 95*(4), 426–434. doi:10.3163/1536-5050.95.4.426 PMID:17971890.

Gurwitsch, A. (1974). *Phenomenology and the theory of science*. Evanston, IL: Northwestern University Press.

Haley, E. (1996). Exploring the construct of organization as source: Consumers' understanding of organizational sponsorship of advocacy advertising. *Journal of Advertising, 25*(2), 21–35.

Hemminger, B. M., Lu, D., Vaughan, K. T. L., & Adams, S. J. (2007). Information seeking behavior of academic scientists. *Journal of the American Society for Information Science and Technology, 58*(14), 2205–2225. doi:10.1002/asi.20686.

Kingma, B. R. (2001). *The Economics of Information*. Westport, CT: Libraries Unlimited.

Kirsop, B., & Chan, L. (2005). Transforming Access to Research Literature for Developing Countries. *Serials Review, 31*, 246–255. doi:10.1016/j.serrev.2005.09.003.

Kirsop, B., Chan, L., & Arunachalam, S. (2007). Access to Scientific Knowledge for Sustainable Development: Options for Developing Countries. *Ariadne, 52*. Retrieved on June 14, 2009, from http://www.ariadne.ac.uk/issue52/

Lindlof, T. R., & Taylor, B. C. (2002). *Qualitative communication research methods* (2nd ed.). Thousand Oaks, CA: Sage.

Majid, S., Anwar, M. A., & Eisenschitz, T. S. (2000). Information needs and information seeking behavior of agricultural scientists in Malaysia. *Library & Information Science Research, 22*, 145–163. doi:10.1016/S0740-8188(99)00051-1.

May, C. (2006). Escaping the TRIPs' Trap: The Political Economy of Free and Open Source Software in Africa. *Political Studies, 54*, 123–146. doi:10.1111/j.1467-9248.2006.00569.x.

McCain, K. W. (1989). Mapping authors in intellectual space: population genetics in the 1980s. (Special Issue: Bibliometric Methods for the Study of Scholarly Communication). *Communication Research, 16*(5), 615–667. doi:10.1177/009365089016005007.

McCraken, G. (1988). *The Long interview*. Newbury Park, CA: Sage.

Meho, L. I., & Tibbo, H. R. (2003). Modeling the Information-Seeking Behavior of Social Scientists: Ellis's Study Revisited. *Journal of the American Society for Information Science and Technology, 54*, 570–587. doi:10.1002/asi.10244.

Meneghini R., Packer A.L., & Nassi-Calò L. (2008). Articles by Latin American Authors in Prestigious Journals Have Fewer Citations. *PLoS ONE, 3*(11), e3804. Retrieved on May 23, 2010, from doi:10.1371/journal.pone.0003804

ONCTI. (2009). *Sobre el Programa de promoción al investigador*. Retrieved on May 16, 2009, from http://oncti.gob.ve/

Peet, R., & Hartwick, E. (1999). *Theories of development*. New York: The Guilford Press.

Powell, R. (1999). Recent trends in research: A methodological essay. *Library & Information Science Research*, *21*(1), 91–119. doi:10.1016/S0740-8188(99)80007-3.

Price, D. J. D. S. (1963). *Little science, big science*. New York: Columbia University Press.

Price, D. J. D. S. (1965). Networks of scientific papers. *Science*, *149*, 510–515. doi:10.1126/science.149.3683.510 PMID:14325149.

Punch, K. (2004). *Introduction to social research: Quantitative & qualitative approaches*. London: Sage Publications.

Schwartz, D. G. (1995). How physicians and biomedical scientists in India learn information-seeking skills. *Bulletin of the Medical Library Association*, *83*, 360–362. PMID:7581195.

Tenopir, C., King, D. W., & Bush, A. (2004). Medical faculty's use of print and electronic journals: Changes over time and in comparison with scientists. *Journal of the Medical Library Association*, *92*(2), 233–241. PMID:15098053.

Tenopir, C., King, D. W., Edwards, S., & Wu, L. (2009). Electronic journals and changes in scholarly article seeking and reading patterns. *Aslib Proceedings*, *61*(1), 5–32. doi:10.1108/00012530910932267.

Thomas, D. R. (2006). A general inductive approach for analyzing qualitative evaluation data. *The American Journal of Evaluation*, *27*(2), 237–256. doi:10.1177/1098214005283748.

Thomson. (2008a). *ISI Web of Knowledge. Journal Citation Report*. Retrieved on April 16, 2008, from http://admin-apps.isiknowledge.com/JCR/JCR

Thomson. (2008b). *The Thomson scientific journal selection process*. Retrieved on April 19, 2008, from http://scientific.thomson.com/free/essays/selectionofmaterial

University of Illinois. (2009). *The cost of journals*. Retrieved on June 15, 2009, from http://www.library.illinois.edu/scholcomm/journalcosts.html

Valenzuela, J. S., & Valenzuela, A. (1978). Modernization and dependency: Alternative perspectives in the study of Latin American underdevelopment. *Comparative Politics*, *10*(4), 535–557. doi:10.2307/421571.

Vickery, B. C. (2000). *Scientific communication in history*. Lanham, MD: Scarecrow Press Inc..

ADDITIONAL READING

Allard, S., Levine, K. J., & Tenopir, C. (2009). Design Engineers and Technical Professionals at Work: Observing Information Usage in the Workplace. *Journal of the American Society for Information Science and Technology*, *60*(3), 443–454. doi:10.1002/asi.21004.

Caputo, C., Requena, J., & Vargas, D. (2012). Life sciences research in Venezuela. *Scientometrics*, *90*(3), 781–805. doi:10.1007/s11192-011-0548-x.

Cardoso, F. (2009). New Paths: Globalization in Historical Perspective. *Studies in Comparative International Development*, *44*(4), 296–317. doi:10.1007/s12116-009-9050-3.

Cortés, M. (2012). Modernización, dependencia y marginalidad: Itinerario conceptual de la sociología latinoamericana. (Portuguese). *Sociologias*, *14*(29), 214–238.

Fraga Medín, C., Canales, C., & Hernández Villegas, S. (2006). Pasado, presente y futuro del proyecto Scielo en España. (Spanish). *El Profesional De La Información*, *15*(1), 23–28. doi:10.3145/epi.2006.jan.04.

Hemminger, B. M., Lu, D., Vaughan, K. L., & Adams, S. J. (2007). Information seeking behavior of academic scientists. *Journal of the American Society for Information Science and Technology*, *58*(14), 2205–2225. doi:10.1002/asi.20686.

Herath, D. (2008). Development Discourse of the Globalists and Dependency Theorists: Do the globalisation theorists rephrase and reword the central concepts of the dependency school? *Third World Quarterly*, *29*(4), 819–834. doi:10.1080/01436590802052961.

Irogbe, K. (2005). Globalization and the development of underdevelopment of the third world. *Journal of Third World Studies*, *22*(1), 41–68.

Iyengar, T. (1992). Science and technology: information services for Third World countries. *Vol 3: Information Systems: Science. Technology (Elmsford, N.Y.)*, 21–30.

Jamali, H. R., & Asadi, S. (2010). Google and the scholar: The role of Google in scientists' information-seeking behavior. *Online Information Review*, *34*(2), 282–294. doi:10.1108/14684521011036990.

Jamali, H. R., & Nicholas, D. (2008). Information-seeking behavior of physicists and astronomers. *Aslib Proceedings*, *60*(5), 444–462. doi:10.1108/00012530810908184.

Meho, L., & Haas, S. (2001). Information-seeking behavior and use of social science faculty studying stateless nations: a case study. *Library & Information Science Research*, *23*(1), 5–25. doi:10.1016/S0740-8188(00)00065-7.

Meneghini, R. (1998). Scientific literature evaluation and the SciELO project (English). *Ciencia Da Informacao*, *27*(2), 219–220.

Miguel, S. (2011). Revistas y producción científica de América Latina y el Caribe: su visibilidad en SciELO, RedALyC y SCOPUS. *Revista Interamericana De Bibliotecología*, *34*(2), 187–199.

Mitha, S. (2009). New information seeking behaviors of academics in the Nelson R. Mandela School of Medicine at the University of KwaZulu-Natal. *Innovation (10258892)*, (39), 19-33.

Moster, B., & Ocholla, D. (2005). Information needs and information seeking behavior of parliamentarians in South Africa. *South African Journal of Libraries & Information Science*, *71*(2), 136–150.

Nel, J. (2001). The information seeking process: is there a sixth sense? *Mousaion*, *19*(2), 23–32.

Nicholas, D., Clark, D., Rowlands, I., & Jamali, H. R. (2009). Online use and information seeking behavior: Institutional and subject comparisons of UK researchers. *Journal of Information Science*, *35*(6), 660–676. doi:10.1177/0165551509338341.

Niu, X., & Hemminger, B. (2012). A study of factors that affect the information-seeking behavior of academic scientists. *Journal of the American Society for Information Science and Technology*, *63*(2), 336–353. doi:10.1002/asi.21669.

Packer, A. (1998). SciELO: uma metodologia para publicação eletrônica. (Portuguese). *Ciencia Da Informacao*, *27*(2), 109–121.

Schwartz, H. (2007). Dependency or Institutions? Economic Geography, Causal Mechanisms, and Logic in the Understanding of Development. *Studies in Comparative International Development*, *42*(1/2), 115–135. doi:10.1007/s12116-007-9000-x.

Schwartzman, K. C. (2006). Globalization from a World-system perspective: A new phase in the Core-A new destiny for Brazil and the semiperiphery. *Journal of World-systems Research*, *12*(2), 264–307.

Sigworth, C. M., & McNamara, T. (2003). Economic Dependency, Education and Gender Inequality: Female Healthy Life Expectancy in Less-Developed Nations. Conference Papers -- American Sociological Association (pp. 1-20).

Smith, T. (1981). The logic of dependency theory revisited. *International Organization*, *35*(4), 755. doi:10.1017/S0020818300034329.

Tenopir, C., Volentine, R., & King, D. W. (2012). Article and book reading patterns of scholars: Findings for publishers. *Learned Publishing*, *25*(4), 279–291. doi:10.1087/20120407.

Tenopir, C., Wilson, C. S., Vakkari, P., Talja, S., & King, D. W. (2010). Cross Country Comparison of Scholarly E-Reading Patterns in Australia, Finland, and the United States. *Australian Academic & Research Libraries*, *41*(4), 26–41.

Wilson, C. S., & Tenopir, C. (2008). Local Citation Analysis, Publishing and Reading Patterns: Using Multiple Methods to Evaluate Faculty Use of an Academic Library's Research Collection. *Journal of the American Society for Information Science and Technology*, *59*(9), 1393–1408. doi:10.1002/asi.20812.

Xuemei, G. (2010). Information-Seeking Behavior in the Digital Age: A Multidisciplinary Study of Academic Researchers. *College & Research Libraries*, *71*(5), 435–455.

KEY TERMS AND DEFINITIONS

International Publications: Are highly cited, high impact academic and research journals published in Europe and the USA.

Leading Scientists and/or "Big Names": Are internationally recognized and highly cited scientists. A preferred strategy for initiating search is to look up "big names" researchers.

Model of Scholarly Communication in Venezuela: Is an inductive-derived model that seeks to understand information seeking behavior and information dissemination in Venezuela.

National Publications: Are scholarly journals published in Venezuela regarded as irrelevant by the Venezuelan scientific community unless they are cited in international journals. The local scientific community perceives those journals as training grounds for aspiring scientists (graduate students).

Reading Abstracts: Is a practice that replaces full-text article reading in a context of limited access to information sources.

Regional Databases: Databases designed in Latin America for the purpose of facilitating access to academic information by the regional scientific community and increasing visibility of research in the region.

Venezuela Scientific Community: Active members of the Venezuelan scientific community affiliated with the Research Incentive Program (PPI) with a "research" rank of level 3 or higher.

Chapter 7
Developing Electronic Information Resources to Promote Social Inclusion of Vulnerable Communities in Uruguay

Martha Sabelli
Escuela Universitaria de Bibliotecología y Ciencias Afines, Universidad de la República, Uruguay

Jorge Rasner
Licenciatura en Ciencias de la Comunicación, Universidad de la República, Uruguay

María Cristina Pérez Giffoni
Escuela Universitaria de Bibliotecología y Ciencias Afines, Universidad de la República, Uruguay

Eduardo Álvarez Pedrosian
Licenciatura en Ciencias de la Comunicación, Universidad de la República, Uruguay

Laura González
Instituto de Computación, Facultad de Ingeniería, Universidad de la República, Uruguay

Raúl Ruggia
Instituto de Computación, Facultad de Ingeniería, Universidad de la República, Uruguay

ABSTRACT

This chapter focuses on multidisciplinary research about needs and the behavior of real and potential information users. The research is carried out in a university context to address social issues as well as to find solutions appropriate to the Uruguayan context, which is rather different from the one in developed countries. The chapter focuses on the discussion of the research results, on the developed electronic information resources, and on the impact on the target population and social mediators. The chapter also focuses on the multidisciplinary work experience, which carries out the research group through meetings and workshops with social actors and decision makers on social policies. This research constitutes a step forward in the development of information and communication sciences as well as to improve the information domain in Uruguay.

DOI: 10.4018/978-1-4666-4353-6.ch007

INTRODUCTION

Despite advances in incorporating communication technologies the information gap constitutes a serious issue in developing countries. According to the report delivered in April 2012 by the World Economic Forum, the digital divide persists between developed and developing countries. For one of the co-authors, Soumitra Dutta, "while technology and infrastructure are important, there are many other aspects that are crucial, including whether the environment is conducive for businesses to use technology and encourages innovation, whether regulations support or inhibit transparency, whether ICT is affordable and accessible, and whether people have the skills to use it." As these aspects have a crucial impact on the effective accessibility and usage of information, their lack generates information gap problems.

This presented work focuses on a multidisciplinary research about needs and the behavior of real and potential information users: adolescents living in disadvantaged communities. The research was carried out in a university context to address social issues as well as to find solutions appropriate to the Uruguayan context, which is rather different from the one in developed countries. The research also represents a scientific contribution to the development of information and communication sciences as well as to improve the information domain in developing countries.

The Republic of Uruguay is a small South American developing country. It covers an area of 176.215 Km^2 and it is the home of 3,251,526 people. Its political system is a presidential democracy. Until the 1960s, Uruguay posed one of the highest rates of social integration, development of middle classes, and literacy of Latin America. This was based on the development of state-based socioeconomic policies, based on a public education system which facilitated social mobility. Furthermore, policies on health and housing promoted the consolidation of the middle classes. The economic and financial crisis of the 1960s and 1970s, together with the authoritarian political regimes (1973-1984), lead to major changes in the social structure as well as in the role of political parties and the labor unions. The return to democracy in 1985 and its consolidation in the 1990s fostered the socioeconomic development, but the poverty levels did not decrease.

Since the end of the 1990s, the country suffered a process of economic and social decline, which led to a crisis in 2002 and 2003. As a result, up to 31% of the population went under the poverty line, provoking the impoverishment of children and teenagers. The Census of 2004 showed a marginalization of a third of the entire population and the lack of basic goods essential to the personal and collective development in the half of the underage population. This context increased the social gaps dramatically followed by digital and information gaps. Such processes strongly affected the most vulnerable communities, which generally live in slums.

In this context, the development of national and local policies to universalize the access to information resources constitutes a major challenge. The Digital Agenda 2011-2015 (ADU11-15) of the AGESIC (Uruguayan Agency for the Electronic Government and the Information Society) showed these strategic lines and action plans. Furthermore, the "Plan Ceibal" (Educational Connectivity on basic IT for online learning), the implementation of the one-laptop-per-child program in Uruguay, has the purpose of strongly reducing the digital gap by covering the entire primary and secondary education centers of the country.

The most recent report about "*El perfil del internauta uruguayo*" [The profile of the Uruguayan Internet user] (Grupo Radar, 2012, pp. 21-22) shows significant figures on Internet penetration in homes: 65% in Montevideo, 52% outside Montevideo, and 61% for the whole country. This report highlights an increase of 94% of Internet penetration in population aged between 12 and 19 years old. The use of Facebook is especially remarkable, covering 50% of this population. In summary, there is about 1,600,000 Internet users in Uruguay, which represents almost half of the population, covering all ages and geographical regions, 40% of them are aged under 20 years old and 30% belong to low socio-economic levels.

Disposing of information in a timely manner is essential for proper decision-making of any nature, from the simplest and everyday ones to those which take relevant meaning for the individual and collective development. In this context, the potential of ICT is out of discussion, but it is clear that access to computers alone does not guarantee social inclusion and access to the Information Society. With their full potential, ICTs can deepen the existing gaps. To address this issue its historical and socio-cultural development has to be considered.

Barja and Gigler (2007) define information and communication poverty as the privation of the basic capabilities to participate in the Information Society, and they consider it an issue that should be a priority on the agenda for designing public policies. Aligned with this approach, we highlight the contributions of Warschauer (2008a; 2008b; 2008c) regarding digital inclusion, access to ICT, social capital, and the role of local needs in ICT projects in the community. Certainly, the unequal access to computers and the Internet are an effect of poverty and of the deep inequalities of income that go across our society, but the lack of access to ICTs is itself a causal factor of impoverishment. Warschauer relates the digital divide to social stratification resulting in an inequality regarding availability of equipment, connectivity, telecommunications, and skills to use ICT. The social practice of having skills to access, use, and produce information and adequate knowledge to social needs is the essence of technology access.

Aligned with this author, we understand that in Uruguay, digital inclusion initiatives, through the access and information literacy, should leverage physical, digital, human, and social resources, public policies and specific local initiatives, effective support of families, the community and institutions, and the involvement of citizens.

In this situation, characterized by improvement and marginalization, the University of the Republic (UdelaR), which is the only public university in Uruguay and its main education and research institution, has decided to address this issue as an academic and social commitment. Researchers have to look for solutions which can help not only to analyze, interpret, and understand them, but also to explore potentially creative and innovative information resources through a multidisciplinary and participative way, involving the subject-object research community with the social mediators.

This Chapter presents the research developed by the Research Group on Information and Communication for Social Inclusion and Integration, created in 2009 in the UdelaR by researchers on Information and Library Science, Communication Science and Computer Science. The subject-object of this research, carried out in the period 2010-2012, are the vulnerable population communities living in disadvantageous neighborhoods of Montevideo. In particular, the research focuses on teenagers and in the way they access, search, and use health-related information. This topic is of great interest given the recent implementation of the Integrated National Health System in the country and the development of health services in primary care which focus on these social sectors.

The rest of the chapter is organized as follows. The next section provides background on the theoretical and methodological framework of the research, highlighting the approaches of information behavior theories, communication paradigms, and computer sciences methods which converge on the research team. Then, the methods and techniques used to collect data and their main results are presented through four main stages: a) on deep interviews with qualified informants and interviews to members of the analyzed community (teenagers in vulnerable situation); b) interviews and observations in primary care services; c) the design and implementation of a Web portal to support teenagers in vulnerable situations, along with the workshops and focus groups implemented with adolescents and social mediators; d) the discussion of solutions and recommendations in dealing with the issues, controversies, or problems presented in the preceding sections. This later section specially describes the methodology applied to design the electronic information resources that aim to facilitate and promote the access and appropriation of information by individuals undergoing information poverty in a developing country. In summary, it focuses on the discussion of the research results related to each of the research phases. Finally, future research directions and conclusions are presented.

Through the dissemination of this paper, the authors aim at receiving feedback and discuss the results of the project with researchers and social workers of other developing countries, especially from Middle East Arab countries, as this will enable a fruitful exchange on the approaches in question.

BACKGROUND

This section provides background on the theoretical and methodological framework of an interdisciplinary research line within a small developing country in Latin America.

Contributions of Information Behavior Theories and Research Experiences in User Studies within a Developing Country

Since the 1990s, teaching and research in EUBCA has started to pay special attention to the population to whom academic and professional work in the Library and Information Science is devoted. This is done by addressing the issues of usage of information by answering questions such as: Do information services know the needs and behaviors of the users? Is this information used to plan eventual changes? Do we take into account the users' social context? Do we know what factors affect information usage? Are non-users taking into account by information systems? Is the production of information resources based on the results of studies on users? Even more, are professionals on information aware that this subject of study, which is highly complex, requires multidisciplinary approaches? Do they take into account the connection between models and processes for human and social communication and those for information search and usage? Are they aware of the impact that ICTs have in the behavior of information and communication?

In the search for answers to these questions, a research line was opened in Uruguay in order to address needs, behavior, and information usage. Since 1992, this research line has been working permanently, addressing different disciplines contexts of activities and daily lives, as well as different kinds of users: academic specialists, productive stakeholders, rural producers, workers associated to unions, decision makers in different organization contexts, women, young people, and teenagers in vulnerable contexts (Sabelli & Rodríguez Lopater, in press).

Our work is guided by, on one hand, current socio-cognitive paradigms, and on the other hand, by personal experiences and theoretical-methodological frameworks in the research and teaching on User Studies previously mentioned, which we have developed in the EUBCA since 1992 (Pérez Giffoni & Sabelli, 2010). We also follow Latin-American perspectives about information appropriation by women in disadvantageous contexts and usage of ICT (Camacho Jiménez, 2000; 2008; Finquelievich, 2000; 2004) as well as the concept of empowerment presented, among others, by G. Sen (1998). It is important to highlight the current research of Juan José Calva, developed in the Library and Information Studies Institute (Instituto de Investigaciones Bibliotecológicas y de la Información-IIBI) of the Autonomous University of Mexico (Universidad Autónoma de México-UNAM). In addition to his PhD thesis about information needs, he examines with greater attention the information needs phenomena and the development of analysis models (Calva, 2004).

Information policies and systems are strongly related to designing fluid communication channels between agents and users. Therefore, this research line also focuses on analyzing how these channels work in addition to generating communication paths, and on the possibility of creating versatile and effective means of transmission of information.

We are interested in the daily life context of the studied communities, which also led to studying with special care the theoretical aspects of information used in daily life, social networks, and its habitus. Socio-constructivist approaches developed by several authors and the application of qualitative methods, like the analysis of the individuals' speech about their skills as information seekers and users, constitute important contributions to the research (Savolainen 1999; 2002; 2005a; 2005b; Hersberger, 2003; 2005; Marteleto, 2010). These approaches help us to understand the factors that impact on the information conceived and offered by professional information services and the preferences about information stated by these communities within their own subculture. Population groups develop social rules and associate them to tactics, which characterize their situation and, ultimately, enable them to solve their needs.

Communicative Interactions in Complex Contexts

A simple theory of the communicative interaction process consists of a transmitter, a receiver, and a channel through which information passes. However, communication problems are not merely technical, solvable by "cleaning" or enhancing the canal. On the contrary, what a speaker transmits to another is an interpretation of the reality, and the message holds and transports these elements which do not necessarily correspond with what the receiver will use to decode the message. This

aspect is inherent in any communicative interaction, and it takes a special relevance when studying the relationships developed in the health area.

In this way, the concern for mediations (Eco, 1993; Barbero, 1991) has replaced the concept of simple and linear communicative interaction between senders and receivers, and of a message which is immediately accessed. Paying attention to mediations necessarily refers to knowing the conceptual environment that favors a message and the coordinates of interpretation employed by potential recipients.

In the primary health care system, communicative interaction usually occurs in a context of profound asymmetry, due to the heterogeneity of the cultural capital of senders and recipients. This situates these actors in very different places: on one side, those who implement or apply public policies and, on the other side, the mere recipients of this proposal, with no other alternative to take it or leave it. Even if they wished, they would not be in a condition to propose on an equal plane some kind of alternative that aims to be valid (Bourdieu, 2001).

It is clear that this deeply asymmetrical situation causes noticeable distortions which cannot be solved by appealing to the creation of new media or improving existing ones. This is for the simple reason that the interpretative coordinates of both are different, regardless of the communication media employed. Without a doubt, trying to improve the communicational flow requires the optimization of the media and tools; however, this is only a necessary condition but not a sufficient one. In this way, it becomes necessary to investigate the perception of the system, which both technical and users/recipients have in specific contexts of interaction.

Therefore, we considered it appropriate to place ourselves in the territory, in order to perceive how those coordinates work and what intelligibility conditions and information access operate in each case. We understood that in this way we could provide elements for not only suggesting the production of better communication media or the optimization of existing ones, but also to gather information on the real needs and behaviors of mediators and target health system users. In particular, what do they understand for health, disease, information and, mainly, by the dynamics of the interactions that occurs between the actors.

This research allowed us to corroborate, in the first place, the alleged asymmetry and, secondly, it allowed us to learn first-hand how some of these interpretive coordinates operate. To this end, we designed a methodological approach that would meet the purposes that motivate the technicians to implement and apply public health policies and also how these policies are perceived by potential recipients. This approach aimed to know the individuals--system mediators and users/recipients--through interviews, and also through the observation of communicative interaction behaviors in the everyday context of clinics of the primary health care network, trying to perceive what they understand and what they expect from the benefits provided by a health system.

Leveraging ICT to Promote Social Inclusion

Recent advances in information and communication technology provide a valuable infrastructure to design and develop electronic information resources to promote the social inclusion of teenagers and young people in vulnerable situations. In particular, the enhancements in Web technologies, geographic information systems, and mobile technologies constitute some of the most relevant developments.

The advances in Web technologies during the last years mainly focus on supporting the Web 2.0 concept, which represents a second generation of the Web, with a strong interactive nature, where users are not only consumers of content but also they participate in its generation. Moreover, users are the center of this new Web, being able to express themselves by sharing, voting, commenting, and classifying information online (Murray et al., 2008).

Some advanced Web technologies that can be leveraged to promote social inclusion are Web portals, social applications, rich Internet applications, and mashups. Web portals are Web applications that integrate information from multiple sources and deliver this information through an aggregated application (Tatnall, 2004). They provide built-in mechanisms to organize information into sections and categories, which facilitates users to find the information they need. Social applications focus on information sharing and collaboration among users. They provide capabilities that allow users to easily create and share content, collaborate online and have real time conversations. Some representative examples of these applications include blogs, wikis (e.g., wikipedia.org), social networks (e.g., facebook.com, linkedin.com) and social bookmarking (e.g., del.icio.us). Rich Internet applications (RIA) provide users with an interactive and lightweight Web experience. Finally, mashups combine content from more than one Web source to provide a new application or service. They leverage existing content and services to deliver a value added application, which can also be enhanced by RIA technologies (López, Álvarez, & González, 2010).

Geographic Information Systems (GIS) deal with geographically referenced information (i.e., information located in the geographic space by latitudinal and longitudinal coordinates). The main purpose of a GIS is to enable users to view, understand, question, interpret, and visualize geographic information (GI) in a natural way. A commonly used way to communicate GI is a map, which is a model of the real world at a particular time. Maps can be leveraged to provide a user friendly way to visualize the geographic placement of interest points. In fact, many governments are driving Spatial Data Infrastructure (SDI) initiatives, in order to provide a framework for sharing and access geographic data and metadata. In Uruguay, for example, IDE-Uruguay is the governmental initiative with this goal. (Rienzi, Sosa, & González, 2010)

Mobile technologies are among the ones which have undergone more improvements during the last years and they have been specially adopted by young people in Uruguay. In fact, Short Message Service (SMS) is the preferred written communication media of this population given its quickness and low cost, among other reasons (Porath, 2011).

Web technologies, GIS, and mobile technologies have been successfully used in many initiatives and projects to enhance how information is delivered to users. Within the health area there are various projects focusing on teenagers and young people, including The Teen Project (http://theteenproject.com/), and Teen Source (http://www.teensource.org/ts/), among others (Bertone, Peluffo, & Katz, 2012), which leverage these technologies to deliver health information in a more friendly way. More concretely, most of these projects provide Web-based applications with a graphic design specifically developed for teenagers and young people (i.e., short texts, audiovisual content, etc.). Additionally, two of the most common services provided by these Web applications are the localization of health centers in maps and the communication via SMS (Le Dantec et al., 2011). Finally, these technologies have also been successfully applied in projects focusing on Latin American countries (Khadraoui, Ruggia, Piedrabuena, & Meinkohn, 2005).

TOWARDS INTERDISCIPLINARY DEVELOPMENT OF ELECTRONIC INFORMATION RESOURCES AND SERVICES FOR DISADVANTAGED COMMUNITIES

This section describes the methods and techniques used to collect data and their main results which were the basis for the interdisciplinary development of electronic information resources and services for disadvantaged communities.

Social Mediators as Qualified Informants of Information Flow and Information Behavior of Adolescents

In the context of this work, health personnel of the Health Center and clinics in the selected area are considered as real and potential mediators of health information and communication; eleven of them (five doctors, two social workers, a nurse, a psychologist, a sociologist and a concierge) were interviewed at the beginning of the investigation by the principal investigators of the team. Among the main topics within the guidelines applied in the in-depth interviews, we highlight the perception of respondents about: a) the health personnel as a possible mediator of information, and b) adolescents in the selected area regarding the following aspects: the main health problems and the types of data and information to produce about these issues, their needs and search strategies in health information, in their daily lives and in their relationship with social networks, the access and use of computers and the Internet, and the capabilities of these tools in the process of appropriation of health information.

Qualitative analysis of the recordings transcripts showed, regarding the first point, that the communication of the health care services has obstacles in the information flow with other external institutions, due to lack of joints in and out of the area. Regarding internal communication, good channels were seen but also some difficulties related to organizational behavior were detected. Answers regarding how health personnel perform health information searches are related to available sources, preferably interpersonal sources such as friends and coworkers.

The perception of the mediators concerning the problems of adolescents and the proposals about the space and information resources that might be provided and used for improving the flow and use of information focus on the following aspects:

- They are the age sector which less consult health services and, in this sector, young women are the ones that do it most often;
- Shortages of formal host spaces and the promotion of social integration of adolescents;
- The best places to convene teens, who do not study or work, are the so called "adolescent spaces" of the health center and clinics, the "youth houses," the community classrooms, public spaces such as plazas, soccer fields, the "corner," social networks, cybercafés, and local radio;
- The main difficulties lie in the lack of life projects in an environment that does not facilitate the identification with the neighborhood and the sense of belonging and self-esteem of adolescents;
- The topics that concentrate most interest are: sexuality, sexually transmitted diseases, reproductive health, oral health, domestic violence, nutrition, and drug and childcare issues in adolescent mothers;
- The information to be produced must be clear, colorful, and attractive; it should leverage ICTs, especially mobile phones and Plan Ceibal computers, and the information resources to be created must incorporate games and music;
- Usage of the waiting rooms of health services;
- Usage of a participatory strategy for information and communication.

The Perception of Adolescents about their Health Information Needs and Information Behavior

As another research activity in data collection, the team performed interviews with 50 adolescents and young people between 13 and 20 years (25 of each sex) in Zone 9 of Montevideo, more precisely,

in the waiting rooms of health centers, in public areas, and community classrooms of the chosen neighborhoods. The community classroom is one of the inclusive institutions of the civil society and it plays a key role in an area that has few spaces of belonging and identity, and meeting and recreation for young people.

The interviews covered these aspects: demographic and characterization of the interviewee, adolescents relationship with health services, use of leisure and recreational interests and habits, knowledge and use of health information, access and terms of use of ICT (particularly the Internet), uses and habits of the respondent on social networks, access and use of the Plan Ceibal computers, and mobile phone use. They are young people in an unfavorable context, belonging to a suburb of Montevideo, with low educational level in relation to age: 18% of them neither study nor work, four respondents that do not study and are aged between 17 and 20 years have children, and two of them do not work either. However, they are "digital natives" with a high percentage of connectivity and ICT.

Additionally, 38% of the respondents expressed no interest in health issues, and those that do have interest highlight the following issues: sexuality, sexually transmitted diseases and their prevention (specifically AIDS) and contraception.

Most of the adolescents (88%) access and use a computer, specifically the Internet, and there is at least one Plan Ceibal laptop in 62% of households. Most of them also participate in social networks, being Facebook (80%) the preferred and most used one (daily or one or more times per week). Finally, 92% of the respondents have a mobile phone which is the primary means of communication. This finding is particularly important considering the potential of this technology as a channel for transmitting information.

The analysis and discussion of these results, in light of the context analysis and the theoretical and conceptual basis of the project, reveal that the issues at stake have a human and social dimension rather than a technological one.

Most of these young people are largely outside of educational institutions and only a low proportion of them are aware of health problems. They are not motivated to find and use information on health issues in formal sources (institutional or in the Web). However, most of them use ICT, have a strong relationship with Facebook, and a high percentage of them express that they read (in particular, readings characterized by brevity of the text).

They also watch videos and they present a keen interest and preference for certain music genres. They participate in online social networks, use mobile telephony every day, and have their own strategies to exchange and share information. They share a territory, interact and build a community that, in turn, builds them.

Although from the point of view of formal systems of information, we cannot define them as real users, in these "non-users" with their cognitive, emotional and socio-cultural characteristics, some informational and communicational practices are perceived. These practices are an essential input for designing products and information services focused on the human factor and in context.

Everyday Mediations in the Primary Health Care Network

We conducted an ethnographic approach focused on the subjectivation processes (Alvarez Pedrosian, 2011) present in the universe of these mediations, which are proper of these local clinics. This approach has expanded in the field of study that concerns us in terms of both users and health system officials (Zhou, 2010). We focus on one of the average clinics, which are those that are attended by members of the local environment itself and by other contiguous ones. Summarizing the conclusions derived from this exploration, we raise a number of important considerations about

the general subject. Firstly, these contexts are small interaction groups, almost exclusively of female character (Ludueña, Olson, Pasco, 2005) where there are women of various generations, adolescents being the major type in everyday places. Secondly, neighborhood ties, although altered and exposed to higher levels of abstraction and anonymity given the growth of coming users, continue guiding the general climate in which constitutes the wait space-time. While consultations are performed in closed offices, the waiting room covers the vast majority of the local, as these offices are very small and on various opportunities the talking within them can be heard.

Administrative management (receipt, delivery number, test results, etc.) is conducted in an open room, and interaction with the waiting room is permanent. It is also important the environment near to the front door, to the point of becoming an open extension of the room, this is important for those who are not interested in interacting with those who wait inside or prefer to perform other activities that are prohibited inside (such as smoking), or that require other social distances, where it is considered that there is a threshold of intimacy to save. Inside, user groups are assembled and disassembled in a dynamic of construction-deconstruction traversed by communication flows. This type of mediations has the face-to-face as the main setting, and constitutes a type of situations conducive to the generation of social networks in the community and beyond it. Some billboards with information on community and health are arranged in the walls and on some sides of the furniture, but they are not much taken into account. They are mainly texts in printed paper and also some freehand writings. There are also some public campaigns posters, and some posters done by medical students about health issues studied there.

The main information channel is undoubtedly the dialogue in these flexible and dynamic groups, which may eventually include more than four women and children. The information displayed on the surfaces of walls acts as stage for such mediations, being objectified, as we could see, when you need to look for a specific data (office hours for example) or when you choose not to exchange looks and to participate at least possible in the relational game with the subjects users which are present.

The difference between visuality and orality is relevant once the spatiality of these small places is made with walls to create different areas. In that sense, what you hear is extended more than what can be seen, while it is a holistic experience (Ong, 1996), situated phenomenologically and which places the subject in the act of perception.

Our research focused on youth and adolescents, and among these, almost exclusively girls, are part of the anthropological landscape of the everyday in the clinics.

The construction of individual and collective identity is a process explicited in their practices, both discursive and, more generally, gestural and bodily, being more complex thanks to the deterritorialization of ICT according to cross-cultural models (Martin-Barbero, 2002).

Design and Implementation of a Web Portal for Vulnerable Communities

This section describes the development of electronic information resources for vulnerable communities within the project, which consisted of designing and implementing a Web portal along with various modules. This design and implementation was performed in an interdisciplinary way, taking as a basis the results of the interviews and observations previously described in this chapter. The work also took into account the characteristics of related projects like The Teen Project and Teen Source. Finally, the portal and its content were enhanced with feedback obtained from workshops with teenagers and young people.

Firstly, it was decided to use a Web portal as the base infrastructure to develop the electronic information resources. This decision was based on the fact that many of the related projects have obtained good results by basing their solutions in Web technologies and on the high proportion of the target population which has Internet access. Additionally, some of the characteristics that were identified as relevant to include in the portal were: audiovisual content (e.g., videos), Web 2.0 tools to promote the participation and appropriation of the site, integration with social networks like Facebook, communication via SMS, didactic games, and a graphic design following specific usability criteria for the target population.

The developed solution consists of a Web portal focusing on health information, more precisely on sexuality and nutrition topics. The portal is based on Web 2.0 tools, interacts with various external systems (e.g., Facebook, Google Maps, YouTube, Twitter, etc.) and includes mechanisms to send information to users via SMS. From a technical point of view, the portal is based on Liferay (http://www.liferay.com/), which is an open source product which provides a standard-based infrastructure to create Web portals.

The main functionalities provided by the Web portal are: maps with health interest points, frequently asked questions regarding sexuality and nutrition, links to other sites containing reliable health information, a search engine to facilitate users to find the content they need, surveys regarding health issues, videos and movie trailers related to health topics, didactic games which give prizes to the best players, interactive tests which give recommendations to the users according to the information they provide, health tips which are sent via SMS, content tagging which allows users to classify content according to their criteria, authentication to the portal via Facebook, and a video-answer functionality which allows users to answer questions uploading a video of themselves, among others (Bertone, Peluffo, & Katz, 2012).

The first version of the Web portal was evaluated in workshops with teenagers and young people who interacted with the portal and the different functionalities it provides. These workshops were very important to enhance the developed electronic information resources. For instance, some terms used in the portal have to be changed given that they were not familiar to the teenagers and young people which participate in the workshops. Additionally, workshops allow validating the effectiveness of some of the modules. In particular, users were very attracted to the maps and video modules.

SOLUTIONS AND RECOMMENDATIONS

During the last years, Uruguay has designed digital inclusion policies, but they have not been articulated with information and communication policies that effectively have a significant impact on the population.

By studying the relationship between young people and adolescents in a vulnerable situation and the use of electronic health information resources, we confirm that facilitating access conditions is not enough: we must awaken the desire to learn about themselves, their environment and context. A policy of preventive information and communication must necessarily promote coordination between the different institutions involved in the given problems.

The health information resources in the country are scarce and they are generally not suitable and/or unknown by the population surveyed. This is a population characterized by the non-use of health information and in which it is perceived a lack of motivation for the use of such information whose utility is unknown. The interviewed health staff perceived that this population does not search for health information.

However, group instances, the animation with participatory techniques, motivate this population and awake the interest. By interpersonal relationships, a gradual involvement is produced, where personalities emerge showing a dynamic leadership in promoting the action (essential phe-

nomenon in the reporting process) of their peers. Adolescents appear as subjects between subject and an artifact--The Web Portal--allowing them different ways of relating with each other, not only in this context but also in other "places" where their role of multipliers for information processes among peers can and must be leveraged. This is an enabling environment to form a community of practice. The community and its networks are a linchpin of the information usage behavior and of the proposed information and communication systems. Reliability is a key factor in evaluating information sources as reliable, credible, and which can solve specific problems.

Understanding information behavior in different contexts is a basic tool to decide on the products and information services to design quality electronic resources and the required mediations to ensure the physical and intellectual access.

FUTURE RESEARCH DIRECTIONS

There are a number of open issues in all the analyzed contexts, which could be the basis for future research directions, specially focusing on the generation of information content using electronic resources to be exploited by different means: electronic devices used in the waiting-rooms of health services (dynamic screens with audiovisual products, computers with Internet access) as well as Plan Ceibal laptops, and mobile phones. Furthermore, a larger future development would consist in the creation of the Local Information Network, within the Primary Health Care Network, which would include "Information Points or Centers."

Another research direction would address the challenges of leveraging the e-Government platform developed by AGESIC to support large-scale operations on the information flows. This approach would facilitate a country-wide deployment of the proposed Information Services in the Health Centers. Finally, ensuring data protection and privacy in the analyzed electronic communications also constitutes a potential research direction.

CONCLUSION

This work presented a multidisciplinary approach to address the needs and behavior of vulnerable population groups on accessing to information. It enabled the identification key factors related to the information and communication with this population, especially in the context of Primary Health Care services.

The presented research line has contributed significantly to the academic development of the involved research groups. In addition, it has enabled the strengthening of the social and political stakeholders that promote social policies on information and communication targeting the most vulnerable population groups.

We expect that these positive results will continue and will provide the basis for exchanging experiences and research results among developing countries.

REFERENCES

AGESIC. (2011). Agenda Digital Uruguay 2011-2015. Retrived on January, 31, 2012, from www.agesic.gub.uy/innovaportal/.../agenda_digital_2011-2015.pdf

Álvarez Pedrosian, E. (2011). *Etnografías de la subjetividad. Herramientas para la investigación*. Montevideo, Uruguay: LICCOM-Universidad de la República.

Barja, G., & Gigler, B. (2007). The concept of information poverty and how to measure it in the Latin American Context. In H. Galperin, & J. Marical, *Digital Poverty. Latin American and Caribbean Perspectives*. Retrieved on February 2, 2012, from http://dirsi.net/sites/default/files/dirsi_07_DP01_en.pdf

Bertone, A. I., Peluffo, G., & Katz, R. (2012, August). *Sistema Colaborativo para la Integración de Información y Servicios en el Área Social y de la Salud: Tu Sitio Salud (Tesis de Grado - Ingeniería en Computación)*. Instituto de Computación, Facultad de Ingeniería, Universidad de la República, Montevideo, Uruguay.

Bourdieu, P. (2001). *Qué significa hablar?* Madrid: Akal.

Calva, J. J. (2004). *Information needs: Theoretical foundations and methods*. México City: UNAM, Centro Universitario de Investigaciones Bibliotecológicas.

Camacho Jimenez, K. (2000). How we approach the assessment of the impact of the Internet in civil society organizations in Central America. *Fundación Acceso*. Retrieved on November 24, 2011, from http://www.acceso.or.cr/publica/telecom/conocimiento22.html.

Eco, U. (1993). El público perjudica a la televisión? In *Sociología de la comunicación de masas (Vol. 2)*. México: Gili.

Finquelievich, S. (2000). *Citizens to the Web! Social ties in the cyberspace*. Buenos Aires, Argentina: CICCUS.

Finquelievich, S. (2004). ICTs in local and regional development: Beyond the metropolis. *INFOLAC, 17*(1), 3–5.

Grupo Radar. (2012). *El perfil del internauta uruguayo*. Montevideo, Uruguay: Radar. Retrieved on November 30, 2012, from http://www.gruporadar.com.uy/01/wp-content/uploads/2012/08/El-perfil-del-internauta-uruguayo-2012.pdf

Hersberger, J. (2003). A qualitative approach to examining information transfer via social networks among homeless populations. *The New Review of Information Behavior Research, 4*, 95–108. doi: 10.1080/14716310310001631462.

Hersberger, J. (2005). The homeless and information needs and services. *Reference and User Services Quarterly, 44*(3), 199–202.

Khadraoui, D., Ruggia, R., Piedrabuena, F., & Meinkohn, F. (2005). *Local-communities insertion network platform: Design and specification.* Paper Presented at the 5th IBIMA International Conference on Internet & Information Technology in Modern Organizations (IBIMA). Cairo, Egypt.

Le Dantec, C. A., Farrell, R. G., Christensen, J. E., Bailey, M., Ellis, J. B., Kellogg, W. A., & Edwards, W. K. (2011). Publics in practice: Ubiquitous computing at a shelter for homeless mothers. In *Proceedings of the 2011 Annual Conference on Human factors in Computing Systems* (pp. 1687–1696). New York: ACM.

López, G., Álvarez, F., & González, L. (2010). *Integrating advanced web technologies in a social security portal.* Paper Presented at the 6th International Policy and Research Conference on Social Security. Luxembourg.

Ludueña, M. C., Olson, J. K., & Pasco, A. (2005). Promoción de la salud y calidad de vida entre madres de preadolescentes. *Una etnografía enfocada. Revista Latino-Americana de Enfermagem, 13*(2), 1127–1134. doi:10.1590/S0104-11692005000800005 PMID:16501782.

Marteleto, R. M. (2010). Redes sociais, mediação e apropiriação de informações: Situando campos, objetos e conceitos na pesquisa. *Ciencia da Informação. Pesq. Bras. Ci. Inf., 3*(1), 27–46.

Martín-Barbero, J. (1991). *De los medios a las mediaciones.* Barcelona, Spain: Gili.

Martín-Barbero, J. (2002). *Jóvenes, comunicación e identidad, en Pensar Iberoamérica. Revista de Cultura, N° 0. Organización de Estados Iberoamericanos.* Retrieved on November 30, 2012, from http://www.oei.es/pensariberoamerica/ric00a03.htm

Murray, P. J., Cabrer, M., Hansen, M., Paton, C., Elkin, P. L., & Erdley, W. S. (2008). Towards addressing the opportunities and challenges of Web 2.0 for health and informatics. *Yearbook of Medical Informatics,* 44–51. PMID:18660875.

Ong, W. (1996). *Oralidad y escritura. Tecnologías de la palabra.* México: FCE.

Pérez Giffoni, M. C., & Sabelli, M. (2010). *Los estudios de usuarios de información: Construcción de una línea de investigación y docencia en el Uruguay.* Montevideo, Uruguay: UdelaR. EUBCA.

Porath, S. (2011). Text Messaging and Teenagers: A Review of the Literature. *Journal of the Research Center for Educational Technology, 7*(2), 86–99.

Rienzi, B., Sosa, R., Foti, P., & González, L. (2010). *Benefits and challenges of using geographic information systems to enhance social security services.* Paper Presented at the 6th International Policy and Research Conference on Social Security. Luxembourg.

Sabelli, M., & Rodríguez Lopater, V. (Eds.) (in press). La información y las jóvenes en contextos desfavorables: Construyendo puentes para la inclusión social desde la investigación. Montevideo, Uruguay: CSIC. UdelaR; EUBCA.

Savolainen, R. (1999). The role of the Internet in information seeking in context. *Information Processing & Management, 35*(6), 765–782. doi:10.1016/S0306-4573(99)00025-4.

Savolainen, R. (2002). Network competence and information seeking on the Internet: From definitions towards a social cognitive model. *The Journal of Documentation, 58,* 211–226. doi:10.1108/00220410210425467.

Savolainen, R. (2005a). Enthusiastic, realistic and critical: discourses of Internet use in the context of everyday life information seeking. *Information Research, 10*(1), paper 198. Retrieved on November 30, 2012, from http://InformationR. net/ir/10-1/paper198.htm

Savolainen, R. (2005b). Everyday life information seeking. In Fisher, K. E., Erdelez, S., & McKechnie, L. (Eds.), *Theories of information Behavior* (pp. 143–148). Medford, NJ: Information Today.

Sen, G. (1998). The empowerment as an approach to poverty. In Arriagada, I., & Torres, C. (Eds.), *Gender and Poverty: New Dimensions*. Santiago, Chile: ISIS Internacional, Ediciones de las Mujeres.

Tatnall, A. (2004). *Web Portals: The New Gateways to Internet Information and Services*. Hershey, PA: Idea Group Publishing. doi:10.4018/978-1-59140-438-5.

Warschahuer, M. (2008a). Laptops and literacy: A multi-site case study. *Pedagogies: An International Journal, 3*, 52-67. Retrieved on April 30, 2012, from http://www.gse.uci.edu/person/warschauer_m/docs/II-pedagogies.pdf

Warschahuer, M. (2008b). *A Literacy Approach to the Digital Divide*. Oakland, CA: University of California. Retrieved April 30, 2012, from http://www.gse.uci.edu/markw

Warschahuer, M. (2008c). Whither the digital divide? In D.L. Kleinman et al. (Eds), *Controversies in Science & Technology: From climate to chromosomes*. New Rochelle, NY: Liebert. Retrieved April 30, 2012, from http://www.gse.uci.edu/person/warschauer_m/docs/whither.pdf

Zhou, X. (2010). *Information in Healthcare: An Ethnographic Analysis of a Hospital Ward*. Unpublished Doctoral thesis. Ann Arbor, MI: University of Michigan. Retrieved on November 30, 2012, from http://deepblue.lib.umich.edu/bitstream/2027.42/78940/1/xmzhou_1.pdf

ADDITIONAL READING

Agosto, D. E., & Hughes-Hassell, S. (2005). People, places, and questions: An investigation of the everyday life information-seeking behaviors of urban young adults. *Library & Information Science Research, 27*(2), 141–163. doi:10.1016/j.lisr.2005.01.002.

Calva González, J. J. (2010). *Necesidades de información y comportamiento en la búsqueda de información de los adolescentes*. México: UNAM, Centro Universitario de Investigaciones Científicas.

Castells, M. (2009). *Comunicación y poder*. Madrid, Spain: Alianza.

Chatman, E. A. (1988). Opinion leadership, poverty and information sharing. *R.Q, 26*(3), 341-353.

Chatman, E. A. (1996). The impoverished life-world of outsiders. *JASIS, 47*(3), 193–206. doi:10.1002/(SICI)1097-4571(199603)47:3<193::AID-ASI3>3.0.CO;2-T.

Chatman, E. A. (1999). A theory of life in the round. *JASIS, 50*(3), 207–217. doi:10.1002/(SICI)1097-4571(1999)50:3<207::AID-ASI3>3.0.CO;2-8.

Daniel, F., Yu, J., Benatallah, B., Casati, F., Matera, M., & Saint-Paul, R. (2006). Understanding UI integration: A survey of problems, technologies, and opportunities. *IEEE INTERNET COMPUTING, MAY/JUNE*(11), 59–66.

Farkas, M. G. (2007). *Social Software in Libraries: Building Collaboration, Communication, and Community Online*. Medford, NJ: Information Today, Inc..

Fischer, T., Bakalov, F., & Nauerz, A. (2009). *An Overview of Current Approaches to Mashup Generation* (pp. 254–259). Wissensmanagement.

Fisher, K. E., Erdelez, S., & McKechnie, L. (2005). *Theories of information behavior*. Medford, NJ: Information Today.

Fisher, K. E., Landry, C. F., & Naumer, C. (2007). Social spaces, casual interactions, meaningful exchanges: 'Information grounds' characteristics based on the college student experience. *Information Research, 12*(2), paper 291. Retrieved on November 30, 2012, from http://InformationR.net/ir/12-1/paper291.htm

Gigler, B. (2004). *Including the Excluded - Can ICTs empower poor communities? Towards an alternative evaluation framework based on the capability approach.* Paper presented at 4th International Conference on the Capability Approach. University of Pavia, Italy. Retrived on February 2, 2012, from http://www.incidenciapolitica.info/biblioteca/EMPB_0052.pdf

González, L., Llambías, G., & Pazos, P. (2010). *Towards an e-health integration platform to support social security services.* Paper Presented at the 6th International Policy and Research Conference on Social Security. Luxembourg.

Hassan, A., & Fleegler, E. W. (2010). Using technology to improve adolescent healthcare. *Current Opinion in Pediatrics, 22,* 412–417. doi:10.1097/MOP.0b013e32833b5360 PMID:20616734.

Pollock, N. (2002). *Conceptualising the information poor: An assessment of the contribution of Elfreda Chatman towards an understanding of behavior within the context of information poverty.* Retrieved on June 3, 2012, from http://npollock.id.au/info_science/chatman.html

Richardson, W. C., Avondolio, D., Vitale, J., Len, P., & Smith, K. T. (2004). *Professional Portal Development with Open Source Tools: JavaTM Portlet API, Lucene, James, Slide.* Wrox.

Sosa, R. (2011, August 19). Integración de Servicios Geográficos en Plataformas de Gobierno Electrónico. PEDECIBA Informática | Instituto de Computación – Facultad de Ingeniería – Universidad de la República.

Spink, A., & Cole, C. (2006). *New directions in human information behavior.* Dordrecht, The Netherlands: Springer. doi:10.1007/1-4020-3670-1.

Tatnall, A. (2004). *Web Portals: The New Gateways to Internet Information and Services.* New York: Idea Group Publishing. doi:10.4018/978-1-59140-438-5.

Tepper, M. (2003). The rise of social software. *NetWorker, 7*(3), 18–23. doi:10.1145/940830.940831.

Wilson, T. D. (1981). On user studies and information needs. *The Journal of Documentation, 37*(1), 3–15. doi:10.1108/eb026702.

Wilson, T. D. (1997). The cognitive approach to information-seeking behavior and information use. *Social Science Information Studies, 4,* 197–204. doi:10.1016/0143-6236(84)90076-0.

KEY TERMS AND DEFINITIONS

Digital Information Resources: Sources and services of information produced and accessible via ICTs.

Everyday Life Information Seeking: Tactics developed by common people regarding information seeking in the context of their everyday lives. Information behavior affected by a wide range of factors related to their way of life, project of life, values, habitus, social capital, cultural and cognitive capital.

Health Information: Resources and services which are accessible via digital networks and that, in a social inclusion strategy, are designed to promote healthcare among the population while contributing to the solution of social, local and personal problems.

Human Information Behavior: It refers to the way in which people in context and communities relate to information contents and interact with them. It constitutes a lifelong social practice and includes the access, search and use of information.

Information and Communication Flow: Complex social process focused on human beings in a socio-cultural context, through which knowledge is transferred to the community. It includes the production, circulation, social use of information resources, as well as the appropriation of contents by the actors involved in the process.

Information Poverty: Citizens in vulnerable situation as users of information, as a result of social inequality along with difficulties in defining their information needs, accessing both physically and intellectually to technology and information resources and communication, and generating, using or applying knowledge to situations which require so.

Information Users: Multidimensional concept that refers to a main actor in the processes of information: the person who either actually or potentially relates to information resources.

Subjectification Processes: Production and reproduction dynamics of ways of being, based on practical and unique experiences, conditioned while at the same time open to changes.

Chapter 8
Digitize or Perish:
Strategies for Improving Access to Indigenous Intellectual Resources in Sub–Saharan Africa

Stephen Asunka
Ghana Technology University College, Ghana

ABSTRACT

In today's knowledge and technology driven society, most scholarly information is increasingly being produced and distributed in digital formats. Yet, in Sub-Saharan Africa, academic libraries have been very slow at joining this digital movement, and hence stand the risk of losing their relevance, particularly with regard to locally generated intellectual material. To better serve the knowledge and information seeking needs of their patrons, librarians need to reinvent services. The challenges are discussed as well as prescriptions of workable strategies that librarians, information scientists, and other stakeholders can adopt to overcome these barriers. Such strategies mostly involve appropriately leveraging the existing Information and Communication Technology (ICT) tools and resources to make library resources more accessible. Consequently, digitizing indigenous intellectual resources may keep libraries from perishing and respond to user needs and information seeking habits in Sub-Saharan Africa.

INTRODUCTION

Decades after several African states had gained their political independence, many Sub-Saharan African academic and research libraries still depended on foreign (mostly European and American) partners and benefactors for access to most intellectual material (books and journals). With such privileges, and given the fact that these libraries operated within poor economies, they largely failed to develop the capacity to provide the resident African user easy access to indigenous and locally generated intellectual material. Thus, even in today's technology driven society, it is fairly easier for information seekers within Africa to locate and access relevant and Africa-related material from foreign sources than from sources within Africa. Meanwhile knowledge generated

DOI: 10.4018/978-1-4666-4353-6.ch008

within Africa, and which might better satisfy the needs of knowledge and information seekers, remain relatively inaccessible, as most of it does not make it into books and scholarly journals.

To the higher education student and researcher, the culminating result of this conundrum is two-fold:

1. There is massive unintentional duplication of research with the attendant wastage of time and financial resources, and
2. Research findings and scholarly writings that can potentially benefit society go unnoticed as they are tucked away in archives with non-existent or poorly managed records.

It is therefore imperative that the African scholarly community begin to evolve common, structured, and cost-effective mechanisms for procuring, storing, organizing, delivering, and sharing indigenous scholarly content in ways that will make them readily accessible, particularly to Africa-based students and scholars. As academic librarians and information scientists are the professionals better equipped to provide leadership in this direction, it behooves them to explore every possible opportunity to do so, now that advances in computer and Internet technologies are offering limitless opportunities.

Indeed, many African institutions, universities, and colleges are already engaged in individual and collaborative activities aimed at facilitating the capture, development, preservation, and dissemination of local scholarly material in digital formats. Such initiatives include online (virtual) libraries, digital repositories, networked information resource centers, and so forth.

However, for these (and similar) initiatives to have the desired impact--which includes making indigenous African scholarly material readily accessible to information seekers in the sub-region--some crucial issues need to be taken into

consideration as the Sub-Saharan African socio-cultural terrain has its own peculiarities.

It is against this backdrop that this chapter:

1. Highlights and provides insights into the current situation with regard to indigenous academic resource availability and use in Sub-Saharan Africa, and;
2. Uses this as a context to evolve best-practice frameworks and strategies that librarians and information science professionals within the sub-continent can adopt to enable them to facilitate the accessibility and usability of digital academic resources in general, and indigenous scholarly output in particular.

THE SUB-SAHARAN AFRICAN INFORMATION RESOURCE AND DIGITAL LITERACY LANDSCAPE

Challenges of the Sub-Saharan African Academic Library

Academic libraries have the task of ensuring that scholars and researchers gain access to whatever material is relevant to their needs whenever they need it (Papin-Ramcharan & Dawe, 2012). Over the past few decades, however, university libraries in many Sub-Saharan African countries have declined in value to academics and students, as they are confronted with limited financial resources, inefficient management practices, and lukewarm attitudes of various governments and stakeholders (Kavulya, 2007; UNESCO, 1995). Additionally, since the establishment of most of these libraries was based on the western model, with little consideration for the needs of African users (Rosenberg, 1993), they have largely failed to re-invent themselves so they can be of better service to scholars, especially when it comes to locally produced intellectual material. Most scholars and researchers have therefore largely lost faith in these libraries as capable of satisfying their intellectual needs, especially with regard to indigenous knowledge (Echezona & Ugwuanyi, 2010), and hence are in a continual and quiet struggle for knowledge and information (Sturges & Neill, 1990). Thus, in Ghana for instance, scholars mostly turn to specialized research libraries such as the George Padmore Research Library for African Affairs, or even the British Council Library for their research needs, rather than university libraries which are presently stocked with outdated and foreign related material.

Significantly however, academic librarians and information professionals in the sub-continent are not throwing their hands up in despair, but are constantly exploring ways of keeping their respective libraries relevant and purposeful to their clientele. Though the philosophy of the academic library as a passive repository is taking longer to change (Rosenberg, 2005), current advances in information and communication technologies (ICTs) are offering struggling libraries a "lifeline," as through these technologies, library material can now be converted into electronic formats and made more visible, and more accessible, to patrons. ICT hardware such as computers, scanners, and digital cameras, together with highly sophisticated multimedia processing software, allow the easy conversion of traditional library material such as books, manuscripts, art works, maps, audio and video recordings, and so forth, into digital formats which can be stored in searchable databases, and made accessible through the Internet to users. With these technologies, libraries can also through collaboration with other institutions, offer the necessary infrastructure and licenses for their respective patrons to access material which is typically beyond the reach of traditional library patrons. More importantly, relevant indigenous knowledge which hitherto could not make it into books and academic journals, as well as antiquated and rare collections, can now also be digitized and made accessible.

Given these potential tremendous benefits of digitization, it is understandable why academic libraries within the sub-continent are embarking on several ICT facilitated document acquisition and delivery initiatives, including digitization. Indeed, there is renewed recognition of the role of the academic library in the enhancement of quality and accessible higher education and research, as they begin to reinvent themselves as digital or electronic libraries. For most of these libraries, the ultimate goal is the attainment of a state where scholars and students can interact electronically with the library's, as well as the world's scholarly content without actually visiting the physical library (Rosenberg, 2005).

Needless to say, Sub-Saharan African academic libraries are very far from attaining this vision, as the technological applications and processes they are developing and harnessing have some accompanying challenges which if not proactively addressed, might result in these libraries stuck somewhere between where they are coming from and where they wish to be. In addition to the pervasive financial and requisite infrastructural constraints, the challenges wrought especially by the current information society include:

1. Lack of appropriate knowledge and skills on the part of most librarians and library staff to deploy, use, and maintain the technological resources required to provide seamless access to intellectual material in electronic form. Most university libraries have, on one hand, trained librarians who are not very adept at using ICT resources and integrating these into their professional activities, and on the other hand, ICT experts who have very little knowledge about how libraries operate, and thus are equally incapable of putting their skills to appropriate use for the benefit of library patrons. The result is the current situation where there are diverse approaches to electronic resource development in terms of scale, scope, and objectives (Tritt, 2008),

a phenomenon which still leaves scholars and researchers struggling for knowledge and information.

2. Limited empirical research literature on digital information seeking behaviors and electronic resource access by potential users of electronic libraries within the sub-continent. Evidence abounds to suggest that ICTs, particularly the Internet and World Wide Web, have changed the information seeking and access behaviors of users of electronic library resources (Kaur & Sharda, 2010). In the traditional library mode, librarians mostly acquired content in the form of books, journals, and so forth, and made these available on shelves for users to access. It was left to the individual user to pick the requisite book or journal and look for the particular information they needed. In the digital era, however, patrons can ask for a single article in a journal or a particular book chapter, and expect to have it rendered on their computers or even handheld devices. Moreover, these information seeking strategies are fluid and situation dependent, where a seeker's actions are influenced by access to information, perceived quality, and trust in the information source (Boyd, 2004).

It is therefore imperative that librarians clearly understand the techniques and strategies that users typically adopt to search and locate library resources and services, so they can deploy these resources in ways that better meet patron needs. Coming to this understanding, however, is a challenge as research works in this direction within the Sub-Saharan African context are largely non-existent. A look at some institutional library Websites attests to this, as very little is offered to the user either by way of search or access to electronic library resources and services.

3. The challenge of ownership. Under the traditional mode, academic libraries had the responsibility of archiving all the printed intellectual material they acquired, and therefore owned this material. In the present era however, publishing has increasingly turned digital, and libraries now only own licenses to electronic publications, with no option for duplication and storage, whilst the content remains with the publisher (Steenbakkers, 2005). In essence, if at any point a publisher decides, or is compelled by circumstances, to fold its operations, all its content will likely cease to be accessible to libraries and their patrons. This represents a big challenge which can only be addressed by libraries or institutions resorting to acquiring and archiving all relevant electronic resources, in addition to publishing and archiving their own e-resources. Thus in the developed world, academic and other research libraries are engaged in major projects to digitize and archive most of their printed collections, particularly those reflecting the history and culture of their respective countries (Igbeka & Ola, 2008).

For Sub-Saharan Africa, however, much of the research output and other intellectual material is in the form of grey literature; that is, unpublished research reports, theses and dissertations, seminar and conference papers, and so forth, which are not well organized and not easily accessible (Kanyengo, 2006). Digitizing these could improve the purposefulness of African libraries towards their users, but it again brings back the issue of financing and the availability of the relevant expertise. It is therefore not surprising that academic libraries within the sub-continent are making a little headway in this direction.

4. In this Web 2.0 paradigm of participatory culture and relatively low barriers to knowledge creation and delivery, the proliferation of self published (non-peer reviewed) content, poses a dilemma for academic librarians

when it comes to evaluating and choosing what to collect and preserve for their user base. Libraries have to maintain standards in collecting works that should be used for research and academic purposes. Thus, even if a knowledge resource appears to be of interest to patrons, librarians cannot always be sure of its credibility if it is in the grey literature domain.

For Sub-Saharan African academic libraries, this is a difficult situation, particularly with regard to indigenous knowledge, as most scholarly works on, or related to, Sub-Saharan Africa, and produced by indigenous scholars, constitutes the largest portion of the sub-continent's scholarly works (Kanyengo, 2006), and is mostly grey literature. Thus, indigenous scholarly works abound (mostly in print form though), yet libraries are incapable of organizing and making them accessible to users.

5.   The presence of other possible barriers to widespread electronic resource acceptance and adoption among users. Despite the numerous advantages inherent in the delivery of electronic intellectual resources, one major drawback is that people still generally find the physical resources more convenient to use (Foster & Remy, 2009). The tactile feedback that users get when flipping through pages of text is a phenomenon which cannot be easily replicated in the electronic environment. This, coupled with copyright and intellectual property (IP) rights issues that make institutions weary of suits and subpoenas (Nelson, 2008), constitute substantial barriers to wholesale adoption and deployment of electronic resources, thus making some libraries quite hesitant to go entirely digital.

The few challenges enumerated above represent substantial barriers to widespread adoption and application ICTs for the procurement, preservation and delivery of electronic scholarly information by libraries in Sub-Saharan Africa. Yet, to remain relevant and not be confined to the dustbin of history, academic and research libraries need to adopt workable strategies that will not only help them overcome these barriers, but enable them to provide the requisite leadership that will help move the sub-continent to a position where its citizens can participate meaningfully and effectively in the global information society. Some of these strategies are discussed in the sections that follow.

STRATEGIES FOR IMPROVING INDIGENOUS ACADEMIC RESOURCE AVAILABILITY, ACCESS AND USE IN SUB-SAHARAN AFRICA

The Infrastructure, Content and Processes

Virtual Libraries: Possible Innovative Strategies

A virtual library (also known as digital library, electronic library, or e-library) is a library where most, or all of the resources and services are made available electronically--frequently over the Internet so that users can access them remotely. As already mentioned, Sub-Saharan African academic libraries are presently decades away from attaining the status of virtual libraries, particularly with regard to locally generated content. By adopting some innovative strategies however, these libraries should be able to leverage the prevalent ICT tools and infrastructure in ways that will enable them deliver on their core mandates, and also be of value to seekers of indigenous scholarly material. One such strategy is the establishment of a Continental Virtual Library.

Through effective collaboration, and harnessing the affordances of ICTs, librarians, publishers, vendors, and all other stakeholders within Sub-Saharan Africa, can work together to create a virtual library that will provide equitable access to critical and relevant scholarly information to users located anywhere within the sub-continent and beyond. Presently, at the individual level, most Sub-Saharan African academic libraries are digitizing local content, and also facilitating online access to thousands of academic databases, e-journals, and e-books published globally. Incidentally, due to copyright or purely administrative decisions, these libraries do not make most of these materials openly accessible to users outside the respective library or university networked systems (e.g., Tritt, 2008).

However, by collaborating to form consortia at the national and ultimately the continental level, libraries can pool resources to establish networked online public access catalogues (OPACs), through which all digital holdings of libraries participating in such consortia can be accessed. This virtual library will therefore be a network of online library databases accessible through a Website interface, and patrons of any library within the network will have access to all collections that all other libraries make available to the network. Each library will therefore, in addition to its peculiar collections, also have a "shadow collections" (i.e., holdings which technically belong to other libraries within the network, but are all accessible to the particular library's patrons Malinconico, 2011]).

Libraries within the sub-region should therefore work towards building such consortia, and paying attention to the proactive strategies to adopt to ensure that such consortia are not only sustainable, but are actively engaged in the creation and sharing of indigenous content as well.

Digitize or Perish: A Case for Open Access Institutional Digital Repositories

An institutional digital repository (often called an institutional repository) is a Web-based database of scholarly material which is institutionally defined, cumulative and perpetual, and openly accessible to members of the institution's community (Mark

Ware Consulting Ltd, 2004). Institutional repositories thus mostly contain the intellectual works of faculty, students and alumni, digitized archival material, as well as records of ongoing scholarly activities and events of the institution itself.

Institutional repositories provide an opportunity to faculty, researchers, administrators, and even alumni who wish to archive their research and other scholarly material in digital formats, and also make them available to the global academic community, to do so. The open access movement, the open archives initiative, the need for changes in scholarly communication to remove barriers to access, and the increasing awareness that universities and research institutions stand to lose valuable digital and print materials if not appropriately preserved, are all factors driving the establishment of institutional repositories (Cullen & Chawner, 2011; Drake, 2004).

In recent times, institutional repositories have increased in popularity among higher education institutions mostly in the developed world. Indeed, the 2012 Top Institutional Repositories Ranking by the Spanish National Research Council (CSIC) Cybermetrics Lab, listed 1,440 open access institutional repositories worldwide, up from a total of 1,172 listed in 2011. Sub-Saharan Africa however lags behind in this aspect as it only contributed 34 out of the 1,440 open access repositories listed by CSIC.

Institutional repositories are being put to several uses, including enhancing communication, facilitating e-learning and e-publishing, collection management, long-term preservation, and even for enhancing institutional prestige (Lynch, 2003; Stevan, 2003). Indications therefore are that institutions that do not currently have repositories are planning on establishing these in the not too distant future (Stuart & Nelson, 2012).

For most institutions, librarians are taking leadership roles in planning and building these repositories, fulfilling their roles as experts in collecting, describing, preserving, and providing stewardship for documents and digital information.

Using open source software, open archive models, established metadata standards, and digital rights management, librarians and information scientists are gathering their respective institutional scholarly output (mostly grey literature), and making these available through repositories. Some institutions allow authenticated users to self archive their personal collections (Asunka, Chae, & Natriello, 2011), thus giving such persons the opportunity to showcase and also share their scholarly works. Partnerships are also emerging that produce distributed digital networks (e.g., MetaArchive) to securely store multiple copies of unique library collections at geographically dispersed sites around the world.

For academic libraries located within Sub-Saharan Africa, institutional open access repositories represent a singular opportune platform for the collection, storage, and dissemination of all aspects of scholarly output which otherwise will remain obscure, unused, or disappear altogether. By simply digitizing all their digitizable holdings, uploading these into their respective repositories, and also encouraging scholars and students to "publish" their works (even if unfinished) on these repositories, libraries will be preserving Africa's knowledge base, and will also be able to render this knowledge available and accessible worldwide. There is even the possibility of integrating these repositories with social networking tools and other library electronic resources to make them more visible and more accessible to the ordinary user.

Admittedly, some technical and administrative issues (e.g., document formats, copyright, document submission processes, etc.) need to be carefully addressed before individual repositories can become operational, but these cannot serve as excuses for academic libraries within the sub-continent to continue hesitating to deploy repositories especially as their development requires minimal infrastructural and human capital investment. The present rate at which Sub-Saharan African research and higher education institutions are buying into the idea of digital content preservation through repositories is simply not acceptable. In Ghana for instance, at the last count in September 2012, only 3 out of over 80 universities and colleges have thus far deployed a repository of some sort.

As a first step, therefore, libraries can begin collecting all digital academic material scattered all over their respective campuses, and formulating policies on how these can be managed. Thankfully, for almost all institutions, students are required to submit research theses and dissertations in digital format (on CD ROM), but rather than simply placing these on shelves like books in the libraries, these can easily be converted to appropriate formats (e.g., PDFs) and uploaded to the repository. Beginning with the most recent, they can then progressively take on the previous years' documents until they get to the point where they have only physical copies. These can then be systematically digitized and uploaded until all theses and dissertations ever produced in that particular institution are digitally archived. The process can then be repeated on all the other categories of library holdings. Ultimately, the majority of the scholarly output of such institutions will not only be safely archived, but will be readily accessible by users. Needless to say, if Sub-Saharan African academic libraries do not provide the right leadership in this direction, their significance will be greatly eroded in the coming years as fewer people will be visiting physical libraries in search of information and knowledge.

Ensuring Equitable Access: A Case for Community Multimedia Centers

One other strategy that academic libraries and indeed governments within Sub-Saharan Africa can adopt to ensure that knowledge generated within academia is accessible to all persons who seek that knowledge is the Community Multimedia (or Media) Center (CMC) approach. At the basic level, a CMC combines community radio by local people in local languages with community telecenter facilities--computers with Internet and e-mail, phone, fax and photocopying services (UNESCO, 2012). CMCs thus operate to meet the information and learning needs of members within a particular community.

Thus, CMC radio presenters search the Web in response to listeners' queries and discuss, on air, the contents of pre-selected websites with studio guests. The CMC can also gradually build up its own database of materials that meet the community's information and education needs. Introducing CMCs in marginalized communities of the developing countries thus helps connect these communities to the global knowledge society. Sub-Saharan Africa abounds in such communities whose residents will likely be seeking information and knowledge that directly impacts their daily lives and development. Paradoxically, universities and development oriented research institutions have typically conducted research in these communities, but have their findings locked up in libraries in the cities.

With CMCs therefore, this knowledge, which should progressively be in digital format and accessible online, now becomes accessible to the persons who need it and will also directly benefit from it. Thankfully also, with mobile telephony penetration in the sub-continent almost at 60% of the population, and an estimated population of about 35% of Africans now browsing the Internet using their mobile phones (Rao, 2012), an opportunity exists for CMCs to override the prevailing technology infrastructural challenges and make a desired impact. Indeed, as CMCs spring up with the support of organizations such as UNESCO, chances are that Sub-Saharan African academic libraries will still remain obscure to indigenes if they are not proactive enough to avail their holdings online, as the Internet is affording access to several other knowledge sources, and library users do not care where the resources are or who owns them; they just want to gain access to whatever

is relevant to their needs (Papin-Ramcharan & Dawe, 2012).

By taking the right initiatives, however, academic librarians can help in ensuring that most Sub-Saharan Africans have equitable access to knowledge generated within the sub-continent, and by scholars within or outside the continent. This will involve liaising with other institutions, organizations, and local governments authorities facilitate the deployment of CMCs within communities whose residents typically do not have access to the Internet and the library's digital resources for that matter.

There is an App for That: Enhancing Mobile Access to Digital Library Resources

As mentioned previously, mobile phone use is growing rapidly in Sub-Saharan Africa, with significant numbers accessing the Internet through their mobile handheld devices. It is, however, common knowledge that due to the small screen sizes, limited processing powers, and graphical limitations of most mobile devices, users spend more than necessary time searching for and accessing content over the Internet through these devices (Motiwalla, 2007). This notwithstanding, the trend shows that mobile computing and mobile resource access over the Internet will be the norm in a few years' time. It therefore behooves librarians and information scientists to begin exploring ways of making their digital holdings accessible and readable over mobile devices.

As a matter of fact, mobile devices are increasing in sophistication and most can render content on their screens the same way the computer does. However, with bandwidth still very expensive in Sub-Saharan Africa, especially over the mobile phone infrastructure, there is the likelihood that library resources, if not appropriately formatted and made mobile friendly, will remain inaccessible to an increasing demographic of users. Academic libraries within the sub-continent therefore need to begin experimenting and honing skills and knowledge in this direction, until they have control over the processes and all the technical ramifications. At that point they should be able to develop customized applications which can be used on mobile devices to facilitate content access, downloads, and so forth.

Ethical and Legal Issues: Navigating the Ill-Structured African Socio-Cultural Terrain

Whilst recommending that academic libraries within Sub-Saharan Africa must embark on aggressive content digitization procedures that will enable them better serve their users who mostly prefer accessing information in electronic formats over the Internet, and on the go, it is worth cautioning that this must be done with care. Most publishers have in place policies that allow online access to their electronic information, but bar institutions from electronically archiving this information within the individual institution's infrastructure (Warner, 2002). Similarly, most scholarly output in print formats have copyright restrictions, hence libraries do not have the freedom to simply digitize these for archiving purposes. Besides, in simply digitizing the scholarly works of others, libraries ought to be sensitive to the respective authors' privacy even though such authors' works might not be copyright protected.

Adding to this, most Sub-Saharan African countries have not evolved clear cut policies to guide electronic scholarly content acquisition, preservation, and distribution (Kanyengo, 2006), though it is clear that enabling policy frameworks would allow libraries to implement various digital record management strategies that are in tune with global best practices. Presently therefore, it is likely that the digitization initiatives being embarked upon by most academic libraries within the sub-continent are either on ad hoc basis, or

based on models that have been developed and are working elsewhere. Of course, some countries have some initiatives in place; for example, the Copyright Society of Ghana has the task of reaching agreements (including paying royalties) with copyright holders so their respective materials can be made freely available online. Incidentally, the impact of this initiative is not being felt.

Therefore, for academic librarians wishing to begin digitization projects, it is advised that they stick to open source applications and open access content at the beginning whilst they work with their respective institutions and governments to develop policy and best practice frameworks that will guide future management of electronic resources. Also, students submitting dissertations could be made to sign undertakings granting the institution the right to copy and redistribute the content. That way, theses and dissertations can be placed in the institutional open access repositories for greater visibility.

On the whole, Sub-Saharan African countries need to individually and collectively develop policy frameworks for acquiring and sharing digital scholarly content. These can even be based on current continental policies such as the NEPAD (The New Partnership for Africa's Development) initiative which is a vision and strategic framework for Africa's renewal, growth, development, and participation in the global economy (nepad.org).

The User

Understanding User Needs: A Framework for Research

Academic libraries within Sub-Saharan Africa are being urged to go digital, but as Kanyengo (2006) points out, one critical issue is that most citizens have not yet fully realized the power of the digital media to demand that resources and services be made available to them via the Internet for faster access and use. Besides, librarians and information scientists have little knowledge of how electronic information seekers wish to see and access scholarly content or library services, but are deploying electronic resources based mostly on what they know about printed material. The result might be a mismatch in activities and behaviors between provider and searcher, leading to inefficiencies such as poor access to available material, misallocation of resources, and so forth.

For maximum satisfaction on both sides, the operations of library information systems and services must be in harmony with the information needs and seeking habits of academics, researchers and students. Librarians and information scientists in institutions therefore need to carry out sensitization programs through which potential library users can be made aware of the resources available, and also be equipped with the requisite searching skills to enable them derive maximum benefits from the library's resources and services. In addition, empirical research studies need to be carried out to ascertain how typical library users search for and retrieve items located in the library's digital collections. Findings of such studies will help inform librarians on what to collect and also refine the ways they organize and render the content to the user.

One popular research approach that is gaining currency is Transaction Log Analysis (TLA). Internet based digital information reside on servers which keep records of all user activities pertaining to searching, opening, and downloading of content. Over any given period of time, these records can be retrieved and analysed to give detailed information on how users interact with the digital content. Such information is of value to librarians as it can help them determine what resources are popular and what are not, what users typically do whenever they visit the library Website, and so forth. TLA has therefore been defined as the study of interactions registered electronically between online systems of information retrieval and persons who search for information contained in

these systems, with the objective of contributing to an improvement in the designs of the system (Villen-Rueda, Senso, & Moya-Anegon, 2007).

Being a non-intrusive and non-interactive method of gathering data (Asunka, Chae, Hughes, & Natriello, 2009), TLA is a very credible method of assessing user behavior, system performance and product performance. Thus, for libraries already operating institutional digital repositories and other digital preservation and delivery mechanisms, librarians need to team up with some other technology experts to periodically carry out TLA of their systems so they can better meet the needs of users.

Developing User Capacity

For citizens in Sub-Saharan Africa to be able to participate meaningfully in the current global information society, there is the need to equip them with the necessary information and digital literacy skills so they can independently seek and find the right information and from the right sources. According to UNESCO (2003);

Information Literacy encompasses knowledge of one's information concerns and needs, and the ability to identify, locate, evaluate, organize and effectively create, use and communicate information to address issues or problems at hand; it is a prerequisite for participating effectively in the Information Society, and is part of the basic human right of lifelong learning (para 3).

Participants at the UNESCO sponsored Information Literacy Meeting of Experts from 23 countries, held in Prague, the Czech Republic in September 2003, proclaimed that Information Literacy is a concern to all sectors of society. They therefore proposed that "governments should develop strong interdisciplinary programs to promote Information Literacy nationwide as a necessary step in closing the digital divide through the creation of an information literate citizenry, an effective civil society and a competitive workforce" (UNESCO, 2003, Para 5).

Clearly, as librarians and other information science professionals in Sub-Saharan Africa work to procure, preserve and make digital scholarly content available and accessible to users, it is likely that these efforts might not pay off if such users have little or no knowledge and skills on how to properly access and use this material purposefully. There is therefore the need for institutions, governments, and other organizations to work towards providing the citizenry with the information literacy skills based on what pertains in the African context, so they can better participate in the knowledge economy. Indeed, organizations like the African Center for Media & Information Literacy are providing leadership in this direction.

In the formal education sector however, emphasis should also be placed on training teachers and library professionals so they can integrate information and digital media literacy into their teaching or professional activities. Academic libraries should also be integrated into such literacy education programs as they can provide the enabling environment and requisite resources to facilitate such training programs.

CONCLUSION

It is general knowledge that academic and research libraries in Sub-Saharan Africa are confronted with challenges which threaten to render them redundant and make them lose their significance as sources of scholarly information for teaching and research purposes. Even in the present digital society where academic libraries in other parts of the world are at the cutting edge, effectively harnessing the affordances of digital technologies to deliver quality services electronically, their counterparts in Sub-Saharan Africa appear to be struggling at the other end of this technological double-edged sword.

All is not lost, however, as these libraries, together with governments and other organizations, can plan and implement some strategic initiatives to overcome the challenges so academic libraries can re-take their place as the premier sources of credible knowledge and information in the African society. Such strategic initiatives should involve libraries digitizing as much content as possible and making these available over the Internet, enacting policies to guide the procurement, preservation and distribution of such digital content, forming partnerships and networking with sister libraries and institutions to leverage their strengths and minimize their weaknesses, and finally involving the ultimate users of these resources in all these operations.

Academic libraries within the sub-continent have little choice but to provide the requisite leadership in this direction, and be at the forefront of adequately addressing the information and knowledge needs of Africans, rather than continuing to rely on foreign models and practices that may only end up making them simply serve as portals to other people's content. At this point, these libraries would have perished into obscurity whilst their roles are taken up by search engines and online databases.

REFERENCES

Asunka, S., Chae, H. S., Hughes, B., & Natriello, G. (2009). Understanding academic information seeking habits through analysis of web server log files: The case of the Teachers College library website. *Journal of Academic Librarianship*, *35*(1), 33–45. doi:10.1016/j.acalib.2008.10.019.

Asunka, S., Chae, H. S., & Natriello, G. (2011). Towards an understanding of the use of an institutional repository with integrated social networking tools: A case study of PocketKnowledge. *Library & Information Science Research*, *33*(1), 80–88. doi:10.1016/j.lisr.2010.04.006.

Boyd, A. (2004). Multi-channel information seeking: A fuzzy conceptual model. *Aslib Proceedings*, *52*(2), 81–88. doi:10.1108/00012530410529440.

Cullen, R., & Chawner, B. (2011). Institutional repositories, open access and scholarly communication: A study of conflicting paradigms. *Journal of Academic Librarianship*, *37*(6), 460–470. doi:10.1016/j.acalib.2011.07.002.

Drake, M. A. (2004). Institutional repositories: Hidden treasures. *Searcher*, *12*(5), 41–45.

Echezona, R. I., & Ugwuanyi, C. F. (2010). African university libraries and Internet connectivity: Challenges and the way forward. *Library Philosophy and Practice*(September), 1-13.

Foster, G., & Remy, E. (2009). E-Books for academe: A study from Gettysburg College. *EDUCAUSE Center for Applied Research: Research Bulletin, 2009*(21), 1-12.

Igbeka, J. U., & Ola, C. O. (2008). The need for digitization of special library materials in Nigerian university libraries. *World Libraries, 18*(1).

Kanyengo, C. W. (2006). *Managing digital information resources in Africa: Preserving the integrity of scholarship*. Paper presented at the Bridging the North-South Divide in Scholarly Communication on Africa: Threats and Opportunities in the Digital Era. Leiden, The Netherlands.

Kaur, H., & Sharda, P. (2010). Role of technological innovations in improving library services. *International Journal of Library and Information Science*, *2*(1), 11–16.

Kavulya, J. M. (2007). Digital libraries and development in Sub-Saharan Africa: A review of challenges and strategies. *The Electronic Library*, *25*(3), 299–315. doi:10.1108/02640470710754814.

Lynch, C. A. (2003). Institutional repositories: Essential infrastructure for scholarship in the digital age. *Association of Research Libraries*, *226*, 1–7.

Malinconico, S. M. (2011). Librarians and user privacy in the digital age. *Scientific Research and Information Technology*, *1*(1), 159–172.

Mark Ware Consulting Ltd. (2004). Pathfinder research on web-based repositories. Bristol, UK: Publisher and Library/Learning Solutions (PALS).

Motiwalla, L. F. (2007). Mobile learning: A framework and evaluation. *Computers & Education*, *49*(3), 581–596. doi:10.1016/j.compedu.2005.10.011.

Nelson, M. R. (2008). E-books in higher education: Nearing the end of the era of hype? *EDUCAUSE Review*, (March/April): 40–56.

Papin-Ramcharan, J., & Dawe, R. A. (2012). Can benevolence and technology bridge the divide between developed and developing countries' libraries? *World Libraries, 20*(1).

Rao, N. (2012). *Mobile Africa Report 2012*. Retrieved on December, 3, 2012, from http://www.mobilemonday.net/reports/MobileAfrica_2012.pdf

Rosenberg, D. (1993). Imposing libraries: The establishment of national public library services in Africa, with particular reference to Kenya. *World Libraries, 4*(1).

Rosenberg, D. (2005). Towards the digital library: Findings of an investigation to establish the current status of university libraries in Africa. *International Network for the Availability of Scientific Publications (INASP), Oxford.* Retrieved on November 28, 2012, from http://www.inasp.info/uploaded/documents/digital-libr-final-format-web.pdf

Steenbakkers, J. F. (2005). Digital archiving in the twenty-first century: Practice at the National Library of the Netherlands. *Library Trends, 54*(1), 33–56. doi:10.1353/lib.2006.0010.

Stevan, H. (2003). Open access to peer-reviewed research through author/institution self-archiving: Maximizing research impact by maximizing online access. In Derek, L., & Andrews, J. (Eds.), *Digital Libraries: Policy Planning and Practice.* London: Ashgate Publishing.

Stuart, N., & Nelson, K. (2012). Trends from the Canadian IR/ETD Survey 2012. Retrieved on November 4, 2012, from http://dspace.library.uvic.ca:8080/bitstream/handle/1828/3845/Stuart_Nelson_Trends_2012.pdf?sequence=7

Sturges, P., & Neill, R. (1990). *The quite struggle: Libraries and information for Africa.* London: Mansell.

Tritt, S. (2008). Report on digital libraries in Ghana. Retrieved November 20, 2012, from http://www.indiana.edu/~libsalc/african/ALN125/125DigLibsGhana.html

UNESCO. (1995). *Policy paper for change and development in higher education.* Paris.

UNESCO. (2003). The Prague Declaration: Towards and information literate society. Retrieved on December 3, 2012, from http://portal.unesco.org/ci/en/ev.php-URL_ID=19636&URL_DO=DO_TOPIC&URL_SECTION=201.html

UNESCO. (2012). Community Multimedia Centers. Retrieved on December 3, 2012, from http://portal.unesco.org/ci/en/ev.php-URL_ID=1263&URL_DO=DO_TOPIC&URL_SECTION=201.html

Villen-Rueda, L., Senso, J. A., & Moya-Anegon, F. D. (2007). The use of OPAC in a large academic library: A transactional log analysis study of subject searching. *Journal of Academic Librarianship, 33*(3), 327–337. doi:10.1016/j.acalib.2007.01.018.

Warner, D. (2002). Why do we need to keep this in print? It's on the web...: A review of electronic archiving issues and problems. *Progressive Librarian*(19-10), 47-64.

ADDITIONAL READING

Adebowale, S. A. (2001). The scholarly journal in the production and dissemination of knowledge on Africa: Exploring some issues for the future. *African Sociological Review, 5*(1), 1–16. doi:10.4314/asr.v5i1.23181.

Agili, V. S., & Moghaddam, I. A. (2008). Bridging the digital divide: The role of librarians and information professionals in the third millennium. *The Electronic Library, 26*(2), 226–237. doi:10.1108/02640470810864118.

Bowdoin, N. T. (2011). Open Access, African scholarly publishing and cultural rights: An exploratory usage and accessibility study. *Library Philosophy and Practice.* Retrieved on December 20, 2012, from http://www.webpages.uidaho.edu/~mbolin/poppeliers.htm

Britz, J., & Lor, P. (2004). A moral reflection on the digitization of Africa's documentary heritage. *IFLA Journal, 30*(3), 216. doi:10.1177/034003520403000304.

Chisenga, J. (2006). *The development and use of digital libraries, institutional digital repositories and open access archives for research and national development in Africa: Opportunities and challenges.* Paper presented at WSIS follow-up Conference on Access to Information and Knowledge for Development. Addis Ababa, Ethiopia.

Ezema, I. (2011). Building open access institutional repositories for global visibility of Nigerian scholarly publication. *Library Review, 60*(6), 473–485. doi:10.1108/00242531111147198.

Fatoki, C. O. (2007). Digitisation of library materials in Nigeria: Issues and considerations for information professionals. *African Journal of Library. Archives and Information Science, 17*(1), 15–21.

Fulkerson, D. M. (2012). Meeting user needs. In Fulkerson, D. (Ed.), *Remote access technologies for library collections: Tools for library users and managers* (pp. 17–32). Hershey, PA: IGI-Global. doi:10.4018/978-1-4666-0234-2.ch002.

Igbeka, J. U., & Ola, C. O. (2010). The need for digitization of special library materials in Nigerian university libraries. *World Libraries, 18*(1). Retrieved on November 10, 2012, from http://www.worlib.org/vol18no1/igbekaprint_v18n1.shtml

Kujenga, A., & de Vries, R. (2011). *Supporting African digital library projects: Experiences from the field*. Paper presented at the Second International Conference on African Digital Libraries and Archives (ICADLA-2). Johannesburg, South Africa.

Limb, P. (2005). The digitization of Africa. *Africa Today, 52*(2), 2–19. doi:10.2979/AFT.2005.52.2.2.

Magara, E. (2002). Applications of digital libraries and electronic technologies in developing countries: Practical experiences in Uganda. *Library Review, 51*(5), 241–255. doi:10.1108/00242530210428746.

Mutula, S. (2004). IT diffusion in Sub-Saharan Africa: Implications for developing and managing digital libraries. *New Library World, 105*(1202/1203), 281–289. doi:10.1108/03074800410551039.

Ojedokun, A. A. (2000). Prospects of digital libraries in Africa. *African Journal of Library. Archives and Information Science, 10*(1), 13–21.

Paulos, A. (2008). Library resources, knowledge production, and Africa in the 21st century. *The International Information & Library Review, 40*, 251–256. doi:10.1016/j.iilr.2008.09.006.

Rosenberg, D. (2006). Towards the digital library in Africa. *The Electronic Library, 24*(3), 289–293. doi:10.1108/02640470610671150.

Seadle, M., & Greifeneder, E. (2007). Defining a digital library. *Library Hi Tech, 25*(2), 169–173. doi:10.1108/07378830710754938.

Sithole, J. (2007). The challenges faced by African libraries and information centers in documenting and preserving indigenous knowledge. *IFLA Journal, 33*(2), 117–123. doi:10.1177/0340035207080304.

Uzuegbu, P. C. (2012). The role of university libraries in enhancing local content availability in the Nigerian community. *Library Philosophy and Practice*. Retrieved on December 10, 2012, from http://unllib.unl.edu/LPP/uzuegbu.pdf

KEY TERMS AND DEFINITIONS

Academic/Research Library: A library that is attached to a research or higher education institution, to serve the teaching and research needs of academics, researchers and students. Academic libraries have the responsibility of acquiring and preserving relevant scholarly material, and making these readily accessible to help address the teaching, learning, research and information needs of their patrons and society at large.

Digitization: The process of converting analogue material such as books, art works, maps, audio, video etc. into digital formats using appropriate hardware devices and software programs so that they can be manipulated by computer, displayed on a screen, transmitted over the Internet etc. Digitization also facilitates the storage and retrieval of information as the digital representations can be stored in searchable databases, and made accessible through the Internet to users.

Indigenous Knowledge (IK): Indigenous knowledge is knowledge that is unique to a given culture or society. It encompasses the skills, experiences and insights of people that form the basis for local-level decision making towards improving the livelihoods of people at the local, community or country level. Indigenous knowledge is thus the basic component of any community's knowledge system, and is some cases, constitutes the main asset with which such communities can gain control of their own lives. The creation and application of such knowledge is thus equally as important for development as the provision of physical infrastructure and financial capital.

Information Access: This is defined as the findability of information regardless of format, channel, or location. Information access thus covers many issues such as copyright, open source/access, privacy, security etc, and also includes activities that involve the application of technologies to help people find and access the right information at the right time and place.

Information and Communication Technologies (ICTs): The integration of telecommunications (telephone lines and wireless signals), computers as well as the necessary enterprise software, middleware, storage, and audio-visual systems, to afford users the opportunity to create, store, transmit, access and manipulate information. The Internet and World Wide Web represent the dominant features of ICTs, and these are profoundly impacting on most human activities as they facilitate the creation and instant distribution of useful information across the globe.

Institutional Digital Repository: This is a Web-based database of electronic scholarly material which is institutionally defined, cumulative and perpetual, and openly accessible to members of the institution's community. Institutional repositories thus mostly contain the intellectual works of faculty, students and alumni, digitized archival material, as well as records of ongoing scholarly activities and events of the institution itself.

Sub-Saharan Africa: Geographically, it is the part of the African continent that lies south of the Sahara. Comprising of forty eight countries, Sub-Saharan Africa is geopolitically distinct from North Africa (considered part of the Arab World) though they occupy a single continent. Over the years, most Sub-Saharan African countries have consistently been confronted with serious political, economic, social and environmental challenges, the consequences of which is the current situation where the region lags behind the rest of the world in all the human development indices.

Virtual Library: A virtual library (also known as digital library, electronic library, or e-library) is library where most, or all of the resources and services are made available electronically - frequently over the Internet so that users can access them remotely. Like the traditional library, a digital library also facilitates access to information and knowledge by comprehensively collecting, managing and preserving relevant digital content, and offering these to its targeted users.

Chapter 9

A Comparison of the Information Needs and Information Seeking Behavior of Entrepreneurs in Small to Medium Sized Enterprises (SMEs) in Developing and Developed Countries:
A Review of the Literature

Linda L. Lillard
Clarion University, USA

ABSTRACT

"Entrepreneurial spirit has been described as the most important economic development stimulus in recent decades" (Chalhoub, 2011, p. 67). In the early 1990s it was estimated that small to medium sized enterprises SMEs employed 22% of the adult population in developing countries and the role of SMEs is viewed as increasingly important in developing countries because of their capacity to create jobs (Okello-Obura, Minishi-Majanja, Cleote, & Ikoja-Odongo, 2007, p. 369). According to Lingelback, de la Viña and Asel (2005), even though entrepreneurship has been linked to wealth and poverty in developing countries and has played an important role in growth and poverty alleviation, it is the least studied significant economic and social phenomenon in the world today. Examining how the information needs and information seeking behavior of entrepreneurs from developing countries may differ from entrepreneurs in developed countries is important as it has been suggested that "entrepreneurship in developing countries is distinctive from that practice in developed countries and that understanding these distinctions is critical to private sector development in developing countries" (Lingelback, de la

DOI: 10.4018/978-1-4666-4353-6.ch009

Vina, & Asel, 2005, p. 2). A review of the studies produced thus serves as a beginning for designing information packages and information services that can benefit a global population. Consequently, this chapter targets the information needs and information seeking behavior of entrepreneurs revealed in studies associated with SMEs in both developed and developing countries and offers conclusions and recommendations for meeting the information needs of this population.

INTRODUCTION

The information needs and information seeking behavior of potential users should be the basis for the design of all high quality information services. Furthermore, it is important to tailor these services to what we know about information seeking behavior of the specific user groups to which they will be targeted. In today's global economy it is important to take a broader perspective of the information user. Most studies of information seeking behavior have been conducted in the English-speaking countries of the developed world and reflect Western culture (Leckie and Pettigrew, 1997; Allen, 1997; Wilson, 1996; Ellis, 1989, Kuhlthau,). LIS specialists cannot be content to design services that only target users from the developed world. Services that appeal to the broader needs of information users in the global economy are essential. In the past few years, some studies have become available that were conducted examining user groups in developing countries. These studies reveal information that allows the LIS community to begin comparing user information needs in both developed and developing countries, thus providing a basis for the design of information services that will appeal to users globally. For example, in a review of the research on information needs and information seeking behavior in developing countries, Dutta (2009) discovered that a study by de Tiratel (2000) concluded that the information-seeking behaviors of university researchers are similar regardless of location or the availability of resources even though developed countries have more advanced information systems and services (p. 46). Furthermore, Dutta's examination of research conducted in Uganda and Ghana concluded that the "information behavior of scholars and educated urbanites is similar to the behavior of information users in developed countries" (p. 46).

This chapter targets the information needs and information seeking behavior of entrepreneurs revealed in studies associated with small to medium sized enterprises (SMEs) in both developed and developing countries. Important to developing countries, of course, is economic development, which involves change and "the entrepreneur becomes the best agent for this change" (Acs & Virgill, 2010, p. 488). Furthermore, regional differences in economic growth have been found by various studies to be linked to levels of entrepreneurship (Acs & Virgill, 2010, p. 489). In 1984, however, Carland, Hoy, Boulton, and Carland stated that there is a distinct difference between SMEs and entrepreneurship and that the concepts are not the same but Thurik & Wennekers (2004) stated that both are important to an economy and that the small business sector is populated by both entrepreneurs introducing new products and by people who own and operate a business for a living (p. 140). In a review of entrepreneurship in developing countries, Acs and Virgill (2010) state that knowledge and information affect entrepreneurship in developing countries by affecting the ability of entrepreneurs to discover what to produce and the technology and processes used in production (p. 500). Citing Mambula (2002) they emphasize that because the cost of this discovery is so high, entrepreneurs will not seek new production areas and markets but will lean toward well established markets. So, lack of information because of the costs attributed to searching likely lead to low levels of entrepreneurship according to

Hausmann and Rodrick (2003). Lack of education resources and information failures are attributed as a major limitation to entrepreneurial development in developing countries.

Within the United States Government, there is no universally accepted definition of an SME. The definition used by the Office of Advocacy of the Small Business Administration serves as the most straightforward definition and it includes all enterprises with fewer than 500 employees (United States International Trade Commission, 2010), while the government of Uganda, for example, classifies SMEs at employing 5-50 people on a small scale and 51-500 people on a medium scale (Okello-Obura et al., 2007, p. 368). Countries that fit into The World Bank (2012) categories of low income economies (those with a gross national income (GNI) per capita of under US$1,105), lower-middle-income economies (those with a GNI per capita of $1,006--$3,975) and upper-middle-income economies (those with a GNI per capita of $3,976--$12,275) will be targeted for this review as countries in those categories are considered to be developing countries by The World Bank. Okella-Obura, Minishi-Majanja, Cloete, and Ikoja-Odongo (2009) describe other characteristics of SMEs such as the fact that their owners may also be the managers and they are often assisted by family members. Furthermore, the nature of operation of SMEs leads them to have a "narrow range of products/services and a relatively simple and unsophisticated management structure with a narrow tolerance range of risk" (p. 2). For this reason, they have difficulties in the advantageous use of market opportunities that require large production quantities. These researchers believe that decisions are made haphazardly in SMEs and these decisions do not make use of accurate business information.

"Entrepreneurial spirit has been described as the most important economic development stimulus in recent decades" (Chalhoub, 2011, p. 67). In the early 1990s it was estimated that SMEs

employed 22% of the adult population in developing countries and the role of SMEs is viewed as increasingly important in developing countries because of their capacity to create jobs (Okello-Obura, Minishi-Majanja, Cleote, & Ikoja-Odongo, 2007, p. 369). In the Middle East, specifically Lebanon, SMEs are said to be "one of the most important factors in the local economy and over 90% of the companies have less than five employees" (Chalhoub, 2011). Increased development of SME's has been attributed to the emergence of the global, knowledge-based economy that allows "speed in new product development, agility in hiring and allocating human resources, and flexibility in internal processes" (Chalhoub, 2011, p. 69) thus overcoming the barriers created by the larger scaled operations and their economies of scale of 30 years ago (Chalhoub, 2011).

According to the 2011 Global Entrepreneurship Monitor, it is estimated that 388 million entrepreneurs were actively engaged in starting and running new businesses in 54 different global economies. Furthermore, 163 million of these were women early-stage entrepreneurs and 165 million were young (between ages 18 and 35) early-stage entrepreneurs. Lingelback, de la Viña, and Asel (2005) refer to the Landes (1998) publication, *The Wealth and Poverty of Nations* when they state that even though the entrepreneurial nature of economies in developing countries has been linked to its wealth and poverty and that plentiful entrepreneurship has played an important role in growth and poverty alleviation, it is the least studied significant economic and social phenomenon in the world today. Examining how the information needs and information seeking behavior of entrepreneurs from developing countries may differ from entrepreneurs in developed countries is important as it has been suggested that "entrepreneurship in developing countries is distinctive from that practice in developed countries and that understanding these distinctions is critical to private sector development in developing countries"

(Lingelback, de la Vina, & Asel, 2005, p. 2). Okella-Obura et al. (2011) believe that in order to enhance productivity and facilitate market access, SMEs need access to adequate information so that long term and sustainable economic growth can be attained (p. 2). Furthermore, these researchers refer to research by Strong, Lee and Wang (1997) that maintains that chaos is created when information is of poor quality. Ladzani (2001) states that information provision is at the top of the priority ranking list of SME needs.

Lingelback et al. (2005) go on to discuss what they believe makes entrepreneurs in developing countries different and these differences fall in the areas of opportunity, financial resources, and apprenticeship and human resources. They believe that opportunities are broader in scope and that the strategy is for entrepreneurs to spread their "resources across several separate but related businesses in order to mitigate systematic risk" (p. 4) playing the same role as a financial investor by managing "portfolio risk by operating several diverse businesses in lieu of investors who might otherwise do the same" (p. 4). This system of interlocking businesses, as they term it, "provide a source of informal information flow, access to a broader pool of skills and resources and, when well implemented, a brand name that can be leveraged across all businesses" (p. 4). Since these interlocking businesses are common in developing markets, Lingelback, de la Vina, and Asel (2005) consider how these businesses start and state that the circumstances usually require these entrepreneurs to begin their businesses "downstream" as they term it, meaning that they have direct access to the end customer. They believe that while these "downstream" businesses reduce initial capital investments they permit "access to customers and information flow that is frequently lacking" and that the availability of this type of information is "often overlooked as a key success factor" (p.4). Futhermore, lack of access to the end customer and the information it provides has been cited by

Fairbanks and Lindsay (1997) as a primary reason that South American businesses fail to move into higher valued added activities.

A review of the studies produced thus far that have examined the information needs and/or information seeking behavior of entrepreneurs in developing countries can serve as a beginning for designing information packages and information services that can benefit a global population. This is an important user group to consider because "SMEs play a key role in the economic growth of–and equitable development in–developing countries" (Okello-Obura et al., 2007, p. 368). Though information is a critical resource for enterprises so that they can gain competitive advantage, many enterprises in developing countries may be operating in an environment of fragmented and incomplete information. Such is the case in Uganda where "an awareness of markets, technology, policies, regulations, and finance is limited" (Okello-Obura et al., 2007, p. 371-372).

Furthermore, it is not enough to design useful services if obstacles exist that prevent the target audience from using these services. Akobundu (2007) also considers the various obstacles to information access and use in developing countries. From a review of the literature, Akobundu cites the work of Uhegbu (2002) who identifies the five obstacles of economic, social, environmental, occupational, and infrastructure and Etim (2000) who lists seven obstacles that include physical infrastructure, technical, and managerial capabilities, among others. They go on to discuss obstacles in the areas of lack of awareness, inaccessibility, information explosion, bibliographic obstacles, environment, poor infrastructure, declining budgets and rising costs, costs for users, staff attitude toward users, and crime. Consequently, this analysis of the literature on information needs and information seeking behavior associated with entrepreneurs in SMEs in developed and developing countries will be undertaken with an eye toward the obstacles noted.

STUDIES OF INFORMATION NEEDS OF SMES IN DEVELOPING COUNTRIES

Uganda

In a very comprehensive study, Okella-Obura, Minishi-Majanja, Cloete, and Ikoja-Odongo (2008) examined the business activities and information needs of SMEs in northern Uganda in order to determine prerequisites for an information system. Uganda falls into The World Bank (2012) classification of a low-income economy below $1,005 GNI per capita. A descriptive research design based on survey techniques was utilized in addition to examining relevant literature on business information provision and SMEs in Uganda. They had a response rate of 87.3 percent of the SME sample of 251 enterprises, a response rate of 72% of the 75 information providers targeted, and an 85% response rate of the targeted 20 business policy makers. This study provided profiles of the respondents in regard to gender, age, education levels, business experience, and language proficiency, the business activities of the SME, and the business information needs of the SME. They provided a final discussion of their results that integrated their research findings with those from their review of the literature and they ended with a detailed recommendation of what should make up a business information system for northern Uganda.

Nigeria

The aim of Popoola's (2009) study of information acquisition and decision making among insurance company managers in Nigeria was to determine the degree of relationship among effective decision-making and self-efficacy, information acquisition, and information utilization. Nigeria lies in The World Bank (2012) classification of a lower-middle income economy with $1,006

to $3,975 GNI per capita. The sample consisted of 153 managers in eleven different insurance companies and data collection involved a self-developed questionnaire consisting of two parts: one that targeted personal information of the respondents such as age, gender, marital status, job tenure, education qualifications and job status, and one that measured self-efficacy. The questionnaire had a response rate of 94.8 percent. Types of information acquired in decision-making and the types of information sources used in addition to managers' level of effective decision-making were determined and then the relationship between effective decision-making, self-efficacy, information acquisition and utilization were reported. The study revealed the major types of information this user group acquire for effective decision making and also determined the major information sources utilized and compared these with previous studies conducted with business managers. The researcher believes that one of the major findings of this study is that "self-efficacy has a significant relationship with effective decision-making of the respondents" (Popoola, 2009, p. 12). Furthermore, these researchers argue that "the more the managers in corporate insurance companies in Nigeria acquire information, the more they are effective in their decision-making (Popoola, 2009, p. 12), which is also corroborated in a study by Ogunlade (2007) in which information from reliable sources is asserted to be responsible for financial institution managers making effective decisions and being innovative. Popoola (2012) believes that "the survival of corporate insurance companies in Nigeria depends on information acquisition and use for the provision of value-added services to their customers (p. 12)" and that the present study found that effective decision-making of the managers in these Nigerian insurance companies was predicted by self-efficacy, information acquisition and information utilization (p. 13). The final conclusion is that effective information systems should be developed for these managers, self-efficacy training should be made available in order to improve decision making and that a program be established to assist managers in becoming information literate (p. 13).

China

A study conducted by Kinnell, Feather, & Matthews (1994) investigated "the need for, and provision of, information services to small and medium-sized (SMEs) in China, (p. 3)" with the intent of making a proposal to develop such a service, implement it, and evaluate the results. China falls in the upper-middle-income economies group in The World Bank (2012) classification with $3,976 to $12,275 GNI per capita. Senior management in thirteen businesses were asked questions about their products, assets, and employees. Access to information sources and services was also considered. A major finding from this study was that "even where there were information services available which might meet some or all of the needs identified, managers were either unaware of their existence, or had used alternative sources" (Kinnell et al., 1994, p. 10). They also discovered that the plethora of economic and technical information available from a local Institute of Scientific and Technical Information and access it provided to foreign business directories and journals was "either not locally accessible because of communication difficulties or not being requested" (p. 10). Furthermore, the "local university library, which held journals and newspapers, and was supporting industrial training for many of the industries in the city, was similarly not being used by local businesses as an information resource" (p. 10). They found that the businesses had their own centers that provided mostly marketing and production information or they gleaned needed information from trade publications or from their research and trade associations. The results of this study, however, were examined in

the context of the UK experience with the result that the researchers also found that the Chinese business managers differed little from UK mangers in their information seeking behavior related to information on product and marketing intelligence.

South Africa

A study by Jiyane and Mostert (2010) examined the use of information and communication technologies by women hawkers and vendors in South Africa. South Africa falls in the upper-middle-income economies group in The World Bank (2012) classification with $3,976 to $12,275 GNI per capita. These researchers make the statement that there is wide acknowledgement "that the use of information and communication technologies (ICTs) by informal sector workers can help them improve their productivity and incomes; consequently they wanted to determine role of ICTs among these women entrepreneurs in the rural areas of South Africa. Information was gathered through observation and interviews of the 42 women selected through purposive sampling. Computer technology appears to be absent but most of the women did display an interest in using it and also owned mobile phones and had access to landlines, radio, and television. A table presented in the article revealed that all of the women used ICTs, in this case radios, televisions, cell phones, and land lines, to make and receive calls to and from friends and relatives, listen and watch business-related programs, make and receive calls to and from business partners, retail stores, product suppliers and distributors, but none of them used ICTs to search for business-related information (Jiyane & Mostert, 2010, p. 1). Conclusions reached were that ICTs were not a major method of obtaining business information for these women which they thought might be attributed to instability of electrical and communication networks, inadequate support and empowerment of these businesses by the government and the focus of these businesses on local and walk by customers. The researchers recommended that training and classes should be made available for these women and that government sponsored Internet cafes located close to their workplaces should be made available and accessible. Training was stressed in the author recommendations.

Zambia

In a case study of Chisokone Market, Kitwe, Zambia, researchers Banda, Mutula, and Grand (2004) determined the information needs of the small scale business community, the types of business conducted, the service providers available in Kitwe and the problems business owners had in seeking information. Using a survey method of data collection, questionnaires were returned from 83.6% of the 250 person sample. Results revealed that most of the information needs of the respondents were in the areas of marketing, management skills, credit and loan facilities, and suppliers. They felt that searching for information was a problem, 76.6% of the respondents, while 78.9% of the respondents "indicated lack of access to information as the major problem" (Banda et al., 2004, p. 102). Very few respondents, 9.1%, were aware they could use the computer to get information and when asked if they would want to use computers for information searching, 66.5% overwhelmingly agreed while 33.0% indicated they would not want to use a computer for any purpose (Banda et al., 2004, p. 102). When questioned about familiarity with sources of information, the radio (13.9%), newspapers (12.4%), and Kitwe City Council (9.6%) were selected but most respondents chose "other" as their answer to this question. "Those who gave 'other' as the answer for their source of information indicated they got information from friends particular business colleagues" (Banda et al., 2004, p. 102). Respon-

dents were also asked what other ways they were interested in receiving information and from the list they were given chose radios and televisions (28.9%), newspapers (18.2%), personal contacts (16.7%), books (6.2%) and seminars (8.6%). The researchers believe that the major problem of information access was a result of lack of knowledge of where to locate information. They also believe that the providers need to design "a collaborative community information system that would harness and document all the information resources available in Kitwe" (Banda et al., 2004, p. 103).

Kenya

A study undertaken by Njoroge, Kiplang'at, and Odero (2011) examines the tourism industry in Kenya and whether micro and small entrepreneurs utilize ICTs to access information. Kenya falls into The World Bank (2012) classification of a low-income economy below $1,005 GNI per capita. A multiple case study method was used and 120 entrepreneurs were identified to participate in this study but only a total of 70 interviews were completed (57%). Though it was extremely important for these businesses to obtain access to relevant business information because of the competitive environment of the tourism industry and new requirements for service delivery, there was limited use of ICTs in what these authors termed the MSE (micro and small enterprises) sector in Kenya. These entrepreneurs were either unaware of the potential of ICTs or lacked knowledge and skills to use them. "They lacked relevant information in the required quantity and quality, and their capacity to continuously access and absorb useful information was directly reducing their incomes and raising operational costs" (Njoroge et al., 2011, p. 133). The researchers concluded that even though these challenges exist, the potential is good for increased use of ICTs by this population. The researchers provide a graphical representation of a model they propose for enhancing ICT utilization by the MSEs in the Kenyan tourism sector. The model recognizes that information needs are an important motivating factor in ICT use to access information. The information needs pinpointed in this study were:

- Marketing information and means of marketing;
- Information about the tourist and tourist destination;
- Training manuals;
- Loan facilities/partnership, source of income, tourism and business licence, tourism movement at any time of the year; and
- Government rules and regulations regarding tours and travel, legal issues and standards of service, among others (Njoroge et al., 2011, p. 126).

Many owners of the MSEs did not have enough experience or financial capital to be starting and running their business. Poor networking was cited by 65.7% of them as a deterrent to access. Most of them agreed that ICT equipment is expensive and availability of finances and manager/owner support had a major affect on adoption of ICTs. When the study respondents were asked what sources of information they used to run their businesses, it was apparent that these entrepreneurs were using the Internet to solve their information needs. Forty-five percent used the Internet and customized databases as important sources and 19.4% said that print and electronic media were most important (Njoroge et al., 2011, p. 128).

South Africa

Kiplang'at, Kwake, and Kariuki (2005) also looked at ICTs and tourism SMEs but in the Durban Region of South Africa. Using a structured questionnaire to interview 51 respondents selected in a purposive sample from tourism stakeholders in Durban who provide lodging or bed and breakfast

facilities for less than 50 people. The Internet was not a major source of information to the respondents in this study as it was found that they consulted other sources of information first. Fax and telephone services were the most accessible ICTs to this population. Overall, e-mail was used the most and the World Wide Web and tourism based information gateways and their computer and Internet operating skills were found to be lacking meaning that the tourism authorities in this region should focus on capacity building in Internet and computer skills. Even with this lack of skills, ICTS were "found to have increased the productivity and facilitated the communication of tourism information. At the same time, ICTs were found to have changed the way tourism stakeholders in the Durban region communicate with their customers (Kiplang'at et al., 2005, p. 139). The authors believe that the tourism stakeholders need to be encouraged to adopt ICTs so that they can utilize the benefits to promote tourism.

Namibia

Chiware (2007) provides a framework for designing and implementing business information services in the SMME sector of Namibia, which falls in the upper-middle-income economies group in The World Bank (2012) classification with $3,976 to $12,275 GNI per capita. Chiware (2007) states that previous studies show that a major deterrent to the development of dynamic SSME sectors is "the accessibility of validated, relevant information services" (p. 136) and that this situation "affects growth and SMME's ability to provide jobs and income opportunities in both urban and remote rural areas" (p. 136). Furthermore, he agrees with Kinnell et al. (1994) in that major impediments to information services in developing countries are underdeveloped computer and communications industries, lack of adequate information sources and low awareness and usage, among others. Several attempts at providing information to the SMME population were in place in Namibia such as the Small Business Information Center (SBIC) that was a one-stop-shop providing information and other advisory services in order to enhance the economic environment for growth of SMMEs that closed down when funding dried up, the market information and support services offered by the Namibia Chamber of Commerce that was underutilized and closed down because it operated on a cost recovery basis, and the trade information center with a functional library provided by the Ministry of Trade and Industry that stopped functioning due to lack of manpower and interest. Chiware makes the statement that "timely and accurate business information services have been identified as a major component in development efforts" (Chiware, 2007, p. 143) and that systematic planning should be behind this type of service delivery and should include study of information needs, patterns of seeking information and assessment of exiting services including the role of ICT in information delivery and use, yet these services failed. Chiware (2007) attributes this to "the lack of formal approaches in the planning design, and implementation of the projects" (p. 139), stating that implementation was usually enacted after the fact or to attract funding. The United Nations Industrial Development Organization (UNIDO) provides a model that "operates on a demand-driven and commercial basis, ensuring SMME's trust and support through strong local ownership by public and private sector business partners" (Chiware, 2007, p. 139) and consists of a one-stop-shop that is a physical location with walk-in business advice and support for entrepreneurs. This should all be developed as a result of evaluation of the overall business support environment.

Malaysia

Kassim (2010) examined Malaysian Bumiputera would-be entrepreneurs in order to determine the types of business information needed, the level of importance of this information to their business needs, to find out how they obtained their information and the sources they used, and to ascertain the importance they attribute to the various sources. Malaysia falls into The World Bank (2012) upper-middle-income economy classification with $3,976 to $12,275 GNI per capita. Surveys were used to collect data from a population of 288 Bumiputera government staff (72% response rate from a list of 600) who took entrepreneurial development courses because of interest in becoming an entrepreneur. Four types of information had more than 80% of the respondents identifying it as needed: information to prepare a business plan, to plan cash flow, to examine business opportunities, and to help in profit planning. Seven types of information were rated as very important to their business needs: information related to planning cash flow, preparing a business plan, profit planning, communications with clients, business opportunities, course on entrepreneurship, and creativeness and innovativeness in business. Individuals were asked what sources, formal or informal, they used to get the needed information with the emphasis not on what sources they should be using but what they actually use. Twelve methods were revealed, with seven of them being targeted by over 70% of the sample: talk with other entrepreneurs (87.4%), share experience with other entrepreneurs (85.6%), discuss with friends/relatives (77.6%), read newspaper and magazines (77.3%), ask clients (76.9%) use Internet/e-mail (75.8%), and advice from government agency officers (70.0%). The bottom of the list consisted of read books (65%), read brochures and pamphlets (61%), talk with experts/business consultants (59.2%), discuss with members of the Malay Chamber of Commerce (41.2%) and last on the list ask librarians (24.4%). Sources used were courses (95.5%), business exhibitions (76.7%), Internet/e-mail (72.6%), business premises (69.1%), and government agencies (63.2%). The bottom half of the list consisted of technical training (52.4%), practical training (48.6%), banks (44.8%), associations/clubs (37.5%), and last on the list (libraries [29.5%]). The importance of the sources were ranked on a scale of 1 to 5 with 1 being not important and 5 being very important. Mean scores were provided and the respondents considered clients (mean score 4.71) and other entrepreneurs (mean score 4.51) as very important sources of business information and libraries (mean score 3.53) and librarians (means score 3.22) received the lowest mean scores. Comparing the data for the sources of business information and the perceived importance of these sources showed that the respondents were consistent about what they considered as sources but this did not translate to perceived importance. For example, 76.7% of the respondents considered business exhibition as a source of information but considered to be only important while Internet/e-mail was considered a source by 72.6% of the respondents but was perceived to be very important. Furthermore, libraries were considered sources by only 29.5% of the respondents, but were perceived as important. The author believes that the implication here is that "a library as one of the sources of information could play an important role in promoting their services to the business communities" (Kassim, 2010, p. 68). He believes that collections of print and electronic sources and well-equipped state-of-the-art information and communications technologies could be made available by the public libraries and that workshops could be planned and conducted to educate and train consumers in a way that would encourage their continuous use of the services.

Uganda, China, Ghana

Okella-Obura and Matovu (2011) discuss the importance of SME development for poverty alleviation, economic development, and the importance of adequate information to enhance productive and facilitate market access. They go on to say that SMEs suffer inadequate provision of business information in most developing countries. They also say that the SMEs in Northern Uganda depend mainly on informal institutions for busi-

ness information provision because they lack an awareness of important information agencies and institutions. In their research, they discovered that the development of information of communication technologies has enhanced the access of business information services and that has given SMEs in developed countries easy access. Newer technologies, especially the Internet, are not being used effectively by SMEs in developing countries to explore business opportunities. Poor Internet connection and speed, costs of technologies and lack of awareness of what the Internet offers are cited as reasons for this low usage. Furthermore, mobile phones are cited as the most widely used ICT in the developing world, their use to conduct business among SMEs is growing, but the impact of their usage on SME Internet usage is uncertain and these authors believe this is something that should examined. Okella-Obura and Matovu (2011) decided to analyze business information provision in a few selected countries in order to better understand situations in terms of designing appropriate information systems. They chose China, which falls into The World Bank (2012) classification of upper-middle income economies with $3,976 to $12,275 GNI per capita, South Africa which also falls into The World Bank (2012) classification of upper-middle income economies with $3,976 to $12,275 GNI per capita, and Ghana, which falls into The World Bank (2012) classification of lower middle-income economies with $1,006 to $3,975 GNI per capita.

China is experiencing fast growth in the business sector due to demand for higher quality goods and services making marketing extremely important. Great amounts of business information on all aspects of products have become necessary so practices have been developed to promote accessibility to business information by the business community. The Institute of Technical Information of China (ISTIC) and the Government of China's Support and Consultation Center for SMEs (SUCCESS) program are important examples. The ISTIC provides township and village enterprises with business and technical information on raw materials, intelligence on commodity markets and management information. SUCCESS collaborates with industrial, trade and professional organizations, private enterprise, and government departments to provide SMEs with comprehensive business information, free access to business electronic databases, a business reference collection in the reference library, and a regular publication on items of interest to SMEs. Workshops and seminar are also presented to expand business knowledge and enhance entrepreneurial skills. Consultation services with expert advisors in addition to a mentorship program are also made available.

In South Africa, the government actively supports the SMEs that account for 84% of all private employment and make up an estimated 80% of the total formal sector. The government's Department of Trade and Industry (DTI) set up the Center for Small Business Promotion (CSBP), which brought into existence other agencies that established support for SMEs. Services were set up and offered by local providers that include training programs for entrepreneurs, mentoring individual firms, marketing, procurement advice, and technology assistance. Local business service centers, owned and managed by local business people offer services such as training, marketing and linkages, counseling and referrals, and information gathering and dissemination. There appears to be a well established procedure in South Africa for the provision of information to SMEs. Okella-Obura and Matovu (2011) state that the integration of libraries into an organized information system to supply business information to the business community is a well thought out strategy.

Okella-Obura and Matovu's (2011) examination of SMEs and information in Ghana revealed that it has a huge SME sector that houses most of the employment opportunities in the country. The major activities in this sector are making soaps and detergents; weaving fabrics; designing clothing and tailoring; producing textiles and leather; village blacksmithing; tin-smiting; firing ceramics;

cutting timber and mining; making bricks and cement; brewing beverages; food processing and baking; creating wooden furniture; assembling electronic products; agro-processing; producing chemical based products; and mechanical activities. Several types of communication centers exist in Ghana to provide information for these activities ranging from a one room facility that provides a narrow range of services to facilities that provide training and a broad range of development activities. These facilities are further categorized into purely commercial facilities to those with an orientation to community/education service. The commercial centers have a profit orientation and almost all of them provide basic telephone access, faxing and photocopying while a great deal of them provide secretarial and computer-based services. They state that the business community does use these services even though a formal study has not been conducted to determine utilization levels. Extended discussion of Business Development Services (BDSs) for SMEs takes note that informal BDSs that include information and advice of relatives, friends or other employees and work related people such as suppliers, contractors, or clients play a key role in business information provision to SMEs. Radio and television programs are also included in the informal BDS category though they may not be documented.

South Africa

Shokane (2002) also looked at information needs of SMEs in South Africa, specifically, Acornhoek. A total of 34 questionnaires were distributed using purposive sampling. The objective of this study was "to determine the extent to which small- and medium-sized enterprises in Acornhoek make use of business information to gain sustainable competitive advantage" (pp. 35-36). Results showed that highest number study participants ranked obtaining information by communicating with colleagues (25), by using e-mail (20), by discussion with subordinates (19) as very important. Ranked not important by the highest number of respondents were asking the librarian (31), conferences (25), e-mail (26), and computerized information (14). Telephone conversations were ranked as somewhat important by 15 study respondents. The importance of various sources of information was also examined. Customers (26), friends, relatives, and associates (20), and suppliers (21) were ranked as used to a very large extent while radio and television (11) were ranked as used to a large extent, local authorities (20) to some extent, with libraries (24), research (24), patents and standards (24), the Internet (23), professional journals (22), and small business information centers (19) being ranked as not applicable. Customers (27) were used most frequently as sources of information, as were suppliers (26), while friends and relatives (22) were cited as frequently used sources. These researchers concluded that:

owing to small- and medium-sized businesses' inability to access information, due to lack of technological resources such as the Internet to facilitate accessibility and information sharing, their business managers to not regard information as a resource that can help them to attain sustainable competitive advantage (p. 46).

They believed that these enterprises did not know where to obtain information.

TYPES OF INFORMATION NEEDED AND SOURCES USED

The studies examined looked at SMEs in a variety of countries that had a wide range of business activities in various markets from tourism to insurance to soap and detergent manufacturing, blacksmithing and tailoring. All studies examined did not provide the types of information needed but of those that did the most frequently appearing information needs were in the areas of, marketing information, funding/finance/capital/ credit/loan information, product development and manufacturing information, business management skills information, supplier information, customer information, information on competitors, banking sources, law information such as government rules and regulations/business laws/taxation, and business opportunities.

Some studies did not identify the sources used by participants to secure the necessary information but these sources ranged from formal organizations such as the Uganda Revenue Authority, the Uganda Ministry of Finance, Planning and Economic Development, Northern Uganda Manufacturers' Association to customers, colleagues, radio and television to an interesting reliance on friends and family members. Some studies revealed that publications and trade literature were used as well as some Internet and CD-ROM databases, but the Internet was used mostly for email contact and libraries were rarely, if ever mentioned. Okella-Obura and Matovu (2011), in fact, mention that although the nationwide existence of public libraries in most countries could be viewed as "coherent measures that are in place to deliver business information services" (p. 10), the "situations in most countries–regarding public libraries as channel through which business information could be accessed by the business enterprises–are deplorable" (p. 10), and that any contributions of business information to business enterprises is almost non-existent.

BARRIERS TO INFORMATION

Not all of the studies identified any barriers experienced by the participants in retrieving the information they needed. However, those that did cited information-poor environment, no meaningful information system in place, word of mouth dependence, lack of physical and human resources such as electricity and trained information professionals, lack of appropriate technology to access electronic information, and information is always in a language that is not understandable, among others (Okella-Obura et al., 2007). Other studies cited unawareness of services, need for more information technology infrastructure and promotion of services available (Kinnell, Feather, & Matthews, 1994); high costs of ICTs, instability of electrical and communications networks, inadequate government support (Jiyane & Mostert, 2010); unawareness of the ability to use the computer to get information, lack of access and lack of knowledge of where to locate information (Banda, Mutula, & Grand, 2004); limited use of ICTs because of expense, lack of skill to use and unawareness of potential of ICTs (Njoroge, Kiplang'at, & Odero, 2011) and finally lack of computer and Internet operating skills, underdeveloped computer and communications industries, and lack of adequate information sources and low awareness of sources (Kiplang'at, Kwake, & Kariuki, 2005).

CONCLUSION AND RECOMMENDATIONS

From these studies it is apparent that there is a basic foundation of information that many of the SME entrepreneurs thought was useful such as marketing information, financial information, product development and manufacturing information, information on suppliers and information on management skills. Furthermore, these SME entrepreneurs like the personal touch and either prefer to get their information from talking with others, or believe that this is the only way to gather the needed information. Talking with other entrepreneurs and colleagues, customers, suppliers, friends and relatives is the most common method of information gathering in these studies. A study conducted by Robinson and Stubberud (2011) examined social networks and entrepreneurial growth. Nine European countries were included in this study consisting of seven developed countries and two developing countries that fell into the World Bank (2012) classification of upper-middle

income economies with $3,976 to $12,275 GNI per capita. The 287,837 business owners included in this study were asked to indicate if they had used the following sources of advice: "informal sources (family and friends; professional acquaintances), formal sources (professional consultants; training course for entrepreneurs; organizations specializing in business start-ups; unemployment administrations; financial institutions) and no sources (no access to relevant sources; no need for advice)" and the results were analyzed according to the number of employees in the business (0 employees, 1-9 employees, and 10 or more employees) (pp. 66-67). Professional acquaintances and family and friends were sources of advice most often sought by all businesses in the study regardless of size. The entrepreneurs who had 10 or more employees were more likely to have relied on professional acquaintances for advice than family and friends or professional consultants. The authors thought this might have been because this group had enough professional acquaintances that they did not need to pay for advice. Even though the participants with no employees or 1-9 employees were deemed to be similar in the sources used and the larger employers (10 or more employees) were considered different, all groups were "more likely to use informal sources of advice (professional acquaintances and family and friends) than formal sources." Overall, the results of the Robinson and Stubberud (2011) study, coupled with the results of the studies examined here, show the importance of talking with somebody for advice as a method of securing business information.

What seems to be an overarching problem in the developing countries is the access to information. The high cost of information and communications technology (ICTs), insufficient IT (information technology) infrastructure, inadequate electricity, lack of appropriate technology, lack of skills in using technology and unawareness of the information services made available through the use of technology all place the SME entrepreneurs in developing countries at a disadvantage. The most commonly used technology is the telephone and the cell phone, which fits with the preference for talking with people to gather information, and e-mail, though lack of other computer and Internet operating skills appears to be high. Jiyane and Mostert (2010) found that of the 42 respondents in their study of women hawkers and vendors in South Africa all owned mobile/cellular phones, landlines/talk boxes, television sets, and radio sets. None of them owned fax machines or computers. Shokane's study (2002) showed that 81.1% of the study respondents rated the importance of the use of radio and television either used to a very large extent (21.8%), to a large extent (34.3%) or to some extent (25%). The very basic of technology seems to be the common means of using ICTs for information gathering in developing countries.

Before the problem of what type of information is needed by the SME entrepreneurs can be addressed, effort needs to be expended in the direction of providing the ICT infrastructure, making IT available at affordable costs, and providing training in the use of the various technologies. Training will most likely have to be made easily available and be taken to the users, possibly in their homes and/or businesses, as suggested by Jiyane and Mostert (2010). These researchers go on to suggest that the governments sponsor Internet cafes in close proximity to the businesses and provide training on request. Perhaps at this time it is not best to concentrate on the type of information needed but on the access to the information. Once these ICT networks are established and in good working order and potential users are trained to use computers and other technology, then it may be determined what kinds of information they need. The question remains, though, will these people use the ICTs? It is important to pay attention to the ways these people acquire their information—the sources they use. The 287,837 respondents in the Robinson and Stubberud (2011) study still preferred networking with others to gather their information, and most of these respondents were in developing countries and they would have ac-

cess to more technology than those in developing countries. Past studies of traditional entrepreneurs in developed countries (Specht, 1987; Smeltzer, Fann, & Nikolaisen, 1988; Schafer, 1990, Brush, 1992) found that entrepreneurs preferred personal or face-to-face sources of information such as family and friends (Lillard, 2002). Nelson (1987) found that entrepreneurs preferred networking and significant others for information sources and Neelameghan (1977) found that they preferred distributors, consultants, customers, employees, and established entrepreneurs as sources of information (Lillard, 2002).

Researchers Kaish and Gilad (1991) found the opposite, in that entrepreneurs preferred nontraditional sources of information such as patent filings and strangers. Executives, however, gravitated toward personal, face-to-face sources such as subordinates, professional acquaintances, customers, and consultants (Lillard, 2002, p. 55).

The preference for networking is an important issue that information providers should not ignore, especially when coupled with the fact that libraries are not considered important sources and librarians are rarely, if ever, consulted. For that reason, it makes sense that information providers consider some relationship marketing. Rather than sitting passively in the library or other information agency and waiting for the entrepreneurs to come in (since they do not), being proactive and going to them seems to be a possibility. Developing a relationship with this group and becoming a trusted source of information that is part of their network could be the way to reach these entrepreneurs.

REFERENCES

Acs, A. J., & Virgill, N. (2010). Entrepreneurship in developing countries. In Acs, Z. J., & Audretsch, D. B. (Eds.), *Handbook of Entrepreneurship Research* (pp. 485–515). New York: Springer. doi:10.1007/978-1-4419-1191-9_18.

Allen, B. (1997). Information needs: A person-in-situation approach. In P. Vakkari, R. Savolainen, & B. Dervin (Eds.), *Information seeking in context: Proceedings of an International Conference on Research in Information Needs, Seeking and Use in Different Contexts* (pp. 99-110). London: Taylor Graham.

Banda, C., Mutula, S. M., & Grand, B. (2004, December). Information needs assessment for small scale business community in Zambia: Case study of Chisokone Market, Kitwe. *Malaysian Journal of Library & Information Science, 9*(2), 95–106.

Brush, C. G. (1992). Research on women business owners: Past trends, a new perspective and future directions. *Entrepreneurship Theory and Practice, 16*(2), 6–30.

Carland, J. W., Hoy, F., Boulton, W. R., & Carland, J. A. (1984). Differentiating entrepreneurs from small business owners: A conceptualization. *Academy of Management Review, 9*(2), 354–359.

Chalhoub, M. S. (2011). Culture, management practices, and the entrepreneurial performance of small and medium enterprises: Applications and empirical study in the Middle East. *Journal of Small Business and Entrepreneurship, 24*(1), 67–84. doi:10.1080/08276331.2011.10593526.

Chiware, E. R. T. (2007). Designing and implementing business information services in the SMME sector in a developing country: The case for Namibia. *IFLA Journal, 33*(2), 136–144. doi:10.1177/0340035207080308.

De Tiratel, S. R. (2000, September). Accessing information use by humanists and social scientists: A study at the Universidad de Buenos Aires, Argentina. *Journal of Academic Librarianship, 26*(5), 346–354. doi:10.1016/S0099-1333(00)00141-5.

Dutta, R. (2009). Information needs and information-seeking behavior in developing countries: A review of the research. *The International Information & Library Review, 41*, 44–51. doi:10.1016/j.iilr.2008.12.001.

Ellis, D. (1989). A behavioral approach to information retrieval design. *The Journal of Documentation, 45*(3), 171–212. doi:10.1108/eb026843.

Etim, E. F. (2001). *Scientific and technological information utilization and industrial Development in Nigeria.* Uyo, Nigeria: Heinemann.

Fairbanks, M., & Lindsay, S. (1997). *Plowing the sea: Nurturing the hidden sources of growth in the developing world.* Cambridge, MA: Harvard Business School.

Hausmann, R., & Rodrik, D. (2003). Economic development as self-discovery. *Journal of Development Economics 14th Inter-American Seminar on Economics, 72*(2), 603-633.

Jiyane, V., & Mostert, J. (2010, April). Use of information and communication technologies by women hawkers and vendors in South Africa. *African Journal of Library, Archives, &. Information Science, 20*(1), 53–61.

Kassim, N. A. (2010, August). Information needs of Malaysian Bumiputera would-be entrepreneurs. *Malaysian Journal of Library & Information Science, 15*(2), 57–69.

Kelley, D. J., Singer, S., & Herrington, M. (2011). Global entrepreneurship monitor: 2011 global report, accessed at www.gemconsortium.org.

Kinnell, M., Feather, J., & Matthews, G. (1994). Business information provision for small and medium-sized enterprises in China: The application of marketing models. *Library Management, 15*(8), 16–24. doi:10.1108/01435129410071363.

Kipling'at, J., Kwake, A., & Kariuki, S. M. (2005). Information and communication technologies (ICT) adoption by small and medium scale enterprise (SME) tourism stakeholders in the Durban Region, South Africa. *African Journal of Library, Archives &. Information Science, 15*(2), 133–140.

Kuhlthau, C. C. (1991). Inside the search process: Information seeking from the user's perspective. *Journal of the American Society for Information Science American Society for Information Science, 42*(5), 361–371. doi:10.1002/(SICI)1097-4571(199106)42:5<361::AID-ASI6>3.0.CO;2-#.

Leckie, G. J., & Pettigrew, K. E. (1997). A general model of the information seeking of professionals. Role theory through the back door? In P. Vakkari, R. Savolainen, & B. Dervin (Eds.), *Information seeking in context: Proceedings of an International Conference on Research in Information Needs, Seeking and Use in Different Contexts* (pp. 99-110). London: Taylor Graham.

Lillard, L. L. (2002). Information seeking in context: An exploratory study of information use online by eBay entrepreneurs. *Dissertation Abstracts International. A, The Humanities and Social Sciences, 63*(02), 1340.

Lingelbach, D. C., de La Viña, L., & Asel, P. (2005). *What's Distinctive about Growth-Oriented Entrepreneurship in Developing Countries?* UTSA College of Business Center for Global Entrepreneurship Working Paper No. 1. Retrieved from http://ssrn.com/abstract=742605

Mambula, C. (2002). Perceptions of SME growth constraints in Nigeria. *Journal of Small Business Management, 40*(1), 58–65. doi:10.1111/1540-627X.00039.

Neelameghan, A. (1977). Information needs and information sources of small enterprises: A synoptic view. *Library Science with a Slant to Documentation, 14*(3-4), 136–139.

Njoroge, G. G., Kiplang'at, J., & Odero, D. (2011). Diffusion and utilization of information and communication technologies by micro and small entrepreneurs in the tourism industry in Kenya. *Mousaion, 29*(2), 117–138.

Ogunlade, O. A. (2007). Information needs and utilization of managers in Nigerian financial institutions. *Journal of Business Management, 10*(2), 80–92.

Okella-Obura, C., & Mantovu, J. (2011). *SMEs and business information provision strategies: An analytica perspective.* Library Philosophy and Practice.

Okella-Obura, C., Minishi-Majanja, M. K., Cloete, L., & Ikoja-Odongo, J. R. (2007). Business activities and information needs of SMEs in northern Uganda. *Library Management, 29*(4/5), 367–391. doi:10.1108/01435120810869138.

Popoola, S. O. (2009, April). Self efficacy, information acquisition and utilization as correlates of effective decision making among managers in insurance companies in Nigeria. *Malaysian Journal of Library & Information Science, 14*(1), 1–15.

Robinson, S., & Stubberud, H. A. (2011). Social networks and entrepreneurial growth. *International Journal of Management & Information Systems, 15*(4), 65–70.

Schafer, S. (1990). Level of entrepreneurship and scanning course usage in very small businesses. *Entrepreneurship Theory and Practice, 15*(2), 19–31.

Shokane, J. K. (2002). Towards meeting the information needs of small- and medium-sized enterprises in Acornhoek. *Mousaion, 20*(20), 34–48.

Smeltzer, L. R., Fann, G. L., & Nikolaisen, V. N. (1988). Environmental scanning practices in small business. *Journal of Small Business Management, 2*(3), 55–62.

Specht, P. H. (1987). Information sources used for strategic planning decisions in small firms. *American Journal of Small Business, 12*, 21–34.

The World Bank. (2012). *Data: Country and lending groups*. Retrieved on June 2, 2012, from http://data.worldbank.org/about/country-classifications/country-and-lending-groups

Thurik, R., & Wennekers, S. (2004). Entrepreneurship, small business and economic growth. *Journal of Small Business and Enterprise Development*, *11*(1), 140–149. doi:10.1108/14626000410519173.

Ugah, A. D. (2007). Obstacles to information access and use in developing countries. *Library Philosophy and Practice*. Retrieved on June 2, 2012, from http://digitalcommons.unl.edu/libphilprac/160

Uhegbu, A. N. (2002). *The information user: Issues and themes*. Enugu, Nigeria: John Jacobs Classics.

United States International Trade Commission. (2010, November). *Small and medium-sized enterprises: Characteristics and performance* (USITC Publication 4189). Retrieved on June 2, 2012, from http://www.usitc.gov/publications/332/pub4189.pdf

Wilson, T. D. (1999). Models of information behavior research. *The Journal of Documentation*, *55*(3), 249–270. doi:10.1108/EUM0000000007145.

ADDITIONAL READING

Avgerou, C. (2008). Information systems in developing countries: A critical research review. *Journal of Information Technology*, *23*, 133–146. doi:10.1057/palgrave.jit.2000136.

Chilmo, W., & Ngulube, P. (2009). Using selected models to explore the connection between information and communication technologies and poverty reduction in developing countries. *Mousaion*, *27*(1), 97–115.

Hayton, J. C., & Cholakova, M. (2012). The role of affect in the creation and intentional pursuit of entrepreneurial ideas. *Entrepreneurship. Theory into Practice*, 41–67.

Holmner, M. (2011). The road to the information and knowledge society: Indigenous knowledge and the millennium development goals. *Mousaion*, *29*(2), 139–157.

Iakovleva, T., Kolvereid, L., & Stephan, U. (2011). Entrepreneurial intentions in developing and developed countries. *Education + Training*, *53*(5), 353–370. doi:10.1108/00400911111147686.

Jennex, M. E., Amoroso, D., & Adelakun, O. (2004). E-commerce infrastructure success factors for small companies in developing economies. *Electronic Commerce Research*, *4*, 263–286. doi:10.1023/B:ELEC.0000027983.36409.d4.

Kaarst-Brown, M. L., & Wang, C. (2003). Doing business in paradise: How small, information intensive firms cope with uncertain infrastructure in a developing island nation (TCI). *Journal of Global Information Management*, *11*(4), 37–57. doi:10.4018/jgim.2003100103.

Kartiwi, M., & MacGregor, R. C. (2007). Electronic commerce adoption barriers in small to medium-sized enterprises (SMEs) in developed and developing countries: A cross-country comparison. *Journal of Electronic Commerce in Organizations*, *5*(3), 35–51. doi:10.4018/jeco.2007070103.

Khavul, S., Bruton, G. D., & Wood, E. (2009). Informal family business in Africa. *Entrepreneurship. Theory into Practice*, 1219–1238.

Markowska, M. (2010). The essence of entrepreneurial learning (summary). *Frontiers of Entrepreneurship Research*, *30*(4), Article 11. Retrieved on June 2, 2012, from http://digitalknowledge.babson.edu/fer/vol30/iss4/11

Meldrum, M., & de Berranger, P. (1999). Can higher education match the information systems learning needs of SMEs? *Journal of European Industrial Training, 23*(8), 323–402. doi:10.1108/03090599910295379.

Minniti, M., & Naude, W. (2010). What do we know about the patterns and determinants of female entrepreneurship across countries? *European Journal of Development Research, 22*(3), 277–293. doi:10.1057/ejdr.2010.17.

Osman, M. H. M., Rashid, M. A., Ahmad, F. S., & Rajput, A. (2011, July). Market orientation – A missing link to successful women entrepreneurship in developing countries: A conspectus of literature. *International Journal of Academic Research, 3*(4), 232–236.

Premkamolnetr, N. (1999). Collaboration between a technological university library and tenant firms in a technology park in Thailand: New challenges for librarianship in a developing country. *Asian Libraries, 8*(12), 451–465. doi:10.1108/10176749910371284.

Robb, A., & Watson, J. (2010). Comparing the performance of female- and male-controlled SMEs: Evidence from the United States and Australia. *Frontiers of Entrepreneurship Research, 30*(8): Article 1. Retrieved on June 2, 2012, from http://digitalknowledge.babson.edu/fer/vol30/iss8/1

Stanger, A. M. J. (2004). Gender-comparative use of small business training and assistance: A literature review. *Education + Training, 46*(8/9), 464–473. doi:10.1108/00400910410569588.

Varis, M., & Littunen, H. (2010). Types of innovation, sources of information and performance in entrepreneurial SMEs. *European Journal of Innovation Management, 13*(2), 128–154. doi:10.1108/14601061011040221.

Wielicki, T., & Arendt, L. (2010). A knowledge-driven shift in perception of ICT implementation barriers: Comparative study of US and European SMEs. *Journal of Information Science, 36*(2), 162–174. doi:10.1177/0165551509354417.

KEY TERMS AND DEFINITIONS

Entrepreneurs: There has been disagreement for years regarding the definition of an entrepreneur. In this paper they are people who make their living by owning and/or operating a business.

ICTs: Information and communication technologies.

MSEs: Used in Njorge, et al. article to describe micro and small enterprises.

SMEs: Small to medium sized enterprises.

SMMEs: Used in Chiware article to describe the small, medium, and micro enterprise sector in Namibia.

Chapter 10

Barriers to Information Access for Specialized Scholars:
An Analysis of Information- Seeking Behavior of Social Scientists in Developing Countries

Lisa Block
Independent Researcher, USA

ABSTRACT

Developing countries must overcome the obstacles to information access so that they can join the global networks of the developed world and become part of the "information age." Studies on the information-seeking behavior and information needs of library users in developing countries are limited. This chapter examines the information-seeking behavior of social science faculty in developing nations in an attempt to explain the barriers to information access for these specialized scholars. Information users in developing countries face different challenges than users in developed nations so it is essential to understand the various obstacles that must be overcome by library and information users in developing nations. Comparisons are made to the information-seeking behaviors and information use of social science faculty in developed nations. Patterns of information-seeking behavior in social science faculty are examined and also compared to existing and proposed models of such behavior.

INTRODUCTION

Several studies exist on the information behavior of social scientists in developing countries. In addition to looking at the studies on social scientists the issues LIS educators and professionals encounter in developing countries and how these issues affect information access of specific users and barriers to information in general for these nations will be addressed. This will allow for recommended criteria for designing library services to meet the information needs of those working in social science programs in developing countries as well as developing appropriate collections for

DOI: 10.4018/978-1-4666-4353-6.ch010

those and other academic programs. Kumar, Singh, and Yadav (2011) describe a social scientist as a person who is involved in teaching and research activities in any of the following areas: Economics, Sociology, Anthropology, Political Science, Psychology, History, Public Administration, and Social Work. This will be the definition used in this chapter unless otherwise indicated in specific studies. By looking at a specialized user–social scientists–it will be possible to identify particular characteristics of this user population. As Wilson's (1996) research demonstrates, any research into information-seeking behavior must emphasize the characteristics of the information seeker as well as the nature of their environment.

A fair amount of research has been done on the information-seeking behavior and needs of social scientists in developed countries and not as much in developing countries. However, enough research exists in developing countries to analyze the information needs of this specialized user group and determine what these needs are and what are the barriers to information access for these users. By identifying the barriers to information access library administrators will be able to eliminate these barriers and design library systems to meet the needs of their particular users. The two are interrelated. Why does the information seeker prefer print sources? Could it be that there is a shortage of computers at the university where he/she works? The barrier to information access defines the information-seeking behavior. Also, it may be that the barriers to information access are the same for social scientists as they are for other user groups. The information seeking-behavior of social scientists may contain unique characteristics but it most likely shares similarities with other library users' information seeking behavior.

By analyzing various studies in several developing countries, a pattern will emerge that can assist LIS administrators and librarians in developing social science collections and in related disciplines as well and serve as design services for their specific user group and other users. The

pattern(s) emerging from analyzing the various studies will be compared to theories/models of information seeking in developing countries (to see how they fit); and to established models of information seeking in developed countries in order to illustrate the differences between library/ information users in developing and developed countries. The barriers to information access exposed in these studies will be analyzed as well and compared to each other to identify similarities. They will also be compared to information access barriers in developed countries to isolate any differences.

LITERATURE REVIEW

Marouf and Anwar (2010) conducted a research study to investigate the information-seeking behavior of social science faculty at Kuwait University. The researchers administered a questionnaire to 77 faculty members and received 54 returns. Faculty members were asked about their purposes for using various sources of information. Faculty members from the following social science disciplines were surveyed: Geography, Political Science, Psychology, Sociology, and Social Work.

Results showed that the participants depend greatly on books and journals for teaching. However, for their research needs they rely on a variety of information sources, the most notable being unpublished research, books, journals, and papers delivered at conferences (2010, p. 534). To stay current in their field they used newspapers and magazines, journals, and conference papers in that order. Results for information-searching skills showed that most faculties believe information searching is critical for faculty members and that these skills are necessary for all academic activities performed by faculty members. Each survey participant used the Internet and rated their use of electronic resources, Internet, and Web resources closer to "good." However, 35% said they were willing to attend appropriate training if it were offered. As for how affective respondents consider the university library service; a majority (61%) view the library service as either ineffective or somewhat effective (2010, p. 536).

Survey respondents were asked about problems they faced during the course of their research and stated that inadequate library staff was the chief problem. Researchers feel that the study respondents understand the significance of the resources they need and have shown the point that the library does not meet their needs to their satisfaction. Staffing issues seem to be the key problem in the library services, with both quality and quantity being viewed as major weak points in terms of staffing. Researchers also found that study participants depended most on formal sources as opposed to informal sources. This pattern is opposite of what was found for Argentine scholars in the study conducted by De Tiratel and Ramanos (2000). Marouf and Anwar say this difference may be explained in terms of a Kuwaiti context because many participants are expatriates on contracts who are "unable to develop strong informal contacts during their stay, have non-existent or low activity of scholarly associations at the national level, and limited funding for travel" (2010, p. 536).

Study respondents also had a preference for print sources. Researchers explain this by the fact that Arabic is the language used for instruction and communication materials at the university and most resources in Arabic are available in print format. A preference for national language materials was also seen in scholars for Argentina, Thai, and Turkish social scientists (2010, p. 536). Researchers noted that materials preferred in digital format, such as abstracts and indexes along with non-book sources mostly originate in the West.

Kumar, Singh, and Yadav (2011) studied the use of information sources by social scientists at Mizoram University in India. The purpose of the study was to determine the use of formal and informal sources of information; to determine the degree to which social scientists make use of various types of information sources; to identify the methods followed by them to keep in touch with the latest developments in their fields; and the availability of information sources and services in Mizoram University (Kumar et. al., 2011). Study participants were social scientists involved in teaching and research at Mizoram University. Researchers randomly distributed 100 questionnaires to participants and 70 were returned. The focus of the study was on formal sources used by the social scientists, informal sources used by social scientists, electronic databases, electronic vs. print resources, journals consulted daily by social scientists, tools and techniques used for current information, methods used by social scientists to obtain journal articles, electronic journals, adequacy of information sources and services, Internet resources, and online public access catalogues (OPACs).

Researchers discovered that the social scientists at Mizoram University depend on many types of formal and informal sources of information. Monographs and textbooks are considered extremely important by the social scientists as are print journals. A clear preference for print documents was evident and electronic databases were found to be less popular. Results of the study also showed that nearly half (42.9%) of the participants felt that information sources were unsatisfactory and did not meet their requirements; slightly less (40%) stated that the sources needed tremendous improvement. Over half (52.9%) of the respondents indicated that the information services need tremendous improvement (Kumar, et.al, 2011).

Bhatti et al. (2011) conducted a study to determine Internet usage of social scientists at the Bahauddin Zakariya University, Maltan, Pakistan. Researchers chose to study Internet usage because libraries in developing countries (including Pakistan) have experienced problems acquiring and providing the latest information sources. Increasing cost of reading materials along with space problems are the major obstacles but the Internet has eliminated these access problems. Related literature reveals that academic libraries around the world use the Internet. Bhatti feels that the Internet use pattern of the users should be studied along with library usage activities. The researchers note that the main library supports every course in the curriculum but most departments have their own departmental libraries located in their own buildings.

A survey questionnaire was given to 70 social scientists from the Faculty of Arts and Social Sciences. Disciplines included Economics, Education, History, Geography, Political Science, and International Relations, Mass communication, Sociology, Applied Psychology, Philosophy, and Pakistan Studies in Gender Studies. Social scientists participating in the study had various reasons for using the Internet. A majority of respondents reported that they use the Internet for teaching, research, doing M.Phil and Ph.D. work, guiding research students, and writing papers for a journal or conference. Databases were the source preferred most by social science faculty followed by e-journals, online abstracting and indexing services, e-dictionaries, and e-encyclopedias. More than half of the social science faculty stated that the Internet is beneficial and nearly half believe that they spend less time searching for needed information because of the Internet. Study participants were asked about problems encountered while using the Internet and a majority complained about a shortage of computers at the university library or in their departments. A lack of knowledge on how to find information on the Internet was also viewed as a major problem.

De Tiratel's (2000) study of the information-seeking behavior of Argentine humanities and social science scholars found no considerable differences between these scholars and the scholars in Anglo-Saxon countries. This was a longitudinal study of the behavior of the researchers at the Facultad de Filosoffa y Letras, Universidad de Buenos Aires (UBA) in nine disciplines in the humanities and social sciences. Social science fields included anthropology, education, geography, history, and library science. To collect data

for the study researchers compiled publications by the scholars (edited between 1990 and 1996) and the references were analyzed. Primary sources and secondary literature were the focus of the study. A total of 180 respondents were surveyed and 124 answered the questionnaires; 61 of the participants were social science researchers. A majority of participants stated that they used the library as a source of information. However, humanities scholars used the library more than social science scholars. As for type of information source, 40.5% of social scientists prefer periodicals, 31.4% prefer books, and 28.2% show equal preference. Respondents in the social sciences favored periodicals while humanities scholars, as Ron Blazek and Elizabeth Aversa confirm, prefer the monograph to the periodical article (De Tiratel, 2000). Although social scientists make less use of the library than humanists, over 70% of both groups stated that libraries make an important contribution to their work.

The most serious obstacles such as the scarcity of books and journals are derived from budgetary deficiencies. Other problems include material on loan to faculty for lengthy periods and the lag time between request and receipt of material originate in the library's organizational defects and can be corrected quite easily. The researchers of this study concluded that there is a common trait to humanities and social science researchers–it is how they access information; their preferences and needs, independently of the material available to them.

Meho and Haas (2001) studied the information seeking behavior of social science faculty studying the Kurds. A questionnaire, citation analysis, and follow-up inquiry were used to gather the data. This study differs from the traditional information-seeking behavior studies that mainly focus on information needs/behavior/use of scholars in the context of their department affiliation. Instead, this study looks at how social science faculty studying a stateless nation, the kerfs, look for government information and what factors influence their information-seeking behavior and use of that information. For this study the researchers considered scholars who worked in the following fields to be social science faculty: Anthropology, area studies, communication, economics, education, geography, history, political science, psychology, sociology, and women's studies.

Researchers thought this study would give them knowledge about the information-seeking behaviors and information use of the social science faculty that would help them meet their information needs. The knowledge gained could lead to the discovery of new information behaviors and user profiles that can be used to enhance existing information models or develop new ones. This is what the researchers had hoped. The study was also done to identify reasons for using and not using this information and the barriers to the use of this information. The questionnaire for this study was composed of 25 questions. Twenty-one participants were identified and all potential participants returned their questionnaire but one wasn't useable as one respondent wasn't a faculty member at any institution (Meho & Haas, 2001). The participants were social science faculty conducting research on the Kurds and affiliated with a western academic institution. None of the scholars were working in developing countries. A majority (94.4%) of the participants reported that they locate the government information they need for their research by finding citations to government information in other works.

Study participants were asked if they are reluctant to ask librarians for help in finding government information. Two-thirds of the social science faculty stated they felt no reluctance while one-third indicated they are sometimes or always reluctant to ask librarians for assistance. Respondents who expressed no unwillingness to seek help from librarians said they asked for help with finding material or information to answer ready-reference type questions; locating publications not held by their library; and assistance in using electronic devices. Social scientists who indicated they are sometimes or always reluctant

to ask librarians for help said the primary reasons were: they felt that their librarians did not appear to be well informed about government publications; they were reluctant to reveal a lack of understanding of library materials/systems; and that previous consultations with library staff had not lead to the desired information. Results show that faculty in this study employed similar methods for locating government information as other social science faculty. These methods include asking or receiving information from colleagues; finding relevant citations in other works; and consulting university library catalogs and printed electronic databases (2001, p. 19).

Al-Suqri (2011) studied the information-seeking behavior of social science scholars at Sultan Qaboos University (SQU) in Oman in order to better understand the barriers facing these scholars in developing countries. The purpose of the study was to discover the barriers or obstacles to information-seeking behavior of social science scholars at SQU. By identifying these barriers the researcher would be able to provide library managers at SQU with ways in which they can better support the social scientists from an administrative perspective. The study was conducted using e-mail and face-to-face interviews. Two research questions were asked; the first concerning the barriers affecting the information-seeking behavior and the second was related to the ways that the SQU main library could address those barriers (Al-Suqri, 2011). Al-Suqri discovered that social science scholars at SQU face two types of barriers–library-related barriers and non-library related barriers. Inadequate library resources, lack of adequate training and information technology limitations were reported as library-related barriers while non-library obstacles included a lack of adequate time, inadequate Internet connections, and language/cultural related barriers.

Dutta (2008) looked at the information needs and information-seeking behavior of the indigenous people of several developing countries. So while this study isn't focusing on social science faculty or university users of any type, understanding the barriers to information access for these users may help LIS professionals in developing countries. Dutta looked at two user groups–urban dwellers and rural dwellers. Similarities and contrasts within the two groups are established and discussed in her paper. A big difference exists between the urban educated and non-educated citizens when compared with those who live in rural areas of developing countries. Poverty, illiteracy, disease, and ignorance are among the factors that hold back the poor people in developing countries.

BARRIERS TO INFORMATION ACCESS

Shen (2007) asked sociology faculty about difficulties experienced while seeking supporting information. One study participant expressed concerns about technology upgrades, stating that, "technology is changing [so] fast that lots of computer files from the 1970s are no longer readable" (Shen, 2007, p.9). Technology problems are an example of the barriers to information access in developing countries but as Shen's study shows, technology can be a barrier in developed countries as well. What can be gained from understanding this is that adequate technology is crucial if library and information users are to have their information needs met. A related technology issue arose in the findings of Shen's study. Another participant commented that the online strategy is great for current information but for older information it's a problem—some research was being written before the online trend began so this older research cannot be found in an online keyword search (Shen, 2007). While a lack of technology or inadequate technology is often discussed as an obstacle to information access in developing countries it is clear that research carried out prior to the digital age is a barrier to information access anywhere if it unsearchable and therefore unfindable by those who seek it out.

Ugah (2007) discusses the obstacles to information access and use in developing countries. Obstacles are addressed by Ugah in these areas: lack of awareness; inaccessibility; information explosion; bibliographic obstacles; environment; poor infrastructure; declining budgets and rising costs; costs for users; staff attitude toward users; and crime. For this chapter the focus will be on inaccessibility, bibliographic obstacles, poor infrastructure, and staff attitude toward users.

Accessibility is critical to a library's success and, notes Ugah, it is not only that resources are available or bibliographically accessible. They must be physically accessible to the users who need them (Ugah, 2007). Ugah contends that failure in library use can typically be categorized as either the library's failure to acquire the material needed by the patron or the reader's failure which has two elements—bibliographic and physical. The reader's inability to find the item in the library catalog constitutes the bibliographic aspect and the physical aspect involves failure to find the materials housed in the library.

Several reasons for inaccessibility in libraries as an obstacle to information access were identified by Aguolu and Aguolu (2002). These are:

- Users do not know precisely what they want; if they do, they cannot articulate their needs accurately to the library staff.
- The bibliographic or intellectual access to the content of the library is inadequate owing to poor indexing system in the library catalog or of the library collection itself.
- The circulation policy of the library is inefficient, shelving methods are in advertent, and guides to the library arrangement are lacking.
- Unnecessary physical and administrative barriers are imposed upon the use of the library material by the library management.

Ugah adds that inability to locate material on the shelves that has been bibliographically indentified in the library catalog is a common frustration for library management. Types of bibliographic obstacles vary and may include incomplete or incorrect bibliographic description, lack of adequate bibliographic description, or lack of information retrieval devices. These devices may include indexes, abstracts, bibliographies, and catalogs. Ugah stated that a lack of information retrieval devices is more serious in developing countries like Nigeria, creating a serious obstacle to information access and use" (Ugah, 2007, p. 3). For libraries, infrastructure can be an obstacle if it is poor because it is the foundation of any information organization. Libraries need effective information so they must have reliable communication facilities such as computers, Internet, telephone, and fax, plus a proper supply of electricity (Ugah, 2007).

A huge potential obstacle is library staff and how they provide service. According to Ugah, the quality of library service depends on the quality of the staff. Ifidon (1995) notes that some library staff seem to lack a clear understanding of their service mission. Dipuolu (1992) observed that some librarians refuse to "soil their hands" and behave as administrators leaving the clerks and secretaries to take care of the library patrons. This behavior results in a failure of librarians to make proper use of their knowledge and skills and results in an obstacle to information access or at least has an effect on access (Ugah, 2007).

PROBLEMS ENCOUNTERED BY SOCIAL SCIENCE FACULTY IN DEVELOPING COUNTRIES

Meho and Haas note that previous studies with regard to government information in particular have identified seven major factors that influence social science faculties' seeking behavior and use of that information, including:

- The relevance of government information to one's research,

- The importance of government information for one's research,
- The researchers' familiarity or unfamiliarity with the arrangement of government publications in libraries,
- The amount of time expended in searching for such materials,
- The researchers' belief that governments publish little or nothing of value in their subject specialization,
- The researchers' unawareness of the existence of relevant information in government publications,
- The unavailability of such publications to the scholars[1].

Participating social scientists were also asked whether they are reluctant to ask librarians for help in locating the government information. Two-thirds of respondents expressed no reluctance while 1/3 said they are sometimes or always reluctant to ask librarians for help. Users who indicated no reluctance in asking librarians for assistance asked for the following:

- Finding materials or information to answer ready-reference types of questions,
- Locating publications not held by their libraries,
- Assistance in using electronic sources.

Respondents who said they are "sometimes" or "always" reluctant to ask librarians for help finding government publications said it was for the following reasons (Meho & Haas, 2001):

- Their librarians appear to not be well informed about government publications.
- They feel reluctant to reveal a lack of knowledge about library materials and systems.
- Consultation with library staff does not lead to desired information.

- They know how to locate the needed information.
- The librarians' lack knowledge about the Kurds.

Half of the participants who answered this question (8 out of 16) said the main barrier is the online catalog – meaning that the catalog does not list all of the government materials acquired by their libraries. Other barriers mentioned were:

- Libraries have small collections of government publications.
- Difficulty determining which publications their libraries have or do not have.
- The classification scheme of government materials is confusing.

Researchers note that not all libraries around the world follow the same classification system for their government publications collections.

In the studies discussed in this chapter, the barriers to information-seeking behavior and information use commonly mentioned by social science faculty in developing countries were: the library staff lacks adequate experience, a shortage of computers in university library and in departments, and the unavailability of Internet facilities in departments. Other obstacles included a lack of searching skills by faculty members and difficulty determining which publications their libraries have or do not have. Social science faculty also` complained of English language materials (not enough materials in Arabic or native language) and information sources in Arabic not up to date. Additional concerns among the studies' findings were a lack of awareness of the availability of materials—publicity of available resources is poor; a shortage of books, journals, and other print resources; and inadequate electronic resources.

Barriers to information use and information-seeking behavior mentioned that are non-library related included lack of time to search for information and e-journal subscriptions that are too expensive. Social scientists also commented that information sources were unsatisfactory and needed tremendous improvement. Information services were thought to be unsatisfactory as well and in need of serious improvement. Staffing issues seem to be the key problem in terms of library services as indicated by the social science faculty in the studies discussed here.

Marouf and Anwar (2010) discovered that the main barrier to information access was inadequate experience by library staff. Insufficient time available to conduct research was reported by faculty as the next biggest barrier to information access. These two obstacles were reported often in other similar studies of social science faculty. Table 1 lists all barriers reported in Marouf and Anwar's study.

Bhatti asked study participants about any difficulties they experienced while using the Internet.

Social scientists in Bhatti's (2011) study also indicated that lack of time was an obstacle, though only 14% of participants reported this as compared to over 60% in Marouf and Anwar's study. In Bhatti's study, respondents reported that a lack of knowledge about Internet information-retrieving techniques (38%) was a serious problem along with a shortage of computers in the university library, which was reported as the main issue (57%). While insufficient time to conduct research on the part of the faculty members is an issue outside of the control of the university library other obstacles such as not enough computers in the library and most certainly library staff who are inadequately trained can be corrected by the library and/or the university. These types of barriers seem to be widespread and often unique to libraries and the experiences of faculty in developing countries.

Other obstacles mentioned in Bhatti's study include e-journal subscriptions are expensive (34%); a shortage of the latest e-book (28%), English language material (27%), slow speed (24%), lack of awareness of the availability of material (21%), unavailability of Internet facility in the departments (20%), and lack of time (overworked) (14%) (Bhatti, 2011).

Al-Suqri (2011) found that barriers to information-seeking behavior by social science scholars at Sultan Qaboos University in Oman could be grouped into two categories–library-related and non-library related. Using these two categories when evaluating obstacles to information seeking in other studies may be useful. Identifying which obstacles to information-seeking are considered library-related barriers will allow library administrators to make any needed improvements that will improve the research process of scholars at their universities. Improvements may also increase library usage by all scholars at the affected universities. Library educators who are trying to improve their LIS curricula and help future LIS professionals could learn from the results of these studies and in particular, from understanding what information-seeking barriers are library related.

BARRIERS TO INFORMATION ACCESS IN LIS EDUCATION

Catherine Johnson (2007) discusses problems with LIS education in developing countries and reviews previous articles submitted to the "International Library Review" in her article, *Library and Information Science Education in Developing Countries*. She asks if the barriers to information access (for both specialized scholars and library users) in developing countries could have their roots in LIS education. Developers of LIS curricula and LIS educators should have a look at Johnson's article to see if this could be where the information access and library user need problems began. This may also be where some solutions lay.

In 2002 Johnson conducted a study in Mongolia for her Ph.D. dissertation. There, she met librarians who wished to improve their skills but found few opportunities to do so. Mongolia, a poor country lacking in resources and their government had just enough funds to keep the libraries open. Making matters worse was that Mongolia's government did not appreciate the value of investing education resources to train people to work in a profession which seemed unnecessary during the tough economic conditions the country faced after the collapse of the Soviet Union. While some students in Mongolia were able to attend short courses and workshops mostly sponsored by international organizations, no one took a second look at the LIS education system to see what changes or improvements could be made. Johnson arranged a panel to find out if other developing countries were experiencing the same

Table 1. Barriers to information access for social scientists (Marouf & Anwar, 2010)

Barrier to Information Access	Percentage
Library staff do not have adequate experience	64.2%
Insufficient time available to me to search information	60.4%
Information resources in Arabic are not up to date	52.8%
Accessing international information resources is difficult	50.9%
Lack of adequate publicity of available resources	49.1%
Inadequacy of electronic information resources	43.4%
I lack information searching skills	41.5%
Inadequacy of print information resources at the library that I need	41.5%
Too much information to deal with	26.4%

problems. She discovered that similar problems existed in other developing countries too.

Johnson also noted that the first issue of the International Library Review (ILR) in 1969 focused little on developing countries. Throughout the 1970s there were 26 articles published that focused on LIS education – five focused on Africa, five on the Middle East, two on Soviet Republics, two on India, and one each on South America and Southeast Asia (specifically Thailand), and 10 on general education issues. LIS education in Middle Eastern countries was popular in the 1980s and 1990s with eight articles focusing on these countries being published during that period (2007, p.66). Most of these articles focused on the progress made in LIS education. Johnson states that, "the most common themes addressed by the authors, at least until the 1990s, were the influence of expatriates in the development of LIS programs, the relevance of the curricula, which were often based on Western programs, and the low status of the profession and libraries which resulted in low pay for librarians and inadequate financial support of libraries by the government" (2007, p.66). Also noteworthy is Keresztesi's (1982) article discussing UNESCO's work in developing library schools was chiefly concerned with the heavy Western influence on the LIS curriculum. Other authors agreed explaining that LIS courses/programs in developing countries should not be duplicates of the curricula in developed or Western countries.

PATTERNS OF INFORMATION-SEEKING BEHAVIOR OF SOCIAL SCIENTISTS IN DEVELOPING COUNTRIES

Social science faculty in developing countries prefers print sources over other sources; monographs and textbooks are particularly important as are print journals. In the studies reviewed in this chapter it is clear that social scientists prefer print documents and electronic databases are less popular. Many social scientists prefer Arabic language resources or sources in their native language over English language sources. Print sources that the faculty most relied on include unpublished research, books, journals, and papers delivered at conferences. Newspapers and magazines along with conference papers were mentioned by faculty as popular choices for staying current in their field. For social scientists that prefer databases they especially like e-journals, online abstracting and indexing services, e-dictionaries, and e-encyclopedias. Using the Internet is popular with many of the social science study participants and in one study nearly half indicated that they believe they spend less time searching for information because of the Internet.

Bhatti's findings show that the Internet was used by social science faculty for reasons including:

Out of the 70 respondents the most common reason given for using the Internet is teaching; other uses are research, doing M.Phil and PhD work, guiding research students, and using it for writing a research paper for a journal or conference. Recreational use, personal purposes, seek-

Table 2. Reasons social scientists use the Internet

Reason for Using the Internet	Percentage
Teaching	48%
M.Phil and Ph.D. work	34%
Research	31%
Guiding research students	25%
Other reasons (non-work related)	
Online chatting	50%
Recreational use	35%
Seeking scholarship for higher studies	34%
Personal purposes	28%
Seeking a job online	2.85%

ing scholarships for higher studies, searching for a job online, and online chatting were also given as reasons for using the Internet. *See Table 2 for the full list of reasons with percentages.*

Sources most preferred by the social science faculty were databases (35%). Other preferred sources include e-journals (34%), online abstracting and indexing services (28%), e-dictionaries (25%), and e-encyclopedias (21%). A majority of the social scientists felt that the Internet is beneficial. Nearly half (48%) think they have to spend less time in searching for their required information because of the Internet.

INFORMATION-SEEKING BEHAVIOR IN DEVELOPING COUNTRIES VERSES DEVELOPED COUNTRIES

Wang (2010) studied the information needs of social scientists in Taiwan and their use of scholarly journals to support scholarly communication and information needs. The study attempted to answer the following research questions:

- What are the main work tasks for social science scientists in Taiwan?
- What kinds of information resources are most used to carry out their tasks?
- How important are scholarly journals to social scientists?
- How do they identify and locate scholarly journals?
- What are their means of access to journals?
- Do scholars prefer print or electronic journals?
- What are the scholarly journal reading patterns of social scientists?
- What are the article deep reading behaviors? What taxonomy emerges for article deep reading behaviors based on reading motivation, process and consequences of reading?

- Do social scientists prefer using electronic journals or using print journals? Do they prefer using Chinese language journals or using English language journals in Taiwan?
- Are social scientists satisfied with the scholarly journal services which libraries provide to meet their information needs?
- Are there scholarly journal seeking, use and reading differences between social scientists and scientists in Taiwan and in United States?

A questionnaire survey and in-depth face-to-face interviews were the two methods used in this study. There were 112 study participants from the following schools/departments: college of social sciences, college of law, and the college of education. In order to understand how the social science faculty read scholarly journals the researchers included article reading patterns in the questionnaire survey. Aspects of reading in the survey included amount of readings, time spent reading, age of articles read, and the value of articles read by social science faculty. Principle purposes of article reading for the faculty included: research (98.2%), teaching (75.5%), writing reports, articles, etc. (66.4%), current awareness (60.9%), lectures (21.8%), professional development (17.3%), personal interest (16.4%), services (10.0%), and administration (4.5%) (2010, p. 277). This study also examined the sources of electronic journals used by social science faculty in Taiwan. Results showed that the following sources for electronic journals were used: library collection (72.7%), free Web journals (21.8%), personal subscriptions (11.8%), and open access journals (4.5%) (2010, p. 280). Wang adds that monograph use was not as important here and this contradicts the study results reported by Line and Brittain (1971).

Shen's (2007) study of sociology faculty at the University of Wisconsin–Madison focused on how social scientists find and use information during the course of their research. Shen gathered data on the information-seeking behavior of social scientists in order to provide empirical evidence on this behavior during scientific research. Three main research questions were addressed: how do social scientists make use of different information sources and channels to satisfy their information needs; what strategies do they apply when seeking information for academic research; and what difficulties are encountered in searching for supporting information? (Shen, 2007). The researcher interviewed the faculty from the department of sociology in their campus offices and all interviews were tape-recorded. Study participants were asked about their strategies for information seeking and strategies used included extracting abstracts, tracking citations, restricting the search to a limited set of sources or types of sources, constantly filtering and interpreting the search results by referring to the summary description of Websites.

Shen also asked the sociology faculty about any difficulties they experienced while seeking information. Common responses included (Shen, 2007):

- Information is scattered in different places and with different qualities (described by patrons as "how tricky computerized search is").
- There is too much information on the Internet to filter, and current search techniques and ranking tools are not intelligent enough to capture relevant information of interest.
- No sources of information or mechanisms assist in the identification of people with similar research interests.
- Technology upgrades and system integration arouse another concern—one participant explained that technology had changed so fast that many computer files from the 1970s were no longer readable.
- There are no digital sources of information for certain historical documents and no retrievable databases for book chapters.

SOLUTIONS AND RECOMMENDATIONS

Several studies found that an inadequate library staff is a main barrier to information access in developing countries. LIS programs and curricula are most likely to blame for these inadequacies in staffing. Analyzing the various studies on barriers to information access may show specifically what is lacking in the librarians abilities but more studies are needed.

Based on Bhatti's findings, the university and the library may need to improve the IT infrastructure so they can bring its services and resources up to the level of those of libraries in developed countries. Other libraries and information centers in developing nations may want to further examine Bhatti's study and see if IT improvements will improve information access for their users.

Studies can often be generalized to other users in developing countries and sometimes form developed countries to the developing nations. Study findings can also be generalized to other user groups such as humanists to social scientists and social scientists other disciplines like medicine. It may be the system that is important to understand more than the specific type of user (i.e., social scientists). However, Dervin and Nilan concluded that "the answers lie not in the system but rather in the understanding that each user's information need is unique" (De Teritel, 2000, p. 352).

Al-Suqri (2011) developed an integrated model of social science information-seeking behavior based on a merging of existing models and tested it against present-day information-seeking of social science scholars at Sultan Qaboos University in Oman. The researcher found that "the information-seeking practices of the study sample could be readily matched to the stages of the model" and that generally, "information-seeking behavior follows universally applicable stages" (Al-Suqri, 2011, p. 1) without regard to changes in the information environment (Al-Suqri, 2011). So this model may be applied to similar future studies in developing countries. Similarly, patterns of information-seeking behavior and barriers to information-seeking could be compared among similar studies in developing countries with the results being compared to future studies and used to improve information-seeking techniques among scholars in these developing countries.

FUTURE RESEARCH DIRECTIONS

A need for studies on information-seeking behaviors of various types of users in developing countries exists. Several studies have been conducted on the information use of and information-seeking behavior of social science faculty in developing countries and while these studies can sometimes be applied to users in other disciplines and even be applied to users more generally, to help LIS professionals meet the needs of all users in developing nations researchers need to examine the information use and behavior of other specific user groups. Library administrators need to design LIS programs and curricula that will help librarians to acquire the skills they need in order to help information users. To do this library administrators need to understand the needs of various users and also the obstacles to information seeking that exist in universities and in their countries as a whole. Johnson (2007) makes the point that many LIS curricula are based on western designs and programs but developing countries need their own LIS curricula designed for them.

As for studying the information behavior and use of social scientists, more studies need to be done in Middle Eastern countries and in any other regions where the number of studies is lacking.

Al-Suqri's (2011) study of social science scholars at SQE in Oman was conducted in order to learn more about this type of scholar is developing countries and to provide information to that university's library that could help the library better serve the scholars. More studies like this need to be done at other universities in developing

nations. If this happens there will be more data on the information-seeking techniques of specialized scholars in the developing world along with information about the obstacles to their information-seeking behavior. It will help researchers in other developing countries and library administrators in these countries' universities to improve their research experiences and achieve more effective research results because it will be specific to the developing world.

CONCLUSION

This is the information age, and while global networks exist, they are found mostly in developed countries. Problems with information accessibility are rising as the volume of information and the world population increases (Aguolu, 1997 p. 25). Developing countries are lacking in information generation and dissemination due to issues such as a lack of awareness of the need for information by the people of these countries and even when information is available for free at libraries and information centers it is not used. Aguolu explains that this is because "the availability of information does not necessarily mean its accessibility" (Aguolu, 1997, p. 26). So while the amount of information increases the problems with access to information are also growing in developing countries.

As Aguolu mentions, other barriers to information accessibility were identified by Doob, Schramm, and Turner and include illiteracy, geographical distance between nations, poverty and underdevelopment (1997, p. 26). It seems that developing countries may continue as just that if they cannot overcome the barriers to information access and join the global information networks of the developed world.

Perhaps a way to overcome these obstacles is by identifying the specific barriers, understanding why they exist, and finding solutions to them. This could be done by focusing on LIS educators and what they are teaching their students—our future information professionals. It can also be achieved by identifying a pattern of information-seeking behavior among a particular user in developing countries and using that to help LIS professionals and educators.

REFERENCES

Aguolu, I. (1997). Accessibility of information: A myth for developing countries? *New Library World*, 25–29.

Al-Suqri, M. N. (2011). Information-seeking behavior of social science scholars in developing countries: A proposed model. *The International Information & Library Review, 43*(1), 1–14.

Al-Suqri, M. N., & Lillard, L. L. (2011). Barriers to Effective Informatoin Seeking of Social Scientists in Developing Countries: The Case of Sultan Qaboos University in Oman. *International Research: Journal of Library & Information Science, 1*(2), 86–98.

Bhatti, R. (2011). Internet Use by Social Scientists at the Bahauddin Zakariya University, Multan, Pakistan: A Survey. Library Philosophy and Practice, 1-12.

De Tiratel, S. R. (2000). Accessing Information Use by Humanists and Social Scientists: A Study at the Universidad de Buenos Aires, Argentina. *Journal of Academic Librarianship, 26*(5), 346–355.

Dutta, R. (2009). Information needs and information-seeking behavior in developing countries: A review of the research. *The International Information & Library Review, 41*(1), 44–51.

Johnson, C. A. (2007). Library and information science education in developing countries. *The International Information & Library Review, 39*(2), 64–71.

Kumar, A., & Singh, S. A. (2011). An Investigation of Use of Information Sources by Social Scientists. *Library Philosophy and Practice*, 1-10.

Marouf, L., & Anwar, M. A. (2010). Information-seeking behavior of the social sciences faculty at Kuwait University. *Library Review, 59*(7), 532–547.

Meho, L. I., & Haas, S. W. (2001). Information-seeking behavior and use of social science faculty studying stateless nations: A case study. *Library & Information Science Research, 23*, 5–25.

Shen, Y. (2007). Information Seeking in Academic Research: A Study of the Sociology Faculty at the University of Wisconsin-Madison. *Information Technology and Libraries*, 4-13.

Ugah, A. D. (2007). Obstacles to Information Access and Use in Developing Countries. *Library Philosophy and Practice*, 1-5.

Wang, M.-L. (2010). Scholarly journal use and reading behavior of social scientists in Taiwan. *The International Information & Library Review, 42*(4), 269–281.

ADDITIONAL READING

Case, D. O. (2006). *Looking for Information: A Survey of Research on Information Seeking, Needs, and Behavior*. Bingley, UK: Emerald Group Publishing.

Fatima, N., & Ahmed, N. (2008). Information seeking behavior of the students at Ajmal Khan Tibbiya College, Aligarh Muslim University: A survey. *Annals of Library and Information Studies, 55*, 141–144.

Folster, M. (1995). Information Seeking Patterns: Social Sciences. *The Reference Librarian, 49-50*, 83–93.

Johnson, C. A. (2007). Social Capital and the Search for Information: Examining the role of social capital in information seeking behavior in Mongolia. *Journal of the American Society for Information Science and Technology*, *58*(6), 883–894.

Majid, S., & Kassim, G. M. (2000). Information-Seeking Behavior of International Islamic University Malaysia Law Faculty Members. *Malaysian Journal of Library & Information Science*, *5*(2), 1–17.

Ramnah, A. T., & Hashim, L. (2011). Information Needs and Information Seeking Behaviors of Social Science Graduate Students in Malaysian Public Universities. *International Journal of Business and Social Science*, *4*(4), 2–5.

Sethi, A. (1990). *Information seeking behavior of social scientists: An Indian conspectus*. New Dehli, India: Hindustan Publishing Corporation.

Shokeen, A. (2002). Information seeking behavior of social scientists of Haryana Universities. *Library Herald*, 29-33.

Wickramanayake, L. (1994). Information-seeking behavior of management and commerce faculty in Sri Lankan universities: An evaluation. *Library Review*, *59*(8), 624–636.

KEY TERMS AND DEFINITIONS

Developing Countries: Poor, non-industrialized countries with low standards of living that seek to develop their resources through industrialization.

Information Access: The ability, right, or permission to obtain or use information.

Information-Access Barriers: Anything that restrains or obstructs access to information.

Information Needs: An individual or group's desire to find and obtain information to satisfy particular requirements or for specific purposes.

Information-Retrieving Techniques: The manner and ability with which someone searches for information.

Information-Seeking Behavior: The manner in which people search for and use information.

Social Scientists: People who study human society and individual relationships in and in relation to society.

ENDNOTES

[1] This reason is primarily found in studies conducted outside the U.S. (Meho & Haas, 2001).

Chapter 11

Where Do Mongolian Scholars Go?

The Information Seeking Behavior within Mongolian Scholarly Communities

Thomas Scheiding
Cardinal Stritch University, USA

Borchuluun Yadamsuren
University of Missouri, USA

Gantulga Lkhagva
Mongolian Libraries Consortium, Mongolia

ABSTRACT

In developing countries, one of the many challenges faced by researchers is increased pressure to conduct research, but inadequate resources provided to do their work. Perhaps nowhere is the inadequacy of research resources more apparent than in the area of access to scholarly research. In this chapter, using survey data, usage statistics, and interviews of researchers, librarians, and research administrators, we describe the information seeking behavior of scholars in Mongolia and how this behavior intersects with the resources made available by research administrators and librarians. Much of the existing research on scholarly communication in developing countries has focused on whether access to scholars should be donated or provided free of charge without restriction. In Mongolia, the issue isn't so much whether access to scholarly communication should be donated or not, but rather whether the scholarly communication system meets researcher needs, is adapted to constraints within the country, and reduces communication dependency. What we find is that the scholarly communication system in Mongolia fails to completely meet researcher needs and makes the country dependent on the scholarly communication products provided by outsiders.

DOI: 10.4018/978-1-4666-4353-6.ch011

INTRODUCTION

Mongolia, prior to the 1990s, was a country closely aligned with the Soviet Union both politically and economically. During this time period all adults were guaranteed a job that was assigned to them by central economic planners. The academic infrastructure within the country was designed to train workers according to the needs of the economy and mimicked the infrastructure that existed in the Soviet Union. Researchers within this academic infrastructure in Mongolia were required to be fluent in Russian, published in research journals internal to Russia and Mongolia, and, like other workers, had their research activities controlled by central planners. The fall of the Soviet Union in 1990 translated into significant economic and political change in Mongolia. These changes, in turn, altered Mongolia's academic infrastructure.

Although the size of the Mongolian economy was already small when it was aligned with the Soviet Union, the economy became even smaller between 1990 and 1993 as the economy transitioned away from Soviet support and influence. The economic challenge since 1993 has been that the increase in the size of the economy has not been accompanied by an increase in employment levels or a diversification of the economy away from agriculture and natural resource extraction. This need to grow and diversify the economy drives the restructuring of the higher education system. In this chapter we focus our attention on how researchers, in this environment, engage with scholarly literature and how this engagement is determined. This engagement process plays a critical role in determining the effectiveness and quality of the research produced. The more effective and the higher the quality of the research, the more likely the research will contribute to economic growth and independence. With an extension of the research methodology in Yadamsuren and Raber (2007), we survey researchers affiliated

with the Mongolian Academy of Sciences, collect usage statistics, and interview researchers, librarians, and research administrators and find that the communication environment in Mongolia is slow to change, is not adapted to the needs of scholars, and is unable to meet the goals of the research patron. In Mongolia, as in other countries, the information seeking behavior of scholars is determined in a complex fashion that cannot be simplified to communication speed or cost. This analysis of the Mongolian scholarly publishing environment suggests that in order to promote economic development and independence that researchers need a scholarly communication process that reflects constraints within the country and fosters the development of a local communication infrastructure.

THE TALE OF THREE TRANSITIONS

Mongolia's economy and culture are both undergoing a significant transition from a socialist planned economy to one more responsive to market forces. This transition, in turn, has had the consequence of increasing higher education enrollment and encouraging researchers to do more research and publish their findings. Beyond the changes specific to Mongolia, the way in which research results are published has also been changing in recent decades with researchers around the world being encouraged to communicate via an electronic medium. In this section, we outline the connections between the changes in the economy, in the research infrastructure, and in the scholarly communication process.

With respect to the economy, Mongolia began its transition from a centrally planned to a market based economy in 1990. The early 1990s represented a particularly turbulent time in the transition with triple digit inflation, high unemployment, and shortages in goods and services as economic output fell by a third. Although the prospects for economic growth would not seem immediately apparent for a developing country that was for so long under the tutelage of the Soviet Union, the Mongolian economy more recently has been one of the fastest growing in the world. And it is the fact that much of the economic growth in the country comes from natural resource extraction that has raised concerns. Given the eventuality of the natural resource being exhausted and economic growth falling, economic authorities in Mongolia have focused on creating the conditions for sustainable growth through the establishment of a knowledge-based economy. Such an economy requires an expanded and well-funded university system and research infrastructure.

With respect to the transition in the research infrastructure, efforts over the past 15 years have been made to privatize the research process by merging and transferring the research and development units within individual government ministries to universities (which themselves have been increasingly privatized) and newly established research corporations. This reorganization of the research and development system towards privatization was designed to make the system self-financing. Businesses, however, have been reluctant to invest in research. With a lack of industrial interest in research and development infrastructure in the country, the research activities conducted within the country remain oriented to encouraging research that satisfies government priorities. Despite this privatization, the expenditures made by the government for research and development still largely reflects a socialist economy with the majority of expenditures devoted to salaries and maintenance costs rather than investments in equipment or training. Although by law scientific research is designated to receive 1.5% of the country's annual output, only 0.3% of the country's annual output has been devoted to research and development activities over the past decade. Since 2007 there has been a renewed intent to increase research and development spend-

ing to the legally designated amount. The type of research being encouraged is that which promotes the development of a well-diversified and thoroughly privatized economy. The government has defined the research priorities as improvements in information technology, promoting traditional technology in agriculture, biotechnology, chemical technology, and metallurgical and machinery technology. Besides encouraging researchers to conduct research in specific areas, the government is also encouraging researchers to increase their engagement with the scholarly communication process.

Over the past two decades the distribution of scholarly literature worldwide has been transformed in nearly every discipline from a paper-based to an electronic medium. Throughout the 1980s and 1990s, scholarly communities in developed countries began to access the scholarly literature through publisher-provided electronic databases of scholarship. Scholars in developing countries, on the other hand, continued to receive their limited access to the scholarship through print journals and indexes. Their access changed somewhat in the latter 1990s, with the extension of Internet access to developing countries, with some access to the scholarly literature occurring through author-posted manuscripts to websites and databases and some access occurring via free of charge electronic-only journals. At the close of the 20th century, however, there remained significant hurdles to scholars in developing countries receiving access to publisher-provided electronic journals and databases. The two largest challenges are the cost to receive access and the lack of technical skills among researchers.

Access to electronic scholarly communication initiatives in Mongolia is achieved primarily through donated access and through open access. Donated access is defined as free or low-cost access to journals and databases that is made available by publishers to researchers in developing countries through charitable programs or targeted funding from government and philanthropic organizations.

Open access is defined as free access to research by scholars in both developing and developed countries either as individual manuscripts in institutional repositories or articles in electronic journals. Some of the donated access to electronic scholarly communication initiatives in Mongolia is achieved through AGORA (Access to Global Online Research in Agriculture), eIFL (Electronic Information for Libraries), OARE (Online Access to Research in the Environment), and HINARI (Access to Health Research). AGORA, OARE, and HINARI are funded by various programs within the United Nations and contain articles from 11,200 journal titles that are available through free access channels as well as articles from traditional journals. Other donated access scholarly communication initiatives include IN-ASP (International Network for the Availability of Scientific Publications) and eIFL (Electronic Information for Libraries) where consortia of institutions within the developing country are formed and bundles of journal titles are licensed to them. Open access electronic scholarly communication initiatives include PubMed Central, Directory of Open Access Journals, Directory of Open Access Repositories, Free Medical Journals Program, and arXiv and rely on financing from the host institution to make access available to all free of charge.

Bringing this all together, in Mongolia, what we find is a developing country that is not only devoting more resources to research, but also a place where the patrons to research have an interest in research that yields economic benefits and where researchers are incentivized to publish more and in specific locations. In the next section we document the determination of the information seeking behavior of researchers and its alignment and resistance to the priorities of research administrators and library professionals. We structure our discussion with a belief that there is plurality in scholarly communication practices across disciplines and cultures. The scholarly communication choices made are determined by technology choices, the needs of scholars and of patrons, and the skills and constraints of information professionals. We will see that it is not simply a matter of scholarly communities across the disciplinary landscape being collectively aligned with the fastest and cheapest form of scholarly communication. Rather, scholarly communities have their communication needs determined by custom, influenced by the resources they have at their disposal, and the incentives and mandates of patrons and librarians.

INFORMATION SEEKING BEHAVIOR OF SCHOLARS IN MONGOLIA

What are the determinants of the kinds of research that Mongolian scholars want and how they obtain it? How is a scholarly communication choice influenced by the motivations of the research administrator and librarians? Finally, to what extent does technology and outsiders influence the communication choices made by researchers, administrators, and librarians? Documenting the needs and behavior of researchers, their administrators, and librarians is important for the purposes of assessing the effectiveness and sustainability of the scholarly communication process in Mongolia in the coming years ahead.

Before outlining the specifics of Mongolian scholarly information needs, it is helpful to have a basis of comparison. In Rowland and Nichols (2006) over 5,500 scholars worldwide were surveyed regarding their scholarly information needs. The generalization among scholars as authors worldwide was that prestige of the journal was of the utmost importance with the nature of the readership and the speed of publication of secondary importance. Scholars reported that whether or not they could retain their copyright or post materials to an institutional repository had little impact on their decision of where to publish their research findings. Scholars perceived the quality of the publication as coming from the peer review process. Scholars did report some dissatisfaction with the peer review process with the perception that the process stifled innovations and ignored challenges to the discipline's boundaries. Scholars in the survey reported as problematic the high price to access the literature and were critical of the fact that too much specialized research is published. Scholars in the survey also reported a greater awareness of open access initiatives and that these initiatives enhanced access to the scholarly literature.

In developing countries the description of the scholarly literature is often clouded by the proselytization of open access scholarly communication initiatives. In research that covers China, India, Malaysia, and countries within Africa, authors describe the potential that open access scholarship presents for economic growth and the creation of autonomous research capacity. With country-specific research suggesting heavily supplementing publisher databases with open access initiatives, the overriding conclusion has been that of convergence in the form that scholarly communication takes in developing countries. These studies over-emphasize the cost benefits to open access scholarship and universalize the scholarly communication practices of researchers. In these studies there are often a lack of conversations with researchers, librarians, and patrons and instead a lengthy discussion of the initiatives and their benefits as perceived by the author.

In Mongolia there is very little research that has been published on the scholarly communication process. First, Mongolian scholars face resource constraints that, when combined with the fact that a sizable number lack English-language and technical skills, limits their international competitiveness. The scholarly literature, traditionally delivered to the researcher via the library in a print format, has become less accessible due to the fact that library professionals lack the training and resources needed to meet researcher needs. Yadamsuren and Raber (2007) surveyed and interviewed researchers to learn how the scholarly

literature is accessed, the format researchers prefer to access the literature, the language they prefer to communicate in, and the barriers they encounter in accessing the literature. Using a survey modified from that used by Francis (2005), Lleperuma (2002) and Tiratel (2000), Yadamsuren and Raber collected survey data from 134 out of the 700 researchers affiliated with the government-financed Mongolian Academy of Sciences responded (with 60% being from the natural and physical sciences and 40% from the humanities and social sciences). More than half of the respondents were less than 40 years old and approximately 60% had a masters or bachelors degree.

Respondents to the survey reported active contributions to the literature with 37% publishing up to 5 articles, 26% up to 10 articles, 19% up to 15 articles, and 18% more than 16 articles. The prestige of the journal was the most important factor followed by the journal's audience and the speed of publication. As readers, the average scholar read the literature for 7 hours a week. The majority of respondents self-evaluated their technical skills as good, over 80% reported fluency in English, over 80% reported using the Internet for research purposes, and 65% reported using the Internet daily. Respondents reported a lack of reliance on the library with nearly half using the library only 2-3 times a month. Most researchers, 72%, used the library at their own research institution with the majority reporting neither satisfaction nor dissatisfaction with library services.

Respondents to the survey reported that they most relied on journals, then textbooks, and finally monographs. Across disciplines, there was no statistically significant difference in their use. With focus on the journal, most researchers relied on getting a copy of an article from a colleague (55%) or from a library (51%). Among the least relied upon methods of obtaining journal articles are using personal subscriptions to an electronic copy of the article (17%) and using the library's electronic copy of the article (21%). There was a statistically significant difference across disciplines with respect to how journal articles were obtained with natural scientists relying on personal subscriptions to the print journal and social scientists overwhelmingly relying on a library's subscription. Overall, there was a slightly stronger preference for print (61%) over electronic (52%). Finally, the majority of respondents revealed that they had never used online databases with less than 10% reporting greater than five uses over a six-month time period.

Although these results are limited to researchers affiliated with the Mongolian Academy of Sciences, they likely reveal the upper-bound estimates of use of the scholarly communication process given the higher research intensity of these individuals. With this survey having been conducted in 2006, the results likely underestimate current use of electronic resources. As such, we complement the survey findings in Yadamsuren and Raber (2007) with usage statistics in order to understand usage from a broader perspective. When we examine one of the first donor-provided databases available to scholars in Mongolia, eIFL access to EBSCO in 2001 and 2002, we see growing usage of the resource. The number of full-text articles decreased from 11,196 articles in 2001 to 5,334 full-text articles in 2002. This decrease indicates an initial hoarding of articles because the number of logins increased from 1,989 in 2001 to 4,403 in 2002 and the number of searchers increased from 8,701 in 2001 to 20,349 in 2002. eIFL set the price of providing access to EBSCO at $20,000 (a price paid for during the trial period

by the Mongolian Foundation for Open Society). With that price, access to a full-text article was estimated at $1.79 in 2001 and $3.75 in 2002. Compared to the other 41 countries participating in the eIFL trial, Mongolia experienced higher access costs than the average country ($0.86 per abstract in 2001 for Mongolia vs. $0.51 average in 2001 and $6.91 per abstract in 2001 for Mongolia vs. $1.84 average). What we can conclude in Mongolia is a high level of initial excitement among a core set of researchers and then growing use of the resource after its establishment.

Access to electronic scholarly communication initiatives in 2002-2003 was no longer donated and academic librarians were either unable or unwilling to pay for access. In 2004, access to electronic scholarly communication initiatives was resumed with access again donated. Through eIFL, access was granted to a number of databases (with EBSCO being a notable exception). The number of licenses to eIFL within the country has steadily increased from 3 in 2004, to 5 in 2005, to 6 in 2007. Despite access to a greater number of databases across more institutions, the number of full-text articles accessed was generally quite low (although increased over time) (see Table 1).

The usage for each database differs significantly by institution. For BioOne, the majority of accesses made were recorded at the National University of Mongolia. By contrast, for the articles provided by Oxford University Press, the Mongolian Academy of Sciences had the largest number of accesses. The usage statistics from

Table 1. Usage of electronic scholarly communication databases in Mongolia, 2004-2007

	BioOne	Cambridge University Press	Institute of Physics	Oxford English Dictionary	Oxford Reference Online	Oxford University Press
2004	7	40	39	--	--	--
2005	84	304	511	116	237	--
2006	142	235	1238	38	206	--
2007	470	403	947	318	76	129

2004 to 2007 reveal so little usage that it would be difficult to justify devoting scarce financial resources to obtain it. If access was no longer donated, it is unlikely librarians would provide their own funding to ensure continued access.

When we consider usage of databases more recently we see extensive use of the JSTOR database from 2007-2009 among researchers in the humanities and the social sciences. During this time period the database was available exclusively at the American Center for Mongolian Studies (ACMS). The ACMS aims to foster academic partnerships in all fields of study related to Mongolia by offering academic resources, student and research support. In 2007 there were 1,548 articles (2,858 pages) accessed, 1,810 articles (1940 pages) accessed in 2008, and 975 articles (3763 pages) accessed in the first half of 2009. The heaviest usage is in the disciplines of Business (11.1% of total usage), Political Science (10.6% of total usage), Math (10.3% of total usage), and Biology (9.5% of total usage). In all four of these disciplines, usage at the ACMS was nearly twice as much as at the average "very small" JSTOR institution.

Finally, we investigate usage at two specialized institutions of higher education in Mongolia–the Institute of Finance and Economics (IFE) and the Academy of Management (AOM). What is notable at these two institutions is that there is some willingness on the part of librarians to devote some resources to receive access. At the IFE, a private institution, EBSCO databases such as Academic Search Premier and Business Source Premier are extensively used. For Academic Search Premier, there were 472 searches from January to July of 2010 across 83 sessions with 259 text downloads. For Business Source Premier there were 1180 searches from January to July 2010 across 315 sessions with 658 text downloads. The most commonly accessed titles were *Harvard Business Review* (representing 130 of the 658 text downloads for Business Source Premier). The second most accessed title was *Library Journal* (representing 69 of the 259 text

downloads for Academic Search Premier). The usage patterns at the AOM, a public institution, reveal that there were 911 searches across 229 sessions with 178 text downloads. For the Business Source Elite database there were 559 searches from January to July 2010 across 131 sessions with 88 text downloads. The titles accessed the most within this database indicate some hoarding with three of the top four titles being in the field of public administration. For both the IFE and the AOM there is evidence that that a large number of researchers are making extensive use of the databases. At both the IFE and AOM, librarians are extensive users of the databases with *Library Journal* being the second most accessed titles at the IFE and the fifth most accessed title at the AOM. This fact highlights the enhanced skill set of librarians at these institutions.

Missing from these usage statistics is the use of open access scholarly communication initiatives. Within Mongolia there are no contributions of journal titles made to the open access scholarly literature. Suber (2007) remarks that research which is easy to find and retrieve should be used and cited more than literature that is harder to find and access. Swan (2010) found 27 studies of open access initiatives that suggest usage is enhanced and only 4 studies that suggest that usage is not enhanced. With focus on developing countries, Dolgin (2009) found that the use of open access initiatives within developing countries is twice that of developed countries. Although lacking Mongolia-specific usage statistics for open access scholarly communication initiatives, it is altogether likely that the use of open access initiatives exceeds that of donor provided access to scholarship. The survey instrument and the collection of usage statistics provides a substantial vision of how Mongolian researchers make use of the literature but neglects to provide a picture of how this usage was determined and whether this use stands in contrast to what research patrons or librarians want. As such, in 2010-2011 we interviewed four researchers, five research administrators, and three librarians (see Appendix 1 for a list of those interviewed).

Interviews with an economist, historian, mining engineer, and international studies researcher revealed a significant generational divide in their research practices. Researchers under the age of 35 were identified by these individuals as being the most likely to possess the technical and language skills needed to make use of the scholarly literature than those over the age of 50. Although younger researchers are more likely to rely and contribute to the scholarly literature, these same researchers report that research that results in a publication is of less importance than commissioned research. The highest skilled and most productive researchers are more likely to privatize and commercialize their research. With respect to the scholarly communication process, the largest users (but perhaps the smallest contributors) are those whose research yields the greatest economic benefit.

Our conversation with librarians at research institutes and universities indicated several challenges that hindered their ability to enhance the information search skills of researchers. These challenges include the deficiencies in the training of librarians, the diminished role the library has within the research institute's administrative and financial structure, and the fact that researchers are not accustomed to relying on the library as a means of obtaining published research. These findings are supported by Johnson and Yadamsuren (2010) where it was revealed that there are significant obstacles facing library development in the country. Librarians at research institutes and universities also reported several challenges in building up the collection of scholarly communication initiatives they make available to researchers. With researchers unaware of what the library offers, librarians frequently are provided with little guidance of what scholarly communication needs are being unmet. Even when librarians are aware of what researchers want, there is often a lack of funding with budget allocations often designated for specific purposes and staffing considered a higher priority than collection building. Moreover, librarians are regularly faced with inadequate funding for the development of internal technology such as catalogs and Websites. Librarians have advocated for the need for additional training and funding and universities have responded because of the threat of losing government accreditation. This accreditation requires certain spending levels, a minimum size in terms of square footage, a document outlining the library's collection philosophy and management structure, and embrace electronic scholarly communication initiatives. This accreditation also requires that librarians possess a certain level of training. To deal with inadequate levels of funding for collection building and an accreditation process that requires the embrace of electronic scholarly communication initiatives, librarians have also been encouraged to participate in consortiums so as to share resources and have embraced open access initiatives to expand what is available to researchers at minimal expense.

Finally, in our conversations with research administrators at the Mongolian Academy of Sciences and the Mongolian Foundation for Science and Technology it was revealed, as is often typical at government research funding agencies worldwide, that there is a concern of not having enough funding to finance all the research that needs to be done. Internally within these organizations, as is also typical at government research agencies worldwide, there was frustration that there was not enough staffing available to administer the research process. Research administrators revealed that scholarly publications and commercial applications are the two most important outputs of a research project. While research institutes in Mongolia each have their own internally circulated research publications, since 1996 the emphasis has been on researchers publishing in field-specific peer reviewed journals that are widely circulated. Both the Mongolian Academy of Sciences and the Mongolian Foundation for Science and Technology have taken steps towards establishing an electronic repository of Mongolian research. This repository would make publicly financed research more accessible and would supplement the scholarly journal publication process. Progress on developing this repository has been slow and reflects the government's lack of financial commitment to the scholarly communication process. Thus, while the administrators of research funding view scholarly communication objects as critical inputs and outputs to the research process, the government as the financier of research does not see it the same way and invests very little in scholarly communication.

When we bring together the survey results, usage statistics, and interviews, we reach several conclusions about how scholarly communication practices are determined. First, we see that researchers have an engagement with the scholarly communication process that is discipline-specific and that the quality of the publication is of utmost importance. Researchers who are the most recently trained are the largest consumers of scholarly research but not necessarily the largest producers of published research given the focus on applied research for industrial customers. Second, we see that librarians play a varying role of assistance to researchers but that even when assistance is provided, the constrained technical skills and finances of the librarians limit the help that researchers receive. Third, we see that although the degree of presence of electronic scholarly communication databases has increased over the past decade, this has not necessarily translated into greater use. Fourth, research administrators have placed a greater priority on the production of research publications but have been unable to secure from the government a financial commitment for it. These conclusions, while likely to hold true in other developing countries, in Mongolia translate into a scholarly communication process that has only slightly changed and remains largely, although not entirely, determined by researchers. The scholarly communication process in Mongolia, as it stands today, is unable to facilitate the transition in the economy and in the research infrastructure. In the last section we outline what some of the needed

changes to the scholarly communication process would need to be to carry out changes to the economy and the research infrastructure.

NEEDED CHANGES TO THE SCHOLARLY COMMUNICATION PROCESS

The central motivating factor in Mongolia that drives almost all other changes is the encouragement and diversification of the source of economic growth. It is economic growth that had made the production of scholarly publications and marketable research applications a priority. The desire for economic growth is the primary and perhaps only inspiration for the government's investment in research. Researchers and librarians are less motivated by economic growth goals but are more willing to adopt the goals of the government because of the personal financial rewards to doing so. With donor-provided access to the scholarly literature, diversification of the economy is encouraged with scholars receiving access to top-quality research that can serve, in turn, as an input in the creation of research and market applications within Mongolia. With open access to the scholarly literature, Mongolians scholars enjoy access to high quality research and, with fewer gatekeepers in some venues, will have an opportunity to contribute scholarship as well. The concern that emerges when donor-provided access is relied upon is that a developing country is provided little opportunity or incentive to develop their own communication infrastructure. Access achieved through open access would encourage the development of the infrastructure and has an advantage over donated access. Open access however has a decentralized structure that requires greater technical skills and a greater reliance on the librarian (both of which are lacking in Mongolia). Thus it is not entirely evident that either form of access is superior to the other or that all disciplines would converge on a single method of access.

Research patrons in Mongolia need to provide scholarly communities with a communication system flexible to the needs of the researchers and the skill levels of librarians while also meeting the need of the patron. This communication system has to accommodate both those doing fundamental and applied research and encourage both the development of a mobile intellectual labor force and protect the development of intellectual property. In a developing country the issue isn't so much whether access is donated or open but rather whether capacity for economic growth is developed. In Mongolia, a country rich in agriculture and natural resources, the type of scholarly communication system used by a scholar will differ from that used by a scholar in a different developing country. Perhaps the greatest challenge is avoiding the temptation to blindly adopt scholarly communication initiatives from developed countries and force researchers to make use of them.

CONCLUDING REMARKS

When we consider the survey results, usage data, and interview reflections we see scholarly research communities in flux. Researchers are contributing more research but remain largely relegated to accessing the literature in a traditional print format due to access and skill constraints. Researchers are slowly making use of electronic databases but these databases have little awareness among researchers and librarians lack the resources to promote their use. Research administrators are understandably concerned about the cost of providing access with a belief that information distributed electronically should be free and seem inclined to accept any access without concern about the development of a local communication infrastructure. The foundation of a developed country is built on a country's research infrastructure and the scholarly communication system plays an integral part in this. In the years going forward, more research is needed on how the needs of researchers, patrons, and librarians in Mongolia can be satisfied with a discipline-specific mixture of donated and open access.

ACKNOWLEDGMENT

Generous funding to conduct this research was provided by the United States-Mongolia Field Research Fellowship Program, sponsored by the American Center for Mongolian Studies (ACMS), the Council of American Overseas Research Centers (CAORC), and the United States Department of Education. The authors would also like to thank all our participants for sharing their thoughts and comments.

REFERENCES

Asian Development Bank. (1992). *Mongolia, a centrally planned economy in Transition*. Hong Kong: Oxford University Press.

Asian Development Bank. (2009). *Private sector assessment for Mongolia*. Retrieved on July 30, 2011, from http://www.adb.org/Documents/Assessments/Private-Sector/MON/PSA-MON-2009.pdf

Auty, R. (1993). *Sustaining development in mineral economies: The resource curse thesis*. London: Routledge.

Bhat, M. (2009). Open access publishing in Indian Premier Research Institutions. *Information Research, 14*(3). Retrieved on July 27, 2011, from http://InformationR.net/ir/14-3/paper409.html

Boumarafi, B. (2010). Electronic resources at the University of Sharjah Medical Library: An investigation of students' information-seeking behavior. *Medical Reference Services Quarterly, 29*(4), 349–362. doi:10.1080/02763869.2010.518921 PMID:21058178.

Chunrong, L., Wang, J., & Zhou, Z. (2010). Regional consortia for e-resources: A case study of deals in the South China Region. *Program: Electronic Library and Information Systems, 44*(4), 328–341. doi:10.1108/00330331011083220.

Dolgin, E. (2009). Online access=more citations. *The Scientist.* Retrieved on September 6, 2010, from http://www.the-scientist.com/blog/display/55437/

Fang, C., & Ziaochun, Z. (2006). The open access movement in China. *Interlending and Document Summary, 34*(4), 186–193. doi:10.1108/02641610610714777.

Fernandez, L. (2006). Open access initiatives in India – An evaluation. *Partnership: the Canadian Journal of Library and Information Practice and Research, 1*(1).

Francis, H. (2005). The information-seeking behavior of social science faculty at the University of the West Indies, St. Augustine Campus. *Journal of Academic Librarianship, 31*(1), 67–72. doi:10.1016/j.acalib.2004.11.003.

Frankel, J. (2010). *The natural resource curse: A survey.* National Bureau of Economic Research Working Paper #15836. Retrieved on July 30, 2011, from http://www.nber.org/papers/w15836

Ghosh, S. B., & Anup, K. D. (2007). Open access and institutional repositories – A developing country perspective: A case study of India. *IFLA Journal, 37*(3), 229–250. doi:10.1177/0340035207083304.

Gul, S., Tariq, S., & Tariq, B. (2010). Culture of open access in the University of Kashmir: A Researcher's Viewpoint. *Aslib Proceedings: New Information Perspectives, 62*(2), 210–222.

Igun, S. (2005). Implications for electronic publishing in libraries and information centers in Africa. *The Electronic Library, 23*(1), 82–91. doi:10.1108/02640470510582763.

Illeperuma, S. (2002). Information gathering behavior of arts scholars in Sri Lankan universities: A critical evaluation. *Collection building, 21,* 22-31

Johnson, C., & Yadamsuren, B. (2010). Libraries in transition: How librarians in Mongolia are re-visioning the role of libraries in the new democracy: A case study. *The International Information & Library Review, 42*(1), 1–7. doi:10.1016/j.iilr.2010.01.003.

Manaf, Z. (2006). The state of digitization initiatives by cultural institutional in Malaysia. *Library Review, 56*(1), 45–60. doi:10.1108/00242530710722014.

Ministry of Education, Culture, and Science. (2007). *Science and technology master plan of Mongolia, 2007-2020.* United Nations Education, Scientific, and Cultural Organizations. Ulaanbaatar, Mongolia.

Rowlands, I., & Dave, N. (2006). The changing scholarly communication landscape: An international survey of senior researchers. *Learned Publishing, 19,* 31–55. doi:10.1087/095315106775122493.

Silver, K. (2002). Pressing the 'Send' Key– Preferential journal access in developing countries. *Learned Publishing, 15*(2), 91–98. doi:10.1087/09531510252848845.

Suber, P. (2007). Comment to report published the Publishing Research Corporation. *Open Access News.* Retrieved on September 6, 2010, from http://www.earlham.edu/~peters/fos/2007_05_13_fosblogarchive.html

Swan, A. (2010). *The open access citation advantage: Studies and results to date.* Technical Report, Scholarly of Electronics and Computer Science, University of Southampton. Retrieved on September 6, 2010, from http://eprints.ecs.soton.ac.uk/18516/

Tiratel, S. R. (2000). Accessing information use by humanities and social scientists: A study at the Universidad de Buenos Aires, Argentina. *Journal of Academic Librarianship, 26*(5), 346–354. doi:10.1016/S0099-1333(00)00141-5.

World Bank. (2007). *Mongolia: Building the skills for the new economy*. Retrieved on July 30, 2011, from http://www.worldbank.org.mn

World Bank. (2011). *Mongolia quarterly economic update*. Retrieved on July 6, 2010, from http://www.worldbank.org.mn

World Vision. (2009). *Mongolia country report*. Retrieved on July 30, 2011, from http://worldvision.org/content.nsf/learn/world-vision-mongolia

Yadamsuren, B., & Raber, D. (2007). Information seeking behavior of Mongolian scholars. *Proceedings of the American Society for Information Science and Technology (ASIS&T) conference, 44*(1), 1-4.

ADDITIONAL READING

Antelman, K. (2004). Do open-access articles have a greater research impact? *College & Research Libraries, 65*(5), 372–382.

Arunachalam, S. (2003). Information for research in developing countries-information technology, a friend or foe? *The International Information & Library Review, 35*(2), 133–147. doi:10.1016/S1057-2317(03)00032-8.

Brown, C., & Abbas, J. M. (2010). Institutional digital repositories for science and technology: A view from the laboratory. *Journal of Library Administration, 50*(3), 181–215. doi:10.1080/01930821003634930.

Cassella, M. (2010). Institutional repositories: An internal and external perspective on the value of IRs for researchers' communities. *Library Quarterly: The Journal of European Research Libraries, 20*(2), 210-225. Retrieved on July 30, 2011, from http://liber.library.uu.nl/publish/articles/000503/article.pdf

Chan, D. L. H. (2009). An integrative view of the institutional repositories in Hong Kong: Strategies and challenges. *Serials Review, 35*(3), 119–124. doi:10.1016/j.serrev.2009.04.002.

Cheng, W., & Shengli, R. (2008). Evolution of open access publishing in Chinese scientific journals. *Learned Publishing, 21*(2), 140–152. doi:10.1087/095315108X288884.

Covey, D. T. (2011). Recruiting content for the institutional repository: The barriers exceed the benefits. *Journal of Digital Information, 12*(3). Retrieved on July 27, 2011, from http://journals.tdl.org/jodi/article/view/2068

Creaser, C. (2010). Open access to research outputs—Institutional policies and researchers' views: Results from two complementary surveys. *New Review of Academic Librarianship, 16*(1), 4–25. doi:10.1080/13614530903162854.

Hide, B. (2008). How much does it cost, and who pays? The global costs of scholarly communication and the UK contribution. *Serials: The Journal for the Serials Community, 21*(3), 194–200. doi:10.1629/21194.

Holmstrom, J. (2004). The cost per article reading of open access articles. *D-Lib Magazine, 10*(1). Retrieved on July 27, 2011, from http://www.dlib.org/dlib/january04/holmstrom/01holmstrom.html

Johnson, I., Hong, W., & Fei, N. (2008). Electronic journal provision and use in China: An initial study. *Serials: The Journal for the Serials Community, 21*(3), 210–221. doi:10.1629/21210.

Kim, H. J. (2001). The transition from paper to electronic journals: Key factors that affect scholars' acceptance of electronic journals. *The Serials Librarian*, *41*(1), 31–64. doi:10.1300/J123v41n01_04.

Kling, R., & Geoffrey, M. (2000). Not just a matter of time: Field differences and the shaping of electronic media in supporting scientific communication. *Journal of the American Society for Information Science American Society for Information Science*, *51*(14), 1306–1320. doi:10.1002/1097-4571(2000)9999:9999<::AID-ASI1047>3.0.CO;2-T.

Kling, R., Geoffrey, M., & Adam, K. (2003). A Bit more To IT: Scholarly communication forums as socio-technical interaction networks. *Journal of the American Society for Information Science and Technology*, *54*(1), 47–67. doi:10.1002/asi.10154.

Krueger, S., & Irina, L. (2007). JSTOR's work in the Russian Federation: A case study. *Slavic & East European Information Resources*, *8*(1), 103–110. doi:10.1300/J167v08n01_12.

Lewis, D. W. (2008). Library budgets, open access, and the future of scholarly communication. *College & Research Libraries News*, *69*(5), 271–273.

Moskovkin, V. (2010). Open access to scientific knowledge. Who receives dividends? *Scientific and Technical Information Processing*, *37*(3), 172–177. doi:10.3103/S0147688210030020.

Schmidt, K. D., Pongracz, S., & Timothy, V. C. (2005). New roles for a changing environment: Implications of open access for libraries. *College & Research Libraries*, *66*(5), 407–416.

Shao, X. (2007). Perceptions of open access publishing among academic journal editors in China. *Serials Review*, *33*(2), 114–121. doi:10.1016/j.serrev.2007.02.002.

Silver, K. (2002). Pressing the 'Send' Key–Preferential journal access in developing countries. *Learned Publishing*, *15*(2), 91–98. doi:10.1087/09531510252848845.

Spinella, M. P. (2007). JSTOR: past, present, and future. *Journal of Library Administration*, *46*(2), 55–78. doi:10.1300/J111v46n02_05.

Tenopir, C. (2000). Online journals and developing nations. *Library Journal*, *1*, 34–36.

Wallenius, L. I. T. (2010). Are electronic serials helping or hindering academic Libraries? *The Acquisitions Librarian*, *19*(1/2), 75–82.

Zhen, X. (2010). Overview of digital library developments in China. *D-Lib Magazine, 16*(5/6). Retrieved on June 6, 2011, from http://www.dlib.org/dlib/may10/zhen/05zhen.html

Zhou, Q. (2005). The development of digital libraries in China and the shaping of digital librarians. *The Electronic Library*, *23*(4), 433–441. doi:10.1108/02640470510611490.

KEY TERMS AND DEFINITIONS

Academic Libraries: An institution that serves as a collection point for scholarly materials and informs a scholar's information seeking behavior.

Donated Access: Access to scholarly communication outlets that are donated to scholars. These donates are directed primarily to scholars in developing countries.

Electronic Scholarly Communication: Scholarly communication outlets that are disseminated to scholars via electronic means.

Information Seeking Behavior of Scholars: The traditions, practices, and training that informs how an individual finds information.

Open Access: Access to scholarly communication outlets that is provided to scholars worldwide free of restrictions.

Scholarly Communication: The outlets that scholars use to communicate with each other.

APPENDIX

In 2010 and 2011 we interviewed the following individuals:

Researchers

- Dr. Tuvshintugs Batdelger, Director of the Economic Research Institute and Professor of Economics, National University of Mongolia
- Dr. Orkhontuul Borya, Deputy Director of the School of Mining Engineering, Mongolian University of Science and Technology
- Zolboo Dashnyam, Researcher of the Institute of International Studies, Mongolian Academy of Sciences
- Tulgaa Togtokhbayar, Senior Researcher, Mongolian Foundation for Science and Technology

Librarians

- Sodgerel Gurbazar, Director of Library, Institute of Finance and Economics
- Dr. Chakerhaan Gulnar, Director of Library, Mongolian University of Science and Technology
- Saranchimeg Davaajantsan, Head of Division of Reading and Service, National Library of Mongolia

Research Administrators

- Dr. Undraa Agvaanluvsan, Advisor, Minister of International Affairs
- Dr. Gan-Erdene Tudev, Head of the Mongolian Foundation for Science and Technology
- Dr. Galbaatar Tuvdendorj, Secretary General, Mongolian Academy of Sciences
- Dr. Shurkhuu Dorj, Scientific Secretary of the Institute of International Studies, Mongolian Academy of Sciences
- Dr. Avid Budeebazar, Head of Department of Research and Monitoring, Mongolian Academy of Sciences
- Dr. Enkhbat Dombon, Head of the Department of Science and Technology, Mongolian University of Science and Technology

Chapter 12
"Lose Your Time in a Useful Way":
Digital Inclusion of the Elderly at a Pensioners' Club in Romania

James M. Nyce
Ball State University, USA

Gail E. Bader
Ball State University, USA

Cheryl Klimaszewski
Bryn Mawr College, USA

ABSTRACT

This chapter looks at the experiences older adults have using computers and the Internet in the context of one e-inclusion effort in Romania. Biblionet – Global Libraries Romania is a project that provides computers to public libraries throughout that country. One of Biblionet's first public access computer centers located outside of a public library opened at a pensioners' club in the city of Zalau. Local librarians who have taken Biblionet-sponsored "train the trainer" courses have adapted instructional methods for older users. Ethnographic research at the pensioners' club has uncovered a variety of experiences around new technology, especially in how computer use is both informed by and extended kin or family work. The project is discussed in the context of NGO-led development initiatives to illustrate the importance of including the wider ICT development landscape (and methods) when studying users, ICTs, and information use.

DOI: 10.4018/978-1-4666-4353-6.ch012

INTRODUCTION

Biblionet – Global Libraries Romania is a project that provides computers to public libraries throughout that country. Funded by The Bill & Melinda Gates Foundation and local Romanian governments and implemented by the International Research and Exchanges Board (IREX), Biblionet works with local communities to create public access computer centers (PACs) in public libraries and at other community sites. Biblionet is an outgrowth of Gates Foundation work in US public libraries as much as it is a response to Romania's e-inclusion and information society policy and development efforts, many of which Romania was required to adopt in preparation for EU membership in 2007 (Klimaszewski & Nyce, 2009). These policies focus on increasing access to information and communication technologies (ICTs) for the underserved. In Romania as in other countries, senior citizens comprise a large part of this population and they are often targets of "active ageing" initiatives that includes ICT access (Ianculescu, 2011).

A pensioners' club (the club) in Zalau, Romania was one of Biblionet's first four pilot sites. The partnership came about because the club already housed a small branch of the public library and because the club was interested in offering technology-related services to its members. Local librarians who had participated in Biblionet-sponsored ICT trainings adapted training courses for pensioners. The first part of this chapter presents the findings of ethnographic research undertaken at the pensioners' club. This research investigates the attitudes and experiences of a small group of pensioners and provides a detailed discussion of the training program for seniors. One of the more notable findings was in how computer use was informed by and extended certain kinds of traditional family work or kin work--work that in Romania is most often done by women.

The success of Biblionet at the pensioners' club was widely celebrated by the project leaders, and for good reason. Researchers found older adults at the club using ICTs that allowed them to, as one user described it, "Lose (their) time in a useful way." However, user experience tells only part of the story. Programs like Biblionet develop as part of larger global ICT access initiatives, in this case one funded by a prestigious, big-name American foundation. This means that the prospects for name recognition and additional funding become an integral part of the project. Therefore, the chapter concludes with a discussion of how these forces can shape development efforts.

BACKGROUND

Older adults have consistently found themselves on the wrong side of the digital divide (McMurtrey, McGaughey, Downey, & Zeltmann, 2010; Morris, Goodman, & Brading, 2007; Wicks, 2003) For this reason, they are the target of many public policy e-inclusion efforts (Gilhooly, Gilhooly, & Jones, 2008; McClean, 2011). They are also the subject of numerous studies on ICT use (and non-use) across disciplines (Dickinson & Gregor, 2006; McMurtrey et al., 2010; Tobias, 1987; Wagner, Hassanein, & Head, 2010). This section will provide a brief introduction to some of the e-inclusion and related policy efforts targeting older users. It will also give a general picture of the trends in and problems with the literature on this user group. It will conclude by discussing the specific problems and issues facing Romania both in terms of older users and e-inclusion policy.

Though studies on older users and ICTs are numerous, they are often problematic in a number of ways. First and foremost, there is a tendency to characterize "the aged" or "the elderly" or "senior citizens" (even in this paper) as a homogenous group when, in fact, differences within this user group will exist based on age (i.e., the young-old vs. the old-old) (Nayak, Priest, & White, 2010; Wicks, 2003); education, work experience, place of residence (i.e., rural or urban) and other socio-economic factors (McMurtrey et al., 2010; Mordini et al., 2009); and perceptions around culture and tradition (Hakkarainen, 2012; Xie, 2006). It does not help that a number of earlier studies were limited to users in developed countries like the U.S. and the UK. These studies have expanded to include a wider range of users from different countries and backgrounds, however many of them are still biased towards including existing computer users. Scholars have begun to look at reasons for non-use of technology among older users and have begun to offer comparative and cross-cultural findings (e.g., Colesca & Dobrica, 2008; Hakkarainen, 2012; Kanayama, 2003; Lin, Tang, & Kuo, 2012; Mikkola & Halonen, 2011; Xie, 2006; Yao, Qiu, Huang, Du, & Ma, 2011).

Early studies often concluded that computer use enhanced the well-being of older users. However, a review of these studies by Dickinson and Gregor (2006) showed little direct causality between computer use itself and well-being in older adults. Instead, these authors found stronger ties between the training associated with computer use and the well-being of older adults perhaps because of the social dimension that training offered these users (Dickinson & Gregor, 2006). Furthermore, additional challenges are present in studying the relationship between quality of life or well-being and ICT use for older users. Gilhooly, Gilhooly, and Jones (2008) outline the difficulties of measuring quality of life or well-being because of the subjective nature of the concepts. While at least one large-scale U.S. study (Ford & Ford, 2009) included several thousand users and showed a decrease in depression among older adults who use computers, it should be noted that the small sample size of most older adult user studies may not provide a thorough enough picture of users cross-demographically or cross-culturally.

Despite inconclusive findings, the assumption persists that computers bring a better quality of life, especially for older users (Gilhooly et al., 2008; McClean, 2011) and e-inclusion of the elderly is generally viewed as an "unqualified good" (Ford & Ford, 2009, p. 4). The EU has numerous policies that attempt to include older users in the developing information and knowledge societies, policies that explicitly and repeatedly state that "ICT can help the older individuals to improve quality of life, stay healthier and live independently for longer." (European Union, Commission of the European Communities, 2007, p. 3; European Union, European Commission, 2007; European Union, European Commission, Information Society and Media, 2008; Ianculescu, 2011). McClean (2011) calls ICTs an "imposed solution" to aging and the digital divide. Her discussion of ethics of e-inclusion and older adults notes that historically the trend has been for others to decide what's best for this group of users:

As Europe moves to embrace strategies for the e-inclusion of older people, it risks repeating this pattern of having stakeholders (in this case, researchers, industrial leaders and policy makers) other than elders themselves decide what elders need and what solutions should be developed (McClean, 2011, p. 314).

This imposed approach has a trickledown effect in countries like Romania that have modeled their e-inclusion efforts after those of the EU (Klimaszewski & Nyce, 2009). Romanians consistently find themselves lagging behind in the statistics that measure computer and Internet dissemination and use, despite great strides in ICT uptake over the past several years. Nita (2011) describes the country as being poorly prepared to take on e-inclusion and he notes that, though e-inclusion is seen as a means to overcome the digital divide, it is more likely a lack of equal access to technology will either reproduce and/

or further legitimize the existing divide. In short, rather than solving the problem, these inclusion efforts merely provide the potential for this divide to continue and introduce new degrees of division and inequality.

This is partially because "ICT access represents just a simple *opportunity* [emphasis in original], and not the capacity of fully using ICT" (Nita, 2011, p. 66; Ţurlea & Ciupagea, 2009). This distinction is often not made in e-inclusion efforts especially those that rely on quantitative analysis to measure growth and development. Therefore, access alone will not be enough. Users need to have meaningful and purposeful reasons (and opportunities) to use ICTs (Ţurlea & Ciupagea, 2009).

In many ways, the discussion of a digital divide itself is inadequate because it implies a gap that can be closed. More likely the nature of the divide will change as technology changes. As Nita (2011) states:

A high level of ICT adoption was supposed to translate into a lower level of social inequalities. Since ICT diffusion and adoption are not sufficient for analyzing the social discrepancies in information society, a broader digital divide paradigm would prove to be more adequate–namely one which focuses on the importance of ICT skills and the quality and meaningfulness of ICT use (Mossberger et al., 2008) and which takes into account more factors of social inclusion/exclusion brought about by ICT spread (Nita, 2011, p. 69).

The digital divide itself has to come to signify more than simply the difference between technology "haves" and "have nots." In addition to changing how "older users" are studied, more widespread but also more nuanced research is needed to supplement the extensive amount of literature on older users. The concept of "older users" also must be widened to take into account the breadth and depth of experience and needs of what is often incorrectly characterized as a homogenous user group.

To this end, the next section presents the findings of another small study of users at a pensioners' club in a city in Romania. In order to place the experiences of these users into a larger context, discussion of the findings will be linked to e-inclusion and development efforts in Romania.

E-INCLUSION FOR PENSIONERS: A CASE STUDY

History and Background

Founded in 1958, the Pensioners' Mutual Care Union of Zalau (CARP Zalau, http://www.carpzalau.ro/en) is a non-profit organization open to all pensioners in Salaj County. CARP has about 9,000 fee-paying members, for whom membership allows access to services ranging from low interest loans to free or low-cost medical treatments to a wide variety of social and cultural activities. One benefit of membership is access to CARP's Pensioners' Club. Located centrally in the city of Zalau (pop. 62,000), the club was established in 2003 as a meeting place visited by 30-40 members daily. The director describes the club as "the pensioners' second home." Male club members gather daily to play cards and games and women often visit and also have special meeting times for their own activities. Since 2005, the club has housed a branch of the Salaj County Library, whose 300-volume collection comprises literature, history, and medical books.

This existing collaboration between the club and the county library enabled the pensioners to have access to ICTs as part of Biblionet. The club's Internet center opened on May 8, 2008 as one of Biblionet's first public access computer centers, which they refer to as the Internet center (the center). The club welcomed the arrival of the center because it could not afford to offer such a service on its own. Biblionet-trained librarians provided free Internet and computer training to club members. CARP's director described the impact of providing Internet access at the club as dramatic:

For most of the people coming here, the Internet was a positive shock, as they couldn't imagine before they would be able to talk to their children in this way. In addition to that, they now search the Internet for everything. They expose themselves to culture, looking for curiosities and new things about the world. This is a very good thing for me. It's surprising and pleasant at the same time.

The next section looks at the role ICTs at the club came to have in the lives of CARP's members.

The Research Project

Fieldwork at the Pensioners' Club took place over a two-week period, as part of a larger, six-week study of public libraries and Biblionet throughout Salaj County, Romania[1]. The study was led by Gail Bader and James M. Nyce, assistant and associate professors of anthropology at Ball State University. The research group included students from Ball State and from the Şcoala Naţională de Studii Politice şi Administrative (SNSPA) in Bucharest. Five researchers had worked with Bader and Nyce in Romania previously. This was the fifth trip Bader and Nyce led to Romania, who began their work there in 2003. Prior community studies have focused on information, knowledge use, and cultural preservation in pre- and post-revolution Romania (Closet-Crane, Dopp, Solis, & Nyce, 2009; Littrell, Nyce, Straub, & Whipple, 2006; Whipple & Nyce, 2007; Klimaszewski & Nyce, 2009; Beasley, B.E., & Nyce, J.M., 2009; Klimaszewski, Bader, Nyce, & Beasley, 2010; Klimaszewski, Bader, & Nyce, 2011, 2012a, 2012b).

Researchers scheduled an appointment with CARP's director to visit the center. When re-

searchers arrived at the Club they found all six computers in use, with male and female pensioners carrying out a variety of online tasks: writing e-mails, reading online newspapers, searching for gardening information and recipes, chatting with friends, watching and listening with headphones to music and video clips. This turned out to be the kind of "staged" experience typical of what researchers experienced to some degree at all scheduled Biblionet site visits both this summer and next. Staging, meaning the presentation of what visitors expected to see that would reflect a "successful" program (i.e., all of the computers being used productively and purposefully), was generally the rule during this and other research visits in Romania. It seems to be a holdover from communist times, when public events were staged to show a program or event in the best light, especially for visitors and which may or may not effectively present the whole truth of the situation (Littrell et al., 2006). While researchers were not surprised by staging, they still had not expected users in this age group to be so technologically engaged. Because this all seemed too good to be true, the experience led researchers to a series of research questions: Can older users really so expertly access computers and the Internet? How did this group of users learn to use the computers? And what motivated them to learn?

Based on the initial visit, it was decided that more in-depth research should be carried out at the club to better understand this group of users. Researchers[2] carried out interviews and informal talks with club members who were regular computers users who had also participated in Biblionet training. These users were also observed during the "Internet morning" and the men's afternoon programs. Semi-structured interviews were carried out at the club with 15 informants: two trainers (the first and current trainer at the Internet Center) and 13 pensioners who were also computer users (8 males, 5 females, 59- to 84-years-old). Each interview was followed by an informal practical computer request in which the interviewee was asked to demonstrate some computer-based activity. This verified the extent to which interview responses were behaviorally grounded. It also proved to be a good strategy, because often interviewees were more comfortable demonstrating their technological skills than talking about them.

Interviews ranged from 20 to 80 minutes and were digitally recorded and later transcribed in Romanian. Relevant quotes were translated into English by a native Romanian speaker fluent in English and then reviewed by a native English speaker. This data was complemented by field notes and information obtained from local newspapers, official library reports, videos, and photographs. The findings present information about the computer training at the club and, despite the small sample size, the data also provides in-depth firsthand information on the older users' attitudes and experiences with technology at this Pensioners' Club.

Training Older Users: A Negotiated Methodology

If you want to be successful, show people that you care about them. (Trainer)

Vision + Resources + A Lot of Patience = Online Success (Biblionet training handout)

Pensioners and trainers who were a part of the study all agreed that free training was the most important element of the club's Biblionet program. More active club members said that their initial motivation for enrolling in the training was to help set an example for other pensioners. Initially, trainers had difficulty coping with the number of pensioners interested in taking the course because they did not expect such a high level of interest from 60 pensioners. Several pensioners said that they "had to queue as in the old times" in order to get a place in the training.

Because their Biblionet training did not specifically cover older users, trainers had to adapt their approach, first conducting a survey that collected basic demographic information along with information about their needs and expectations for training. Fifty-eight pensioners (who were among the most active club members) completed the survey, which overall showed that participants had little or no prior experience with computers. 62% of pensioners surveyed indicated either that they already had a computer at home that they didn't know how to use or that they intended to purchase a computer in the near future. Their most common reason for learning to use the computer was to be able to communicate with relatives and friends living abroad.

The training course lasted three weeks, ran four days a week, and was presented to club members as a new service of the library. Each session began with computer skills practice, followed by a topic-related information search on the Internet. As the training progressed, other digital devices were introduced such as webcams, CDs and DVDs, as well as software for downloading pictures and music from the Internet. Other topics of interest were also covered to ensure that participants "would not get bored." This included health and medical information, e-government services, online newspapers, and online shopping. To add an element of fun, certificates and prizes were awarded in such categories as "First Website Opened," "Most Active Participant," "Best Online News Searcher," and "Most Emotional E-Mail Received."

Neither trainer had had previous experience working with the elderly, nor were the Biblionet courses they had taken specifically targeted for dealing with this category of user. Consequently instruction at the club became, as one trainer described it, "a negotiation between explaining meanings, listening to life-stories and giving support." This kind of introduction to using computers and the Internet was just as much a learning experience for the trainers, as one described it:

The basic idea was that you have to listen to what older people have to say, to emphatically understand them. You talk less . . . and you have to collaborate in different domains of interest to them, for instance, from religious icons on glass to oil extraction in Norway, from political comments to recipes of all kinds and even marriage notices. I am not good at everything, but I had to listen and I found sometimes that I had a lot to learn as well. That's this generation...

Trainers reported that user difficulties generally fell into one of four categories: remembering what they had learned; physical difficulties performing tasks; not understanding terminology; and fear of making mistakes. Trainers took different tactics so that users would not become discouraged. They also had to keep a sense of humor about their work. For instance, users often had problems remembering passwords, so trainers developed simple strategies for overcoming this problem:

I had to do something: I wrote down in my notebook all (the user's) passwords. I do remember a funny moment when one of the gentlemen, who usually forgot his password, asked for it and I tried to whisper it to its ear. Having a bad hearing as well he repeated it loudly and then (said that) all his colleagues would know it and next time help him with it.

Health problems that challenged older users' computer use and training included loss of eyesight and eyestrain and some users reported having difficulty staying at the computer for more than an hour at a time. If users forgot their glasses, this also challenged their ability to see the screen. Other physical problems were more difficult for users and trainers to overcome. Trainers coped with these problems by slowing down the pace of the training and taking into account the fact that some users had difficulty learning and performing new hand movements.

While physical challenges were expected with users in this age bracket, trainers also faced challenges introducing users to new terms and technical jargon, some of which was in English. Trainers dealt with this by simplifying terms or by creating new, more meaningful terms that users could better understand. As one trainer explained:

We had to adapt all this language, to use words as simple and understandable as possible, so (users would) easily understand. We also let them describe things in their own words; otherwise they wouldn't remember it next time. For instance, the desktop was called the TV screen (ecran de televizor). Another example were the sign commands such as "the glove" (manusa) or "the hand" (manuta). I also tried to make them understand that when we begin to write we have to be sure that the line-cursor is "blinking" (sa clipoceasca). This way of expression was very useful in order for them to understand. This was in no way considered a negative estimate of their intellectual or professional qualities, but rather a useful and necessary strategy of adapting [these users] to the computer. There were no complaints about this.

Users still encountered difficulties as they began to work with Internet-based applications, like G-mail or Yahoo! Mail. While the computers had Romanian versions of operating systems and software installed locally, English words like "send," "inbox," and "attach" had to be explained to users, which was difficult because few of them knew English.

Finally, trainers had to constantly assure elder users that it was unlikely they would damage the equipment or make catastrophic mistakes as they used the computers. One trainer said:

At the beginning their fears were great. The fear of the unknown was the biggest. They were afraid to put their hand on the mouse, to touch the keyboard. I had to assure them that nothing bad will happen, to convince them to press the buttons and trust that nothing will break. At the beginning they had this huge fear of breaking (the computer), but after a few sessions they got used to it.

What use the pensioners put their Biblionet training and computers to is taken up next.

User Experiences

In this study, the most remarkable findings were how the Internet was used to extend and expand traditional gendered work. This was particularly the case with kin work, the kind of labor that is generally undertaken by women to help maintain and support their families and to create and maintain different kinds of male-female relations. While access to different forms of information and learning opportunities increased the most important and meaningful use that computers brought to the club generally related to increased contact with family members and members of the opposite sex.

As one 62-year-old female user commented:

I enrolled at the Internet center (at the Pensioners' Club) immediately after they opened it. I took the training classes in order to learn how to communicate through email and messenger with my children. I have seven children, four in France, one in Spain, one in Bucharest and one in Zalau. I missed them a lot so I had to do something. So in less than two weeks I learned how to send and receive messages from my children. Now we are permanently in touch and the fact that the telephone bill has lowered considerably is also an extraordinary thing.

For most of the pensioners, especially the women, this kind of kin work was perhaps the primary use club members made of the computers and Internet access Biblionet had provided. Women also used the Internet to cultivate romantic relationships. One 67-year-old woman told of a relationship she was cultivating online with an American man. She began using the Internet four years ago after the death of her husband. She mentioned that she often used the Internet at home, staying up late to chat with her male suitor online. She explained:

In my house the Internet shuts down at 9 in the evening or even later if the gentleman from America tells me he is signing in. I've met him on the Neogen network where I have my profile… There you can talk, have conversations, and it can also happen that somebody will fall in love with you, as it happened to me.

The connection the Internet brings often fills a social gap experienced by older users, allowing them to stay in touch with their family and peers for little or no cost to them. As one 60-year-old female pensioner said:

The Internet has so beautiful things to offer for the pensioners. For instance, I was so impressed by (some things) I received [there] that I sent them around to the people I knew and now we are a group of friends sending each other things. I think it's important that all the pensioners are in contact in order to receive things that make you feel better, bring you peace and quiet. That's what the old people need.

In addition to kin work, nearly all of the users more readily accessed information relevant to them. Several pensioners even believed the Internet to be the "best" source of information. It was certainly the most convenient. One 65-year-old computer user talked about how she managed her household needs through online searching:

For me, recipes and gardening are the most important. For instance, I checked information about not so common plants such as chick-pea and lentil and then I went and bought the seeds. I also looked for information regarding the conditions (the plants need to grow) and how to take care of them. For the recipes as well, you can find whatever you like. I just type (the name of the recipe) and I get it.

Both men and women used the Internet to find information about their health conditions and prescription medicines. One respondent commented:

I looked through the Internet for a doctor who operated me a long time ago in the Mureş County and to my great surprise I found [him]. I told him that I am a former patient of him and that I needed some advice, as some of the medical problems had reappeared. He responded and recommended certain treatments and some of the products, namely creams, [which] I found and ordered through the Internet. I am now actually waiting for the order.

Many users indicated that they felt like they got the most up-to-date information via the Internet, especially those that were interested in the news, current events, and popular entertainment. Some indicated they also liked to see the posts and comments from other Internet users, as well, "to see how others think." Club members also talked about how their use of the Internet gave them the confidence to try new things. As one 65-year-old male explained:

For me (finding information on the Internet) means a lot. For instance, I've booked a ticket for a treatment resort and then I checked everything about it on the Internet: how to get there by train, where to sleep, how it looks and what can I do there. Now I know everything, I'm prepared to go

and that gives me confidence. Otherwise where would I find all that information? It helps a lot, not only the young people, but also the old people, who especially need to be prepared.

These older users were also aware that information use and access, not to mention how they spend their free time, were changing. As one 62-year pensioner noted:

The Internet opens access to information and makes you want more. Before, I used to read a lot. It's true that I read less now and this could be a negative side of it. But on the other hand, the information that I now have access to has increased maybe ten times more than before.

Users appreciated the Internet as an information source because, unlike the television, they had a choice about what they could see or do:

At TV you get to see only what they want to show you. They don't give you everything. If you have Internet you have everything. At TV you have only the news. On the Internet you can access information about everything you are interested in: medical treatments, booking flights. And it's not hard to do it either. If you want to see landscapes from France you find them there, from Spain as well. You are well informed.

Users were also aware that the Internet had the potential downside. It could lead, as a club member noted above, users to read less. This observation from a 70-year-old male user generally sums up the feelings of most of the informants on this issue:

It's an enormous source of information in all domains… Here you find everything in one place. People always try to get something as easily as possible. I need a week to read a book and here at the Internet in a couple of hours I resolve my problem. That's rapid information. Once we were forced to read until it became a pleasure, now we want to learn the computer because it is very useful. It is the computer that generated the lack of interest for books and this is not good for the young generation.

However, users were able to "take home" their knowledge and share it with family members and friends, which added value. One 67-year-old male talked about how his Biblionet computer training allowed him to help his neighbors:

I have some neighbors, pensioners as well, not necessarily older than me, but for which the computer is not a 'passion.' And they ask me to look for information regarding their disease, the medicine they take or about a certain law. So I look it up on the Internet, note it down and then give them the right information. I can honestly say that it brings me a great joy to be able to help the others with their problems.

The 62-year-old user above explained why she thought the Biblionet training program and Internet access at the center was so important:

We wanted to have it here because not everybody can afford to have a computer at home. And when you are old you want to do something, to lose your time in some way: reading the press, playing games or seeing the cities from all over the world, landscapes. So at the beginning people came and they liked it and they are still coming now.

However, it is important to note that few of these users had any desire to become competent or proficient at the computer; it was enough, as club members believed, for them for them to know how to get some basic tasks done. As one 70-year-old user put it: "I now know exactly what I need to know. I don't need to be a 'super-performer' in computers."

SUMMARY OF FINDINGS

This small-scale study of pensioners using ICTs reveals some ways that technology can be beneficial for older users. However, it is not simply access to ICTs that allowed these pensioners to learn and continue to use computers (Nita, 2011; Ţurlea & Ciupagea, 2009). Continued use was encouraged through personalized instruction in a community setting where skills were developed to meet specific user needs. Users often described how the Internet "changed their lives" and all of them understood at some level that using ICTs allowed them to "keep up" with their families and with life in general. Contact with family members was often the main motivation for learning to use ICTs, which led to the creation of technologically diffuse households[3]. The free, direct, and immediate nature of the communication maintained and increased family ties across and between generations. As children and grandchildren were impressed by their parents'/grandparents' newfound technological competence, positive reinforcement encouraged these older users to further their technological engagement.

The literature suggests that fewer women especially older women than men engage with computers. This seems generally not to be the case in this Internet center and elsewhere in Romania (Ianculescu, 2011). For women in particular, the Internet provided additional avenues by which women could communicate with family members, with friends, and male suitors, allowing them to expand and maintain social networks. As women and men continue to "bring home" their ICT knowledge and competence, this could lead to a waterfall effect, one the literature has not picked up on, as familiarity with, confidence in, and a desire to experiment with ICT resources could disseminate across and within, as well as up and down (in age) kinship lines.

The pensioners seemed to perceive the Internet as a one-stop-shop for information, often the "best" source of information, and certainly the most convenient. They saw information available on the Internet as being different from and usually better than the information found on television or in newspapers because the Internet was thought to be largely not under anyone's control. That this group saw television and newspapers in Romania as more controlled likely has ties to Romania's communist past, when information was controlled by the state, a legacy from which public libraries still suffer (Anghelescu et al., 2009). In other words, these pensioners tended to see information on the Internet as not influenced in any direct way (by a particular ideology for example) which to them made the content seem more reliable. This indicates the need for information literacy training, a topic that was generally seen as outside the scope of, or secondary to, the programs Biblionet offered in Romania that emphasized access (i.e., quantity over quality).

The training Biblionet provided though was welcomed and valued by this group of users, likely because over time it became more and more tailored to the needs of these users. However, Biblionet trained only 176 club members over two years, which represents only 2% of CARP's total membership. Further, the numbers trained at the club have been decreasing from 76 in 2008 to 20 in 2009 and 30 by May, 2010. After May 2010, training continued but on an individual basis. This raises the question of how the club and library together can more effectively promote computer training.

EVALUATING BIBLIONET AS AN NGO DEVELOPMENT INITIATIVE

The Biblionet-sponsored Internet center at the pensioners' club in Zalau was considered a success by both US and Romanian Biblionet and IREX staff. While the success or failure of the program is not in question here, one problem researchers

observed was that program staff tended to focus heavily on one-off, one-event, exceptional ICT "success stories" (Klimaszewski et al., 2011). These widely promoted and disseminated stories of the "triumphs" of individual users tend to overlook the more gradual and subtle developments (some of which have been highlighted here) that can have the potential to shepherd more lasting and nuanced developments around ICTs (Klimaszewski et al., 2011). The attention Biblionet gives to "short term" success seems to reflect more the needs of this NGO to generate legitimacy and credibility for itself in the development community than it does on local social or community needs in Romania.

This focus on success as a marketing tool is not limited to this project. Most if not all NGOs have a need for institutional legitimacy, especially in a challenging economic climate (for, who will want to be associated with an "unsuccessful" program?). In a similar way, those who plan and implement these projects will need more and more proof of how "successful" those projects have "actually" been. This "proof" usually takes the form of a statistical set of occurrences and frequencies (number of users; number of connections, etc.) that are punctuated by the "success stories." For Biblionet, examples of this can be seen in Chiranov (2010) and Fried, Kochanowicz & Chiranov (2010).

This need for legitimization-through-success creates something of a "feedback loop" that tends to validate the NGO's local staff and project work as well as how the NGO defines and constructs its overall policies and procedures. One result is that while an NGOs pragmatic and policy efforts may be well-intentioned, in the end what drives international development work and its evaluation is a kind of entitlement and institutional championship. This tends often unintentionally to exclude any number of stakeholder cohorts (McClean, 2011) which in turn can weaken whatever benefits an NGO brings to local target communities. It does not help that most NGOs regardless of rank or stature are at the same time involved in a kind of "war against all" in the competition for funding. There is a certain irony that the relationships between NGOs often have more in common with late 19th century capitalism than the kind of disinterested or collaborative "involvement" they portray as having with one another.

The challenge all this raises for researchers is that when studying and evaluating ICT projects internationally and cross-culturally they must learn to be aware of and operate within the legitimization-success "feedback loop." This means that researchers should be willing to consider the NGOs need for legitimization-through-success critically while working to bring a wider range of stakeholder voices into evaluation and impact assessment (beyond metrics and "success stories"). This also suggests a need for the NGO community to rethink its approach toward impact assessment, which would likely mean developing a more critical and nuanced position on what is taken as evidence and fact in policy, project, and assessment efforts. Some distancing from this current NGO practice and belief would make it possible to move, for example, beyond the belief that the presence of technology in and of itself can everywhere be transformational (Day, 1998).

FUTURE RESEARCH DIRECTIONS

Studies around "active ageing" and e-inclusion would be enriched by going beyond user experience to focus also on NGO and policy initiatives that encourage ICT access and uptake. A wider range of stakeholder voices should be included in the research generally. Quantitative assessment should be supplemented by qualitative and ethnographic studies of the effects of Western development initiatives based in non-Western or less developed areas. Both short- and long-term effects of ICTs and related development efforts need to be studied in some depth to better gauge

more subtle shifts and changes over time, as opposed to those changes noted immediately after "access" to technology has been granted. More attention should be paid to the policy implications of e-inclusion and a more critical look at the discrepancies between policy and reality would be welcome. Finally, those working for the good (i.e., researchers, development workers and policy makers) must be willing to be critical of their own work in addition to championing their successes (Klimaszewski et al., 2012a).

REFERENCES

Anghelescu, H. G. B., Lukenbill, J., Lukenbill, W. B., & Owens, I. (2009). Acceptance of social marketing concepts by selected Romanian librarians: Culture and context. *Advances in Library Administration and Organization*, *27*, 123–150. doi:10.1108/S0732-0671(2009)0000027012.

Beasley, B. E., & Nyce, J. M. (2009). *A more perfect Poundbury? Prince Charles' reinvention of Viscri, Romania*. Presented at the Indiana University Romanian Studies Conference, Bloomington, Indiana.

Chiranov, M. (2010). Real life impact of the global libraries: Biblionet Romania Program. *Performance Measurement and Metrics*, *11*(1), 93–106. doi:10.1108/14678041011026900.

Colesca, S. E., & Dobrica, L. (2008). Adoption and use of e-government services: The case of Romania. *Journal of Applied Research and Technology*, *3*, 204–217.

Day, M. T. (1998). Transformational discourse: Ideologies of organizational change in the academic library and information science literature. *Library Trends*, *46*(4), 635–667.

Dickinson, A., & Gregor, P. (2006). Computer use has no demonstrated impact on the well-being of older adults. *International Journal of Human-Computer Studies, 64*(8), 744–753. doi:10.1016/j.ijhcs.2006.03.001.

European Union, Commission of the European Communities (2007). *Ageing well in the Information Society: An i2010 Initiative* (Communication No. COM (2007) 332 final). Brussels, Belgium. Retrieved on June 23, 2012, from http://eur-lex.europa.eu/LexUriServ/site/en/com/2007/com2007_0332en01.pdf

European Union, European Commission. (2007). *European i2010 initiative on e-Inclusion: "To be part of the information society"* (Communication No. COM (2007) 694 final). Retrieved on June 23, 2012, from http://ec.europa.eu/information_society/activities/einclusion/docs/i2010_initiative/comm_native_com_2007_0694_f_en_acte.pdf

European Union, European Commission, Information Society and Media. (2008). *Senoirwatch 2: Assessment of the Senior Market for ICT Progress and Developments.* Bonn and Brussels, Belgium. Retrieved on June 23, 2012, from http://ec.europa.eu/information_society/activities/einclusion/docs/swa2finalreport.pdf

Ford, G., & Ford, S. (2009). *Internet Use and Depression Among the Elderly.* Retrieved on June 23, 2012, from http://papers.ssrn.com/sol3/papers.cfm?abstract_id=1494430

Fried, S., Kochanowicz, M., & Chiranov, M. (2010). Planning for impact, assessing for sustainability. *Perform, 11*(1), 56–74.

Gilhooly, M. L. M., Gilhooly, K. J., & Jones, R. B. (2008). Quality of life: Conceptual challenges in exploring the role of ICT in active ageing. In Cabrera, M., & Malanowski, N. (Eds.), *Information and Communication Technology for Active Ageing: Opportunities and Challenges for the European Union* (pp. 49–76). Amsterdam, The Netherlands: IOS Press.

Hakkarainen, P. (2012). *No Good for Shovelling Snow and Carrying Firewood: Social Representations of Computers and the Internet by Elderly Finnish Non-Users. New Media & Society.* Thousand Oaks, CA: Sage Publications.

Ianculescu, M. (2011). The imperative role of ICT for supporting aging with dignity. In *Proceedings of the 15th WSEAS International Conference on Computers* (pp. 124–128). Stevens Point, Wisconsin: World of Scientific and Engineering Academy and Society. Retrieved on June 23, 2012, http://dl.acm.org/citation.cfm?id=2028325

Kanayama, T. (2003). Ethnographic Research on the Experience of Japanese Elderly People Online. *New Media & Society, 5*(2), 267–288. doi:10.1177/1461444803005002007.

Klimaszewski, C., Bader, G. E., & Nyce, J. M. (2011). "Success stories" as an evidence form: Organizational legitimization in an international technology assistance project. *Martor, 16.*

Klimaszewski, C., Bader, G. E., & Nyce, J. M. (2012a). Hierarchy, complicity and culture in the library and information science preservation agenda: Observations from Romania. *Journal of Librarianship and Information Science.*

Klimaszewski, C., Bader, G. E., & Nyce, J. M. (2012b). Studying up (and down) the cultural heritage preservation agenda: Observations from Romania. *European Journal of Cultural Studies, 15*(4), 479–495. doi:10.1177/1367549412455495.

Klimaszewski, C., Bader, G. E., Nyce, J. M., & Beasley, B. E. (2010). Who wins? Who loses? *Library Review, 59*(2), 92. doi:10.1108/00242531011023853.

Klimaszewski, C., & Nyce, J. M. (2009). Does universal access mean equitable access? What an information infrastructure study of a rural Romanian community can tell us. *New Library World, 110*(5/6), 219–236. doi:10.1108/03074800910954253.

Lin, C. I. C., Tang, W. H., & Kuo, F. Y. (2012). Mommy wants to learn the computer: How Middle-aged and elderly women in Taiwan learn ICT through social support. *Adult Education Quarterly, 62*(1), 73–90. doi:10.1177/0741713610392760.

Littrell, M. A., Nyce, J. M., Straub, J., & Whipple, M. (2006). A study of the information infrastructure of a Transylvanian village. *New Library World, 107*(7/8), 321–331. doi:10.1108/03074800610677290.

McClean, A. (2011). Ethical frontiers of ICT and older users: Cultural, pragmatic and ethical issues. *Ethics and Information Technology, 13*, 313–326. doi:10.1007/s10676-011-9276-4.

McMurtrey, M., McGaughey, R. E., Downey, J. P., & Zeltmann, S. M. (2010). Seniors and information technology: Much ado about something? In *2010 Conference Proceedings*. Presented at the Southwest Decision Institute Conference, Dallas, TX. Retrieved June 21, 2012, from http://www.swdsi.org/swdsi2010/SW2010_Preceedings/papers/PA130.pdf

Mikkola, K., & Halonen, R. (2011). *"Nonsense?" ICT perceived by the elderly* (pp. 306–317). A paper Presented at the European, Mediterranean & Middle Eastern Conference on Information Systems. Athens, Greece. Retrieved June 21, 2012, from http://www.iseing.org/emcis/EMCISWebsite/EMCIS2011%20Proceedings/SCI1.pdf

Mordini, E., Wright, D., Wadhwa, K., De Hert, P., Mantoyani, E., Thestrup, J., & Vater, I. (2009). Senior citizens and the ethics of e-inclusion. *Ethics and Information Technology, 11*, 203–220. doi:10.1007/s10676-009-9189-7.

Morris, A., Goodman, J., & Brading, H. (2007). Internet use and non-use: Views of older users. *Universal Access in the Information Society, 6*, 43–57. doi:10.1007/s10209-006-0057-5.

Nayak, L. U. S., Priest, L., & White, A. P. (2010). An application of the technology acceptance model to the level of Internet usage by older adults. *Universal Access in the Information Society, 9*, 367–374. doi:10.1007/s10209-009-0178-8.

Nita, V. (2011). An Extended Approach to E-Inclusion and its Implications for Romania. *SSRN eLibrary*. Retrieved June 21, 2012, from http://papers.ssrn.com/sol3/papers.cfm?abstract_id=1794346

Tobias, C. L. (1987). Computers and the Elderly: A Review of the Literature and Directions for Future Research. *Proceedings of the Human Factors and Ergonomics Society Annual Meeting, 31*(8), 866–870.

Țurlea, G., & Ciupagea, C. (2009). Happy e-Inclusion? The case of Romania. *Romanian Journal of Economic Forecasting, 110*.

Vintilă, M. (2000). La maisnie diffuse, du communisme au capitalisme: Questions et hypotheses. *Balkanaulogie, 4*(2).

Wagner, N., Hassanein, K., & Head, M. (2010). Computer use by older adults: A multi-disciplinary review. *Computers in Human Behavior, 26*, 870–882. doi:10.1016/j.chb.2010.03.029.

Whipple, M., & Nyce, J. M. (2007). Community analysis needs ethnography: An example from Romania. *Library Review, 56*(8), 694–706. doi:10.1108/00242530710818027.

Wicks, D. A. (2003). Building bridges for seniors: Older adults and the digital divide. Retrieved June 21, 2012, from http://www.cais-acsi.ca/proceedings/2003/Wicks_2003.pdf

Xie, B. (2006). Perceptions of computer learning among older Americans and older Chinese. *First Monday, 11*(10). Retrieved June 21, 2012, from http://www.firstmonday.org/htbin/cgiwrap/bin/ojs/index.php/fm/article/view/1408/1326

Yao, D., Qiu, Y., Huang, H., Du, Z., & Ma, J. (2011). A survey of technology accessibility problems faced by older users in China. *Universal Access in the Information Society, 10*(4), 373–390. doi:10.1007/s10209-011-0222-3.

ADDITIONAL READING

Anghelescu, H. G. B., Lukenbill, J., Lukenbill, W. B., & Owens, I. (2009). Acceptance of social marketing concepts by selected Romanian librarians: Culture and context. *Advances in Library Administration and Organization, 27*, 123–150. doi:10.1108/S0732-0671(2009)0000027012.

Checchi, R. M., Loch, K. D., Straub, D. W., Sevcik, G. R., & Meso, P. (2012). National ICT policies and development: A stage model and stakeholder theory perspective. *Journal of Global, 21*(1), 57–79.

Colesca, S. E., & Dobrica, L. (2008). Adoption and use of e-government services: The case of Romania. *Journal of Applied Research and Technology*, (3), 204–217. Retrieved June 21, 2012, from http://redalyc.uaemex.mx/redalyc/pdf/474/47413023006.pdf

Dickinson, A., & Gregor, P. (2006). Computer use has no demonstrated impact on the well-being of older adults. *International Journal of Human-Computer Studies, 64*(8), 744–753. doi:10.1016/j.ijhcs.2006.03.001.

European Commission. (2012). Digital Agenda for Europe. *Digital Agenda for Europe: A Europe 2020 INitiative*. Retrieved on November 26, 2012, from https://ec.europa.eu/digital-agenda/

European Commission. (2012). Europe's information society thematic portal. Retrieved on November 26, 2012, from http://ec.europa.eu/information_society/activities/einclusion/index_en.htm

Ford, G., & Ford, S. (2009). Internet use and depression among the elderly. Retrieved on November 26, 2012, from http://papers.ssrn.com/sol3/papers.cfm?abstract_id=1494430

Gilhooly, M. L. M., Gilhooly, K. J., & Jones, R. B. (2008). Quality of life: Conceptual challenges in exploring the role of ICT in active ageing. In Cabrera, M., & Malanowski, N. (Eds.), *Information and Communication Technology for Active Ageing: Opportunities and Challenges for the European Union* (pp. 49–76). Amsterdam, The Netherlands: IOS Press.

IGI Global, & Information Resources Management Association (2012). *Digital democracy concepts, methodologies, tools, and applications*. Hershey, Pa: IGI Global. Retrieved on November 26, 2012, from http://www.library.drexel.edu/cgi-bin/r.cgi?url=http://services.igi-global.com/resolvedoi/resolve.aspx?

Jordan, L., Tuijl, P. V., & Edwards, M. (2006). *NGO Accountability Politics Principles and Innovations*. London: Routledge.

Klimaszewski, C., & Nyce, J. M. (2009). Does universal access mean equitable access? What an information infrastructure study of a rural Romanian community can tell us. *New Library World, 110*(5/6), 219–236. doi:10.1108/03074800910954253.

Loos, E., Haddon, L., & Mante-Meijer, E. A. (2008). *The social dynamics of information and communication technology*. Aldershot, England; Burlington, VT: Ashgate Pub. Company. McClean, A. (2011). Ethical frontiers of ICT and older users: Cultural, pragmatic and ethical issues. *Ethics and Information Technology, 13*, 313–326.

Mordini, E., Wright, D., Wadhwa, K., De Hert, P., Mantoyani, E., & Thestrup, J. et al. (2009). Senior citizens and the ethics of e-inclusion. *Ethics and Information Technology*, (11): 203–220. doi:10.1007/s10676-009-9189-7.

Morris, A., Goodman, J., & Brading, H. (2007). Internet use and non-use: Views of older users. *Universal Access in the Information Society, 6*, 43–57. doi:10.1007/s10209-006-0057-5.

Nita, V. (2011). An Extended Approach to E-Inclusion and its Implications for Romania. *SSRN eLibrary*. Retrieved on November 26, 2012, from http://papers.ssrn.com/sol3/papers.cfm?abstract_id=1794346

Pertot, J. C., McClure, C. R., & Jaeger, P. T. (2010). Public libraries and the Internet: Roles, perspectives, and implications. Santa Barbara, CA: Libraries Unlimited.

Tanner, S. (2012, October 23). When the Data hits the Fan!: The Balanced Value Impact Model. *When the Data Hits the Fan!* Retrieved on November 19, 2012, from http://simon-tanner.blogspot.com/2012/10/the-balanced-value-impact-model.html

Ţurlea, G., & Ciupagea, C. (2009). Happy e-Inclusion? The case of Romania. *Romanian Journal of Economic Forecasting, 110*. Retrieved on November 26, 2012, from http://89.38.230.246/rjef/rjef3_09/rjef3_09_9.pdf

Vetta, T. (2009). Democracy puilding in Serbia: The NGO effect. *Southeastern Europe. L'Europe du Sud-Est, 33*(1), 26–47. doi:10.1163/187633309X421148.

Wagner, N., Hassanein, K., & Head, M. (2010). Computer use by older adults: A multi-disciplinary review. *Computers in Human Behavior, 26*, 870–882. doi:10.1016/j.chb.2010.03.029.

Whipple, M., & Nyce, J. M. (2007). Community analysis needs ethnography: An example from Romania. *Library Review, 56*(8), 694–706. doi:10.1108/00242530710818027.

World Bank Group. (2012). The World Bank Romania. Retrieved on November 26, 2012, from http://www.worldbank.org/en/country/romania

World Summit on the Information Society. (2012). *World Summit on the Information Society*. Retrieved on November 26, 2012, from http://www.itu.int/wsis/index.html

KEY TERMS AND DEFINITIONS

Active Ageing: Policies and programs that strive to enhance quality of life for people as they age by providing increased opportunities for involvement in daily life and for increased independence.

Cross-Cultural Development: The process by which (usually Western-based or sponsored) NGOs work with stakeholders in developing countries to improve quality of life.

E-Inclusion: Policies and practices that aim to provide more equitable access to ICTs.

Impact Assessment: The methods and processes used to measure the actual effects of development projects against the project's stated goals and objectives. Note that quality impact assessment considers both positive and negative impacts of a program or project.

Information Society: Society where the creation, distribution, use, integration and manipulation of information is a significant economic, political and cultural activity.

Older Adults: Adults at or close to retirement age.

User Experience: Includes a person's thoughts and feelings about their actual experience of using technology as well as their perceptions about using technology.

User Training: The process by which users learn to use technology.

ENDNOTES

[1]   This research study was funded in part by IREX.

[2]   The bulk of the research at the pensioners' club was undertaken by Corina Cimpoieru, doctoral student at the Şcoala Natională de Studii Politice şi Administrative (SNSPA) in Bucharest.

[3]   The *diffuse household* networks emerged as a consequence of the work migration and other forms of geographic and social mobility. Linking together rural and urban residents, the diffused household emerged as a functional unit during communism and it was based on a specific distribution of work and redistribution of resources to which their members had access due to their particular occupation. Urbanization and migratory labor has created a new class of laborers who chose to move geographically and socially from their village in order to cope with the needs of the subsistence economy practiced by their households. These displaced members that became urban industrial workers were still connected to their countryside through the diffuse household networks (*see* Vintilă, 2000).

Chapter 13

Contextual Factors Influencing Information Seeking Behavior of Social Scientists:
A Review of the Literature

Mohammed Nasser Al-Suqri
Sultan Qaboos University, Oman

ABSTRACT

Many researchers in the area of information seeking behavior have highlighted the importance of context in influencing information-seeking behavior. However, few have elaborated on how contextual factors influence information-seeking in practice. This chapter explores the impact of disciplinary traditions of non-western, developing country external environments on patterns of information seeking and retrieval. Conditions that influence information seeking behaviors of social science scholars in non-western, developing countries impact research traditions, publication patterns, and subsequent formats are examined. This chapter draws on existing literature to examine the impact of contextual factors on information seeking by social science scholars as well as, on relevant findings based on research with other categories of researchers. The chapter concludes that there is substantial evidence from previous research to indicate the importance of contextual factors in influencing the information-seeking behavior of social scientists. Some of these factors are related to the nature of social science as a domain of study, while others are related to researcher's external environment, including constraints on the availability of particular types of information.

INTRODUCTION

Many researchers in the area of information seeking behavior have highlighted the importance of context in influencing information-seeking behavior. However, few have elaborated on how

contextual factors influence information-seeking in practice. Wilson, who developed one of the earliest models of information seeking, later acknowledged that his 1981 model paid insufficient attention to contextual factors. He writes "the limitation of this kind of model, however, is that

DOI: 10.4018/978-1-4666-4353-6.ch013

it does little more than provide a map of the area and draw attention to gaps in research: it provides no suggestion of causative factors in information [behavior] and, consequently, it does not directly suggest hypotheses to be tested" (Wilson, 1999, p. 251).

Although Wilson and others have taken steps to incorporate contextual factors into their models of information seeking, this is still an area in which there are gaps in understanding, and as a result no comprehensive theory of information seeking has yet been developed which can be readily applied to different contextual situations, such as different disciplinary groups or geographical or cultural environments. More modeling is therefore necessary in order to advance our understanding of information seeking. As Bates (2005) noted, "Models are most useful at the description and prediction stages of understanding a phenomenon. Only when we develop an explanation for a phenomenon can we properly say we have a theory. Consequently, most of theory in LIS is really still at the modeling stage" (Bates, 2005).

In order to investigate the role of contextual factors on information seeking, this chapter discusses relevant findings from previous studies and explores the impact of disciplinary traditions of non-western, developing country external environments on patterns of information seeking and retrieval. Specifically, the following issues are addressed:

1. Research traditions and the publication patterns and formats and their impacts on the social science scholars information seeking.
2. Conditions influence information seeking behaviors of social science scholars in non-western, developing countries.

In discussing these issues, this paper also highlights the ways in which the technological information environment has undergone dramatic changes since the earlier models of information seeking were developed, and how this is having a

major impact on patterns of information-seeking, although perhaps to a greater or lesser extent for different categories of researchers. This study focuses specifically on the impact of contextual factors on information seeking by social science scholars, but also draws on relevant findings based on research with other categories of researchers where these are particularly significant.

RESEARCH TRADITIONS AND THE PUBLICATION PATTERNS AND FORMATS

Many earlier studies found that although there were some differences between researchers of different disciplines in their information-seeking behavior, there were also many similarities (e.g., APA, INFROSS, cited in Brittain, 1984; Ellis, Cox & Hall, 1993; Folster, 1989; Romanos de Tiratel, 2000; Ellis & Haugan, 1997).

In the 1970s, a major program of research conducted at Bath University, as in Brittain (1984), in the UK investigated the information-seeking behaviors of social science scholars and practitioners. Often referred to simply as 'The Bath Studies', the Investigation into Information Requirements of the Social Sciences (INFROSS) and the Design of Information Systems in the Social Sciences (DISISS) were the first major studies conducted from an Information Science perspective which aimed to determine social science user requirements in terms of library and information services. However, the current practical relevance of findings from the Bath studies is very limited, since the studies were conducted long before the information-seeking environment was transformed by the development and widespread use of electronic resources, particularly the Internet.

Ellis and Haugan (1997), who conducted a study of the research activities of engineers and research scientists at Statoil's Research Center in Norway, were able to readily map the engineers' and scientists' information-seeking activities to the eight generic stages of research already identified by Ellis for social scientists: surveying; chaining; monitoring; browsing; distinguishing; filtering; extracting and ending. Ellis and Haugan concluded that Ellis' information-seeking model was robust in relation to the information-seeking patterns of scientists, engineers and social scientists in both an academic and an industrial research environment and over a period of time in which there had been considerable developments in the information environment as a result of rapid technological change (Ellis & Haugan, 1997).

However, there is a growing body of research evidence indicating that there are indeed significant differences in the information-seeking behavior of researchers in different disciplines, which can be related largely to the research traditions and the dominant publication patterns and formats in their domain of study. This evidence has significant implications for the delivery of library and information services and for the advancement of models and theories of information seeking.

The Use of Formal Sources

Ucak and Kurbanoglu (1998) carried out a study of engineers, scientists, social scientists, and humanities scholars in a Turkish University and found significant differences between all four groups in their information seeking behavior, with the engineers and humanities scholars exhibiting the most dissimilar pattern of information-seeking behavior. The most important differences between the groups related to their use of books compared with periodicals for research, and the researchers observed that this was due to the relative importance to the groups of having up-to-date information. This was most important for the engineers and scientists, who relied most heavily on periodicals, and least important for the humanities scholars, with social scientists having a general preference for books but also using journals more than humanities scholars. As a consequence, the scientists and engineers also used electronic re-

trieval systems and various databases, indices and abstracts more frequently and intensively than the humanities or social science researchers.

Similarly, Tenopir (2003) noted that many previous studies have observed that although scientists in all fields of work read peer-reviewed journal articles, there are significant differences in their level of use of such articles and whether they obtain them in print or electronic format (Pullinger & Baldwin, 2002; Tenopir & King, 2000; Kling & McKim, 1999; Kling & McKim, 2000, cited in Tenopir, 2003). For example, physicists, it is observed, have traditionally been heavy users of preprint articles and have adapted and make much use of e-print services, because their research tends to be highly collaborative, while engineers tend to read fewer journal articles than scientists, but highly value them and spend more time on those that they do read (Tenopir, 2003).

Quigley, Peck, Rutter, McKee, and Williams' (2002) survey of 230 science faculty and researchers at the University of Michigan also observed different levels of use of preprint literature and noted the important tradition of using this publication format in certain scientific disciplines, notably mathematics (78%) and astronomy (70%). In disciplines where preprinted literature was used less frequently, such as geology (13.3%) and chemistry (9.1%), the research team noted that it is sometimes the case that the use of preprint literature is actively discouraged by their respective professions.

Use of Informal Sources

Research has found that both social scientists and humanities scholars tend to favor informal methods of obtaining information such as consulting colleagues, browsing and following references or citations (chaining) from other works (Bouazza, 1986; Watson-Boone, cited in Bass, Fairlee, Fox, & Sullivan, 2005; Hobohm, 1999, Ucak & Kurbanoglu, 1998). They are also less likely than other categories of researchers to consult reference librarians or bibliographic reference tools (Duff & Johnson, 2002). In the case of humanities scholars, one explanation which has been given for this tradition of using informal sources is that they are already experts in their respective fields and do not have a need for help or advice when searching for information, or that they are reluctant to acknowledge a lack of information or knowledge of important sources (Ucak & Kurbanoglu, 1998).

A number of studies and articles have indicated that social science research tends to be less systematic and more informal than in other research domains, such as the physical sciences and humanities (INFROSS, 1970, cited in Wilson, 2000; Brittain, 1984; Bouazza, 1986). Line (1999) has argued that the "relative lack of coherence and consistency in the social sciences" (p. 132) and the instability of the subject matter has meant that "the penalties for ignorance of previous work in supposedly similar areas are far less than in the pure or applied sciences" (p. 132). The inference is that social scientists have less rigorous information-seeking behavior than other types of researchers and have also been less likely to demand improved library and information services to meet the needs of their disciplines. Following this line of argument, it is possible to contend that information-seeking and retrieval by social science scholars is less systematic and rigorous through necessity, due to a lack of sufficient information in their subject areas, and that they have to make do with whatever is available to them (Line, 1999).

Research topics in social science frequently span many different sub-disciplines, such as geography, history, psychology, and sociology, rather than being clearly delineated in the way that physical science research topics often are. Moreover, as Line (1999) notes, since social science is concerned with human beings interacting or acting in groups, "the interaction of largely unpredictable with other largely unpredictable beings produces great scope for instability and uncertainty" (Line, 1999, p. 131). These inherent

characteristics of social science research often require a great deal of flexibility and innovation in information-seeking behavior, which leads to the use of informal sources of information such as colleagues, and the use of various chaining strategies to follow up references in what may often appear to be an unsystematic fashion.

Since social science is the study of people and societies which are themselves in a constant state of development and change, this means that the concepts, terminologies and findings of research in this domain tend to change much more frequently than those of other disciplines, and there are fewer definitive sources of reference information available. Moreover, social scientific research is more often conducted from a specific theoretical or ideological perspective, and the findings of previous studies, therefore, have to be regarded much more cautiously and interpreted more carefully than in research domains where there is a greater degree of consensus or inherent objectivity, such as the physical sciences. This may be one of the factors leading social science scholars to rely more heavily on references in books rather than citations in periodical articles, since the latter may be regarded as less authoritative given the relative ease of publication in journals rather than books.

In general, previous studies have found that social science scholars utilize a wide variety of sources in their information-seeking, including books, journals, monographs, archives, citations, indexes and abstract, personal collection, and electronic sources (Brittain, 1970; Stoan, 1991; Folster, 1989; Meho, 2001; Case, 2002). However, a number of studies have found that social scientists are particularly likely to use informal methods of searching for information sources, compared with their counterparts in other academic disciplines.

One of the main findings of the Bath Studies (in Brittain, 1984), for example, was that compared with scholars of other disciplines, social science scholars were less likely to use a formalized approach to information retrieval and preferred personal recommendations, browsing, and chain citations over the traditional bibliographies and reference databases used by their non-social science peers.

Similarly, the social science researchers as well as the scientists in Ellis, Cox, and Hall's (1993) study employed personal contacts as an initial source of information when approaching a new topic. Both groups were found to rely equally heavily on starter references, personal contacts, reviews or review type material, and secondary services. In comparison, the humanities scholars tended to rely more heavily on formal sources when seeking information, such as printed bibliographies, subject catalogues and research guides (Broadbent, 1986; Stoan, 1991; Sievert & Sievert, 1989; Wiberley & Jones, 1989). Given the observed similarities between scientists and social scientists in their heavy use of personal contacts in information-seeking, the findings of research by Brittain (1970) on the role of informal networks in the science community may also help to shed light on their role among social scientists. Brittain (1970) found that the informal networks is a quick way in bringing new developments to researchers, help to keep researchers aware of the latest state of knowledge in their field, and the information disseminated by the informal networks is current. Informal networks were also seen to be important as an informal arena in which scientists are willing to speculate about their work, discuss their mistakes as well as their successes, and range over a broad area of interests which in a more rigorous framework may appear only tangential to their specific findings, and, finally, it allows them to direct a communication and select the information they need.

The research highlighted above was conducted long before the establishment of the Internet and other electronic means of communication, and it may be the case that the relative importance or nature of informal networks within academic communities has changed as a result. However,

more recent research with scientists (Ucak & Kurbanoghu, 1998) also found that scientific conferences and meetings provided this group with an important platform for the acquisition of informal information through discussions with colleagues encountered at such gatherings. When the respondents in Ucak and Kurbanoghu's (1998) study were asked as to why they attend scientific meetings, all indicated that such meetings were beneficial, not only for the knowledge gained from listening to presentations and discussions, but also for developing social contacts and relationships. It may be that the establishment of the Internet has facilitated the process of informal networking among various groups of academics, complementing rather than detracting from the importance of face to face gatherings. This view was supported by research by Borgman (2000) who noted that "The invisible college…has embraced the ease in communicating informally in a virtual environment" (p. 145).

Similarly, Tenopir (2003) noted that many previous studies have observed that although scientists in all fields of work read peer-reviewed journal articles, there are significant differences in their level of use of such articles and whether they obtain them in print or electronic format (Pullinger & Baldwin, 2002; Tenopir & King, 2000; Kling & McKim, 1999; Kling & McKim, 2000, cited in Tenopir, 2003). For example, physicists, it is observed, have traditionally been heavy users of preprint articles and have adapted and make much use of e-print services, because their research tends to be highly collaborative, while engineers tend to read fewer journal articles than scientists, but highly value them and spend more time on those that they do read (Tenopir, 2003).

Quigley, Peck, Rutter, McKee, and Williams' (2002) survey of 230 science faculty and researchers at the University of Michigan also observed different levels of use of preprint literature and noted the important tradition of using this publication format in certain scientific disciplines, notably mathematics (78%) and astronomy (70%). In disciplines where preprinted literature was used less frequently, such as geology (13.3%) and chemistry (9.1%), the research team noted that it is sometimes the case that the use of preprint literature is actively discouraged by their respective professions.

As the social sciences are interdisciplinary in nature, a number of studies have found that social scientists tend to fall somewhere between other disciplines such as science and humanities, using a wider range of formal and informal sources (Case, 2002, p. 238). As such, social science scholars rely on a wide variety of both formal (e.g., journal articles, books) and informal sources (e.g., personal contacts, colleagues) of information. They often have to depend on literature (e.g., printed documents, archival materials, government publications, newspapers, statistics) from other disciplines not indexed in social sciences literature per se which require "a great deal of creative ingenuity on the part of the researcher to conceptualize as significant and then track down" (Stoan, 1991, p. 244).

Publications

These characteristics of social science have also resulted in different publication patterns and formats which affect the availability of information and how it can be used. In many physical sciences, for example, there is a well-established terminology and definitive research findings which have facilitated the development of databases, handbooks, indices and abstracts, which are as a result widely used in information-seeking within these disciplines and less so in the social science and humanities domains, where encyclopedias and dictionaries are more frequently used as reference sources (Ucak & Kurbanoglu, 1998).

The lack of consensus in the social sciences may also necessitate the use of broader-ranging information searches and the consultation of a larger number of sources in order to effectively interpret and evaluate the findings of previous work on a particular subject. Nevertheless, a number of studies have found that journals articles are one of the most popular sources of information overall for social scientists, more so than for humanities scholars (Folster, 1989; Romanos de Tiratel, 2000), perhaps because of the greater need in social science for up to date information given the rate of development of social science knowledge.

Compared with the physical sciences, it has also been much more difficult to develop a coherent and comprehensive established body of research in the social sciences due to the parochial nature of many social science studies and the tendency for social science researchers to write in their own native languages rather than English (Line, 1999). The body of research which does exist tends to consist predominantly of material published in the English language and from Western countries. It has also been observed that there has been a general tendency for parochialism within social science in Western and Eastern Europe and the United States (Brittain, 1986), with research from the U.S. being most predominant in availability and accessibility all over the world, while research from outside these three main areas is virtually ignored in other parts of the world. Publication patterns and accessibility of sources to social science researchers around the world, therefore, influence their information-seeking behavior by encouraging a focus on American and other English-language sources and the research findings they contain, at the expense of non-Western research findings published in other languages, which might have taken information-seekers in different directions, both in their continuing search for information and the conclusions they arrive at in their own research. Although Brittain's (1986) comments on the parochialism of social science research were made before the development of the

World Wide Web which has improved the ease of international communications between social science researchers, it remains likely that research published in the English language will receive a greater audience than material in other languages.

The Use of Primary Research

A further difference in information-seeking between social scientists and other researchers is that social scientists often undertake ground-breaking research in particular topics, or alternative need to generate up-to-date findings, for example on people's attitudes or experiences. As a result, they can rely less heavily on secondary sources of material than, say, humanities researchers and spend more time generating new information or data from primary sources rather than seeking existing information. This is one of the reasons why studies of information-seeking have found that social science scholars spend less time consulting library sources than researchers in other disciplines (e.g., Romanos de Tiratel, 2000).

Location of Information

Several studies have found that researchers from various disciplines mainly use information located in libraries, personal collections, or among their network of colleagues or other contacts. For social scientists, the inter-disciplinary nature of their work means that the books and journals they need are often spread throughout a library, and it can be difficult to use library resources efficiently, even with the assistance of a librarian (Turner, 2000). Perhaps for this reason, few of the social scientists surveyed by Abouserie (2003) indicated that they read from sources located in the central and department libraries. While a slightly higher percentage reported using sources in their own homes, the majority stated that they read from sources located in their offices. Similarly, a

study by Folster (1989) revealed that consulting a librarian was a very low priority for social scientists engaging in information-seeking. Folster (1995) found that libraries are utilized only as a last resort by social scientists and are viewed as sources for acquiring material previously identified as relevant, rather than as a primary source for identifying relevant information. Instead, social scientists have been shown to greatly value and heavily rely on personal collections for their research (Soper, 1976; Folster, 1989; Hartmann, 1995; Hobohm, 1999). Several studies on information needs and information-seeking behavior of users have indicated that the process of seeking information always starts with the personal collection (Hobohm, 1999). Both scientists and social scientists in Soper's (1976) study reported that convenience was the main reason for putting effort and money into building their personal collections. Other reasons cited were easier to use due to the ability to arrange the collection to meet and reflect their needs and interests and the flexibility, responsiveness, and accessibility of personal collections more than other collection of materials (Soper, 1976).

This is another area in which existing research findings are less likely to be relevant to a developing country context. It is likely to be the case that libraries in developing countries will have smaller collections of relevant materials, particularly in the relatively young subject areas of the social sciences. This may lead to an increased reliance on personal collections, but at the same time it may be difficult to build these personal collections due to budgetary constraints and the difficult of purchasing academic resources locally. Again, research is needed in this area to understand the role of location of information on patterns of information-seeking, which is likely to have wider applicability to understand human behavior in information-seeking.

Use of Electronic Resources

Electronic sources have revolutionized the way research can be done. Those seeking information no longer have to physically go to the library but can stay at home or the office and merely need to log on to access online library information resources. The ease in which information can be retrieved online "can enable innovation in teaching and increase timeliness in research as well as increase discovery and creation of new fields of inquiry" (Renwick, 2005, p. 21), and research has shown that many information-seekers prefer to use electronic resources and the Internet to obtain information quickly and easily (Dalgleish & Hall, 2000). Tenopir (2003) conducted a study of the ways in which students and faculty in an academic setting use the Internet and other electronic resources. This revealed that relevant articles were generally printed out rather than saved or book marked, and that hyperlinks were used by scholars to locate and view related research. Tenopir (2003) also discovered that library subscriptions to e-journals were increasing over time as scholars from different disciplines increasingly relied on them, while library and personal subscriptions to print journals were decreasing.

Some studies have found that social scientists lag behind their counterparts in other academic disciplines in their use of technology (Hobohm, 1999). Even at the time of the Bath studies, social science scholars were found to be less likely than those in other academic disciplines to make use of new technology in their information seeking (Line, 1971). By the late 1980s, studies were indicating that social scientists' use of technology had still not increased significantly since the Bath studies; possible reasons for this according to Preschel and Woods (1989, p. 282) were "costs, the interdisciplinary structure, imprecise terminology and fuzzy-edged concepts of the subject areas, and the possibly poor prospectus for return on investment," suggesting that it may have been

at least in part a lack of adequate technology provision in libraries which was contributing to the low of usage among social scientists. However, many studies have provided evidence that social scientists actually prefer to use print resources for information (Hernon, 1984; Folster, 1989; Hobohm, 1999; Folster, 1995; Tenopir, 2003; Francis, 2005) and are less likely to use electronic sources (Bouazza, 1986; Hobohm, 1999). According to these studies, social scientists mainly rely on books, journals, conferences proceedings, bibliographies, government publication, and dissertations for their information.

In general, it seems that traditional print sources of information continue to be important to social scientists, along with other academic researchers, despite the growth in the availability of electronic-format information. This was predicted in 1992 by the participants in Reichel's study of humanists, scientists, and social science scholars in a university environment. When interviewed about their perceptions of how technological resources will affect the information-seeking process by the year 2001, the scholars indicated that even though they believed that electronic access to information would be dominant by 2001, traditional sources would continue to be important and the overall impact will be additional types of information sources, not replacement of formats. Similarly, Curtis, Weller, and Hurd's (1993) study of health sciences faculty at the University of Illinois at Chicago found that although new electronic formats were becoming available for accessing literature, the traditional formats of information resources continued to be used.

Nevertheless, there does seem to have been a significant increase over time in the use of electronic resources by social science scholars, reflecting a general trend in information-seeking behavior, which has had an impact on academic research generally. Meho & Haas' (2001) research topic based analysis revealed that besides using traditional methods for locating relevant information, social science scholars used the World Wide Web and electronic mail in their information-seeking. More than 88% of the social scientists in this study indicated that they had electronic resources in their research of the Kurds, including several core social science indexes and abstracts (Meho & Haas, 2001, p. 20). These findings mirror those of similar research with science researchers. According to Curtis, Weller, and Hurd (1997), the use of electronic resources by scientists had increased since their first study in 1991. Faculty used electronic resources in higher percentages and used a wider of electronic resources in 1995 than they did in 1991, and this trend towards electronic resources was expected to continue.

Similarly, a survey of science faculty at the University of Oklahoma conducted by Brown (1999) found that less than 50% of the science faculty were using electronic journals for teaching and research. Another survey by Lenares (1999) found that the percentage of the use of electronic journals by scientists from different disciplines had jumped to 61%. Lenares' (1999) study found that the number of faculty using electronic journals had increased in all disciplines, with the greatest growth in use among scholars in the physical and biological sciences. Ninety percent of respondents in the physical sciences reported that they use electronic journals.

Research since then has supported Meho and Haas' (2001) findings that social science faculty generally utilize information technology to support their research (Hughes & Buchanan, 2001; Tenopir et al., 2003; Heterick, 2002; Tombros, Ruthven, & Jose, 2005). A study by Heterick (2002) indicated that social scientists comfortable using electronic resources and they believe that variety of electronic resources such as databases are very important for their research. Francis' (2005) study of social scientists' information-seeking behaviors at the University of the West Indies revealed a preference for journal articles in electronic format over print articles, which demonstrates that social scientists

"have embraced electronic publishing and [have] electronic access capabilities" (Francis, 2005, p. 71). It was reported that the awareness of new information technology among the social scientists in this study was demonstrated not only by their knowledge and use of the Internet and e-mail, but also by their utilization of a wide range of other relevant electronic databases.

The main limitation of previous research in this area is the reduced applicability of much of the work to present-day information-seeking, given the extremely rapid changes in the nature of the technological environment which are taking place. Even since the publication of the Meho and Haas study in 2001, it can be expected that there may have been an increase in the use of electronic information-seeking, as technology becomes faster and easier to use, more resources become available in electronic format, and individuals become more skilled in the use of information technology. The major significance of the technological environment to Library and Information Science research presents challenges to this area, since there is a constant need to update the findings of previous studies and to explore the impact of technology in a range of different subject areas and geographical environments.

Factors Influencing the Use of Electronic Resources

The retrieval techniques required with the use of technology are often incompatible with the way social scientists search for information. Hobohm (1999) describes this problem as twofold, due to

...the rigid methods of the computer with regard to storing and retrieving information, and the fuzzy object and informal scientific behavior of the scholars. Information retrieval is inherently uncertain and incomplete because on the input side you never really know for which circumstances a document indexed will find a future use, and

on the output side–the moment of information retrieval–you do not know which context has produced documents you will find. And necessarily it has been different in most of the aspects, not only in terms of the date of creation. And finally there is the indexing process itself which is problematic regardless if it has been done by human in intellectual indexing or by a machine in automatic indexing (p.125).

Moreover, the specialized nature of social science research often impedes social science scholars' success in finding adequate information in electronic format. For example, social science research that is historically focused requires the examination of archival materials (Meho & Tibbo, 2003, p. 575). It is among these scholars that reliance on personal collections, archives, and fieldwork may be more appropriate than the use of electronic resources. However, other research has found that electronic resources are more useful to social scientists than to humanities scholars (Wiberley & Jones, 1994) since humanistic evidence is not easily categorized or entered into relational databases is not readily subject to statistical analysis in the way that much of social science material is (Wiberley & Jones, 1994).

Personal characteristics and previous experience also have an impact on the extent of use of electronic resources among academic scholars. In a study of medical science faculty at the University of the West Indies (Renwick, 2005), it was found that "how faculty attain [computer] skills and knowledge depends on many factors, such as their disciplines, academic status and ranks, ages, access (hardware and location) to electronic resources, and training. Factors motivating use can be, for example, what level of importance they allocate to e-resources, how useful they have found them, and for which purposes they use e-resources" (p.22).

Renwick (2005) argued that the library plays a leading role in terms of orientation and training in the use of information resources, including

electronic resources. However, an earlier study by Stoan (1991) reported that "[Social science scholars'] rates of use do not improve even when [they] are trained in database searching and given more convenient access" (p. 248). Although the use of information technology has increased generally since the time of Stoan's study, it is likely that there is still a disparity between those scholars in the social sciences or other disciplines who are more or less technologically literate and are at ease with the Internet and other electronic sources.

The availability of electronic-format information within a particular field of study will also have an impact on the use of electronic resources in information searching in that field. In this context, there has been a major increase in recent years in the availability of electronic journals, in many different academic areas, reflecting the increasingly important role that journals occupy in academic research, whether in print or electronic format (Tomney & Burton, 1998; Tenopir & King, 2001; Fry & Talja, 2004). Tenopir and King (2001) found that about a third of the journal articles being read by scientists in their study were from electronic resources or digital databases, and that reading of journals had increased in recent years and had become diversified to cover a wide variety of journals. Among the West Indian social scientists in Francis' (2005) study, it was found that a number of electronic databases were very popular, including EbscoHost, Emerald, OCLC FirstSearch, and Proquest. However, between a quarter and one-third of the participants had never heard of each of these sources, indicating that there is still a wide diversity of practice within social science in terms of electronic information-seeking.

Comparing the usage of electronic resources among various disciplines, the SuperJournal project indicated that social scientists are more task-driven (browse or search depending on the task) than scientists in their use of electronic journals. More specifically, social science scholars search for current and relevant articles when prompted by tasks while scientists browse electronic journals on a regular basis to keep up to date (Pullinger & Baldwin, 2002).

Studies, which have investigated the impact of factors influencing the use of electronic resources, have been valuable in highlighting the influence of personal factors such as age, occupational seniority and previous experience. This is a perspective which has been lacking more generally in research on information-seeking with the majority of studies simply describing behavior, or, at most, comparing it between researchers of different disciplines. There is a pressing requirement for research on information-seeking, which examines the relationships between socio-demographic factors and information-seeking behavior and its outcomes. This was a major focus of the current study, which investigated patterns of information-seeking behavior by variables such as age, gender, length of service, rank, department, college, and preferred search language.

Diversity within Social Science

Despite these general observations about the influence of research traditions and publication formats in the social science domain, it is important to note that there is considerable diversity between different social science disciplines, which will also influence patterns of information-seeking. For example, as Line (1999) notes, econometrics, a branch of economics, is closely related to mathematics and research in this area thus shares similarities with the natural sciences, while survey research is regarded as being a 'soft' discipline, with a high degree of variability in the findings of different studies. Additionally, individual characteristics such as the researcher's own level of experience and purpose for conducting research will interact with disciplinary characteristics to affect patterns of information seeking and the resources used.

CONDITIONS INFLUENCE INFORMATION SEEKING BEHAVIORS OF SCHOLARS IN NON-WESTERN, DEVELOPING COUNTRIES

Most studies of information-seeking behavior have been conducted in Western, English-speaking countries, and the research participants have often been selected from large academic institutions with abundant information resources. However, these are unlikely to be representative of scholars around the world. Many academic researchers are based in non-Western, developing countries where the availability of research materials may be more limited and where there may be other types of constraints on information seeking and retrieval. There are a limited number of research studies, which have focused on information-seeking by researchers in developing countries. This section discusses the key findings of a number of these studies in order to highlight the conditions that may influence information-seeking behavior in such countries. It is intended to shed further light on how models of information-seeking behavior may need to be refined in order to adequately incorporate contextual factors in order to move towards a comprehensive theory of information-seeking.

Similarities with Developed Countries

Some studies of information-seeking behavior in non-Western, non-English speaking countries have found that there are few differences between information seeking in these countries and in the west, and that the various models of information-seeking behavior, such as Ellis' (1989) can be readily applied to researchers in developing countries.

For example, on the basis of a three-year longitudinal study of the information-seeking behaviors of social science and humanities scholars at the

University of Buenos Aires in Argentina, Romanos de Tiratel (2000) concluded that there were no significant differences between these researchers and those in Anglo-Saxon countries. When initiating research, both groups demonstrated a preference for using informal information search methods such as consulting colleagues. Taking a social constructionist perspective, Romanos de Tiratel (2000) concluded that neither geographical nor disciplinary differences account for different patterns of information seeking, since each user's information need is unique and his or her information is formed and interpreted through interactions with other individuals and the diverse social and organizational contexts in which the research is conducted.

Other studies have also found that the information-seeking behavior of social scientists in developing countries is very similar to that of social scientists in Western, English-speaking countries, but have concluded that this is because the main influence on information seeking is the discipline of the researcher, regardless of their geographical location.

For example, Francis' (2005) study of social science faculty at the University of the West Indies, Augustine, found that, as in the Anglo-Saxon world, social scientists in this university favor the use of journal articles to inform their research and keep them up to date with developments in their specialist area. Like the Argentinean researchers in Romanos de Tiratel's (2000) study, the West Indian social scientists also relied heavily on informal sources of information such as recommendations by colleagues. Francis concluded that regardless of the location and information environment in which social science scholars' work, journals in particular are an essential information resource for them, and that information-seeking patterns in the social sciences are universal in nature. Similarly, Ucak and Kurbanoglu (1998), who conducted

research with scholars in science, engineering, social sciences and humanities in a Turkish University, came to the conclusions that the main differences in information-seeking behavior are between disciplines, not between countries.

Despite the similarities which these studies have found between the actual information-seeking practices of researchers in developing countries and in Western, developed countries, there is also research evidence of particular conditions often found in less developed countries which are likely to impose constraints or other influences on the ways in which social science scholars in particular, as well as other academic researchers in developing countries, obtain their research material.

Format and Location of Information Used

Existing studies on social science scholars in developing countries indicate that despite dissimilar working environments and differences in the quality and quantity of available resources, social scientists in developing and developed countries share common characteristics in their information needs and seeking behaviors (Romanos de Tiratel, 2000; Lleperuma, 2002; Patitungkho & Deshpande, 2005). For example, Romanos de Tiratel (2000) investigated the information-seeking behaviors of Argentine social science and humanities scholars at the University of Buenos Aires and found no substantial differences between them and scholars in Anglo-Saxon countries. When initiating research, this group of social scientists tended to use informal sources such as consultation with colleagues before utilizing formal sources, such as journals, just like their colleagues in developed countries (Ellis et al., 1993; Hallmark, 1994).

Francis (2005) highlighted the importance of informal networking among social scientists in developing countries, since "much of the information social scientists from developing countries would find useful cannot be found in external databases" (p. 71). A number of studies have highlighted the importance of personal communication with colleagues in one's region, and in other parts of the world, as a vital information resource for scholars in developing countries (Lleperuma, 2002; Menou, 1993). The most practical method for personal communication with colleagues, particularly those in other countries, is through the use of e-mail. However, although scholars in some developing nations utilize e-mail, access to the Internet and other electronic resources appears to vary among countries, and research on the topic is scarce (Younis, 2002).

Social scientists in developing countries have also been found to express a preference for formal compared with informal sources of information, despite also using the latter frequently. For example, the social science scholars in Lleperuma's (2002) study exhibited a distinct preference for formal sources of information and considered maps, atlases, and access to databases as the least important sources. Likewise, social science scholars in Haryana, India indicated that they prefer formal sources than the informal. Current journals were the most used sources, followed by books (Shokeen & Kushik, 2002). In a study of the information-seeking behaviors of education, humanities, and social science faculty members from six universities in Bangkok, Thailand, textbooks were found to be the most popular type of information source for all faculty members (Patitungkho and Deshpande, 2005). In Romanos de Tiratel's (2000) study, both social scientists and humanities scholars reported that they preferred to use materials written in their mother tongue or translated into it.

Research among social scientists in developing countries also highlights a heavy dependence among this group on the use of official government publications, which has similarly been identified among social scientists in the Western world. For example, in a study of social science faculty at the University of Botswana, 97.3% indicated that they consult government publications for research (89%) and teaching (86%) (Mooko & Aina, 1998). When asked about the specific types of government documents utilized, respondents in Mooko and Aina's (1998) study reported the heaviest use of annual and statistical reports, national development plans, government policy documents, reports of commissions and committees, and population census reports. The least used publications were statutes and law reports and this is because they are used primarily by the Department of Law. Similar results have been obtained by studies of social science scholars in developed countries. For example, a study by Buttlar and Wynar (1992), which surveyed social science scholars' published articles in ethnic studies journals, found that government documents were one of the most valued sources of information. Likewise, social science scholars surveyed by Meho and Haas (2001) reported frequent use of government documents, and regarded them as very important sources of information.

Whereas it has been observed that Western social scientists make relatively little use of library resources, preferring to rely on their personal collections of research material and information sources of information (Folster, 1989; Hobohm, 1999; Romanos de Tiratel, 2002), research indicates that scholars in developing countries are heavy users of library resources. The majority of the social scientists in Shokeen and Kushik's (2002) Indian study, for example, reported visiting the library daily, while more than half of the social science scholars interviewed by Mooko and Aina (1998) indicated that they were heavily dependent on the University of Botswana Library for their information needs. This may be due to the inability of social scientists in developing countries to build up adequate personal collections of research material due to cost constraints, and in some countries, to less well developed networks of personal contacts, perhaps because there are fewer people working in the same specialist area.

Barriers to Information-Seeking

Western Dominance of the Social Sciences

In many developing countries where English is not the main language, scholars are often hindered in their research by a paucity of material in their own language, and a lack of previous research conducted in similar developing country contexts. For example, in the social science field the majority of studies have been published in English, with a dominance of U.S.-based research. Moreover, there has been a tendency for social scientists in the UK, other European countries, and North America to be quite insular in their work, rarely taking account of studies conducted outside these regions (Brittain, 1984). Overall, North American research has dominated the social sciences in recent decades, and relatively little consideration has been given within this academic field to developments in non-Western regions of the globe.

Several studies of social science researchers in developing countries have a revealed a preference for reading research texts in their own language, in contrast with researchers in other fields who place lower importance on the availability of own-language material (Romanos de Tiratel, 2000; Al-Suqri, 2011, Al-Suqri & Lillard, 2012). For example, Ucak and Kurbanoglu (1998) compared the views of respondents in four different academic fields within a major university in Turkey. They found that, compared with scientists and engineers, social scientists as well as humanities researchers expressed a preference for reading research material in Turkish. These researchers often understood the original language of publi-

cation, but favored reading the translated texts. Similarly, in a study of academics in Thailand, Patitungkho and Deshpande (2005) almost 75% of respondents from various disciplines expressed a preference for reading literature in their native Thai language, with the remainder favoring texts in English.

The lack of sufficient native-language sources along with the relative lack of research conducted in developing country environments is likely to hinder progress in social science within the non-Western, non-English speaking world. Scholars in these regions may have considerable difficulty staying informed of global developments in their field, or locating literature that provides suitable background for their own research.

Budgetary Constraints

Financial factors also often present barriers to effective information-seeking among social scientists in developing countries. Universities in these countries often have tight financial budgets which limit their ability to purchase books, journals, and technology. The implications of this for social scientists in particular have been documented in several studies. For example, research conducted by Romanos de Tiratel in Argentina (2000) observed that financial constraints had severely limited the availability of research materials and were regarded by social science faculty interviewed to be the main barrier to effective information-seeking.

In Pakistan, Saeed, Asghar, Anwar, and Ranzam's (2000) survey of 40 academic libraries found evidence of inadequate technological facilities resulting from budgetary constraints. Only half of the libraries had Internet access at all and of those who were connected, many had insufficient numbers of computers, frequent connectivity problems, or inadequate technical skills among library staff. More generally, several studies have highlighted the adverse impact of financial constraints on technological infrastructures and information systems, which are in turn hindering the work of social scientists (e.g., Ma Wengfeng & Wang Liqing, 1999). This can have an economic impact on the countries concerned: researchers have provided evidence of a correlation between the amount of social science research being conducted within a country and its GDP (Kishida and Matsui, 1997). Moreover, the quality of social science research is likely to be affected if scholars are unable to secure access to the most reliable or suitable sources of data, and have to make do with material readily available to them. Over time, the increased availability of and access to the Internet in developing countries is improving the situation, but since the majority of online resources are in English, social science researchers in developing countries still often face difficulties in locating material relevant to interests and needs.

Access to Information

In some countries, formal policies or regulations have been introduced which prevent overseas scholars from securing access to national data, especially when it is perceived that this might be used for political or economic gain by other countries (Hobohm, 1999). This presents an added difficulty for social scientists in developing countries, who often have the greatest need for the type of data and information being withheld, especially when this relates to countries with similar characteristics to their own.

One implication of the restricted access to official data is the common tendency of social scientists in the non-Western world to obtain information through informal means, such as networking and direct communication with personal contacts, both within their own region and overseas. In recent years, this international networking has been facilitated by the increasing use of the Internet and email communications. The use of informal methods of information-seeking was documented among social science researchers at the University of the West Indies (Francis,

2005) who reported a heavy reliance on conference participation, meetings with peers, and direct personal communications for securing access to important information for their research.

A particular problem faced by many social science researchers in developing countries and regions is the limited availability of local, national and regional data, for example relating to populations, labor markets and the economy. This type of information is generally produced by national statistical departments or financial institutions, or by regional inter-governmental bodies, but is often unavailable to researchers either because of delays in publication, or by regulations restricting access to and use of the data. The heavy reliance on official data of this type, and the problems created by its non-availability, were highlighted by social science faculty at the University of the West Indies, interviewed by Francis (2005).

In general, freedom of information is more restricted in developing countries than in the West, particularly in volatile political environments where governments fear that data might be used by their opponents or other hostile groups to destabilize the country or threaten the existing regime. In some extreme cases, the work of social science researchers may be tightly controlled, and their findings censored or suppressed if they are not favorable to the government. In such circumstances, the process of information-seeking and data collection may even put the personal safety of researchers at risk; at the very least they will need to consider trade-offs regarding the time and effort involved in securing information not available within their own countries.

Adaptations and Progress

Overall, the literature indicates that social scientists in developing countries tend to adapt their information-seeking practices to the barriers that they face. The evidence from countries including Sri Lanka (Lleperuma, 2002), India (Shokeen and Kushik, 2002) and Thailand (Patitungkho and

Dashpande, 2005) suggests that these researchers are similar to their counterparts in the developed world in preferring formal sources such as books, journal articles, and official statistics. However, the unavailability of or limited access to these types of sources results in a widespread tendency for social scientists in the developing world to rely heavily on personal contacts and informal methods of obtaining information (Francis, 2005; Romanos de Tiratel, 2000).

Similarly, social scientists in developing countries differ from their Western counterparts in their use of libraries. In the developing world, social science researchers rely heavily on library resources in their work, as illustrated by Mooko and Aina's (1998) study of social science faculty in Botswana, and Shokeen and Kushik's (2002) research with Indian social scientists who were found to be visiting their university library at least once a day. In contrast, it has been reported that social scientists in the developed world prefer to utilize their own collections of research resources rather than visiting the library (Folster, 1989; Hobohm, 1999; Romanos de Tiratel, 2002). This may reflect the greater difficulty of building personal collections of resources in developing countries, due to the barriers and problems discussed earlier. In some countries, these difficulties are exacerbated since the field of social science is fairly undeveloped, making it more difficult to build a personal network of peers in order to help generate resources.

Technological progress and the growth of the Internet are dramatically changing the nature of the information-seeking environment for social scientists in developing countries, generally for the better. Now that many organizations post information online, it is becoming much easier to obtain access to local, national and regional data for research purposes, as well as other information from around the world that was previously out of reach. Studies have shown that social science faculty and other academic researchers in developing countries make frequent use of the Internet for research and communications purposes. Francis (2005) found

for example that social science researchers in the University of the West Indies were regular users of data from the Websites of regional organizations such as the Caribbean Community and Common Market (CARICOM); the Economic Commission for Latin America and the Caribbean (ECLAC); and the Organization of American States (OAS). In the Arabian Gulf, Siddiqui (2003) reported evidence that most users of university libraries were regularly accessing the Internet and utilizing email as a form of communication, and in Thailand, a study of social science faculty (Patitungkho and Deshpande, 2005) also found evidence of frequent Internet and email usage.

CONCLUSION

This paper has demonstrated that there is substantial evidence from previous research to indicate the importance of contextual factors in influencing the information-seeking behavior of social scientists. Some of these factors are related to the nature of social science as a domain of study, while others are related to researcher's external environment, including constraints on the availability of particular types of information. Models of information seeking need to take into account the impact of these contextual factors, and must be sufficiently flexible to incorporate their effects. External factors such as the constraints on information-seeking experienced by social scientists in some developing countries may affect the applicability of existing models of information seeking, since they may necessitate substantial changes in cognitive processes to cope with the external constraints and significant modifications to information-seeking strategies.

Similarly, it is clear from the current literature on information-seeking among social scientists and other scholars in developing countries that local conditions do appear to have a significant impact on information-seeking behavior. The available evidence seems to suggest that, overall, social science researchers in the developing world exhibit similar preferred patterns of information-seeking behavior to their counterparts in the developed world, but that these have to be modified as a result of local conditions such as the unavailability or restricted access to preferred sources of information.

REFERENCES

Aber, S. W. (2005). *Information needs and behaviors of Geoscience education: A ground theory study*. Unpublished doctoral dissertation, Emporia State University, Emporia, KS.

Abouserie, H. E. M. R. (2003). *Information-seeking and communicating behavior of social science faculty in an academic environment with special reference to the use of electronic journals: A field study*. Unpublished doctoral dissertation, University of Pittsburgh, Pittsburgh, PA.

Al-Suqri, M. N. (2011). Information Seeking Behavior of Social Science Scholars in Developing Countries: A Proposed Model. *The International Information & Library Review, 43*, 1–14. doi:10.1016/j.iilr.2011.01.001.

Al-Suqri, M. N., & Lillard, L. (2011). Barriers to Effective Information Seeking of Social Scientists in Developing Countries: The Case of Sultan Qaboos University in Oman. *International Research: Journal of Library & Information Science, 1*(2), 86–100.

Bass, A., Fairlee, J., Fox, K., & Sullivan, J. (2005). *The Information Behavior of Scholars in the Humanities and Social Sciences*. University of Washington, LIS 510 November 17, 2005.

Bates, M. J. (2005) Information and knowledge: An evolutionary framework for information science. *Information Research, 10,* 4. Retrieved on September 22, 2006, from http://informationr.net/ir/10-4/paper239.html

Borgman, C. L. (2000). Scholarly communication and bibliometrics revisited. In Cronin, B., & Atkins, H. B. (Eds.), *The Web of Knowledge: A Festschrift in Honor of Eugene Garfield* (pp. 145–150). Medford, NJ: Information Today, Inc..

Bouazza, A. (1986). *Use of information sources by physical scientists, social scientists, humanities scholars at Carnegie-Mellon University*. Unpublished doctoral dissertation, University of Pittsburgh, Pittsburgh, PA.

Brittain, J. M. (1970). *Information and its users: A review with special reference to the social science*. New York: Wiley Inter-science.

Brittain, J. M. (1984). Internationality of the social sciences: Implications for information transfer. *Journal of the American Society for Information Science American Society for Information Science, 35*(1), 11–18. doi:10.1002/asi.4630350103.

Broadbent, E. (1986). A study of humanities faculty library information-seeking behaviour. *Cataloging & Classification Quarterly, 6*, 23–37. doi:10.1300/J104v06n03_03.

Brown, C. M. (1999). Information seeking behavior of scientists in the electronic information age: Astronomers, chemists, mathematicians, and physicists. *Journal of the American Society for Information Science American Society for Information Science, 50*(10), 929–943. doi:10.1002/(SICI)1097-4571(1999)50:10<929::AID-ASI8>3.0.CO;2-G.

Buttlar, L., & Wynar, L. R. (1992). Cultural pluralism and ethnic diversity: Authors as information users in the field of ethnic studies. *Collection Management, 16*(3), 13–33. doi:10.1300/J105v16n03_02.

Case, D. O. (2002). *Looking for information: A survey of research on information seeking, needs, and behavior*. New York: Academic Press.

Curits, K. L., Weller, A. C., & Hurd, J. M. (1993). Information-seeking behavior: A survey of health sciences faculty use of indexes and databases. *Bulletin of the Medical Library Association, 81*(4), 383–392. PMID:8251974.

Dalgleish, A., & Hall, R. (2000). Uses and perceptions of the World Wide Web in an information seeking environment. *Journal of Library and Information Science, 32*(3), 104–116.

Duff, W. M., & Johnson, C. A. (2002). Accidentally found on purpose: Information- seeking behavior of historians in archives. *The Library Quarterly, 72*(4), 472–496.

Ellis, D. (1989). A behavioral approach to information retrieval design. *The Journal of Documentation, 45*, 171–212. doi:10.1108/eb026843.

Ellis, D., Cox, D., & Hall, K. (1993). A comparison of the information seeking patterns of researchers in the physical and social sciences. *The Journal of Documentation, 49*(4), 356–369. doi:10.1108/eb026919.

Ellis, D., & Haugan, M. (1997). Modelling the information seeking patterns of engineers and research scientists in an industrial environment. *The Journal of Documentation, 53*(4), 384–403. doi:10.1108/EUM0000000007204.

Folster, M. B. (1989). A study of the use of information sources by social science researchers. *Journal of Academic Librarianship, 15*, 7–11.

Folster, M. B. (1995). Information seeking patterns: Social sciences. *Library Users and Reference Services, 32*, 83–93. doi:10.1300/J120v23n49_06.

Francis, H. (2005). The information-seeking behavior of social science faculty at the University of the West Indies, St. Augustine Campus. *Journal of Academic Librarianship, 31*, 67–72. doi:10.1016/j.acalib.2004.11.003.

Fry, J., & Talja, S. (2004). The cultural shaping of scholarly communication: Explaining e-journal use within and across academic fields. *Proceedings of the American Society for Information Science and Technology, 41*(1), 20–30. doi:10.1002/meet.1450410103.

Hallmark, J. (1994). Scientists' access and retrieval of references cited in their recent journal articles. *College & Research Libraries, 55*, 199–209.

Hartmann, J. (1995). Information needs of anthropologists. *Behavioral & Social Sciences Librarian, 13*, 13–24. doi:10.1300/J103v13n02_02.

Hernon, P. (1984). Information needs and gathering patterns of academic social scientists with special emphasis given to historians and their use of U.S. government publications. *Government Information Quarterly, 1*, 401–429. doi:10.1016/0740-624X(84)90005-4.

Heterick, B. (2002). Faculty attitudes towards electronic resources. *EDUCAUSE Review, 37*(4), 10–11.

Hobohm, H. (1999). Social science information & documentation: Time for a state of the art? *INSPEL, 3*, 123–130.

Hughes, C. A., & Buchanan, N. L. (2001). Use of electronic monographs in the humanities and social sciences. *Library Hi Tech, 19*(4), 368–375. doi:10.1108/EUM0000000006541.

Kishida, K., & Matsui, S. (1997). International publication patterns in social sciences: A quantitative analysis of the IBSS file. *Scientometrics, 40*, 277–298. doi:10.1007/BF02457440.

Lenares, D. (1999). *Faculty use of electronic journals at research institutions.* Paper presented at the ACRL Ninth National Conference. New Orleans, LA. Retrieved March 13, 2006, from http://www.ala.org/ala/acrl/acrlevents/lenares99.pdf#search='lenares%20and20999%20and%20electronic%20journals'

Line, M. B. (1999). Social science information – The poor relation. *INSPEL, 33*, 131–136.

Lleperuma, S. (2002). Information gathering behavior of arts scholars in Sri Lankan Universities: A critical evaluation. *Collection Building, 21*, 22–31. doi:10.1108/01604950210414698.

Meho, L. I. (2001). *The information-seeking behavior of social science faculty studying stateless nations.* Unpublished doctoral dissertation, University of North Carolina, Chapel Hill, NC.

Meho, L. I., & Haas, S. W. (2001). Information-seeking behavior and use of social science faculty studying stateless nations: A case study. *Library & Information Science Research, 23*, 5–25. doi:10.1016/S0740-8188(00)00065-7.

Meho, L. I., & Tibbo, H. R. (2002). Modeling the information-seeking behavior of social scientists: Ellis's study revisited. *Journal of the American Society for Information Science and Technology, 54*(6), 570–587. doi:10.1002/asi.10244.

Menou, M. (1993). *Measuring the impact of information on development.* Ottawa, Canada: IDRC.

Mooko, N. P., & Aina, L. O. (1998). The use of government publications: The case of social scientists at the University of Botswana. *Journal of Government Information, 25*(4), 359–365. doi:10.1016/S1352-0237(98)00015-X.

Niedźwiedzka, B. (2003). A proposed general model of information behavior. *Information Research, 9*(1). Retrieved on June 20, 2006, from http://InformationR.net/ir/9-1/paper164.html

Patitungkho, K., & Deshpande, N. J. (2005). Information-seeking behavior of faculty members of Rajabhat Universities in Bangkok. *Webology, 2*(4). Retrieved on May 10, 2006, from http://www.webology.ir/2005/v2n4/a20.html

Preschel, B. M., & Woods, L. J. (1989). Social science information. *Annual Review of Information Science & Technology, 24*, 267–292.

Pullinger, D., & Baldwin, C. (2002). *Electronic journals and user behaviour: Learning for the future from the SuperJournal Project.* Cambridge, UK: Deedot Press.

Quigley, J., Peck, D.R., Rutter, S., & McKee Williams, E. (2002). Making choices: Factors in the selection of information resources among science faculty at the University of Michigan. Results of a survey conducted July-September, 2000. *Issues in Science and Technology Librarianship, 34*.

Renwick, S. (2005). Knowledge and use of electronic information resources by medical sciences faculty at the University of the West Indies. *Journal of the Medical Library Association, 93*(1), 21–31. PMID:15685270.

Romanos de Tiratel, S. (2000). Accessing information use by humanists and social scientists: A study at the Universidad de Buenos Aires, Argentina. *Journal of Academic Librarianship, 26*(5), 346–354. doi:10.1016/S0099-1333(00)00141-5.

Shokeen, A., & Kushik, S. K. (2002). Information-seeking behavior of social scientists of Haryana universities. *Library Herald, 40*(1), 8–11.

Siddiqui, M. A. (2003). Adoption of the Internet for resource sharing by the Gulf academic libraries. *The Electronic Library, 21*(1), 56–62. doi:10.1108/02640470310462425.

Sievert, D., & Sievert, M. E. (1989). Philosophical research: Report from the field. In *Proceedings of the Humanists at Work symposium* (pp. 79-94). Chicago, IL: Institute for Schema.

Soper, M. E. (1976). Characteristics and use of personal collections. *The Library Quarterly, 46*(4), 397–415. doi:10.1086/620584.

Tenopir, C. (2003). *Use and users of electronic library resources: An overview and analysis of recent research studies.* Washington, DC: Council on Library and Information Resources. Retrieved on May 12, 2005, from http://www.clir.org/pubs/abstract/pub120abst.html

Tenopir, C., & King, D. (2001). *Electronic journals: How user behaviour is changing in online information*. Oxford, London: Learned Information Europe Ltd..

Tenopir, C., King, D. W., Boyce, P., Grayson, M., Zhang, Y., & Ebuen, M. (2003). Patterns of journal use by scientists through three evolutionary phases. *D-Lib Magazine, 9*(5). doi:10.1045/may2003-king.

Tombros, A., Ruthven, I., & Jose, J. (2005). How users assess web pages for information-seeking. *Journal of the American Society for Information Science and Technology, 56*(4), 327–344. doi:10.1002/asi.20106.

Tomney, H., & Burton, P. F. (1998). Electronic journals: A study of usage and attitudes among academics. *Journal of Information Science, 24*(6), 419–429. doi:10.1177/016555159802400605.

Ucak, O. N., & Kurbanoglu, S. S. (1998). Information need and information seeking behavior of scholars at a Turkish university. *64ʰ IFLA General Conference*. Retrieved on June 20, 2006, from http://www.ifla.org/IV/ifla64/041-112e.htm

Wengfeng, M., & Liqing, W. (1999). *Toward Twenty First Century: Research of social science information services of University Libraries in China*. Paper presented at the 65th IFLA Conference. Bangkok, Thailand.

Wiberley, S., & Jones, W. G. (1989). Patterns of information seeking in the humanities. *College & Research Libraries, 50*, 638–645.

Wilson, T. D. (1999). Models of information behavior research. *The Journal of Documentation, 55*(3), 249–270. doi:10.1108/EUM0000000007145.

Wilson, T. D. (2000). Human information behavior. *Informing Science, 3*(2), 49–55.

Wilson, T. D., & Streatfield, D. R. (1981). *Action research and users' needs*. Retrieved on June 16, 2006, from http://informationr.net/tdw/publ/papers/action81.html

ADDITIONAL READING

Al-Suqri, M. N. (2007). *Information Needs and Seeking Behavior of Social Science Scholars at Sultan Qaboos University in Oman: A Mixed-Method Approach.* Unpublished Doctoral Dissertation. Emporia State University, Emporia, KS.

Al-Suqri, M. N. (2010). Socio-Demographic Differences in Information Seeking Behavior of Social Science Scholars in Developing Countries: The Case of Sultan Qaboos University. *Information Studies, 9*, 51–68.

Badu, E. E., & Markwei, E. D. (2005). Internet Awareness and Use in the University of Ghana. *Information Development, 21*(4), 260–268. doi:10.1177/0266666905060069.

Bass, A., Fairlee, J., Fox, K., & Sullivan, J. (2005). The information behavior of scholars in the humanities and social sciences. Retrieved December 2, 2005, from http://ischool.washington.edu/harryb/courses/LIS510/Assign_2/Team_2_Scholar.pdf

Bu-Merafi, B. M. (2001). Use of Internet by the teaching staff at the university of Al-Sharqa. *Risalat Al-Maktaba, 36*(1/2), 74–90.

Busha, C. H., & Harter, S. P. (1980). *Research Methods in Librarianship: Techniques and interpretations*. New York: Academic Press.

Buttlar, L., & Wynar, L. R. (1992). Cultural pluralism and ethnic diversity: Authors as information users in the field of ethnic studies. *Collection Management, 16*(3), 13–33. doi:10.1300/J105v16n03_02.

Ford, G. (1973). Progress in documentation: Research in user behaviour in university libraries. *The Journal of Documentation, 29*, 85–106. doi:10.1108/eb026552.

Gleeson, A. C. (2001). *Information seeking behavior of scientists and their adaptation to electronic journals*. Unpublished Master's thesis, University of North Carolina at Chapel Hill, NC.

Goldberg, A. L. (1971). Information needs of social scientists and ways of meeting them. *International Social Science Journal, 23*, 273–284.

Hughes, C. A., & Buchanan, N. L. (2001). Use of electronic monographs in the humanities and social sciences. *Library Hi Tech, 19*(4), 368–375. doi:10.1108/EUM0000000006541.

Hurd, J. M., Weller, A. C., & Curits, K. L. (1992). Information-seeking behavior of faculty: Use of indexes and abstracts by scientists and engineers. *American Society for Information Science Process, 29*, 136–143.

Jirojwong, S., & Wallin, M. (2002). Use of formal and informal methods to gain information among faculty at an Australian regional university. *Journal of Academic Librarianship, 28*(1–2), 68–73. doi:10.1016/S0099-1333(01)00284-1.

Kingrey, K. P. (2002). Concepts of information seeking and their presence in the practical library literature. *Library Philosophy and Practice, 4*(2), 1–13.

Krikelas, J. (1983). Information seeking behavior: Patterns and concepts. *Drexel Library Quarterly, 19*, 5–20.

Lazinger, S. S., Bar-Ilan, J., & Peritz, B. C. (1997). Internet Use by Faculty Members in Various Disciplines: A Comparative Case Study. *Journal of the American Society for Information Science American Society for Information Science, 48*(6), 508–518. doi:10.1002/(SICI)1097-4571(199706)48:6<508::AID-ASI4>3.0.CO;2-Y.

Lomax, E. C., & Lowe, H. J. (1998). Information needs research in the era of the digital medical library. In *Proceedings of the American Medical Informatics Association Symposium* (658-662).

Mahé, A. (2004). Beyond usage: understanding the use of electronic journals on the basis of information activity analysis. *Information Research, 9*(4) paper 186. Retrieved April 24, 2006, from http://InformationR.net/ir/9-4/paper186.html

Paisley, W. (1968). Information needs and uses. *Annual Review of Information Science & Technology, 3*, 1–30.

Younis, A. R. M. (2002). The perception and administrative effect of Internet usage in Jordanian university libraries. *Online Information Review, 26*(3), 193–208. doi:10.1108/14684520210432477.

KEY TERMS AND DEFINITIONS

Barrier: Any condition or challenges that affect the information seeking behavior of social science scholars.

Contextual Factors: Factors influencing the information-seeking behavior of users, such as their own characteristics, the nature of the information environment and the available sources.

Electronic Resources: All types of library materials that are available in electronic format, such as e-books, e-journals, etc.

Information Seeking: The behavior and thought processes of individuals involved in searching for information and resources to meet their needs.

Social Sciences: The academic field that includes the following disciplines: psychology, political science, sociology and social work, anthropology, geography, history, economics, finance, education, communication, law, library and information science, criminology, and women's studies.

Users' Information Needs: Users desire to obtain information to fill a gap in their knowledge.

Chapter 14
Undergraduate Students Information Behavior in the Changing Technological Era:
An Investigating of Sultan Qaboos University, Oman

Naifa Eid Al-Saleem
Sultan Qaboos University, Oman

ABSTRACT

There has been a great deal of research conducted to investigate the information-seeking behavior of difference group of users. A search of current literature, however, reveals few studies dealing with information-seeking strategies of undergraduates in the electronic era. This chapter presents the results of a preliminary study of information-seeking among 675 undergraduates at Sultan Qaboos University (SQU). The study was designed to 1) explore undergraduates' information-seeking behavior with e-resources; 2) identify the role of faculty members and librarians in assisting undergraduates to attain search skills; and 3) discover the differences between undergraduates in terms of their age, gender, academic year, and college. The study results indicated that only 3% of undergraduates use the electronic services and databases subscribed to by the SQU main library. In addition, the results showed that 57.7% of the undergraduate students at SQU used the Google search engine for their initial search. There is a statistical difference between undergraduate students in terms of their age and use of e-resources. Finally, this study found the role of faculty members and librarians in assisting undergraduates to learn search strategies is almost absent.

DOI: 10.4018/978-1-4666-4353-6.ch014

INTRODUCTION

It is a universal phenomenal that students throughout all their educational stages need information. They need it to support their classes, their assignments, projects, and their research aims (Case, 2002). According to Halder et al. (2010) that, during the last decade, information has become essential due to vast developments in the World Wide Web (WWW) and in information and communication technologies (ICT), a tremendous population explosion, and the increased complexities of organizations. Information has become a key in various fields including education, psychology, information management, and library science (Majid & Kassim, 2000; Nicholas et al., 2010; Solomon, 2005).

Students are encouraged to become information literate, life-long learners in order to deal with the challenges of the fast-paced society, knowledge explosion, technological advancement, culture of information revolution, and new academic and vocational opportunities. Because of the importance of information seeking behavior for students, institutions of higher education in Oman need to facilitate a culture of information seeking and to improve the employment of resource support, such as library and documentation services. With knowledge changing rapidly and the ready access to technology, students must upgrade their knowledge and skills in order to cope with an overflow of knowledge (Eskola, 1998; Griffiths & Brophy, 2002). Also, there are global changes in the educational system that have required researchers to study in earnest undergraduate information needs and their information-seeking behavior. These changes have also affected the educational system in Oman. Some of these changes deal with the role of the student, either as an information recipient or an information producer. There is also a strong push to make information technologies like the Internet available and accessible to uni-

versity and school students (Nesset, 2008). The form of information resources has also changed, from printed to electronic materials. To make their collections available around the world, libraries subscribe to electronic databases, but without student use of these databases, libraries will not succeed. To help students use the electronic collection properly, the libraries and information centers have to know their users and what their information needs are, as well as how they use databases (by determining their search strategies). Faculty members can help libraries and information centers by training undergraduate students in specific search strategies.

STUDY BACKGROUND

Sultan Qaboos University (SQU) in Oman is the only public university which includes 17,070 students. It has nine colleges: Agricultural & Marine Sciences, Arts & Social Sciences, Economic & Political Science, Education, Engineering, Law, Medicine & Health Science, Science, and the College of Nursing. It has research and academic programs in most of the major hard sciences, engineering, and the humanities and social sciences. Close to 15,645 undergraduates were enrolled in the 2011/2012 academic year, aged 18-22. They are identified by their academic class, which is designated by their department and their specialization.

Because of the importance of undergraduate information-seeking behavior, it is necessary to study the students' information needs and their information-seeking behavior, so as to help the information center and campus library better serve them with information compatible to their needs. Because SQU educates through technology, it requires the students to use different resources for their projects and homework--in particular the electronic (E) resources. Using e-resources enables students to retrieve texts and information from thousands of databases. To find their way, the students must learn information search skills or search strategies. Faculty members and librarians at SQU play an important role in providing students with the search skills for e-resources, especially during the undergraduate stage when the number of resources the students collect is less important than the search strategy they use.

SQU has three main libraries and information centers: the main library, the medical library, and the commerce information center, along with small libraries attached to each college. The three main libraries have different collections of printed materials in addition to a number of official important databases: e-journal, e-dissertation and -theses, e-reference, e-books. Within each of these databases exist sub-databases. For example, within the e-journal database, the user will find Science Direct, Academic Search Complete, Willy Online Library, Springer Link, and so forth.

THE PROBLEM OF THE STUDY

Although the libraries and information centers at SQU put a lot of effort and money into subscribing to different information databases, in addition to keeping printed materials, from time to time we hear, as faculty members of the information studies department, complaints from the Main library at SQU that the undergraduate students do not benefit from the databases as intended. One colleague commented that students from different colleges, especially the scientific colleges, have remarkable scientific databases, though they know nothing about them. The inevitable conclusion is that the undergraduate students do not know how to find information in the databases to which the Main Library subscribes. On numerous occasions, when asked to review literature for their final project, the undergraduate students answered that they had not found resources because they queried only the Google search engine. This anecdote is in

agreement with the research finding that students lack strategies for thinking and planning when seeking necessary information, especially during the early stages of their development (Cooper, 2002; Kuhlthau, 2004). It appears that the libraries, information centers, and faculty members of SQU subscribed to databases without assessing the skill levels or information-seeking behaviors of their undergraduate students.

Because the undergraduates students at SQU lack information-search strategies, more research must be conducted in the area of undergraduate information-seeking behavior, especially with students in their first year.

THE STUDY RESEARCH QUESTIONS AND AIMS

According to the problems discussed above, this study aims to answer the following questions:

1. What information-seeking behavior do the SQU undergraduate students utilize when they use e-resources?
2. How can the faculty members and librarians at SQU assist undergraduate students with the skills and search strategies they need to use e-resources?
3. Are there any statistically significant differences between the SQU undergraduate students in terms of their gender, academic year, specialization, college, level of English, Information communication technology (ICT) skills, or awareness of search strategy?

This study aims to:

1. Identify SQU undergraduate students' information-seeking behavior with e-resources.
2. Explore the role of faculty members and libraries in assisting undergraduates with search strategies.

3. Explore the differences between undergraduate students in terms of age, gender, academic year, and college.

SIGNIFICANCE OF THE STUDY

A study involving undergraduate student information-seeking behavior is important for the following reasons:

Importance of Understanding Information-Seeking Behavior for E-Resources

The proliferation of e-learning and the call for information resources and information literacy in education supports the significance of this study. According to Hart (2008), recent issues describe the necessity of supporting e-learning while making sure that undergraduate students are adequately trained in the use of online content. The results of this study will help faculty members to understand the importance of assessing undergraduate students' skills and search strategies in relation to seeking information in e-resource databases. The study is important because it will help libraries and information centers at SQU to identify users and their needs, and adjust accordingly.

STUDY LIMITATIONS

This study has the following limitations:

1. Substantive limitation: this study covers the subject of undergraduate information needs and their information-seeking behavior in an e-learning environment.
2. Spatial boundaries: SQU in the Sultanate of Oman.
3. Timeline limit: the study was conducted in the spring of 2012.

REVIEW OF THE LITERATURE

We have to believe that there are individual differences between undergraduate students in their individualized information-seeking behaviors. The literature review that follows is largely apprehensive with the finding of studies based on surveys and interviews which relate themselves with undergraduates' students' information seeking behavior in technological era. The literature shows that psychologists have struggled to categorize and predict human behavior related to information processing in an objective, consistent, and valid manner (Halder et al., 2010). Such studies can recognize the basis of individual differences and predict behavioral patterns with respect to situations and context. The recognition of individual differences is increasingly becoming an important consideration in user information-seeking studies (Dresang, 2005; Tella, 2009). Kuhlthau (2004) thinks understanding why people search for information in different ways is significant to designing information retrieval systems and user support services so that search behavior can be more holistically understood and generalized. Also Zaborowski (2008) believes that to understand the way in which undergraduate students seek information in e-resources it is necessary to explain undergraduate students' information-seeking process. The information-seeking process starts with the student identifying a topic for his/her assignment, project etc. As Malliari et al. (2011) suggest, once the faculty members explain the issues at play, it is the undergraduates' (or seekers') personal characteristics that affect search strategies and overall information-seeking ability. These characteristics include demographic aspects, as well as cognitive and psychological variables. Demographic variables and their relationship with information-seeking choices and strategies have been studied mostly in terms of age/generation (Weiler, 2005; Haglund & Olsson, 2008; Hargittai, 2010), gender (Hargittai & Shafer, 2006; Rowlands & Nicholas, 2008; Whitmire, 2002) and academic status (Branch, 2003; Banwell & Coulson, 2004; Barrett, 2005; Callinan, 2005; Chen, 2009). Others have noted the existence of significant variation between different institutions (Nicholas et al., 2007; Nicholas et al., 2009) due to different "faculty models of research behavior" (Barrett, 2005).

In relation to cognitive processes and the academic environment, some studies have found that discipline plays a significant role in information-seeking strategies (George et al., 2006; Kerins et al., 2004; Makani & WooShue, 2006; Nicholas, Clark, Rowlands, & Jamali, 2009; Whitmire, 2002; Sadler & Given, 2007; Talja & Maula, 2003; Urquhart et al., 2005. However, a number of studies also found little or no correlation between discipline and information-seeking behavior (Ellis et al., 1993; Heinström, 2003; Korobili et al., 2011). Other factors that have been demonstrated to influence information-seeking include domain knowledge (Hölscher & Strube, 2000; Jenkins et al., 2003; Marchionini, 1997), computer and Web experience (Aula, 2005; Aula et al., 2005; Eshet-Alkalai & Chajut, 2009; Hölscher & Strube, 2000; Hargittai, 2002; Jenkins et al., 2003; Korobili et al., 2011), search experience (Chen, 2009; Hsieh-Yee, 1993), and frequency of e-source use (Griffiths & Brophy, 2005; Haglund & Olsson, 2008; George et al., 2006; Korobili et al., 2006). Some studies have revealed the importance of other people (tutors, instructors, colleagues, librarians, friends, etc.) to the information-seeking process (Branch, 2003; Barrett, 2005; George et al., 2006; Griffiths & Brophy, 2005; Patitungkho & Deshpande, 2005; Vezzosi, 2009).

The literature shows that undergraduate students opt for the easiest and most convenient method of information seeking (Nicholas et al., 2009), and appreciate the time saving characteristics of electronic resources (Dalgleish & Hall, 2000). Students are said to rely heavily on simple search engines, such as Google, to find what they want (Dalgleish & Hall, 2000; Becker, 2003; Drabenstott, 2003). Fast and Campbell (2004) carried out an exploratory study of how

university students perceive and interact with web search engines compared to web-based OPACs. A qualitative study was conducted involving just sixteen students, eight of whom were first-year undergraduates and eight of whom were graduate students in library and information science. The participants performed searches on Google and on a university OPAC. The interviews and "think-afters" revealed that while students were aware of the problems inherent in web searching and of the many ways in which OPACs are organized, they generally preferred Web searching. The coding of the data suggests that the reason for this preference lies in psychological factors associated with the comparative ease with which search engines can be used, and system and interface factors which made searching the Web much easier and less confusing.

Kennedy et al. (2010) carried out a study on gender differences as per the digital divide, and their results showed that when searching for information, women participating in the study preferred social collaboration, contextual information, and personal identification. As in Roy et al. (2003) states, they examined how students look for, browse, and learn specific information when performing an online (Web) versus an off-line (library) search. The results of their study revealed that males tended to employ a different search pattern from females and that this variation in search behavior was related to the pattern of performance outcomes. Nicholas et al. (2010) found gender differences in information-seeking behavior in library use, suggesting in their study that due to the socio-cultural background of gender, women may be more prone to computer anxiety and feelings of lower self-efficacy.

Selwyn (2008) carried out a study with 1,222 undergraduate students studying at UK higher education institutions. The data was collected through surveys. The aim of the study was to address students' engagement with the Internet as a source of academic information for their studies. In particular, the study seeks to explore how academic use of the Internet is patterned by a range of potential influences such as students' wider Internet use, access and expertise, their year of study, gender, age, and ethnic and educational background. Analysis of these data suggests that students' academic internet use is most strongly patterned along the lines of gender and subject-specialism rather than other individual characteristics or differences in technology access or expertise. The study therefore considers how these differences can be addressed by those seeking to encourage ICT-based learning across all sectors of the undergraduate population.

Nicholas et al. (2009) conducted a study aiming to provide evidence for the actual information-seeking behavior of students in a digital scholarly environment--not what they thought they did. It also compared student information-seeking behavior with that of other academic communities, as well as for some "real world" cases. The data were gathered as part of CIBER's ongoing Virtual Scholar program. In particular, log data from two digital journals, Blackwell Synergy and OhioLINK, and one e-book collection (Oxford Scholarship Online) were utilized. The study showed a distinctive type of information-seeking behavior associated with students and was able to delineate the differences between them and other members of the academic community. For example, students constituted the biggest users in terms of sessions and pages viewed, and they were more likely to undertake longer online sessions. Undergraduates and postgraduates were the most likely users of library links to access scholarly databases, suggesting an important "hot link" role for libraries.

In a study by Mahajan (2009) into the information-seeking behavior of different user groups. Different academic libraries must understand the information needs of faculty and students in order to address those needs. Mahajan's study explores the information-seeking behavior of undergraduates, postgraduates, and researchers into the sciences, social sciences, and humanities at the Panjab University, Chandigarh, India. The data was collected through questionnaires, and consisted of

100 undergraduates, 100 postgraduates, and 50 researchers from sciences, social sciences, and humanities. With regard to the students' purposes for information-seeking 100% of undergraduate students and 98% of postgraduates seek information to prepare notes for examinations, whereas 0% of researchers seek information related to their research. Seeking information for discussions and general awareness is favored more heavily by the researchers 62% than by other respondents. With regard to the formal source of information, the study found that undergraduate students rely more on books than other sources 94%, whereas researchers rely more on journals, conference proceedings, and databases because they need information current to their research areas. informal sources of information, including email and discussion with teachers, were preferred by most respondents: undergraduates (96%), postgraduates (98%), and researchers (100%), all of whom feel that friends and teachers direct them with various sources of information that may be useful. Teachers even provide journal articles and books. Researchers also attend seminars and conferences to acquire information by establishing new contacts or participating in lectures and discussions. It is interesting to note that discussion with librarians as providers of information was not heavily favored.

METHODOLOGY

This study used a qualitative methodology to investigate three research questions: 1) what information-seeking behavior do the undergraduate students at SQU undertake when they use e-resources? 2) how do the faculty members and the librarians at SQU assist undergraduate students with the skills and search strategies they need to use e-resources? 3) are there any statistically significant differences between the undergraduate students at SQU in terms of their gender, academic year, specialization, college, level of English, ICT skills, or awareness of search strategies? The reason for using a qualitative methodology is that as an exploratory study, it aims to explore the reality of undergraduate students' information-seeking behavior. In the view of Shenton (2004), with any methodology, whether qualitative or quantitative, the researcher must be aware of the fact that the research process will be affected by any decisions made regarding how to proceed.

In order to accomplish the above set of research questions, a survey was administered to all undergraduate students at the nine colleges at (SQU): Agricultural & Marine Sciences, Arts & Social Sciences, Economic & Political Science, Education, Engineering, Law, Medicine & Health Science, Science, and College of Nursing. The survey was carried out during the spring semester of the 2012 academic period. The survey was a designed, structured questionnaire: students were invited to complete the questionnaire through their university e-mail. The undergraduate student population was 15,645 and the response rate obtained was approximately 23.1%. The procedure produced 675 fully answered and therefore usable questionnaires.

The first part of the questionnaire contained the following demographic variables of the respondents: gender, age, college, academic year, level of CT, level of English. The second part of the questionnaire contained questions about the use of electronic services available at the Website of libraries and information centers at SQU and undergraduate information-seeking behavior, which was intended to measure the most commonly adopted practices when starting a search process. The third part of the questionnaire consisted of one question which referred to the role of the faculty members and the librarians at SQU in assisting undergraduate students in acquiring those skills.

Descriptive statistical indices, including frequency and correlation, were used to present the data. Only the results in which the observed significance level (p-value) was found to be statically significant (at the 0.01 level) are reported and discussed.

FINDINGS

Profile of SQU Undergraduates Students

Descriptive statistics indicated that 45.6% of the sample was male while 54.4% were female. With regard to academic year, 4.9% of them were in the FP (foundation program), and 23.1% were in their 1st year, compared to 6.2% who were in their 5th year–most of whom were undergraduates from the College of Medicine or from the College of Science. The majority of the undergraduate students (48.6%) were aged from 18-20 years old, and the older students, aged from 24-26 years old, were in the minority (24.4%). With regard to college, the lowest sample in this study was from College of Law (3.7%), while the highest was from College of Engineering (22.8%). See Table 1 for the general characteristics of the study sample.

Undergraduates ICT Skills and Their Level of English

To identify undergraduate students, we had to study their ICT skills and their level of English, as some studies assumed a relationship between undergraduates' ICT skills and their level of English (Dee & Stanley, 2005; Selwyn, 2008). The results showed that the majority of the undergraduate students in this study have a medium level of ICT (53.3%) while only a few of them had low ICT skills (1.6%) (see Table 2).

The study went further in an attempt to determine a statistical difference between the undergraduate students in terms of their age, academic year, college, gender, and ICT skills. The correlation test showed there to be a difference between the undergraduates in two variables: age and college.

Table 3 shows that there is a negative relationship between students' age and their ICT skills, meaning that as the students grow, their ICT skills go down. The results also indicate a positive relationship between undergraduate students' colleges and their ICT skills.

Table 1. General characteristics of the study sample

General Characteristics of the Study Sample			
Variables		**Frequency**	**Percentage**
Sex	Male	308	45.6%
	Female	367	54.4%
Acad. Year	FP.	33	4.9%
	1st	156	23.1%
	2nd	139	20.6%
	3rd	150	22.2%
	4th	155	23.0%
	5th	42	6.2%
Age	18-20	328	48.6%
	21-23	182	27.0%
	24-26	165	24.4%
College	Foundation	43	6.4%
	Arts	138	20.4%
	Agri.	39	5.8%
	Com.	52	7.7%
	Education	100	14.8%
	Eng.	154	22.8%
	Law	25	3.7%
	Med.	53	7.95%
	Science	71	10.5%
Total		**675**	

Table 2. Sample ICT skills and their level of English

Sample ICT Skills and their Level of English			
Skills	**Level**	**Frequency**	**Percentage**
ICT	High	304	%45.0%
	Medium	360	%53.3%
	Low	11	%1.6%
English	High	102	%15.1%
	Medium	421	%62.4%
	Low	152	%22.5%

Table 3. The correlation between undergraduates' age, college and ICT skills

Measure	**Age**	**College**
Computer skills	-. 144**	.103**

**p <. 001

Table 4. The correlation between undergraduates' academic year, college, and their English level

Measure	**Academic Year**	**College**
English skills	.126**	.207**

* p<. 01 ** p <. 001

In developing countries where the English language is not the first language, students learning English are at a disadvantage as the vast majority of the sources they depend on for writing their assignments are in English. The students with little English fluency will behave differently from the students who have a moderate or high level of English fluency. The results showed that 62.4% of the students surveyed had moderate level of English, while 22.5% of the students had little English.

As the study tested the relationship between variables such as age, college, academic year, and so forth, and their effect on ICT skills, the study also tested the impact of the previously discussed variables on the undergraduate students' English level. The correlation test illustrated that there was no statistical difference between undergraduates' age and gender. However, there was a statistical difference found between undergraduates' academic year, their college, and their level of English. Table 4 displays this information in greater detail.

Table 4 demonstrates that there is a relationship between academic year and the undergraduates' level of English. The relationship is positive, meaning that if the undergraduates' move to a higher level or term, his/her English will continue to develop.

Undergraduate's Information Seeking Behavior

This part of the questionnaire aims to identify undergraduates' information-seeking behavior. However, to achieve this we have to describe the undergraduates' use of the library services available on the SQU campus. Because SQU assures that most of the library's services and collection are in electronic form, the study does not look at whether the students go to the library building or not; rather, the study aims to explore the undergraduates' information-seeking behavior in the electronic era.

Table 5 shows that 97% of the undergraduates did not use the library electronic services, such as the databases, while 3% of them did.

After we explored the undergraduate students' use or non-use of the library electronic services available at SQU, we considered what practices were commonly adopted when starting a search process, or how students gather information for their assignments. We asked the undergraduates to report their most commonly used sources of information. The results demonstrated that after the faculty members explained the purpose of the paper, the undergraduates looked for information in the following places:

Table 6 shows that 57.7% of the undergraduates depend on Google for information gathering. The last source they consulted was the librarian.

Some resources were not commonly used by a large number of the sample including librarian consultation (7.1%), e-books (7.8%), databases (8.7%), and e-journals (8.7%).

The study sought to find out if the faculty or the librarian assisted the undergraduates' with the search skills or search strategy (see Table 7).

The results illustrated that from the view point of the undergraduates in this study, the librarian at the SQU library and information centers assisted the undergraduate students more than faculty members did: the percentage of undergraduates who thought the faculty members assisted them was 24.9%, compared to 32.1% of undergraduates students who thought they were assisted by librarians.

The study also aimed to explore the statistical differences between the undergraduate students in terms of their age, gender, academic year, and college compared to their use of resources. It was found that there was a statistical difference between undergraduates, as shown in Table 8.

DISCUSSION

In order to identify the information-seeking behavior of undergraduates at SQU, this study considered the following factors: the information-seeking process of undergraduates, the role of the faculty members at the SQU colleges, and

Table 5. Undergraduates use of SQU library electronic services

Yes	Frequency 20
	Percentage 3.0%
No	Frequency 655
	Percentage 97.0%

Table 6. The sources used by the undergraduate students - information-seeking at SQU

Sources	Frequency	Percentage
Google	390	57.7%
e-dissertation & theses	69	10.2%
e-journals	59	8.7%
Databases	55	8.1%
e-books	53	7.8%
Librarian consultation	48	7.1%

Table 7. Assistance from faculty members and librarians

Assistant		Frequency Percentage
Faculty members	Yes	168 24.9%
	No	493 74.5%
Librarians	Yes	213 32.1%
	No	448 66.3%

Table 8. The correlation between undergraduate students' age and use of e-resources

Correlations	Age	Sour
age Person Correlation Sig. (2-tailed) N	1 675	.118** .002 675
age Person Correlation Sig. (2-tailed) N	.118** .002 675	1 675

** Correlation is Significant at the 0.01 level

the role of the campus librarian in assisting undergraduates with information-search strategies. With regard to gender, this study found that 54.4% of the study sample was female while 45.6% were male, which agreed with Chen (1996) whose study sample included 58.2% female students and 41.7% male students, though it disagreed with Malliari et al. (2011), in whose study (52%) of the study population were males. The high percentage of female undergraduate students in this study can be explained in that the last five years produced a great number of female high school graduates. Regarding the academic year, the highest percentage of respondent undergraduate students were in their 1st year (23.1%), compared to the lowest percentage of students who were at foundation programme (FP) 4.9%. Perhaps the lack of representation of FP students in this study can be explained by the fact that until they finish their FP,

they do not belong to any college, so distributing the questionnaire to them was difficult. With regard to students' colleges, the greatest percentage (22.8%) of the students participating in this study came from the Engineering College. This may be due to the fact that high numbers of high school graduates enroll at this college because the job market at Oman attracts engineering graduates. On the other hand, the lowest number (3.7%) of participants came from the College of Law, which may be because the law specialization is still new at Oman and there is little awareness of what such studies entail after graduation.

With regard to undergraduates' students ICT skills, this study found that the highest percentage of respondents (53.3%) had medium ICT skills, while the undergraduates with low skills were in the minority (1.6%). This result is acceptable and it suggests that the undergraduate students at SQU heavily depend on ICT, probably because they use ICT for their assignments. On the other hand, the students with low ICT skills may be the undergraduates from FP who just enrolled at SQU, meaning that until the study began they did not have the urgency to use ICT. The correlation test showed there to be a negative relationship. A positive relationship between the undergraduates' college and ICT skills may mean that some colleges at SQU require their students to use ICT skills more than other colleges due to the specialization of the college. For example, it may be assumed that the students from the College of Science use ICT a great deal because computer science is part of their college's curriculum, as are other technical subjects. In the Dee & Stanley (2005) study about the information-seeking behavior of nursing students and clinical nurses, they found that 20% of the nursing students felt they lacked the technological skills to search electronic databases.

The results revealed that there were more undergraduate students with moderate English abilities (62.4%) than there were students with other levels of English ability. In fact, the educational system in Oman uses English as a medium of instruction, therefore, the students face problems using the language from the start. In addition, the correlation test suggested that there was a positive relationship between undergraduates' academic year, college, and level of English, suggesting that as the undergraduate progresses to higher level or term his/her English will continue to develop and grow, as he/she will come into contact with many different resources, most of which are in English, and he/she will also learn to write assignments for colleges where a good level of English is expected. These results agree with Sarkodie-Mensah (2000) and Curry & Copeman (2005), who specialized in the factors that affect undergraduates' information-seeking behavior relating to English language capability. Sookhtanlo et al. (2010) also found statistical differences between the information-seeking behavior of Agricultural students working on Bachelors of Sciences and Masters of Science in Iran, and it was found that English language ability created significant differences. The mean for undergraduates' capability in English language was 11.46%, while for postgraduates the mean was 16.57.

Although the libraries at SQU subscribe to many popular databases, it seems these databases have gone untapped. The results of this study provide ample evidence for this statement, showing that 97% of the students surveyed did not use the SQU library electronic services. These services may have gone unused due to students either collecting the needed information from other sources or being unaware of critical information-seeking strategies into formal channels of information such as databases. This assessment agrees with Jarvelin & Ingwersen (2004) who found that low-level information-seeking skills may affect individuals' ability to recognize the need for information as well as the value of libraries or other information providers. However, it disagrees with Nicholas et al. (2009) who concluded at their study that undergraduates and postgraduates were the most likely users of library links to access scholarly databases. Approximately 3% of the undergradu-

ates surveyed used the library's electronic services. Those students may have taken an orientation course on how to use the services available in the libraries. They may have been trained by faculty members or they had assistance from SQU librarians. This understanding agrees with Whitmire (2001), who examined the differences in library use attributed to students at different class levels through a survey investigating the library experiences of undergraduate students during three years of study. The frequency of asking the librarian was the one type of experience that decreased between the first and the third year undergraduate students. Also in agreement with Drabenstott (2003), who examined strategies used by 14 undergraduates in a single search session, employing a so-called information gateway, a university library's home page on the Web that provides a single point of access to the library's online resources. She concluded that few undergraduates were able to enlist search strategies commonly taken by domain experts (i.e., subject experts like professors) and when they did, domain-expert strategies were used infrequently and ineffectively.

Since undergraduates did not use the databases available at the SQU libraries, they must have collected information from other sources. The results showed that 57.7% of the undergraduate students at SQU used the Google search engine for their initial search. This result is confirmed by Malliari et al. (2011) who found that 84% of the postgraduate students at the University of Macedonia start their search with search engines like Google. It may be that the undergraduates who depend on Google do so because in Google it is easier for them to not follow criteria and it enables them to translate any article they do not understand. Seiden et al. (2012) found that 32 out of the 39 students in their study sample had experience using the Web and 60% of those noted that they used it for research. One reason for choosing the Web that Seiden et al. (2012) students consistently pointed to was the success they had when searching it, although the students were using the Web, the results indicate that most of the students have a relatively poor understanding of the information environment, and that the "digital library" exaggerates and magnifies these problems. In this study only 7.1% of the sample asked for help from the librarians. Usually undergraduates lack both confidence in themselves and communication skills, so they prefer not to ask for help, even from librarians, for fear of someone laughing at them. This finding agrees with Lathey & Hodge (2001), who found that many health professionals were reluctant to use libraries.

The role of faculty members and librarians in assisting undergraduates to learn search strategies is almost absent. Approximately 32.1% of the surveyed undergraduate students reported being assisted by the SQU librarian, particularly in terms of guiding them to use resources and gain search strategy skills, while 66.3% of the undergraduate students believe they had not received help or assistance from the SQU librarian before. Similarly, 24.9% of the undergraduates said they were assisted by faculty members while 74.5% thought they had not received any assistance from faculty members. This finding disagreed with that of Seiden et al.(2012) whose survey sample, when asked if any faculty encouraged or required computer-based searching subjects, mentioned a wide variety of courses and faculty. The role of faculty members and librarians is wider than merely pointing out appropriate resources or explaining the assignments for undergraduates. They often begin with explaining the homework or the paper, but they also teach students step-by-step search strategies and resource evaluation. The following studies have indicated the influence of library instruction or other information literacy programs on information-seeking behavior the influential role of librarians: Branch (2003),runton (2007), Craig & Corrall (2007), Tramullas & Casabon (2010), Urquhart & Rowley (2007).

With regard to the role of the librarian, at the beginning of each semester, the Main Library at SQU runs a section on the use of the databases that the library subscribes to as well as search strategies appropriate to these databases. However, a common complaint among librarians at SQU is that these sections are very poorly attended by undergraduates.

This study found a statistical difference between undergraduate students in terms of their age and the use of e-resources, namely a positive relationship, indicating that as students mature their use of e-resources increases. This agrees with Nicholas et al. (2009) who concluded that students get better at searching as their skills progress to the higher stages of their studies.

CONCLUSION

Information-seeking behavior is important to understanding how users look for information and how they evaluate it. Without understanding users' information-seeking behavior, libraries will fail. We live in an electronic era in which electronic resources dominate other resources. This study aimed to explore the electronic resource information-seeking behavior of undergraduate students at SQU. The results of the study show that students tend to start their search using Google search engine more than other resources. The study also examined the role of faculty members and librarians in assisting undergraduates with search strategy and information-seeking skills, which is almost absent.

REFERENCES

Al-Suqri, M. N. (2007). *Information Needs and Seeking Behavior of Social Science Scholars at Sultan Qaboos University in Oman: A Mixed-Method Approach*. Emporia, KS: Emporia State University.

Al-Suqri, M. N. (2011). Information Seeking Behavior of Social Science Scholars in Developing Countries: A Proposed Model. *The International Information & Library Review, 43*, 1–14. doi:10.1016/j.iilr.2011.01.001.

Becker, N. J. (2003). Google in perspective: Understanding and enhancing student search skills. *New Review of Academic Librarianship, 9*(1), 84–100. doi:10.1080/13614530410001692059.

Broskoske, S. L. (2005). Making a case for writing research papers. *Teaching Professor*, 4.

Case, D. O. (2002). *Looking for information: A survey of research on information seeking behavior, needs*. Amsterdam, The Netherlands: Academic Press.

Chen, J. F. (1996). Gender Differences in Taiwan Business Writing Errors. *The Internet TESL Journal, 2*(10). Retrieved on August 23, 2012, from http://iteslj.org/Articles/Chen-GenderDifs/

Cooper, L. Z. (2002). A case study of information seeking behavior in 7 year-old children in a semistructured situation. *Journal of the American Society for Information Science and Technology, 53*(11), 904–922. doi:10.1002/asi.10130.

Curry, A., & Deborah, C. (2005). Reference Service to International Students: A Field Stimulation Research Study. *Journal of Academic Librarianship, 31*(5), 409–420. doi:10.1016/j.acalib.2005.05.011.

Dalgleish, A., & Hall, R. (2000). Uses and perceptions of the World Wide Web in an information-seeking environment. *Journal of Librarianship and Information Science, 32*(3), 104–116.

Dee, C., & Stanley, E. E. (2005). Information-seeking behavior of nursing students and clinical nurses: Implications for health sciences librarians. *Journal of the Medical library Association, 93*(2), 213–222. Retrieved on December 16, 2012, from http://www.ncbi.nlm.nih.gov/pmc/articles/pmc1082938/

Drabenstott, K. M. (2003). Do nondomain experts enlist the strategies of domain experts? *Journal of the American Society for Information Science and Technology, 54*(9). doi:10.1002/asi.10281.

Fast, K. V., & Campbell, G. (2004). I still like Google: University student perceptions of searching OPACs and the Web. In *Proceedings of the 67th ASIS&T Annual Meeting, 41*, 138-146.

Halder, S., Ray, A., & Chakrabarty, P. K. (2010). Gender differences in information seeking behavior in three universities in West Bengal, India. *The International Information & Library Review, 42*(4), 242–251. doi:10.1016/j.iilr.2010.10.004.

Hart, C. T. (2008). *Exploring the information-seeking behavior of the staff and students of the Florida Virtual School: A case study*. Unpublished Doctoral dissertation, Florida State University, Tallahassee, FL.

Jarvelin, K., & Ingwersen, P. (2004). Information-seeking research needs extension towards tasks and technology. *Information Research, 10*(1).

Kennedy, T., Wellman, B., & Klement, K. (2003). Gendering the digital divide. *IT and Society, 1*(5), 72-96. Retrieved on December 17, 2012, from http://www.stanford.edu/group/siqss/itandsociety/v01i05/v01i05a05.pdf

Kuhlthau, C. C. (2004). *Seeking Meaning* (2nd ed.). Westport, CT: Libraries Unlimited,Inc..

Lathey, J. W., & Hodge, B. (2001). Information seeking behavior of occupational health nurses: How nurses keep current with health information. *AAOHN Journal, 49*(2), 87–95. PMID:11760270.

Mackay, D. M. (1960). What makes a question? *Listener (London, England), 63*, 789–790.

Mahajan, P. (2009). Information-Seeking Behavior: A Study of Panjab University, India. *Library Philosophy and Practice*. Retrieved on December 27, 2012, from http://unllib.unl.edu/LPP/mahajan4.htm.%20

Majid, S., & Kassim, G. M. (2000). Information-seeking behaviour of International Islamic University, Malaysia law faculty members. *Malaysian Journal of Library & Information Science*, *5*(2), 1–17.

Malliari, A., Korobili, S., & Zapounidou, S. (2011). Exploring the information seeking behavior of Greek graduate students: A case study set in the University of Macedonia. *The International Information & Library Review*, *43*(2), 79–91. doi:10.1016/j.iilr.2011.04.006.

Nesset, V. (2009). *The information-seeking behavior of grade-three Elementary School students in the context of a class project*. Unpublished Doctoral dissertation.

Nicholas, D., Huntington, P., Jamali, H. R., Rowlands, I., & Fieldhouse, M. (2009). Student digital information-seeking behaviour in context. *Journal of Documentation*, *65*(1). Retrieved on December 28, 2012, from http://www.emeraldinsight.com/journals.htm?articleid=1766885&show=abstract

Nicholas, D., Rowlands, I., & Jamali, H. R. (2010). E-textbook use, information seeking behaviour and its impact: Case study business and management. *Journal of Information Science*, *36*(2), 263–280. doi:10.1177/0165551510363660.

Roy, M., Taylor, R., & Chi, M. T. H. (2003). Searching for information on-line and off-line: Gender differences among middle school students. *Journal of Educational Computing Research*, *29*, 229–252. doi:10.2190/KCGA-3197-2V6U-WUTH.

Sarkodie, M. K. (2000). The international student on campus: History, trends, visa classification, and adjustment issues. In Jacobson, T. E., & Williams, H. C. (Eds.), *Teaching the New Library To Today's Users: Reaching International, Minority, Senior Citizens, Gay/Lesbian, First Generation, At-Risk, Graduate and Returning Students, and Distance Learners*. New York: Neal-Shuman.

Seiden, P., Szymborski, Z., & Norelli, B. (2012). Undergraduate Students in the Digital Library: Information Seeking Behavior in an Heterogeneous Environment. *Association of College & Research Libraries*. Retrieved on December 18, 2012, from http://www.ala.org/acrl/publications/whitepapers/nashville/seidenszymborski

Selwyn, N. (2008). An investigation of differences in undergraduates' academic use of the Internet. *Active Learning in Higher Education*, *9*(1), 11-22. Retrieved on December 27, 2012, from http://alh.sagepub.com/content/9/1/11.short

Solomon, P. (2002). Discovering information in context. In Cronin, B. (Ed.), *Annual Review of Information Science and Technology, 36, 229-264*.

Sookhtanlo, M., Mohammadi, H. M., & Rezvanfar, A. (2010). A comparative study of the information-seeking behavior of bachelor of science and master of science agricultural extension and education students. *Library philosophy and practice*. Retrieved on December 27, 2012, from http://unllib.unl.edu/lpp/sookhtanlo-mohammadi-rezvanfar.htm

Weiler, A. (2005). Information-seeking behavior in Generation Y students: Motivation, critical thinking, and learning theory. *Journal of Academic Librarianship*, *31*(1), 46–53. doi:10.1016/j.acalib.2004.09.009.

Whitmire, E. (2001). The relationship between undergraduates' background characteristics and college experiences and their academic library use. *College & Research Libraries*, *62*(6), 528–540.

Zaborowski, B. A. (2008). Identifying the information-seeking behaviors of students, the expectations of faculty, and the role of librarians in writing assignments that require students to use information sources in selected Pennsylvania community colleges: A model for instruction. Unpublished Doctoral dissertation, Pennsylvania.

ADDITIONAL READING

Amiel, T., & Sargent, S. L. (2004). Individual differences in Internet usage motives. *Computers in Human Behavior, 20*(6), 711–726. doi:10.1016/j.chb.2004.09.002.

Chowdhury, S., Gibb, F., & Landoni, M. (2011). Uncertainty in information seeking and retrieval: A study in an academic environment. *Information Processing & Management, 47*(2), 157-175. Retrieved on December 6, 2012, from http://ac.elscdn.com/S0306457310000798/1-s2.0-S0306457310000798-main.pdf?_tid=724740a4-57f8-11e2-be46-00000aab0f01&acdnat=1357473715_17a9ff11907c715cbdb12885ed9d0727

Chowdhury, S., & Landoni, M. (2006). News aggregator services: User expectations and experience. *Online Information Review, 30*(2), 100–115. doi:10.1108/14684520610659157.

Halder, S., Ray, A., & Chakrabarty, P. K. (2010). Gender differences in information seeking behavior in three universities in West Bengal, India. *The international information & library Review, 42*, 242-251. Retrieved on February 12, 2013, from http://ac.els-cdn.com/S1057231710000639/1-s2.0-S1057231710000639-main.pdf?_tid=aad4f41e-7532-11e2-b7900000aacb361&acdnat=1360687305_5b2d311dbcbf901f213e2f23ca015635

Heinstro¨m, J. (2006). Fast surfing for availability or deep diving into quality-motivation and information seeking among middle and high school students. *Information Research, 11*(4). Retrieved on December 28, 2012, from http://informationr.net/ir/11 4/paper265.html

Hembrooke, H. A., & Granka, L. A., Gay, Geraldine, K., & Liddy, E. D. (2005). The effects of expertise and feedback on search term selection and subsequent learning. *Journal of the American Society for Information Science and Technology, 56*(8), 861–871. doi:10.1002/asi.20180.

Hsieh-Yee, I. (2001). Research on web search behaviour. *Library & Information Science Research, 23*(2), 167–185. doi:10.1016/S0740-8188(01)00069-X.

Jamali, H. R., & Asadi, S. (2010). Google and the scholar: The role of Google in scientists' information-seeking behaviour. *Online Information Review, 34*(2), 282–294. doi:10.1108/14684521011036990.

Kai-Wah Chu, S., & Law, N. (2008). The development of information search expertise of research students. *Journal of Librarianship and Information Science, 40*(3), 165–177. doi:10.1177/0961000608092552.

McKechnie, E. F., Goodall, G. R., Lajoie-Paquette, D., & Julien, H. (2005). How human information behaviour researchers use each other's work: A basic citation analysis study. *Information Research, 10*(2). Retrieved on December 28, 2012, from http://InformationR.net/ir/10-2/paper220.html

Palmer, J. (1991). Scientists and information: II. Personal factors in information behaviour. *The Journal of Documentation, 47*(3), 254–275. doi:10.1108/eb026880.

Palmquist, R. A., & Kim, K. S. (2000). Cognitive style and online database search experience as predictor of web search performance. *Journal of the American Society for Information Science American Society for Information Science, 51*(6), 558–566. doi:10.1002/(SICI)1097-4571(2000)51:6<558::AID-ASI7>3.0.CO;2-9.

Ramirez, A., Walther, J. B., Burgoon, J. K., & Sunnafrank, M. (2002). Information-seeking strategies, uncertainty, and computer-mediated communication. Toward a conceptual model. *Human Communication Research, 28*(2), 213–228.

Rieh, S. Y. (2002). Judgment of information quality and cognitive authority in the web. *Journal of the American Society for Information Science and Technology, 53*(2), 145–161. doi:10.1002/asi.10017.

Samson, S. (2010). Information literacy learning outcomes and student success. *Journal of Academic Librarianship, 36*(3), 202–210. doi:10.1016/j. acalib.2010.03.002.

Sharifabadi, S. R. (1996). Information seeking and communication among researchers and the impact of electronic networks: A literature review. In *Effects of the Internet on research activities, information seeking and communication behaviour of Australian academic psychologists* (Ch. 3, pp. 45e86). Sydney, Australia: University of New South Wales. Retrieved on December 28, 2012, from http://www. alzahra.ac.ir/rezaei/PDF/CHAP3.pdf

Thatcher, A. (2008). Web search strategies: The influence of web experience and task type. *Information Processing & Management, 44*(3), 1308–1329. doi:10.1016/j.ipm.2007.09.004.

White, R. W., Dumais, S. T., & Teevan, J. (2009). *Characterizing the influence of domain expertise on web search behavior*. Paper presented at the 2nd ACM international Conference on web Search and data mining. Barcelona, Spain. Retrieved on December 3, 2012, from www.wsdm2009.org/papers/p132-white.pdf

Wildemuth, B. M. (2004). The effects of domain knowledge on search tactic formulation. *Journal of the American Society for Information Science and Technology, 55*(3), 246–258. doi:10.1002/asi.10367.

Williamson, K., Bernath, V., Wright, S., & Sullivan, J. (2008). Research students in the Electronic Age: Impacts of changing information behavior on information literacy needs. *Communications in Information Literacy, 1*(2). Retrieved on December 3, 2012, from http://www.comminfolit.org/index. php/cil/article/view/Fall2007AR1/48

Zhang, X., Anghelescu, H. G. B., & Yuan, X. (2005). Domain knowledge, search behavior, and search effectiveness of engineering and science students: An exploratory study. *Information Research, 10*(2). Retrieved on December 3, 2012, from http://InformationR.net/ir/10-2/paper217. html

KEY TERMS AND DEFINITIONS

Electronic Services: The services that are available on the website of the SQU libraries and information centers, such as the e-journal, e-books, e-dissertation, etc.

Search Strategy: The strategy that users use to seek information.

Undergraduate Information-Seeking Behavior: The way undergraduate students look for information or the search strategy that they use and how they use it.

Undergraduate Students: University students in years one to four.

User Studies: The study that focuses on how users benefit from the services that are available at libraries and information centers.

Compilation of References

Abdullahi, I., Kajberg, L., & Virkus, S. (2007). Internationalization of LIS education in Europe and North America. *New Library World, 108*(1/2), 7–24. doi:10.1108/03074800710722144.

Aber, S. W. (2005). *Information needs and behaviors of Geoscience education: A ground theory study*. Unpublished doctoral dissertation, Emporia State University, Emporia, KS.

Abouserie, H. E. M. R. (2003). *Information-seeking and communicating behavior of social science faculty in an academic environment with special reference to the use of electronic journals: A field study*. Unpublished doctoral dissertation, University of Pittsburgh, Pittsburgh, PA.

Acs, A. J., & Virgill, N. (2010). Entrepreneurship in developing countries. In Acs, Z. J., & Audretsch, D. B. (Eds.), *Handbook of Entrepreneurship Research* (pp. 485–515). New York: Springer. doi:10.1007/978-1-4419-1191-9_18.

AGESIC. (2011). Agenda Digital Uruguay 2011-2015. Retrieved on January, 31, 2012, from www.agesic.gub.uy/innovaportal/.../agenda_digital_2011-2015.pdf

Aguolu, I. (1997). Accessibility of information: A myth for developing countries? *New Library World*, 25–29.

Alabi. (2004, April 30). Evolving Role of ICT's in Teaching, Research and Publishing. *Nigerian Tribune*.

Al-Ansari, H., Rehman, S., & Yousef, N. (2001). Faculty in the library schools of the Gulf Co-operation Council member nations: an evaluation. *Libri, 51*(3), 173–181. doi:10.1515/LIBR.2001.173.

Alimohammadi, D., & Jamali, H. R. (2011). Common problems of Library and Information Science education in Asian developing countries: a review article. *International Journal of Information Science and Management, 9*(2), 79–92.

Allen, B. (1997). Information needs: A person-in-situation approach. In P. Vakkari, R. Savolainen, & B. Dervin (Eds.), *Information seeking in context: Proceedings of an International Conference on Research in Information Needs, Seeking and Use in Different Contexts* (pp. 99-110). London: Taylor Graham.

Al-Mulhim, A. (2012, June 1). Gulf states and an era of cooperation. *ArabNews.com*. Retrieved July 16, 2012 from http://www.arabnews.com/gulf-states-and-era-cooperation

Al-Suqri, M. N., Al-Saleem, N. E., & Gharib, M. E. (2012). Understanding the Prospects and Potential for Improved Regional LIS Collaboration in the Developing World: An Empirical Study of LIS Departments in the GCC States. World Library and Information Congress 2012, 78th IFLA General Conference and Assembly: Libraries Now! - Inspiring, Surprising, Empowering. Helsinki, 11-17 August 2012, Helsinki, Finland.

Al-Suqri, M. N. (2007). *Information Needs and Seeking Behavior of Social Science Scholars at Sultan Qaboos University in Oman: A Mixed-Method Approach*. Emporia, KS: Emporia State University.

Al-Suqri, M. N. (2010). Collaboration in library and information science education in the Gulf Co-operation Council (GCC): current status, challenges and future trends. *The Emporia State Research Studies, 46*(2), 48–53.

Al-Suqri, M. N. (2011). Information Seeking Behavior of Social Science Scholars in Developing Countries: A Proposed Model. *The International Information & Library Review, 43*, 1–14. doi:10.1016/j.iilr.2011.01.001.

Al-Suqri, M. N., & Afzal, W. (2007). Digital age: challenges for libraries. *Information. Social Justice (San Francisco, Calif.), 1*(1), 43–48.

Al-Suqri, M. N., & Lillard, L. (2011). Barriers to Effective Information Seeking of Social Scientists in Developing Countries: The Case of Sultan Qaboos University in Oman. *International Research: Journal of Library & Information Science*, *1*(2), 86–100.

Álvarez Pedrosian, E. (2011). *Etnografías de la subjetividad. Herramientas para la investigación*. Montevideo, Uruguay: LICCOM-Universidad de la República.

Ameen, K. (2011). Changing scenario of librarianship in Pakistan: managing with the challenges and opportunities. *Library Management*, *32*(3), 171–182. doi:10.1108/01435121111112880.

American Library Association. (1989). *American Library Association Presidential Commission on Information Literacy. Final report*. Chicago, Ill.: American Library Association.

Anderson, J. D. (2003). *Analysing the role of knowledge organization in scholarly communication: An inquiry into intellectual foundation of knowledge organization*. Retrieved on July 3, 2011, from http://arizona.open-repository.com/arizona/bitstream/10150/105100/1/jackandersen-phd.pdf.

Anghelescu, H. G. B., Lukenbill, J., Lukenbill, W. B., & Owens, I. (2009). Acceptance of social marketing concepts by selected Romanian librarians: Culture and context. *Advances in Library Administration and Organization*, *27*, 123–150. doi:10.1108/S0732-0671(2009)0000027012.

Annan, K. (2004). Science for all Nations. *Science Magazine*, *303*, 925. PMID:14963291.

Anonymous (2010, October 29). Spanish investors encouraged to tap into Oman market. Asia Pulse.

Anonymous. (2012, April 29). Saudi Arabia to launch $21 billion education projects. *Albawaba.com*. Retrieved on July 15, 2012 from http://www.albawaba.com/business/saudi-arabia-university-education-projects-422936.

Anonymous. (2012, May 13). UAE hosts highest number of international branch campuses worldwide. *UAEInteract.com*. Retrieved on July 15, 2012 from http://www.uaeinteract.com/docs/UAE_hosts_highest_number_of_International_Branch_Campuses_worldwide/49461.htm

Aqili, S. V., & Moghaddam, A. I. (2008). *Bridging the digital divide: The role of Librarians and Information Professionals in the third millennium*. Retrieved on April, 27, 2011, from http://www.emeraldinsight.com/0264-0473.htm.

Aristeguieta-Trillos, S., & Maura Sardo, M. (2006). *A bibliometric study on scientific production in Venezuela from 1994 to 2003 based on Science Citation Index*. Retrieved on April 17, 2008, from http://www.congreso-info.cu/

Arnold, L., Sadler, L., Balkan, S. M., & Humphreys, R. L. (1997). *Machine Translation: An Introductory Guide*. London: Blackwell.

Arunachalam, S. (2003). Information for research in developing countries: Information technology--A friend or foe? *The International Information & Library Review*, *35*, 133–147. doi:10.1016/S1057-2317(03)00032-8.

Asian Development Bank. (1992). *Mongolia, a centrally planned economy in Transition*. Hong Kong: Oxford University Press.

Asian Development Bank. (2009). *Private sector assessment for Mongolia*. Retrieved on July 30, 2011, from http://www.adb.org/Documents/Assessments/Private-Sector/MON/PSA-MON-2009.pdf

Asunka, S., Chae, H. S., Hughes, B., & Natriello, G. (2009). Understanding academic information seeking habits through analysis of web server log files: The case of the Teachers College library website. *Journal of Academic Librarianship*, *35*(1), 33–45. doi:10.1016/j.acalib.2008.10.019.

Asunka, S., Chae, H. S., & Natriello, G. (2011). Towards an understanding of the use of an institutional repository with integrated social networking tools: A case study of PocketKnowledge. *Library & Information Science Research*, *33*(1), 80–88. doi:10.1016/j.lisr.2010.04.006.

Auty, R. (1993). *Sustaining development in mineral economies: The resource curse thesis*. London: Routledge.

Baldwin, R. C. (1998). *Technology's impact on faculty life and work. The Impact of Faculty Life and Work: New Directions in Teaching and Learning*. San Fransisco, CA: Jossey-Bass.

Ballesteros, L., & Croft, W. (1998). Resolving ambiguity for cross-language retrieval. *In Proceedings of SIGIR Conference*. Melbourne, Australia: ACM.

Banda, C., Mutula, S. M., & Grand, B. (2004, December). Information needs assessment for small scale business community in Zambia: Case study of Chisokone Market, Kitwe. *Malaysian Journal of Library & Information Science*, *9*(2), 95–106.

Barja, G., & Gigler, B. (2007). The concept of information poverty and how to measure it in the Latin American Context. In H. Galperin, & J. Marical, *Digital Poverty. Latin American and Caribbean Perspectives*. Retrieved on February 2, 2012, from http://dirsi.net/sites/default/files/dirsi_07_DP01_en.pdf

Baron, S. (2011, March). Why we need a UK National Digital Library. *Update*.

Barry, C. L. (1994). User-defined relevance criteria: An exploratory study. *Journal of the American Society for Information Science and Technology*, *45*(3), 149–159. doi:10.1002/(SICI)1097-4571(199404)45:3<149::AID-ASI5>3.0.CO;2-J.

Bass, A., Fairlee, J., Fox, K., & Sullivan, J. (2005). *The Information Behavior of Scholars in the Humanities and Social Sciences*. University of Washington, LIS 510 November 17, 2005.

Bates, M. J. (2005) Information and knowledge: An evolutionary framework for information science. *Information Research*, *10*, 4. Retrieved on September 22, 2006, from http://informationr.net/ir/10-4/paper239.html

Bates, M. J. (1989). The design of browsing and berrypicking techniques for the online search interface. *Online Review*, *13*(5), 407–424. doi:10.1108/eb024320.

Bates, M. J. (1991). The berry-picking search: User interface design. In Dillon, M. (Ed.), *Interfaces for information retrieval and online systems: The state of art* (pp. 55–61). New York: Greenwood Press.

Beasley, B. E., & Nyce, J. M. (2009). *A more perfect Poundbury? Prince Charles' reinvention of Viscri, Romania*. Presented at the Indiana University Romanian Studies Conference, Bloomington, Indiana.

Becker, N. J. (2003). Google in perspective: Understanding and enhancing student search skills. *New Review of Academic Librarianship*, *9*(1), 84–100. doi:10.1080/13614530410001692059.

Beheshti, J., Large, A., & Tam, M. (2010). Transaction logs and search patterns on a children's portal. *Canadian Journal of Information and Library Science*, *34*(4), 391–402. doi:10.1353/ils.2010.0011.

Belkin, N. J. (1980). Anomalous states of knowledge as a basis for information retrieval. *Canadian. Journal of Information Science*, *5*, 133–143.

Belkin, N. J., Oddy, R. N., & Brooks, H. (1982). ASK for Information retrieval Part I. *The Journal of Documentation*, *38*(2), 61–72. doi:10.1108/eb026722.

Belkin, N. J., Oddy, R. N., & Brooks, H. (1982). ASK for Information retrieval Part II. *The Journal of Documentation*, *38*(3), 145–164. doi:10.1108/eb026726.

Belkin, N. J., & Vickery, A. (1985). *Interaction in information system: A review of research from document retrieval to knowledge-based system*. London: The British Library.

Bertone, A. I., Peluffo, G., & Katz, R. (2012, August). *Sistema Colaborativo para la Integración de Información y Servicios en el Área Social y de la Salud: Tu Sitio Salud (Tesis de Grado - Ingeniería en Computación)*. Instituto de Computación, Facultad de Ingeniería, Universidad de la República, Montevideo, Uruguay.

Bhat, M. (2009). Open access publishing in Indian Premier Research Institutions. *Information Research, 14*(3). Retrieved on July 27, 2011, from http://InformationR.net/ir/14-3/paper409.html

Bhatti, R. (2011). Internet Use by Social Scientists at the Bahauddin Zakariya University, Multan, Pakistan: A Survey. Library Philosophy and Practice, 1-12.

Bhatt, R. K. (2010). Use of UGC-Infonet Digital Library Consortium resources by research scholars and faculty members of the University of Delhi in History and Political Science: A study. *Library Management*, *31*(4/5), 319–343. doi:10.1108/01435121011046371.

Borgman, C. L. (1984). Psychological research in human-computer interaction. *Annual Review of Information Science & Technology, 19*, 33–64.

Borgman, C. L. (1996). Why are online catalogs still hard to use? *Journal of the American Society for Information Science American Society for Information Science, 47*, 493–503. doi:10.1002/(SICI)1097-4571(199607)47:7<493::AID-ASI3>3.0.CO;2-P.

Borgman, C. L. (2000). Scholarly communication and bibliometrics revisited. In Cronin, B., & Atkins, H. B. (Eds.), *The Web of Knowledge: A Festschrift in Honor of Eugene Garfield* (pp. 145–150). Medford, NJ: Information Today, Inc..

Bouazza, A. (1986). *Use of information sources by physical scientists, social scientists, humanities scholars at Carnegie-Mellon University.* Unpublished doctoral dissertation, University of Pittsburgh, Pittsburgh, PA.

Bouazza, A., & Al-Mahrooqi, H. (2010). Use of the Internet by Arts and Social Science students as a source of information: the case of the Sultanate of Oman. *Digest of Middle East Studies, 18*(2), 72–84. doi:10.1111/j.1949-3606.2009.tb01106.x.

Boumarafi, B. (2010). Electronic resources at the University of Sharjah Medical Library: An investigation of students' information-seeking behavior. *Medical Reference Services Quarterly, 29*(4), 349–362. doi:10.1080/02763869.2010.518921 PMID:21058178.

Bourdieu, P. (2001). *Qué significa hablar?* Madrid: Akal.

Boyd, A. (2004). Multi-channel information seeking: A fuzzy conceptual model. *Aslib Proceedings, 52*(2), 81–88. doi:10.1108/00012530410529440.

Brady, M. (2005). *Blogging: Personal participation in the public knowledge-building on the web.* Colchester, UK: University of Essex.

Brittain, J. M. (1970). *Information and its users: A review with special reference to the social science.* New York: Wiley Inter-science.

Brittain, J. M. (1984). Internationality of the social sciences: Implications for information transfer. *Journal of the American Society for Information Science American Society for Information Science, 35*(1), 11–18. doi:10.1002/asi.4630350103.

Broadbent, E. (1986). A study of humanities faculty library information-seeking behaviour. *Cataloging & Classification Quarterly, 6*, 23–37. doi:10.1300/J104v06n03_03.

Broskoske, S. L. (2005). Making a case for writing research papers. *Teaching Professor, 4.*

Brown, C. M. (1999). Information Seeking Behavior of Scientists in the Electronic Information Age: Astronomers, Chemists, Mathematicians, and Physicists. *Journal of the American Society for Information Science American Society for Information Science, 50*(10), 929–943. doi:10.1002/(SICI)1097-4571(1999)50:10<929::AID-ASI8>3.0.CO;2-G.

Brush, C. G. (1992). Research on women business owners: Past trends, a new perspective and future directions. *Entrepreneurship Theory and Practice, 16*(2), 6–30.

Buck, S., & Nichols, J. (2012). Beyond the search box. *Reference and User Services Quarterly, 51*(3), 235–245. doi:10.5860/rusq.51n3.235.

Bush, V. (1945). As We May Think. *The Atlantic Monthly* (Vol. 176, No. 1). Retrieved on August 26, 2004, from http://www.theatlantic.com/unbound/flashbks/computer/bushf.htm

Business Monitor International. (2010). *Oman infrastructure report: Q3 2010.* Business Monitor International.

Buttlar, L., & Wynar, L. R. (1992). Cultural pluralism and ethnic diversity: Authors as information users in the field of ethnic studies. *Collection Management, 16*(3), 13–33. doi:10.1300/J105v16n03_02.

Calva, J. J. (2004). *Information needs: Theoretical foundations and methods.* México City: UNAM, Centro Universitario de Investigaciones Bibliotecológicas.

Camacho Jimenez, K. (2000). How we approach the assessment of the impact of the Internet in civil society organizations in Central America. *Fundación Acceso.* Retrieved on November 24, 2011, from http://www.acceso.or.cr/publica/telecom/conocimiento22.html.

Cardoso, F., H. (1972). Dependent Capitalist Development in Latin America. *New Left Review, 74*(I), 83–95.

Carland, J. W., Hoy, F., Boulton, W. R., & Carland, J. A. (1984). Differentiating entrepreneurs from small business owners: A conceptualization. *Academy of Management Review, 9*(2), 354–359.

Carr, J. A. (2003). Exploring cultural challenges to the integration of technology. In *Leadership, Higher Education and The Information Age: A new Era for Information Technology Libraries*. London: Neal Schuman.

Case, D. O. (2002). *Looking for information: A survey of research on information seeking, needs, and behavior.* New York: Academic Press.

Casey, M. E., & Savastinuk, L. C. (2006). Library 2.0: Service for the next generation library. *Library Journal, 131*(14), 40–42.

Chalhoub, M. S. (2011). Culture, management practices, and the entrepreneurial performance of small and medium enterprises: Applications and empirical study in the Middle East. *Journal of Small Business and Entrepreneurship, 24*(1), 67–84. doi:10.1080/08276331.2011.10593526.

Chan, L., Kirsop, B., & Arunachalam, S. (2005). Open access archiving: The fast track to building research capacity in developing countries. *Science and Development Network.* Retrieved on January 27, 2010, from http://www.scidev.net/ms/openaccess/

Chatman, E. A. (1986). Diffusion theory: A review and test of a conceptual model in information diffusion. *Journal of the American Society for Information Science American Society for Information Science, 37*(6), 377–386.

Chen, J. F. (1996). Gender Differences in Taiwan Business Writing Errors. *The Internet TESL Journal, 2*(10). Retrieved on August 23, 2012, from http://iteslj.org/Articles/Chen-GenderDifs/

Cheng, Y. (2004). *Thoughts, feelings, and actions: Quantitative comparisons of interactions and relationships among three factors in college students' information seeking.* Unpublished Doctoral Dissertation, Indiana University, Bloomington, IN.

Chiranov, M. (2010). Real life impact of the global libraries: Biblionet Romania Program. *Performance Measurement and Metrics, 11*(1), 93–106. doi:10.1108/14678041011026900.

Chiware, E. R. T. (2007). Designing and implementing business information services in the SMME sector in a developing country: The case for Namibia. *IFLA Journal, 33*(2), 136–144. doi:10.1177/0340035207080308.

Chiware, E. R. T. (2010). Positioning the technological university library in higher education and human resources development in Africa. *Library Management, 31*(6), 391–403. doi:10.1108/01435121011066153.

Chowdhury, G. (2003). Natural language processing. [ARIST]. *Annual Review of Information Science & Technology, 37*, 51–89. doi:10.1002/aris.1440370103.

Choy, F. C. (2011). From library stacks to library-in-a-pocket: will users be around? *Library Management, 32*(1/2), 62–72. doi:10.1108/01435121111102584.

Chunrong, L., Wang, J., & Zhou, Z. (2010). Regional consortia for e-resources: A case study of deals in the South China Region. *Program: Electronic Library and Information Systems, 44*(4), 328–341. doi:10.1108/00330331011083220.

CIA. (2009). *South America: Venezuela.* Retrieved on June 15, 2009, from https://www.cia.gov/library/publications/the-world-factbook/geos/VE.html

Colesca, S. E., & Dobrica, L. (2008). Adoption and use of e-government services: The case of Romania. *Journal of Applied Research and Technology, 3*, 204–217.

Cooperation Council for The Arab States of the Gulf. (1981). *The Charter.* Retrieved from http://www.gcc-sg.org/eng/indexfc7a.html?action=Sec-Show&ID=1

Cooper, L. Z. (2002). A case study of information seeking behavior in 7 year-old children in a semistructured situation. *Journal of the American Society for Information Science and Technology, 53*(11), 904–922. doi:10.1002/asi.10130.

Corbin, J. M., & Strauss, A. C. (2007). *Basics of qualitative research: Techniques and procedures for developing grounded theory.* Newbury Park, CA: Sage.

Corrall, S. (2010). Educating the academic librarian as a blended professional: a review and case study. *Library Management, 31*(8/9), 567–593. doi:10.1108/01435121011093360.

Cosijn, E., & Ingwersen, P. (2000). Dimensions of relevance. *Information Processing & Management, 36*, 533–550. doi:10.1016/S0306-4573(99)00072-2.

Cullen, R., & Chawner, B. (2011). Institutional repositories, open access and scholarly communication: A study of conflicting paradigms. *Journal of Academic Librarianship*, *37*(6), 460–470. doi:10.1016/j.acalib.2011.07.002.

Curits, K. L., Weller, A. C., & Hurd, J. M. (1993). Information-seeking behavior: A survey of health sciences faculty use of indexes and databases. *Bulletin of the Medical Library Association*, *81*(4), 383–392. PMID:8251974.

Curry, A., & Deborah, C. (2005). Reference Service to International Students: A Field Stimulation Research Study. *Journal of Academic Librarianship*, *31*(5), 409–420. doi:10.1016/j.acalib.2005.05.011.

Dagli, A. (2005). *Culture and information needs in web-based learning: An instrumental case study of multilingual graduate students.* Unpublished Doctoral Dissertation, Florida State University, Tallahassee, FL.

Dalgleish, A., & Hall, R. (2000). Uses and perceptions of the World Wide Web in an information-seeking environment. *Journal of Librarianship and Information Science*, *32*(3), 104–116.

Davids, G. (2011, February 5). Gulf states lag world in university participation rates. *Arabianbusiness.com*. Retrieved on July 12, 2012 from http://www.arabianbusiness.com/gulf-states-lag-world-in-university-participation-rates-378740.html

Davis, M., & Ogden, W. (1997). QUILT: Implementing a Large-Scale Cross-Language Text Retrieval System. In *Proceedings of the 20th Annual International ACM SIGIR Conference on Research and Development in Information Retrieval* (pp. 92-98). Philadelphia, PA: ACM.

Day, M. T. (1998). Transformational discourse: Ideologies of organizational change in the academic library and information science literature. *Library Trends*, *46*(4), 635–667.

De Tiratel, S. R. (2000). Accessing Information Use by Humanists and Social Scientists: A Study at the Universidad de Buenos Aires, Argentina. *Journal of Academic Librarianship*, *26*(5), 346–355.

Dee, C., & Stanley, E. E. (2005). Information-seeking behavior of nursing students and clinical nurses: Implications for health sciences librarians. *Journal of the Medical library Association*, *93*(2), 213–222. Retrieved on December 16, 2012, from http://www.ncbi.nlm.nih.gov/pmc/articles/pmc1082938/

Dervin, B. (1983). *An overview of sense-making: Concepts, methods and results to date.* Paper presented at the International Communication Association Annual Meeting. Dallas, TX.

Dervin, B. (1992). From the mind's eye of the user: The sense-making qualitative-quantitative methodology. In Glazier, J. D., & Powell, R. R. (Eds.), *Qualitative research in information management* (pp. 61–84). Englewood, CO: Libraries Unlimited.

Dervin, B. (1997). Given a context by any other name: Methodological tools for taming the unruly beast. In Vakkari, P., Savolainen, R., & Dervin, B. (Eds.), *Information seeking in context* (pp. 13–38). London: Taylor Graham.

Dervin, B. (1999). On studying information seeking methodologically: The implications of connecting metatheory to method. *Information Processing & Management*, *35*(6), 727–750. doi:10.1016/S0306-4573(99)00023-0.

Dervin, B., Foreman-Wernet, L., & Lauterbach, E. (2003). *Sense-making methodology reader: Selected writings of Brenda Dervin.* New York: Hampton Press.

Dervin, B., & Nilan, M. (1986). Information needs and uses. *Annual Review of Information Science & Technology*, *21*, 3–33.

Dickinson, A., & Gregor, P. (2006). Computer use has no demonstrated impact on the well-being of older adults. *International Journal of Human-Computer Studies*, *64*(8), 744–753. doi:10.1016/j.ijhcs.2006.03.001.

Dolgin, E. (2009). Online access=more citations. *The Scientist*. Retrieved on September 6, 2010, from http://www.the-scientist.com/blog/display/55437/

Drabenstott, K. M. (2003). Do nondomain experts enlist the strategies of domain experts? *Journal of the American Society for Information Science and Technology*, *54*(9). doi:10.1002/asi.10281.

Drake, M. A. (2004). Institutional repositories: Hidden treasures. *Searcher*, *12*(5), 41–45.

Duff, W. M., & Johnson, C. A. (2002). Accidentally found on purpose: Information- seeking behavior of historians in archives. *The Library Quarterly*, *72*(4), 472–496.

Dutta, R. (2009). Information needs and information-seeking behavior in developing countries: A review of the research. *The International Information & Library Review*, *41*(1), 44–51.

Echezona, R. I., & Ugwuanyi, C. F. (2010). African university libraries and Internet connectivity: Challenges and the way forward. *Library Philosophy and Practice*(September), 1-13.

Economist Intelligence Unit. (2009). *The GCC in 2020: the Gulf and its people*. The Economist Intelligence Unit Limited. Sponsored by the Qatar Financial Center Authority.

Eco, U. (1993). El público perjudica a la televisión? In *Sociología de la comunicación de masas* (*Vol. 2*). México: Gili.

Ellis, D. (1989). A behavioral approach to information retrieval design. *The Journal of Documentation, 45*(3), 171–212. doi:10.1108/eb026843.

Ellis, D. (1989). A behavioral model for information retrieval system design. *Journal of Information Science, 15*, 237–247. doi:10.1177/016555158901500406.

Ellis, D., Allen, D., & Wilson, T. (1999). Information science and information systems: Conjunct subjects disjunct disciplines. *Journal of the American Society for Information Science and Technology, 50*(12), 1095–1107. doi:10.1002/(SICI)1097-4571(1999)50:12<1095::AID-ASI9>3.0.CO;2-Z.

Ellis, D., Cox, D., & Hall, K. (1993). A comparison of the information seeking patterns of researchers in the physical and social sciences. *The Journal of Documentation, 49*(4), 356–369. doi:10.1108/eb026919.

Ellis, D., & Haugan, M. (1997). Modelling the information seeking patterns of engineers and research scientists in an industrial environment. *The Journal of Documentation, 53*(4), 384–403. doi:10.1108/EUM0000000007204.

Etim, E. F. (2001). *Scientific and technological information utilization and industrial Development in Nigeria*. Uyo, Nigeria: Heinemann.

European Union, Commission of the European Communities (2007). *Ageing well in the Information Society: An i2010 Initiative* (Communication No. COM (2007) 332 final). Brussels, Belgium. Retrieved on June 23, 2012, from http://eur-lex.europa.eu/LexUriServ/site/en/com/2007/com2007_0332en01.pdf

European Union, European Commission, Information Society and Media. (2008). *Senoirwatch 2: Assessment of the Senior Market for ICT Progress and Developments*. Bonn and Brussels, Belgium. Retrieved on June 23, 2012, from http://ec.europa.eu/information_society/activities/einclusion/docs/swa2finalreport.pdf

European Union, European Commission. (2007). *European i2010 initiative on e-Inclusion: "To be part of the information society"* (Communication No. COM (2007) 694 final). Retrieved on June 23, 2012, from http://ec.europa.eu/information_society/activities/einclusion/docs/i2010_initiative/comm_native_com_2007_0694_f_en_acte.pdf

Fairbanks, M., & Lindsay, S. (1997). *Plowing the sea: Nurturing the hidden sources of growth in the developing world*. Cambridge, MA: Harvard Business School.

Fang, C., & Ziaochun, Z. (2006). The open access movement in China. *Interlending and Document Summary, 34*(4), 186–193. doi:10.1108/02641610610714777.

Fast, K. V., & Campbell, G. (2004). I still like Google: University student perceptions of searching OPACs and the Web. In *Proceedings of the 67th ASIS&T Annual Meeting, 41*, 138-146.

Fatuyi, E. O. A., & Al-Suqri, M. N. (2009). Information security and privacy in digital libraries. In Theng, L., Foo, S., Goh, D., & Na, J. C. (Eds.), *Handbook of research on digital libraries: Design, development, and impact*. Singapore: IGI Global.

Fernandez, L. (2006). Open access initiatives in India – An evaluation. *Partnership: the Canadian Journal of Library and Information Practice and Research, 1*(1).

Finquelievich, S. (2000). *Citizens to the Web! Social ties in the cyberspace*. Buenos Aires, Argentina: CICCUS.

Finquelievich, S. (2004). ICTs in local and regional development: Beyond the metropolis. *INFOLAC, 17*(1), 3–5.

Fisher, K. E., Erdelez, S., & McKechnie, L. (2005). *Theories of information behavior*. Medford, NJ: Information Today.

Folster, M. B. (1989). A study of the use of information sources by social science researchers. *Journal of Academic Librarianship, 15,* 7–11.

Folster, M. B. (1995). Information seeking patterns: Social sciences. *Library Users and Reference Services, 32,* 83–93. doi:10.1300/J120v23n49_06.

Foo, S., & Ng, J. (2008). Library 2.0, Libraries and Library School. Paper presented at Proceedings Of Library Association of Singapore Conference 2008. Singapore.

Ford, G., & Ford, S. (2009). *Internet Use and Depression Among the Elderly.* Retrieved on June 23, 2012, from http://papers.ssrn.com/sol3/papers.cfm?abstract_id=1494430

Foster, G., & Remy, E. (2009). E-Books for academe: A study from Gettysburg College. *EDUCAUSE Center for Applied Research: Research Bulletin, 2009*(21), 1-12.

Foster, A. (2004). A nonlinear model of information-seeking behavior. *Journal of the American Society for Information Science and Technology, 55*(3), 228–237. doi:10.1002/asi.10359.

Francis, H. (2005). The information-seeking behavior of social science faculty at the University of the West Indies, St. Augustine Campus. *Journal of Academic Librarianship, 31*(1), 67–72. doi:10.1016/j.acalib.2004.11.003.

Frankel, J. (2010). *The natural resource curse: A survey.* National Bureau of Economic Research Working Paper #15836. Retrieved on July 30, 2011, from http://www.nber.org/papers/w15836

Fried, S., Kochanowicz, M., & Chiranov, M. (2010). Planning for impact, assessing for sustainability. *Perform, 11*(1), 56–74.

Fry, J., & Talja, S. (2004). The cultural shaping of scholarly communication: Explaining e-journal use within and across academic fields. *Proceedings of the American Society for Information Science and Technology, 41*(1), 20–30. doi:10.1002/meet.1450410103.

Gajendara, S., Sun, W., & Ye, Q. (2010). Second Life: A strong communication Tool in Social Networking and Business. *Information Technology Journal, 9*(3), 254–534.

Ghosh, S. B., & Anup, K. D. (2007). Open access and institutional repositories – A developing country perspective: A case study of India. *IFLA Journal, 37*(3), 229–250. doi:10.1177/0340035207083304.

Gilhooly, M. L. M., Gilhooly, K. J., & Jones, R. B. (2008). Quality of life: Conceptual challenges in exploring the role of ICT in active ageing. In Cabrera, M., & Malanowski, N. (Eds.), *Information and Communication Technology for Active Ageing: Opportunities and Challenges for the European Union* (pp. 49–76). Amsterdam, The Netherlands: IOS Press.

Grefsheim, S. F., & Rankin, J. A. (2007). Information needs and information seeking in a biomedical research setting: a study of scientists and science administrators. *Journal of the Medical Library Association, 95*(4), 426–434. doi:10.3163/1536-5050.95.4.426 PMID:17971890.

Grupo Radar. (2012). *El perfil del internauta uruguayo.* Montevideo, Uruguay: Radar. Retrieved on November 30, 2012, from http://www.gruporadar.com.uy/01/wp-content/uploads/2012/08/El-perfil-del-internauta-uruguayo-2012.pdf

Gul, S., Tariq, S., & Tariq, B. (2010). Culture of open access in the University of Kashmir: A Researcher's Viewpoint. *Aslib Proceedings: New Information Perspectives, 62*(2), 210–222.

Gurwitsch, A. (1974). *Phenomenology and the theory of science.* Evanston, IL: Northwestern University Press.

Ha, Y. (2008). *Accessing and using multilanguage information by users searching in different information retrieval systems.* Unpublished Doctoral Dissertation, Rutgers University, Newark, NJ.

Haddad, W. D., & Draxler, A. (2002). *Technologies for Education: Potentials, Parameters, and Prospects.* Paris: United Nations, Educational, Scientific and Cultural Organization.

Hakkarainen, P. (2012). *No Good for Shovelling Snow and Carrying Firewood: Social Representations of Computers and the Internet by Elderly Finnish Non-Users. New Media & Society.* Thousand Oaks, CA: Sage Publications.

Halder, S., Ray, A., & Chakrabarty, P. K. (2010). Gender differences in information seeking behavior in three universities in West Bengal, India. *The International Information & Library Review*, *42*(4), 242–251. doi:10.1016/j.iilr.2010.10.004.

Haley, E. (1996). Exploring the construct of organization as source: Consumers' understanding of organizational sponsorship of advocacy advertising. *Journal of Advertising*, *25*(2), 21–35.

Hall, E. T. (1976). *Beyond Culture*. Garden City, NY: Anchor Press/Doubleday.

Hall, E. T. (1984). *The dance of life: The other dimension of time*. Garden City, NY: Doubleday.

Hallmark, J. (1994). Scientists' access and retrieval of references cited in their recent journal articles. *College & Research Libraries*, *55*, 199–209.

Hart, C. T. (2008). *Exploring the information-seeking behavior of the staff and students of the Florida Virtual School: A case study*. Unpublished Doctoral dissertation, Florida State University, Tallahassee, FL.

Hartmann, J. (1995). Information needs of anthropologists. *Behavioral & Social Sciences Librarian*, *13*, 13–24. doi:10.1300/J103v13n02_02.

Hasan, H., & Pfaff, C. C. (2006). The Wiki: An environment to revolutionize employees' interaction with corporate knowledge. In *Proceedings of OZCHI*. Sydney, Australia.

Hassan, H., & Ditsa, G. (1999). The Impact of Culture on the Adoption of IT: An Interpretive Study. *Journal of Global Information Management*, *7*(1), 26–37.

Hausmann, R., & Rodrik, D. (2003). Economic development as self-discovery. *Journal of Development Economics 14th Inter-American Seminar on Economics*, *72*(2), 603-633.

Hawkins, R. J. (1998). Ten Lessons for ICT and Education in the Developing World. In *World Bank Development Indicators* (pp. 38–43). New York: World Bank.

Hemminger, B. M., Lu, D., Vaughan, K. T. L., & Adams, S. J. (2007). Information seeking behavior of academic scientists. *Journal of the American Society for Information Science and Technology*, *58*(14), 2205–2225. doi:10.1002/asi.20686.

Hernon, P. (1984). Information needs and gathering patterns of academic social scientists with special emphasis given to historians and their use of U.S. government publications. *Government Information Quarterly*, *1*, 401–429. doi:10.1016/0740-624X(84)90005-4.

Hersberger, J. (2003). A qualitative approach to examining information transfer via social networks among homeless populations. *The New Review of Information Behavior Research*, *4*, 95–108. doi:10.1080/14716310310001631462.

Hersberger, J. (2005). The homeless and information needs and services. *Reference and User Services Quarterly*, *44*(3), 199–202.

Heterick, B. (2002). Faculty attitudes towards electronic resources. *EDUCAUSE Review*, *37*(4), 10–11.

Hickman, L. A. (1990). *Technology as a human affair*. New York: McGraw-Hill.

Hobohm, H. (1999). Social science information & documentation: Time for a state of the art? *INSPEL*, *3*, 123–130.

Hofstede, G. (1991). *Cultures and organizations: Software of the mind. Intercultural cooperation and its importance for survival*. London: McGraw-Hill.

Hofstede, G. (2001). *Culture's consequences: International differences in work-related values* (2nd ed.). Beverly Hills, CA: SAGE.

Holliday, A. (1992). Tissue rejection and informal orders in ELT projects: Collecting the right information. *Applied Linguistics*, *13*(4), 403–424. doi:10.1093/applin/13.4.403.

Hughes, C. A., & Buchanan, N. L. (2001). Use of electronic monographs in the humanities and social sciences. *Library Hi Tech*, *19*(4), 368–375. doi:10.1108/EUM0000000006541.

Hyldegård, J. (2006). Collaborative information behavior – Exploring Kulthau's Information Search Process model in a group-based educational setting. *Information Processing & Management, 42*, 276–298. doi:10.1016/j.ipm.2004.06.013.

Hyman, K. (2000). Struggling in a one-stop shopping world, or people want what they want. In Laughlin, S. (Ed.), *Library Networks in the New Millenium: Top Ten trends*. Chicago, IL: Association of Specialized and Cooperative Libraries.

Ianculescu, M. (2011). The imperative role of ICT for supporting aging with dignity. In *Proceedings of the 15th WSEAS International Conference on Computers* (pp. 124–128). Stevens Point, Wisconsin: World of Scientific and Engineering Academy and Society. Retrieved on June 23, 2012, http://dl.acm.org/citation.cfm?id=2028325

Igbeka, J. U., & Ola, C. O. (2008). The need for digitization of special library materials in Nigerian university libraries. *World Libraries, 18*(1).

Igun, S. (2005). Implications for electronic publishing in libraries and information centers in Africa. *The Electronic Library, 23*(1), 82–91. doi:10.1108/02640470510582763.

Iivonen, M., & White, M. D. (2001). The choice of initial Web search strategies: A comparison between Finnish and American searchers. *The Journal of Documentation, 57*, 465–491. doi:10.1108/EUM0000000007091.

Illeperuma, S. (2002). Information gathering behavior of arts scholars in Sri Lankan universities: A critical evaluation. *Collection building, 21*, 22-31

Ingwersen, P. (1982). Search procedures in the library analyzed from the cognitive point of view. *The Journal of Documentation, 38*, 165–191. doi:10.1108/eb026727.

Jabr, N. H. (2010). Measuring Omani information professionals' competencies: From the professionals' perspectives. *The Electronic Library, 28*(2), 263–275. doi:10.1108/02640471011033620.

Jarvelin, K., & Ingwersen, P. (2004). Information-seeking research needs extension towards tasks and technology. *Information Research, 10*(1).

Jiao, Q. G., & Onwuegbuzie, A. J. (1997). Antecedents of library anxiety. *The Library Quarterly, 67*, 372–389. doi:10.1086/629972.

Jiyane, V., & Mostert, J. (2010, April). Use of information and communication technologies by women hawkers and vendors in South Africa. *African Journal of Library, Archives, &. Information Science, 20*(1), 53–61.

Johnson, C. A. (2007). Library and information science education in developing countries. *The International Information & Library Review, 39*(2), 64–71.

Johnson, C., & Yadamsuren, B. (2010). Libraries in transition: How librarians in Mongolia are re-visioning the role of libraries in the new democracy: A case study. *The International Information & Library Review, 42*(1), 1–7. doi:10.1016/j.iilr.2010.01.003.

Kanayama, T. (2003). Ethnographic Research on the Experience of Japanese Elderly People Online. *New Media & Society, 5*(2), 267–288. doi:10.1177/1461444803005002007.

Kankaanranta, M. (2005). International Perspectives on the Pedagogically Innovative Uses of Technology. *Human Technology, 1*(2), 111–116.

Kanyengo, C. W. (2006). *Managing digital information resources in Africa: Preserving the integrity of scholarship*. Paper presented at the Bridging the North-South Divide in Scholarly Communication on Africa: Threats and Opportunities in the Digital Era. Leiden, The Netherlands.

Kassim, N. A. (2010, August). Information needs of Malaysian Bumiputera would-be entrepreneurs. *Malaysian Journal of Library & Information Science, 15*(2), 57–69.

Katz, E., Levin, M. L., & Hamilton, H. (1963). Traditions of research on the diffusion of innovations. *American Sociological Review, 28*, 237–253. doi:10.2307/2090611.

Kaul, S. (2010). DELNET – the functional resource sharing library network: a success story from India. *Interlending & Document Supply, 38*(2), 93–101.

Kaur, H., & Sharda, P. (2010). Role of technological innovations in improving library services. *International Journal of Library and Information Science, 2*(1), 11–16.

Kavulya, J. M. (2007). Digital libraries and development in Sub-Saharan Africa: A review of challenges and strategies. *The Electronic Library, 25*(3), 299–315. doi:10.1108/02640470710754814.

Keesing, R. M., & Keesing, F. M. (1971). *New perspectives in cultural anthropology*. New York: Holt, Rinehart Winston.

Kelley, D. J., Singer, S., & Herrington, M. (2011). Global entrepreneurship monitor: 2011 global report, accessed at www.gemconsortium.org.

Kelly, G. A. (1963). *A theory of personality: The psychology of personal constructs*. New York: W.W. Norton.

Kennedy, T., Wellman, B., & Klement, K. (2003). Gendering the digital divide. *IT and Society, 1*(5), 72-96. Retrieved on December 17, 2012, from http://www.stanford.edu/group/siqss/itandsociety/v01i05/v01i05a05.pdf

Kerrigan, K., Lindsey, G., & Novak, K. (1994). Computer networking in International Agricultural Research Experience of the CGNET. New Information technologies in Agriculture. *Quarterly Bulletin of the International Association of Agricultural Information Specialists, XXXIX*(1&2), 182–193.

Khadraoui, D., Ruggia, R., Piedrabuena, F., & Meinkohn, F. (2005). *Local-communities insertion network platform: Design and specification*. Paper Presented at the 5th IBIMA International Conference on Internet & Information Technology in Modern Organizations (IBIMA). Cairo, Egypt.

Khan, S. A., & Bhatti, R. (2012). A review of problems and challenges of library professionals in developing countries including Pakistan. *Library Philosophy and Practice (e-journal)*. Paper 757. Retrieved on July 18, 2012 from http://digitalcommons.unl.edu/libphilprac/757

Kigongo-Bukenya, I., & Musoke, M. (2011). *LIS Education and training in developing countries: developments and challenges with special reference to Southern Sudan and Uganda*. Paper delivered at the Satellite Pre-Conference of SIG LIS Education in Developing Countries, IFLA Puerto Rico, 11th -12th August 2011. Retrieved on February 11, 2012 from http://edlib.b.uib.no/files/2011/08/IFLA_2011_pre_conf_paper_with_KB.pdf

Kim, Y.-W. (2004). *Typology of user of user uncertainty in Web-based information seeking: Insight into the information seeking context of scholarly researchers in the field of science*. Unpublished Doctoral Dissertation, Rutgers University, Newark, NJ.

Kim, K.-S. (2002). Information seeking on the Web: Effects of user and task variables. *Library & Information Science Research, 23*, 233–255. doi:10.1016/S0740-8188(01)00081-0.

Kingma, B. R. (2001). *The Economics of Information*. Westport, CT: Libraries Unlimited.

Kinnell, M., Feather, J., & Matthews, G. (1994). Business information provision for small and medium-sized enterprises in China: The application of marketing models. *Library Management, 15*(8), 16–24. doi:10.1108/01435129410071363.

Kipling'at, J., Kwake, A., & Kariuki, S. M. (2005). Information and communication technologies (ICT) adoption by small and medium scale enterprise (SME) tourism stakeholders in the Durban Region, South Africa. *African Journal of Library, Archives &. Information Science, 15*(2), 133–140.

Kirsop, B., Chan, L., & Arunachalam, S. (2007). Access to Scientific Knowledge for Sustainable Development: Options for Developing Countries. *Ariadne, 52*. Retrieved on June 14, 2009, from http://www.ariadne.ac.uk/issue52/

Kirsop, B., & Chan, L. (2005). Transforming Access to Research Literature for Developing Countries. *Serials Review, 31*, 246–255. doi:10.1016/j.serrev.2005.09.003.

Kishida, K., & Matsui, S. (1997). International publication patterns in social sciences: A quantitative analysis of the IBSS file. *Scientometrics, 40*, 277–298. doi:10.1007/BF02457440.

Klimaszewski, C., Bader, G. E., & Nyce, J. M. (2011). "Success stories" as an evidence form: Organizational legitimization in an international technology assistance project. *Martor, 16*.

Klimaszewski, C., Bader, G. E., & Nyce, J. M. (2012). Hierarchy, complicity and culture in the library and information science preservation agenda: Observations from Romania. *Journal of Librarianship and Information Science*.

Klimaszewski, C., Bader, G. E., & Nyce, J. M. (2012). Studying up (and down) the cultural heritage preservation agenda: Observations from Romania. *European Journal of Cultural Studies, 15*(4), 479–495. doi:10.1177/1367549412455495.

Klimaszewski, C., Bader, G. E., Nyce, J. M., & Beasley, B. E. (2010). Who wins? Who loses? *Library Review, 59*(2), 92. doi:10.1108/00242531011023853.

Klimaszewski, C., & Nyce, J. M. (2009). Does universal access mean equitable access? What an information infrastructure study of a rural Romanian community can tell us. *New Library World, 110*(5/6), 219–236. doi:10.1108/03074800910954253.

Koltay, T. (2007). A new direction for library and information science: the communication aspect of information literacy. *Information Research, 12*(4) paper colise06. Retrieved on July 16, 2012 from http://InformationR.net/ir/12-4/colise06.html

Komlodi, A. (2005). Cultural models of Hofstede and Hall. In Fisher, K. E., Erdelez, S., & McKechnie, L. (Eds.), *Theories of information behavior* (pp. 108–112). Medford, NJ: Information Today.

Kroeber, A. L., & Kluckhohn, C. K. M. (1952). Culture: A critical review of concepts and definitions. Papers of the Peabody Museum of American Archaeology and Ethnology, vol. XLVII, no. 1. Cambridge: The Museum.

Kuhlthau, C. C. (1983). *The Library Research Process: Case Studies and Interventions with high School Seniors in Advanced Placement English Classes Using Kelly's Theory of Constructs.* Doctoral dissertation, Rutgers University, Newark, NJ.

Kuhlthau, C. C. (1988). Developing a model of the library search process: Cognitive and affective aspects. *RQ, 28,* 232-242.

Kuhlthau, C., Spink, A., & Cool, C. (1992). Exploration into stages in the information search process in online information retrieval. In *Proceedings of the ASIS Annual Meeting* (pp. 67-71).

Kuhlthau, C. C. (1988). Longitudinal case studies of the information search process of users in libraries. *Library & Information Science Research, 10*(3), 257–304.

Kuhlthau, C. C. (1988). Perceptions of the information search process in libraries: A study of changes from high school through college. *Information Processing & Management, 24*(4), 419–428. doi:10.1016/0306-4573(88)90045-3.

Kuhlthau, C. C. (1991). Inside the search process: Information seeking from the user's perspective. *Journal of the American Society for Information Science American Society for Information Science, 42*(5), 361–371. doi:10.1002/(SICI)1097-4571(199106)42:5<361::AID-ASI6>3.0.CO;2-#.

Kuhlthau, C. C. (1993). *Seeking meaning: A process approach to library and information services.* Norwood, NJ: Ablex publishing corporation.

Kuhlthau, C. C. (1993). A principle of uncertainty for information seeking. *The Journal of Documentation, 49*(4), 339–355. doi:10.1108/eb026918.

Kuhlthau, C. C. (1994). *Seeking meaning: A process approach to library and information services.* Norwood, NJ: Ablex Publishing.

Kuhlthau, C. C. (1999). The role of experience in the Information search Process of an early career information worker: Perceptions of uncertainty, complexity, construction, and sources. *Journal of the American Society for Information Science American Society for Information Science, 50*(5), 399–412. doi:10.1002/(SICI)1097-4571(1999)50:5<399::AID-ASI3>3.0.CO;2-L.

Kuhlthau, C. C. (1999). Accommodating the user's information search process: Challenges for information retrieval system designers. *Bulletin of the American Society for Information Science,* (February/March): 12–16.

Kuhlthau, C. C. (2004). *Seeking meaning: A process approach to library and information services.* Westport, CT: Libraries Unlimited.

Kuhlthau, C. C. (2005). Kuhlthau's Information Search Process. In Fisher, K. E., Erdelez, S., & McKechnie, L. (Eds.), *Theories of Information Behavior.* Medford, NJ: Information Today Inc..

Kumar, A., & Singh, S. A. (2011). An Investigation of Use of Information Sources by Social Scientists. *Library Philosophy and Practice,* 1-10.

Lajoie-Paquette, D. (2005). Diffusion theory. In Fisher, K. E., Erdelez, S., & McKechnie, L. (Eds.), *Theories of information behavior* (pp. 118–122). Medford, NJ: Information Today.

Large, A., & Moukdad, H. (2001). Multilingual access to web resources: An overview. *Program, 34*, 43–58. doi:10.1108/EUM0000000006938.

Lathey, J. W., & Hodge, B. (2001). Information seeking behavior of occupational health nurses: How nurses keep current with health information. *AAOHN Journal, 49*(2), 87–95. PMID:11760270.

Lavrenko, V., Choquette, M., & Croft, W. B. (2002). Cross-lingual relevance models. In M. Beaulieu, R. Baeza-Yates, S.H. Myaeng, & K. Järvelin (Eds), *Proceedings of the 25th Annual International ACM-SIGIR Conference on Research and Development in Information Retrieval* (pp. 175–182). New York: ACM.

Le Dantec, C. A., Farrell, R. G., Christensen, J. E., Bailey, M., Ellis, J. B., Kellogg, W. A., & Edwards, W. K. (2011). Publics in practice: Ubiquitous computing at a shelter for homeless mothers. In *Proceedings of the 2011 Annual Conference on Human factors in Computing Systems* (pp. 1687–1696). New York: ACM.

Leckie, G. J., & Pettigrew, K. E. (1997). A general model of the information seeking of professionals. Role theory through the back door? In P. Vakkari, R. Savolainen, & B. Dervin (Eds.), *Information seeking in context: Proceedings of an International Conference on Research in Information Needs, Seeking and Use in Different Contexts* (pp. 99-110). London: Taylor Graham.

Lederman, A., Warnick, W., Hitson, B., & Johnson, L. (2010). Breaking down language barriers through multilingual federated search. *Information Services & Use, 30*(3/4), 125–132.

Lenares, D. (1999). *Faculty use of electronic journals at research institutions*. Paper presented at the ACRL Ninth National Conference. New Orleans, LA. Retrieved March 13, 2006, from http://www.ala.org/ala/acrl/acrlevents/lenares99.pdf#search='lenares%20 and 20 999%20 and%20electronic%20journals'

Leuski, A., Lin, C., Zhou, L., Germann, U., Och, F., & Hovy, E. (2003). Cross-lingual C*ST*RD: English access to Hindi information. *ACM Transactions on Asian Language Information Processing, 2*(3), 245–269. doi:10.1145/979872.979877.

Lillard, L. L. (2002). Information seeking in context: An exploratory study of information use online by eBay entrepreneurs. *Dissertation Abstracts International. A, The Humanities and Social Sciences, 63*(02), 1340.

Lin, C. P. (2004). *The challenges and opportunities of regional co-operation in LIS education in East Asia*. World Library and Information Congress: 70th IFLA General Conference and Council 22-27 August 2004, Buenos Aires, Argentina. Retrieved on February 9, 2012 from http://archive.ifla.org/IV/ifla70/papers/065e-Lin.pdf

Lin, C. I. C., Tang, W. H., & Kuo, F. Y. (2012). Mommy wants to learn the computer: How Middle-aged and elderly women in Taiwan learn ICT through social support. *Adult Education Quarterly, 62*(1), 73–90. doi:10.1177/0741713610392760.

Lincoln, Y., & Guba, E. (1985). *Naturalistic inquiry*. New York: Sage.

Lindlof, T. R., & Taylor, B. C. (2002). *Qualitative communication research methods* (2nd ed.). Thousand Oaks, CA: Sage.

Line, M. B. (1999). Social science information – The poor relation. *INSPEL, 33*, 131–136.

Lingelbach, D. C., de La Viña, L., & Asel, P. (2005). *What's Distinctive about Growth-Oriented Entrepreneurship in Developing Countries?* UTSA College of Business Center for Global Entrepreneurship Working Paper No. 1. Retrieved from http://ssrn.com/abstract=742605

Littrell, M. A., Nyce, J. M., Straub, J., & Whipple, M. (2006). A study of the information infrastructure of a Transylvanian village. *New Library World, 107*(7/8), 321–331. doi:10.1108/03074800610677290.

Lleperuma, S. (2002). Information gathering behavior of arts scholars in Sri Lankan Universities: A critical evaluation. *Collection Building, 21*, 22–31. doi:10.1108/01604950210414698.

López, G., Álvarez, F., & González, L. (2010). *Integrating advanced web technologies in a social security portal*. Paper Presented at the 6th International Policy and Research Conference on Social Security. Luxembourg.

Ludueña, M. C., Olson, J. K., & Pasco, A. (2005). Promoción de la salud y calidad de vida entre madres de preadolescentes. *Una etnografía enfocada. Revista Latino-Americana de Enfermagem, 13*(2), 1127–1134. doi:10.1590/S0104-11692005000800005 PMID:16501782.

Lynch, C. A. (2003). Institutional repositories: Essential infrastructure for scholarship in the digital age. *Association of Research Libraries, 226*, 1–7.

Machlup, F. (1972). *The production and distribution of knowledge in the United States*. Princeton, NJ: Princeton University.

Mackay, D. M. (1960). What makes a question? *Listener (London, England), 63*, 789–790.

Mahajan, P. (2009). Information-Seeking Behavior: A Study of Panjab University, India. *Library Philosophy and Practice*. Retrieved on December 27, 2012, from http://unllib.unl.edu/LPP/mahajan4.htm.%20

Majid, S., Anwar, M. A., & Eisenschitz, T. S. (2000). Information needs and information seeking behavior of agricultural scientists in Malaysia. *Library & Information Science Research, 22*, 145–163. doi:10.1016/S0740-8188(99)00051-1.

Majid, S., & Kassim, G. M. (2000). Information-seeking behaviour of International Islamic University, Malaysia law faculty members. *Malaysian Journal of Library & Information Science, 5*(2), 1–17.

Malinconico, S. M. (2011). Librarians and user privacy in the digital age. *Scientific Research and Information Technology, 1*(1), 159–172.

Malliari, A., Korobili, S., & Zapounidou, S. (2011). Exploring the information seeking behavior of Greek graduate students: A case study set in the University of Macedonia. *The International Information & Library Review, 43*(2), 79–91. doi:10.1016/j.iilr.2011.04.006.

Mambula, C. (2002). Perceptions of SME growth constraints in Nigeria. *Journal of Small Business Management, 40*(1), 58–65. doi:10.1111/1540-627X.00039.

Manaf, Z. (2006). The state of digitization initiatives by cultural institutional in Malaysia. *Library Review, 56*(1), 45–60. doi:10.1108/00242530710722014.

Maness, J. (2006). Library 2.0 Theory: Web 2.0 and Its Implications for Libraries. *Webology, 3*(2).

Mark Ware Consulting Ltd. (2004). Pathfinder research on web-based repositories. Bristol, UK: Publisher and Library/Learning Solutions (PALS).

Marouf, L., & Anwar, M. A. (2010). Information-seeking behavior of the social sciences faculty at Kuwait University. *Library Review, 59*(7), 532–547.

Marteleto, R. M. (2010). Redes sociais, mediação e apropiriação de informações: Situando campos, objetos e conceitos na pesquisa. *Ciencia da Informação. Pesq. Bras. Ci. Inf., 3*(1), 27–46.

Martín-Barbero, J. (2002). *Jóvenes, comunicación e identidad, en Pensar Iberoamérica. Revista de Cultura, N° 0. Organización de Estados Iberoamericanos*. Retrieved on November 30, 2012, from http://www.oei.es/pensariberoamerica/ric00a03.htm

Martín-Barbero, J. (1991). *De los medios a las mediaciones*. Barcelona, Spain: Gili.

May, C. (2006). Escaping the TRIPs' Trap: The Political Economy of Free and Open Source Software in Africa. *Political Studies, 54*, 123–146. doi:10.1111/j.1467-9248.2006.00569.x.

McCain, K. W. (1989). Mapping authors in intellectual space: population genetics in the 1980s. (Special Issue: Bibliometric Methods for the Study of Scholarly Communication). *Communication Research, 16*(5), 615–667. doi:10.1177/009365089016005007.

McClean, A. (2011). Ethical frontiers of ICT and older users: Cultural, pragmatic and ethical issues. *Ethics and Information Technology, 13*, 313–326. doi:10.1007/s10676-011-9276-4.

McCraken, G. (1988). *The Long interview*. Newbury Park, CA: Sage.

Mchombu, K. J. (1991). Which way African Librarianship? *IFLA Journal, 17*(1), 43–50. doi:10.1177/034003529101700108.

McMurtrey, M., McGaughey, R. E., Downey, J. P., & Zeltmann, S. M. (2010). Seniors and information technology: Much ado about something? In *2010 Conference Proceedings*. Presented at the Southwest Decision Institute Conference, Dallas, TX. Retrieved June 21, 2012, from http://www.swdsi.org/swdsi2010/SW2010_Preceedings/papers/PA130.pdf

Meho, L. I., & Haas, S. W. (2001). Information-seeking behavior and use of social science faculty studying stateless nations: A case study. *Library & Information Science Research, 23*, 5–25. doi:10.1016/S0740-8188(00)00065-7.

Meho, L. I., & Tibbo, H. R. (2002). Modeling the information-seeking behavior of social scientists: Ellis's study revisited. *Journal of the American Society for Information Science and Technology, 54*(6), 570–587. doi:10.1002/asi.10244.

Meho, L. I., & Tibbo, H. R. (2003). Modeling the Information-Seeking Behavior of Social Scientists: Ellis's Study Revisited. *Journal of the American Society for Information Science and Technology, 54*, 570–587. doi:10.1002/asi.10244.

Meneghini R., Packer A.L., & Nassi-Calò L. (2008). Articles by Latin American Authors in Prestigious Journals Have Fewer Citations. *PLoS ONE, 3*(11), e3804. Retrieved on May 23, 2010, from doi:10.1371/journal.pone.0003804

Menou, M. (1993). *Measuring the impact of information on development*. Ottawa, Canada: IDRC.

Metcalfe, J., & Gilmore, J. (1990). Information Technology in Agricultural development. In Speedy, A. (Ed.), *Development World Agriculture*. London: Grosvenor Press International.

Mezey, M. (2011, March). The challenges of creating ambidextrous organizations. *Update*.

Mikkola, K., & Halonen, R. (2011). *"Nonsense?" ICT perceived by the elderly* (pp. 306–317). A paper Presented at the European, Mediterranean & Middle Eastern Conference on Information Systems. Athens, Greece. Retrieved June 21, 2012, from http://www.iseing.org/emcis/EMCISWebsite/EMCIS2011%20Proceedings/SCI1.pdf

Miller, R. L. (2008). *The intercultural transfer of professional knowledge in international partnerships: A case study of the American Bulgarian Library Exchange*. Unpublished Doctoral Dissertation, Emporia State University, Emporia, KS.

Ministry of Education, Culture, and Science. (2007). *Science and technology master plan of Mongolia, 2007-2020*. United Nations Education, Scientific, and Cultural Organizations. Ulaanbaatar, Mongolia.

Mizoue, C., Matsumoto, M., Nakayama, S., Ishii, H., & Joho, H. (2010). Ideas for the International Collaboration in the LIS Education and Research at Tsukuba. In *Proceedings of the Workshop on Global Collaboration of Information Schools (WIS 2010)*, JCDL/ICADL 2010, Queensland, Australia.

Mooko, N. P., & Aina, L. O. (1998). The use of government publications: The case of social scientists at the University of Botswana. *Journal of Government Information, 25*(4), 359–365. doi:10.1016/S1352-0237(98)00015-X.

Mordini, E., Wright, D., Wadhwa, K., De Hert, P., Mantoyani, E., Thestrup, J., & Vater, I. (2009). Senior citizens and the ethics of e-inclusion. *Ethics and Information Technology, 11*, 203–220. doi:10.1007/s10676-009-9189-7.

Morris, A., Goodman, J., & Brading, H. (2007). Internet use and non-use: Views of older users. *Universal Access in the Information Society, 6*, 43–57. doi:10.1007/s10209-006-0057-5.

Motiwalla, L. F. (2007). Mobile learning: A framework and evaluation. *Computers & Education, 49*(3), 581–596. doi:10.1016/j.compedu.2005.10.011.

Mphidi, H. (2004). *Digital divide or digital exclusion? The role of Librarians in bridging the digital divide*. Paper presented at LISA 7th Annual conference. Pholokwane, South Africa. Retrieved on April 27, 2012, from http://www.liasa.org.za/conference/conferences2004/papers/LIASA-conference

Murray, P. J., Cabrer, M., Hansen, M., Paton, C., Elkin, P. L., & Erdley, W. S. (2008). Towards addressing the opportunities and challenges of Web 2.0 for health and informatics. *Yearbook of Medical Informatics*, 44–51. PMID:18660875.

Nahl, D. (2004). Measuring the affective information environment of web searchers. *Proceedings of the 67th ASIS&T Annual meeting*, (41), 191-197.

Nahl, D., & Tenopir, C. (1996). Affective and cognitive searching behavior of novice end-users of a full-text database. *Journal of the American Society for Information Science American Society for Information Science*, *47*, 276–286. doi:10.1002/(SICI)1097-4571(199604)47:4<276::AID-ASI3>3.0.CO;2-U.

Nawe, J. (1993). The realities of adaptation of western librarianship to African situation. *Journal of Libraries. Archives and Information Science*, *2*(9), 1–9.

Nayak, L. U. S., Priest, L., & White, A. P. (2010). An application of the technology acceptance model to the level of Internet usage by older adults. *Universal Access in the Information Society*, *9*, 367–374. doi:10.1007/s10209-009-0178-8.

Neelameghan, A. (1977). Information needs and information sources of small enterprises: A synoptic view. *Library Science with a Slant to Documentation*, *14*(3-4), 136–139.

Nelson, M. R. (2008). E-books in higher education: Nearing the end of the era of hype? *EDUCAUSE Review*, (March/April): 40–56.

Nesset, V. (2009). *The information-seeking behavior of grade-three Elementary School students in the context of a class project*. Unpublished Doctoral dissertation.

Nicholas, D., Huntington, P., Jamali, H. R., Rowlands, I., & Fieldhouse, M. (2009). Student digital information-seeking behaviour in context. *Journal of Documentation*, *65*(1). Retrieved on December 28, 2012, from http://www.emeraldinsight.com/journals.htm?articleid=1766885&show=abstract

Nicholas, D., Rowlands, I., & Jamali, H. R. (2010). E-textbook use, information seeking behaviour and its impact: Case study business and management. *Journal of Information Science*, *36*(2), 263–280. doi:10.1177/0165551510363660.

Niedźwiedzka, B. (2003). A proposed general model of information behavior. *Information Research, 9*(1). Retrieved on June 20, 2006, from http://InformationR.net/ir/9-1/paper164.html

Nita, V. (2011). An Extended Approach to E-Inclusion and its Implications for Romania. *SSRN eLibrary*. Retrieved June 21, 2012, from http://papers.ssrn.com/sol3/papers.cfm?abstract_id=1794346

Njoroge, G. G., Kiplang'at, J., & Odero, D. (2011). Diffusion and utilization of information and communication technologies by micro and small entrepreneurs in the tourism industry in Kenya. *Mousaion*, *29*(2), 117–138.

Oard, D. W. (1997). Serving users in many languages: Cross-language information retrieval for digital libraries. *D-Lib Magazine*. Retrieved on April 12, 2011, from http://www.dlib.org/dlib/december97/oard/12oard.html

Oard, D., & Resnik, P. (1999). Support for interactive document selection in cross language information retrieval. *Information Processing & Management*, *35*, 363–379. doi:10.1016/S0306-4573(98)00066-1.

Occholla, D. (2009). Are African Libraries active participants in today's Knowledge and Information Society? *South African Journal of Library and Information Science*, *75*(1), 20–27.

Ocholla, D. (2010). *Is African Information ethic unique?* Retrieved on April 30, 2011, from http://www.lis.uzulu.ac.za/2011/Ocholla%20Prolissa%202011%20information%20ethics%20Feb%2018.pdf

Ocholla, D. (2007). The current status and challenges of collaboration in library and information studies (LIS) education and training in Africa. *New Library World*, *109*(9/10), 466–479. doi:10.1108/03074800810910496.

Ogden, D., & Davis, M. (2000). Improving Cross-Language Text Retrieval with Human Interactions. *Hawaii International Conference on System Sciences*. Maui, HI: IEEE.

Ogden, D., Cowie, J., Davis, M., Ludovik, E., Molina-Salado, H., & Shin, H. (1999). G*etting information from documents you cannot read: An interactive cross-language text retrieval and Summarization System.* Joint ACM Digital Library/SIGIR Workshop on Multilingual Information Discovery and Access (MIDAS).

Ogden, D., Cowie, J., Davis, M., Ludovik, E., Nirenburg, S., Molina-Salgado, H., & Sharples, N. (1999). *Keizai: An interactive cross-language text retrieval system.* Paper presented at the Workshop on Machine Translation for Cross-language Information Retrieval, Machine Translation Summit VII. Sinagpore.

Ogunlade, O. A. (2007). Information needs and utilization of managers in Nigerian financial institutions. *Journal of Business Management, 10*(2), 80–92.

Ojala, M. (2005). Blogging for knowledge sharing, management and dissemination. *Business Information Review, 22*(4), 269–276. doi:10.1177/0266382105060607.

Okella-Obura, C., & Mantovu, J. (2011). *SMEs and business information provision strategies: An analytica perspective.* Library Philosophy and Practice.

Okella-Obura, C., Minishi-Majanja, M. K., Cloete, L., & Ikoja-Odongo, J. R. (2007). Business activities and information needs of SMEs in northern Uganda. *Library Management, 29*(4/5), 367–391. doi:10.1108/01435120810869138.

ONCTI. (2009). *Sobre el Programa de promoción al investigador.* Retrieved on May 16, 2009, from http://oncti.gob.ve/

Ong, W. (1996). *Oralidad y escritura. Tecnologías de la palabra.* México: FCE.

Onwuegbuzie, A. J., & Jiao, Q. G. (1998). The relationship between library anxiety and learning styles among graduate students: Implications for library instruction. *Library & Information Science Research, 20*(3), 235–249. doi:10.1016/S0740-8188(98)90042-1.

Papin-Ramcharan, J., & Dawe, R. A. (2012). Can benevolence and technology bridge the divide between developed and developing countries' libraries? *World Libraries, 20*(1).

Parry, K. (2011). Libraries in Uganda: Not just linguistic imperialism. *Libri: International Journal of Libraries & Information Services, 61*(4), 328–337.

Patitungkho, K., & Deshpande, N. J. (2005). Information-seeking behavior of faculty members of Rajabhat Universities in Bangkok. *Webology, 2*(4). Retrieved on May 10, 2006, from http://www.webology.ir/2005/v2n4/a20.html

Peet, R., & Hartwick, E. (1999). *Theories of development.* New York: The Guilford Press.

Peplinski, C. (2007). *Oral Traditions and Weapons of Resistance: The Modern Africa Filmmaker as Griot.* Retrieved on April 4, 2011, from http://ccms.ukzn.ac.za/index.php?option=com_content&task=view&id=382&Itemid=48

Pérez Giffoni, M. C., & Sabelli, M. (2010). *Los estudios de usuarios de información: Construcción de una línea de investigación y docencia en el Uruguay.* Montevideo, Uruguay: UdelaR. EUBCA.

Petrelli, D., Beaulieu, M., Sanderson, M., Demetriou, G., Herring, P., & Hansen, P. (2004). Observing users, designing clarity: A case study on the user-centered design of a cross-language information retrieval system. *Journal of the American Society for Information Science and Technology, 55*, 923–934. doi:10.1002/asi.20036.

Pettigrew, K., Fidel, R., & Bruce, H. (2001). Conceptual frameworks in information behavior. *Annual Review of Information Science & Technology, 35*, 43–78.

Popoola, S. O. (2009, April). Self efficacy, information acquisition and utilization as correlates of effective decision making among managers in insurance companies in Nigeria. *Malaysian Journal of Library & Information Science, 14*(1), 1–15.

Porath, S. (2011). Text Messaging and Teenagers: A Review of the Literature. *Journal of the Research Center for Educational Technology, 7*(2), 86–99.

Postman, N. (1997). Science and the story that we need. Retrieved on April 4, 2011, from http://www.firstthings.com/ftissues/ft9701/articles/postman.html

Postman, N. (1998). Five things we need to know about technological change. Retrieved on April 14, 2011, from http://itrs.scu.edu/tshanks/pages/Comm12/12Postman

Powell, R. (1999). Recent trends in research: A methodological essay. *Library & Information Science Research*, *21*(1), 91–119. doi:10.1016/S0740-8188(99)80007-3.

Preschel, B. M., & Woods, L. J. (1989). Social science information. *Annual Review of Information Science & Technology*, *24*, 267–292.

Price, D. J. D. S. (1963). *Little science, big science*. New York: Columbia University Press.

Price, D. J. D. S. (1965). Networks of scientific papers. *Science*, *149*, 510–515. doi:10.1126/science.149.3683.510 PMID:14325149.

Pullinger, D., & Baldwin, C. (2002). *Electronic journals and user behaviour: Learning for the future from the SuperJournal Project*. Cambridge, UK: Deedot Press.

Punch, K. (2004). *Introduction to social research: Quantitative & qualitative approaches*. London: Sage Publications.

Quigley, J., Peck, D.R., Rutter, S., & McKee Williams, E. (2002). Making choices: Factors in the selection of information resources among science faculty at the University of Michigan. Results of a survey conducted July-September, 2000. *Issues in Science and Technology Librarianship, 34*.

Ranganathan, S. R. (1957). *The five laws of library science*. London: Blunt and Sons, Ltd..

Rao, N. (2012). *Mobile Africa Report 2012*. Retrieved on December, 3, 2012, from http://www.mobilemonday.net/reports/MobileAfrica_2012.pdf

Rehman, S. (2008). Quality assurance and LIS education in the Gulf Cooperation Council (GCC) countries. *New Library World*, *109*(7/8), 366–382. doi:10.1108/03074800810888186.

Rehman, S., & Marouf, L. (2007). MLIS program at Kuwait University: Perceptions and reflections. *Library Review*, *57*(1), 13–24. doi:10.1108/00242530810845026.

Renwick, S. (2005). Knowledge and use of electronic information resources by medical sciences faculty at the University of the West Indies. *Journal of the Medical Library Association*, *93*(1), 21–31. PMID:15685270.

Rieh, S. Y., & Xie, H. (2001). Patterns and sequences of multiple query reformulations in Web searching: A preliminary study. In E. Aversa, & C. Manley (Eds.), In *Proceedings of the 64th Annual Meeting of the American Society for Information Science and Technology, 38* (pp. 246–255). Medford, NJ: Information Today.

Rieh, H. Y., & Rieh, S. Y. (2005). Web searching across languages: Preference and behavior of bilingual academic users in Korea. *Library & Information Science Research*, *27*(2), 249–263. doi:10.1016/j.lisr.2005.01.006.

Rieh, S. Y. (2004). On the Web at home: Information seeking and Web searching in the home environment. *Journal of the American Society for Information Science and Technology*, *55*, 743–753. doi:10.1002/asi.20018.

Rienzi, B., Sosa, R., Foti, P., & González, L. (2010). *Benefits and challenges of using geographic information systems to enhance social security services*. Paper Presented at the 6th International Policy and Research Conference on Social Security. Luxembourg.

Robinson, S., & Stubberud, H. A. (2011). Social networks and entrepreneurial growth. *International Journal of Management & Information Systems*, *15*(4), 65–70.

Rogers, E. M. (1962). *Diffusion of innovations*. Glencoe, IL: Free Press.

Rogers, E. M. (1995). *Diffusion of innovations*. New York: Free Press.

Rogers, E. M. (2003). *Diffusion of innovations* (5th ed.). New York: Free Press.

Rogers, E. M., & Shoemaker, F. F. (1971). *Communication of innovations*. New York: Free Press.

Romanos de Tiratel, S. (2000). Accessing information use by humanists and social scientists: A study at the Universidad de Buenos Aires, Argentina. *Journal of Academic Librarianship*, *26*(5), 346–354. doi:10.1016/S0099-1333(00)00141-5.

Rosenberg, D. (1993). Imposing libraries: The establishment of national public library services in Africa, with particular reference to Kenya. *World Libraries, 4*(1).

Rosenberg, D. (2005). Towards the digital library: Findings of an investigation to establish the current status of university libraries in Africa. *International Network for the Availability of Scientific Publications (INASP), Oxford*. Retrieved on November 28, 2012, from http://www.inasp.info/uploaded/documents/digital-libr-final-format-web.pdf

Rowlands, I., & Dave, N. (2006). The changing scholarly communication landscape: An international survey of senior researchers. *Learned Publishing, 19*, 31–55. doi:10.1087/095315106775122493.

Roy, M., Taylor, R., & Chi, M. T. H. (2003). Searching for information on-line and off-line: Gender differences among middle school students. *Journal of Educational Computing Research, 29*, 229–252. doi:10.2190/KCGA-3197-2V6U-WUTH.

Sabelli, M., & Rodríguez Lopater, V. (Eds.) (in press). La información y las jóvenes en contextos desfavorables: Construyendo puentes para la inclusión social desde la investigación. Montevideo, Uruguay: CSIC. UdelaR; EUBCA.

Samba Financial Group. (2011). *The GCC: prospering in uncertain times. Samba Report Series*. Riyadh: Samba Financial Group.

Saracevic, T. (1996). Relevance reconsidered. In P. Ingwersen, & N. Ple Pors (Eds.), *2nd International Conference on Conceptions of Library and Information Science* (pp. 201-218). Copenhagen, Denmark: Royal School of Librarianship.

Sarkodie, M. K. (2000). The international student on campus: History, trends, visa classification, and adjustment issues. In Jacobson, T. E., & Williams, H. C. (Eds.), *Teaching the New Library To Today's Users: Reaching International, Minority, Senior Citizens, Gay/Lesbian, First Generation, At-Risk, Graduate and Returning Students, and Distance Learners*. New York: Neal-Shuman.

Savolainen, R. (2005). Enthusiastic, realistic and critical: discourses of Internet use in the context of everyday life information seeking. *Information Research, 10*(1), paper 198. Retrieved on November 30, 2012, from http://InformationR.net/ir/10-1/paper198.htm

Savolainen, R. (1999). The role of the Internet in information seeking in context. *Information Processing & Management, 35*(6), 765–782. doi:10.1016/S0306-4573(99)00025-4.

Savolainen, R. (2002). Network competence and information seeking on the Internet: From definitions towards a social cognitive model. *The Journal of Documentation, 58*, 211–226. doi:10.1108/00220410210425467.

Savolainen, R. (2005). Everyday life information seeking. In Fisher, K. E., Erdelez, S., & McKechnie, L. (Eds.), *Theories of information Behavior* (pp. 143–148). Medford, NJ: Information Today.

Sawahel, W. (2010, December 12). Arab States: e-books still at an early stage. *University World News* Retrieved on July 16, 2012 from http://www.universityworldnews.com/article.php?story=20101210215454146

Sawahel, W. (2011, April 3). Gulf States: virtual universities on the rise. *University World News* Retrieved on July 16, 2012 from http://www.universityworldnews.com/article.php?story=20110401190727550http://www.universityworld

Schafer, S. (1990). Level of entrepreneurship and scanning course usage in very small businesses. *Entrepreneurship Theory and Practice, 15*(2), 19–31.

Schamber, L. (1991). Users' criteria for evaluation in a multimedia environment. In J.-M. Griffiths (Eds.), In *Proceedings of the 54th Annual Meeting of the American Society for information Sciences* (pp. 126-133). Medford, NJ: Learned Information.

Schamber, L., Eisenberg, M., & Nilan, M. (1990). A reexamination of relevance: Toward a dynamic, situational definition. *Information Processing & Management*, (26): 755–776. doi:10.1016/0306-4573(90)90050-C.

Schiltz, M., Truyen, F., & Coppens, H. (2007). Cutting the trees of knowledge: Social software, information architecture and their epistemic consequences. *Thesis Eleven, 89,* 94-114.

Schwartz, D. G. (1995). How physicians and biomedical scientists in India learn information-seeking skills. *Bulletin of the Medical Library Association, 83,* 360–362. PMID:7581195.

Seiden, P., Szymborski, Z., & Norelli, B. (2012). Undergraduate Students in the Digital Library: Information Seeking Behavior in an Heterogeneous Environment. *Association of College & Research Libraries.* Retrieved on December 18, 2012, from http://www.ala.org/acrl/publications/whitepapers/nashville/seidenszymborski

Selwyn, N. (2008). An investigation of differences in undergraduates' academic use of the Internet. *Active Learning in Higher Education, 9*(1), 11-22. Retrieved on December 27, 2012, from http://alh.sagepub.com/content/9/1/11.short

Sen, G. (1998). The empowerment as an approach to poverty. In Arriagada, I., & Torres, C. (Eds.), *Gender and Poverty: New Dimensions.* Santiago, Chile: ISIS Internacional, Ediciones de las Mujeres.

Serageldin, I. (2008). Joining the Fast Lane. *Nature, 456,* 18–20. doi:10.1038/twas08.18a PMID:18987709.

Serola, S., & Vakkari, P. (2005). The anticipated and assessed contribution of information types in references retrieved for preparing a research proposal. *Journal of the American Society for Information Science American Society for Information Science, 55*(4), 373–381.

Shannon, C. E., & Weaver, W. (1949). *The mathematical theory of communication.* Urbana, IL: University of Illinois Press.

Shariful, I. M., & Nazmul, I. M. (2006). Information and Communication Technology (ICT) for Librarianship. *Asian Journal of Information Technology, 5*(8), 809–817.

Shen, Y. (2007). Information Seeking in Academic Research: A Study of the Sociology Faculty at the University of Wisconsin-Madison. *Information Technology and Libraries,* 4-13.

Sheshadri, K. N., Shivalingaiah, D., & Manjunatha, K. (2011) *Library consortia in United Arab Emirates: an opinion survey.* Paper presented at the Asia-Pacific Conference On Library & Information Education & Practice 2011 (A-LIEP2011): Issues, Challenges and Opportunities, 22-24 June 2011, Pullman Putrajaya Lakeside, Malaysia.

Shokane, J. K. (2002). Towards meeting the information needs of small- and medium-sized enterprises in Acornhoek. *Mousaion, 20*(20), 34–48.

Shokeen, A., & Kushik, S. K. (2002). Information-seeking behavior of social scientists of Haryana universities. *Library Herald, 40*(1), 8–11.

Siddiqui, M. A. (2003). Adoption of the Internet for resource sharing by the Gulf academic libraries. *The Electronic Library, 21*(1), 56–62. doi:10.1108/02640470310462425.

Sievert, D., & Sievert, M. E. (1989). Philosophical research: Report from the field. In *Proceedings of the Humanists at Work symposium* (pp. 79-94).Chicago, IL: Institute for Schema.

Silver, K. (2002). Pressing the 'Send' Key–Preferential journal access in developing countries. *Learned Publishing, 15*(2), 91–98. doi:10.1087/09531510252848845.

Smeltzer, L. R., Fann, G. L., & Nikolaisen, V. N. (1988). Environmental scanning practices in small business. *Journal of Small Business Management, 2*(3), 55–62.

Solomon, P. (2002). Discovering information in context. In Cronin, B. (Ed.), *Annual Review of Information Science and Technology, 36, 229- 264.*

Sonnenwald, D. H. (1999). Evolving perspectives of human information behavior: Contexts, situations, social networks and information horizons. In Wilson, T., & Allen, D. (Eds.), *Exploring the contexts of information behavior* (pp. 176–190). London: Taylor Graham.

Sookhtanlo, M., Mohammadi, H. M., & Rezvanfar, A. (2010). A comparative study of the information-seeking behavior of bachelor of science and master of science agricultural extension and education students. *Library philosophy and practice.* Retrieved on December 27, 2012, from http://unllib.unl.edu/lpp/sookhtanlo-mohammadi-rezvanfar.htm

Soper, M. E. (1976). Characteristics and use of personal collections. *The Library Quarterly, 46*(4), 397–415. doi:10.1086/620584.

Specht, P. H. (1987). Information sources used for strategic planning decisions in small firms. *American Journal of Small Business, 12*, 21–34.

Spink, A., & Jansen, B. J. (2004). *Web search: Public searching of the Web.* Boston, MA: Kluwer Academic Publishers.

Spink, A., Ozmutlu, H. C., & Ozmutlu, S. (2002). Multitasking information seeking and searching processes. *Journal of the American Society for Information Science American Society for Information Science, 53*(8), 639–652. doi:10.1002/asi.10124.

Steenbakkers, J. F. (2005). Digital archiving in the twenty-first century: Practice at the National Library of the Netherlands. *Library Trends, 54*(1), 33–56. doi:10.1353/lib.2006.0010.

Stephens, M., & Collins, M. (2007). Web 2.0, Library 2.0 and the Hyperlinked Library. *Serials Review, 33*(4), 253–256. doi:10.1016/j.serrev.2007.08.002.

Stevan, H. (2003). Open access to peer-reviewed research through author/institution self-archiving: Maximizing research impact by maximizing online access. In Derek, L., & Andrews, J. (Eds.), *Digital Libraries: Policy Planning and Practice.* London: Ashgate Publishing.

Stuart, N., & Nelson, K. (2012). Trends from the Canadian IR/ETD Survey 2012. Retrieved on November 4, 2012, from http://dspace.library.uvic.ca:8080/bitstream/handle/1828/3845/Stuart_Nelson_Trends_2012.pdf?sequence=7

Sturges, P., & Neill, R. (1990). *The quite struggle: Libraries and information for Africa.* London: Mansell.

Suber, P. (2007). Comment to report published the Publishing Research Corporation. *Open Access News.* Retrieved on September 6, 2010, from http://www.earlham.edu/~peters/fos/2007_05_13_fosblogarchive.html

Sun, Hao-Chang, Chen, Kuan-nien, Tseng, C., Tsai, Wen-Hui. (2011). Role changing for librarians in the new information technology era. *New Library World, 112*(7/8), 321–333. doi:10.1108/03074801111150459.

Swan, A. (2010). *The open access citation advantage: Studies and results to date.* Technical Report, Scholarly of Electronics and Computer Science, University of Southampton. Retrieved on September 6, 2010, from http://eprints.ecs.soton.ac.uk/18516/

Tatnall, A. (2004). *Web Portals: The New Gateways to Internet Information and Services.* Hershey, PA: Idea Group Publishing. doi:10.4018/978-1-59140-438-5.

Taylor, R. S. (1962). The process of asking questions. *American Documentation, 13*(4), 391–396. doi:10.1002/asi.5090130405.

Taylor, R. S. (1968). Questioning-negotiation and information seeking in libraries. *College & Research Libraries, 29*, 178–194.

Taylor, R. S. (1991). Information use environments. In Derwin, B., & Voigt, M. J. (Eds.), *Progress in Communication Sciences* (pp. 217–255). Norwood, NJ: Ablex.

Tenopir, C. (2003). *Use and users of electronic library resources: An overview and analysis of recent research studies.* Washington, DC: Council on Library and Information Resources. Retrieved on May 12, 2005, from http://www.clir.org/pubs/abstract/pub120abst.html

Tenopir, C., & King, D. (2001). *Electronic journals: How user behaviour is changing in online information.* Oxford, London: Learned Information Europe Ltd..

Tenopir, C., King, D. W., Boyce, P., Grayson, M., Zhang, Y., & Ebuen, M. (2003). Patterns of journal use by scientists through three evolutionary phases. *D-Lib Magazine, 9*(5). doi:10.1045/may2003-king.

Tenopir, C., King, D. W., & Bush, A. (2004). Medical faculty's use of print and electronic journals: Changes over time and in comparison with scientists. *Journal of the Medical Library Association, 92*(2), 233–241. PMID:15098053.

Tenopir, C., King, D. W., Edwards, S., & Wu, L. (2009). Electronic journals and changes in scholarly article seeking and reading patterns. *Aslib Proceedings, 61*(1), 5–32. doi:10.1108/00012530910932267.

The World Bank. (2012). *Data: Country and lending groups*. Retrieved on June 2, 2012, from http://data. worldbank.org/about/country-classifications/country-and-lending-groups

Thomas, D. R. (2006). A general inductive approach for analyzing qualitative evaluation data. *The American Journal of Evaluation, 27*(2), 237–256. doi:10.1177/1098214005283748.

Thomas, V. K., Satpathi, C., & Satpathi, J. N. (2010). Emerging challenges in academic librarianship and role of library associations in professional updating. *Library Management, 31*(8/9), 594–609. doi:10.1108/01435121011093379.

Thomson. (2008). *ISI Web of Knowledge. Journal Citation Report*. Retrieved on April 16, 2008, from http://admin-apps.isiknowledge.com/JCR/JCR

Thomson. (2008). *The Thomson scientific journal selection process*. Retrieved on April 19, 2008, from http://scientific.thomson.com/free/essays/selectionofmaterial

Thurik, R., & Wennekers, S. (2004). Entrepreneurship, small business and economic growth. *Journal of Small Business and Enterprise Development, 11*(1), 140–149. doi:10.1108/14626000410519173.

Tiratel, S. R. (2000). Accessing information use by humanities and social scientists: A study at the Universidad de Buenos Aires, Argentina. *Journal of Academic Librarianship, 26*(5), 346–354. doi:10.1016/S0099-1333(00)00141-5.

Tobias, C. L. (1987). Computers and the Elderly: A Review of the Literature and Directions for Future Research. *Proceedings of the Human Factors and Ergonomics Society Annual Meeting, 31*(8), 866–870.

Tombros, A., Ruthven, I., & Jose, J. (2005). How users assess web pages for information-seeking. *Journal of the American Society for Information Science and Technology, 56*(4), 327–344. doi:10.1002/asi.20106.

Tomney, H., & Burton, P. F. (1998). Electronic journals: A study of usage and attitudes among academics. *Journal of Information Science, 24*(6), 419–429. doi:10.1177/016555159802400605.

Tritt, S. (2008). Report on digital libraries in Ghana. Retrieved November 20, 2012, from http://www.indiana. edu/~libsalc/african/ALN125/125DigLibsGhana.html

Ţurlea, G., & Ciupagea, C. (2009). Happy e-Inclusion? The case of Romania. *Romanian Journal of Economic Forecasting, 110*.

Ucak, O. N., & Kurbanoglu, S. S. (1998). Information need and information seeking behavior of scholars at a Turkish university. *64th IFLA General Conference*. Retrieved on June 20, 2006, from http://www.ifla.org/IV/ifla64/041- 112e.htm

Ugah, A. U. (2007). Obstacles to information access and use in developing countries. *Library Philosophy and Practice*. Retrieved June 23, 2011, from http://digitalcommons.unl.edu/libphilprac/160

Uhegbu, A. N. (2002). *The information user: Issues and themes*. Enugu, Nigeria: John Jacobs Classics.

Ukoha, O. (n.d.). *Igwe Harnessing Information Technology for the 21st Century: Library Education in Nigeria*. Retrieved April 15, 2011, from http://www.webpages. uidaho.edu/~mbolin/igwe.htm

UNESCO. (1995). *Policy paper for change and development in higher education*. Paris.

UNESCO. (1998). Harnessing Information Technology for Development in Africa. Retrieved on April 5, 2011, from http://www.unesco.org/education/educprog/Iwf/doc/IAI.html

UNESCO. (2003). The Prague Declaration: Towards and information literate society. Retrieved on December 3, 2012, from http://portal.unesco.org/ci/en/ev.php-URL_ID=19636&URL_DO=DO_TOPIC&URL_SECTION=201.html

UNESCO. (2012). Community Multimedia Centers. Retrieved on December 3, 2012, from http://portal.unesco. org/ci/en/ev.php-URL_ID=1263&URL_DO=DO_TOPIC&URL_SECTION=201.html

United States International Trade Commission. (2010, November). *Small and medium-sized enterprises: Characteristics and performance* (USITC Publication 4189). Retrieved on June 2, 2012, from http://www.usitc.gov/publications/332/pub4189.pdf

University of Illinois. (2009). *The cost of journals*. Retrieved on June 15, 2009, from http://www.library.illinois.edu/scholcomm/journalcosts.html

Vakkari, P. (2000). Relevance and contributing information types of searched documents in task performance. In *Proceedings of SIGIR 2000 conference, Athens* (pp. 2-9). New York: ACM.

Vakkari, P. (2001). A theory of task-based information retrieval. *The Journal of Documentation, 57*(1), 44–60. doi:10.1108/EUM0000000007075.

Vakkari, P. (2003). Task-based information searching. *Annual Review of Information Science & Technology, 37*, 413–464. doi:10.1002/aris.1440370110.

Vakkari, P., Pennanen, M., & Serola, S. (2003). Changes of search terms and tactics while writing a research proposal: A longitudinal case study. *Information Processing & Management, 39*(3), 445–463. doi:10.1016/S0306-4573(02)00031-6.

Valenzuela, J. S., & Valenzuela, A. (1978). Modernization and dependency: Alternative perspectives in the study of Latin American underdevelopment. *Comparative Politics, 10*(4), 535–557. doi:10.2307/421571.

Vickery, B. C. (2000). *Scientific communication in history*. Lanham, MD: Scarecrow Press Inc..

Villen-Rueda, L., Senso, J. A., & Moya-Anegon, F. D. (2007). The use of OPAC in a large academic library: A transactional log analysis study of subject searching. *Journal of Academic Librarianship, 33*(3), 327–337. doi:10.1016/j.acalib.2007.01.018.

Vintilă, M. (2000). La maisnie diffuse, du communisme au capitalisme: Questions et hypotheses. *Balkanaulogie, 4*(2).

Virkus, S. (2007). Collaboration in LIS education in Europe: Challenges and opportunities. Proceedings of the World Library and Information Congress: 73rd IFLA General Conference and Council. Libraries for the future: Progress, Development and Partnerships, 19-23 August 2007, Durban, South Africa.

Vreins, D. (2005). Information and Communication Technology: Tools for competitive inteligence. Encyclopedia of Information Science and Technology, 3, 1-6.

Wagner, N., Hassanein, K., & Head, M. (2010). Computer use by older adults: A multi-disciplinary review. *Computers in Human Behavior, 26*, 870–882. doi:10.1016/j.chb.2010.03.029.

Walters, T. N., Kadragic, A., & Walters, L. M. (2006). Miracle or mirage: is development sustainable in the United Arab Emirates? *Middle East Review of International Affairs, 10*(3), 79.

Wang, M.-L. (2010). Scholarly journal use and reading behavior of social scientists in Taiwan. *The International Information & Library Review, 42*(4), 269–281.

Wang, P., Berry, M., & Yang, Y. (2003). Mining longitudinal Web queries: Trends and patterns. *Journal of the American Society for Information Science and Technology, 54*, 743–758. doi:10.1002/asi.10262.

Wang, P., Hawk, W. B., & Tenopir, C. (2000). Users' interaction with World Wide Web resources: An exploratory study using a holistic approach. *Information Processing & Management, 36*, 229–251. doi:10.1016/S0306-4573(99)00059-X.

Warner, D. (2002). Why do we need to keep this in print? It's on the web...: A review of electronic archiving issues and problems. *Progressive Librarian*(19-10), 47-64.

Warschahuer, M. (2008). Laptops and literacy: A multi-site case study. *Pedagogies: An International Journal, 3*, 52-67. Retrieved on April 30, 2012, from http://www.gse.uci.edu/person/warschauer_m/docs/II-pedagogies.pdf

Warschahuer, M. (2008). *A Literacy Approach to the Digital Divide*. Oakland, CA: University of California. Retrieved April 30, 2012, from http://www.gse.uci.edu/markw

Warschahuer, M. (2008). Whither the digital divide? In D.L. Kleinman et al. (Eds), *Controversies in Science & Technology: From climate to chromosomes*. New Rochelle, NY: Liebert. Retrieved April 30, 2012, from http://www.gse.uci.edu/person/warschauer_m/docs/whither.pdf

Weiler, A. (2005). Information-seeking behavior in Generation Y students: Motivation, critical thinking, and learning theory. *Journal of Academic Librarianship, 31*(1), 46–53. doi:10.1016/j.acalib.2004.09.009.

Wengfeng, M., & Liqing, W. (1999). *Toward Twenty First Century: Research of social science information services of University Libraries in China.* Paper presented at the 65th IFLA Conference. Bangkok, Thailand.

Whipple, M., & Nyce, J. M. (2007). Community analysis needs ethnography: An example from Romania. *Library Review, 56*(8), 694–706. doi:10.1108/00242530710818027.

Whitaker, B. (2009). *What's really wrong with the Middle East.* London: Saqi Books.

Whitmire, E. (2001). The relationship between undergraduates' background characteristics and college experiences and their academic library use. *College & Research Libraries, 62*(6), 528–540.

Wiberley, S., & Jones, W. G. (1989). Patterns of information seeking in the humanities. *College & Research Libraries, 50*, 638–645.

Wicks, D. A. (2003). Building bridges for seniors: Older adults and the digital divide. Retrieved June 21, 2012, from http://www.cais-acsi.ca/proceedings/2003/Wicks_2003.pdf

Widen-Wuilff, G., Huvilla, I., & Holmberg, K. (2008). Library 2.0 as a new participatory context. In Pagani, M. (Ed.), *Encyclopedia of Multimedia Technology and Networking* (pp. 842–848). Hershey, PA: IGI Global. doi:10.4018/978-1-60566-014-1.ch115.

Willson, R., & Given, L. M. (2010). The effect of spelling and retrieval system familiarity on search behavior in online public access catalogs: A mixed methods study. *Journal of the American Society for Information Science and Technology, 61*(12), 2461–2476. doi:10.1002/asi.21433.

Wilson, T. D. (1996). *Information behavior: An interdisciplinary perspective.* Sheffield, UK: University of Sheffield. Retrieved June 10, 2012, from http://informationr.net/tdw/publ/infbehav/cont.html

Wilson, T. D., & Streatfield, D. R. (1981). *Action research and users' needs.* Retrieved on June 16, 2006, from http://informationr.net/tdw/publ/papers/action81.html

Wilson, T. D., Ford, N. J., Ellis, D., Foster, A. E., & Spink, A. (2000, August). *Uncertainty and its correlates.* Paper presented at Information Seeking in Context. Gothenburg, Sweden.

Wilson, B. (1992). *Information Technology: The Basics.* London: Macmillan.

Wilson, T. D. (1981). On user studies and information needs. *The Journal of Documentation, 37*(1), 3–15. doi:10.1108/eb026702.

Wilson, T. D. (1999). Models of information behavior research. *The Journal of Documentation, 55*(3), 249–270. doi:10.1108/EUM0000000007145.

Wilson, T. D. (2000). Human information behavior. *Informing Science, 3*(2), 49–55.

Wise, M. (1985). *Aspects of African Librarianship: A collection of writings.* London: Mansell.

World Bank. (2007). *Mongolia: Building the skills for the new economy.* Retrieved on July 30, 2011, from http://www.worldbank.org.mn

World Bank. (2011). *Mongolia quarterly economic update.* Retrieved on July 6, 2010, from http://www.worldbank.org.mn

World Vision. (2009). *Mongolia country report.* Retrieved on July 30, 2011, from http://worldvision.org/content.nsf/learn/world-vision-mongolia

Xie, B. (2006). Perceptions of computer learning among older Americans and older Chinese. *First Monday, 11*(10). Retrieved June 21, 2012, from http://www.firstmonday.org/htbin/cgiwrap/bin/ojs/index.php/fm/article/view/1408/1326

Yadamsuren, B., & Raber, D. (2007). Information seeking behavior of Mongolian scholars. *Proceedings of the American Society for Information Science and Technology (ASIS&T) conference, 44*(1), 1-4.

Yao, D., Qiu, Y., Huang, H., Du, Z., & Ma, J. (2011). A survey of technology accessibility problems faced by older users in China. *Universal Access in the Information Society, 10*(4), 373–390. doi:10.1007/s10209-011-0222-3.

Yoon, K. (2002). *Certainty, uncertainty and the role of topic and comment in interpersonal information seeking interactions.* Unpublished Doctoral Dissertation, Syracuse University, Syracuse, NY.

Yuan, W. (1997). End-user searching behavior in information retrieval: A longitudinal study. *Journal of the American Society for Information Science American Society for Information Science, 48*(3), 218–234. doi:10.1002/(SICI)1097-4571(199703)48:3<218::AID-ASI4>3.0.CO;2-#.

Zaborowski, B. A. (2008). Identifying the information-seeking behaviors of students, the expectations of faculty, and the role of librarians in writing assignments that require students to use information sources in selected Pennsylvania community colleges: A model for instruction. Unpublished Doctoral dissertation, Pennsylvania.

Zhou, X. (2010). *Information in Healthcare: An Ethnographic Analysis of a Hospital Ward.* Unpublished Doctoral thesis. Ann Arbor, MI: University of Michigan. Retrieved on November 30, 2012, from http://deepblue.lib.umich.edu/bitstream/2027.42/78940/1/xmzhou_1.pdf

About the Contributors

Mohammed Nasser Al-Suqri is an assistant professor and the Head of the Department of Information Studies, College of Arts and Social Sciences, Sultan Qaboos University. He received his Ph.D. in Library and Information Management from Emporia State University, School of Library and Information Management, Emporia, USA; a Master's degree in Library and Information Science from Pratt Institute, School of Information and Library Science, New York, USA; and a Bachelor's degree in Library and Information Science from Sultan Qaboos University, Department of Library and Information Science, Sultanate of Oman. Mohammed Nasser Al-Suqri conducts research in the area of user studies, knowledge management and sharing, information industries, impact of new technology on academic libraries, digital divide, digital libraries, and LIS education and collaboration in the Middle East.

Linda L. Lillard holds undergraduate and graduate degrees in Business Education and an M.L.S. and Ph.D. in Library and Information Management from Emporia State University in Kansas. She was on the faculty at University of Central Missouri, University of Kentucky, and Emporia State University before she came home to Pennsylvania to Clarion University. Dr. Lillard's dissertation research was on the information seeking behaviors and information needs of people working in online environments, specifically eBay entrepreneurs. As an entrepreneur herself on several occasions: Taos Candy Factory in Taos, New Mexico, and Pak-n-Ship in Emporia, KS, Dr. Lillard has always been interested in the information needs of entrepreneurs. The advent of the online environment broadened her research interests to people working in an online environment and thus she has also studied embedded librarianship and worked with LIS students to embed them in online courses to assist other students with their information needs.

Naifa Eid Al-Saleem is an assistance professor at the Department of information studies and the assistant dean of training and community services, Sultan Qaboos University. He has a BA in Library Science and Documentation (1993). In 2001, she obtained her MA in Information Management from the University of Sheffield in the United Kingdom. She got her Ph.D. from the University of Exeter in the United Kingdom in 2006. Dr. Naifa's areas of interests are: e- learning, research methodology, and information seeking behavior. She published several articles in both Arabic and English in refereed journals.

* * *

Ismail Abdullahi is a Professor of Global Library and Information Science. He is a graduate of the Royal School of Library and Information science in Denmark. He has an MLS from North Carolina Central University and a Ph.D. from the University of Pittsburgh. Dr. Abdullahi is a recipient of many awards. Among them are: The Harold Lancour Award for Excellence in International and Comparative Study in Library and Information Science; The Meyers Center Award for the Study of Human Rights in the United Sates; Emerald Literati Award for Internationalization of Library Education in Europe and North America. Dr. Abdullahi has published two books, E. Josey: an Activist Librarian, Scarecrow, 1992; Global Library and Information Science: A Textbook for Students and Educators, IFLA Publications 136-137, K.G. Saur 2009 and numerous chapters in books and articles. His research interest includes Global Library and Information Science, Management and Leadership, Internationalization of Library Education, and Diversity and Intercultural Communication.

Simon Aristeguieta-Trillos was born in Caracas, Venezuela. In 1984, he graduated from the University of California, Berkeley. In 2002, he contributed to establishing the Scientific Electronic Library Online (SciELO), the Sistema Regional de Información en Línea para Revistas Científicas de América Latina, el Caribe, España y Portugal (Latindex) and the Curriculum Vitae en Ciencia y Tecnología (CVLAC). In 2003, he traveled to San Juan, Puerto Rico, where he studied Information Science at the University of Puerto Rico. There he focused his attention on citation analysis and bibliometric research. In 2010, he finished a Ph.D in Communication and Information from the University of Tennessee, Knoxville. His research led to develop a model of scholarly communication in a context of dependency. In 2011, he joined the Library Science faculty at Clarion University of Pennsylvania.

Stephen Asunka holds MA and Ed.D degrees in Instructional Technology and Media from Teachers College, Columbia University, New York, and is currently the Dean/Director of the Kumasi Campus of the Ghana Technology University College, Ghana. Stephen is passionate about the integration of digital technologies into all levels of education, with particular emphasis on higher education in the developing world where institutions have to contend with inadequate technology infrastructure and limited resources. His research work therefore focuses on evolving best practice frameworks and strategies for the efficient deployment of technology tools and resources in ways that will not only make knowledge and skills acquisition more accessible, but also result in more positive learning outcomes under developing world conditions.

Gail E. Bader, an assistant professor at Ball State University, received her Ph.D. from Brown University (Providence, Rhode Island, USA) in 1984. Bader, a cultural anthropologist, currently studies issues related to education and informational technology in contemporary American and Romanian life.

Lisa Block has worked as an academic librarian in the areas of access services, instruction, reference, and law. She has worked as a medical information consultant and is currently the Medical Librarian at the Atlanta Medical Center. Ms. Block earned her Master of Science degree in Library & Information Studies from Florida State University and her Bachelor's degree from Ohio University. She also works as a freelance writer and is a book reviewer for Library Journal. Her research interests include information needs of library users, barriers to information access, "library as place," eBooks, and digital publishing.

Collence Takaingenhamo Chisita is a principal lecturer of Library and Information Science. He is a graduate of the National University of Science and Technology Zimbabwe. He has an MLS from NUST and is completing a Ph.D. in Information Science. Chisita is a well renowned Information Science specialist who has done collaborations with a number of scholars within and outside Southern Africa. Chisita has raised the profile of LIS Education and profession in Zimbabwe and beyond. He strongly believes in the immense potential of collaboration. Collence Chisita has published the book *Perceptions shaping preferences: Print versus Electronic resources*. His papers are included in the *La solidarité intergénérationnelle dans les bibliothèques, The Road to Information Literacy,* all IFLA Publications K.G. Saur 2012 series and various other articles. Chisita's research interests include digital literacy, Use of social media, information retrieval, convergence of technology, and culture, curriculum, Digital preservation and access, comparative librarianship, knowledge Management intercultural communication.

María Cristina Pérez Giffoni was born in Montevideo in 1951. She graduated in Library Science, School of Library Science and Related Areas (EUBCA), Universidad de la República (UdelaR, Uruguay). She received a Graduate Diploma in Library and Archives, Scuola Vaticana di Biblioteconomia, and Scuola di Paleografia, Diplomatica e Archivistica, Città del Vaticano (1981-1982). She is an associate professor and researcher in the Department of Reference, Bibliography, and User Information Studies. She is an Academic Coordinator of Bachelor in Library Science, EUBCA. She is a researcher in the Scholar Development Program of Information and Communication. PRODIC–UdelaR. She has presented papers at national and international events and is the author of several publications. Her recent book is *Los estudios de usuarios de información: Construcción de una línea de investigación y docencia en el Uruguay* (Information user studies: constructing a research and teaching field in Uruguay), co-author: Martha Sabelli. Montevideo: CSIC /UdelaR, 2010.

Laura González is Computer Engineer (University of the Republic, Uruguay) and she holds a Master's degree in Computer Science. She is an associate professor of the Computer Science Department at the University of the Republic of Uruguay, where she lectures on Enterprise Application Platforms, Information Systems, and Middleware. Since 2004, she has worked in consulting, research projects, and teaching activities at this department. Her research interests include middleware technologies, enterprise application integration, interoperability, service oriented computing, e-government, and digital inclusion. She is currently working on her Ph.D. thesis in the area of integration platforms for service based systems.

YooJin Ha earned a Ph.D. in Library and Information Science from Rutgers University in 2008 and an MLS at the State University of New York at Buffalo in 2003. She also has a Bachelor's of Art in Library and Information Science from Yonsei University, Seoul, Korea, in 1991. Currently YooJin Ha works in the Department of Library Science at Clarion University of Pennsylvania, USA, since Fall 2009. Her work experience includes serving as a reference librarian at the East Brunswick Public Library in New Jersey, a metadata indexer for two digital library projects at the Scholarly Communication Center (SCC) within the Rutgers University Library system, and a cataloger at the central library of Yonsei University in Korea. Her research interests include users' information seeking behavior, user studies including needs assessment, access to multilingual bibliographic information, library system evaluation, evaluation of online retrieval systems, and information organization.

Manir Abdullahi Kamba is a lecturer with the Department of Library and Information Sciences, Bayero University, Kano, Nigeria. Dr. Kamba obtained his Ph.D. from the International Islamic University, Malaysia. He has also published articles in reputable journals both internationally and nationally. Dr.

Kamba has also presented papers at both international and national conferences. His areas of specialization are information seeking behaviour, research methodology, and statistics in library and information science, with special interest to ICT application and information science.

Cheryl Klimaszewski is a librarian and researcher based in Philadelphia, Pennsylvania. She has been studying various issues in ICT policy, information use, and cultural heritage preservation in Romania since 2007. She holds an MS-LIS from the iSchool at Drexel University and currently works as the Digital Collections Specialist at Bryn Mawr College.

Gantulga Lkhagva is the executive director of Mongolian Libraries Consortium, a non-government organization which is responsible for e-resources license negotiations, open access resources development, and building local capacity in Mongolia. He is the country coordinator of the EIFL and INASP. His research interests are in the open access, library science, and bibliometric analysis. His focus specifically is centered on conducting a bibliometric analysis for Mongolian researchers and the role played by open access and the development of institutional repositories in Mongolia.

Rebecca L. Miller holds a MLS and Ph.D. in Library and Information Management from Emporia State University, Emporia, Kansas, USA. During her doctoral work, she was a lead organizer on an international library conference held biennially in Sofia, Bulgaria. This work led her to study the diffusion of professional knowledge between American and Bulgarian librarians for her dissertation. She has been a director of an undergraduate information studies program, an assistant professor in library science, and currently is working with a think tank in Afghanistan. She is Founder and Principal of Realm Advising, LLC, a research consultancy firm.

James M. Nyce is an associate professor at Ball State University and received his Ph.D. from Brown University in 1987. Nyce, a cultural anthropologist, studies how information technologies emerge and are used in different workplaces and organizations. A docent (in Informatics) at Linköping University, Sweden, Nyce is also adjunct associate professor in the Department of Radiology, Indiana University School of Medicine, Indianapolis, IN.

Eduardo Álvarez Pedrosian was born in Montevideo in 1975. He has a Ph. D. in Philosophy: History of Subjectivity from the University of Barcelona (UB, Catalonia, Spain) and Diplomaed in Advances Studies for the same University. He graduated in Anthropological Sciences, Universidad de la República (UdelaR, Uruguay). He is a professor and researcher in the Department of Human and Social Sciences (LICCOM-UdelaR) and different postgraduate programs. He is a researcher in the Scholar Development Program of Information and Communication (PRODIC, UdelaR). He's also a member of the National System of Researches (SNIANII) and the Uruguayan Association of Social Anthropology (AUAS). He has lectured and published books, chapters, and papers in Uruguay, Argentina, Brazil, Chile, and Spain on philosophy of humanities and social sciences, processes of subjectivation, and contemporary ethnography.

Jorge Rasner was born in Montevideo, Uruguay on December 16, 1957. He is married and he is the father of three sons. He holds a Bachelor's degree in Philosophy and a Master's degree in Human Sciences, Universidad de la República (UdelaR), Uruguay. He has been an associate professor at UdelaR since 1990, where he lectures on Science, Technology and Society (Facultad de Ingeniería) and *Epistemology of communication sciences* (Licenciatura en Ciencias de la Comunicación, LICCOM). He also performs postgraduate teaching activities at Instituto de Perfeccionamiento y Estudios Superiores (Administración Nacional de Educación Pública). He coordinates the Communication Theory area at LICCOM. He has also published papers and books on his area.

Raúl Ruggia is Computer Engineer (University of the Republic, Uruguay) and received his Ph.D. in Computer Science from the University of Paris VI (France). He is a full professor in the Computer Science Department of the University of the Republic of Uruguay, where he lectures on information systems, supervises graduate students, and directs research activities on middleware, data quality management, and data warehousing. He has also supervised technological projects on eGovernment and telecommunications domains joint with Uruguayan government agencies.

Martha Sabelli is professor and senior researcher at the Information and Society Department, School of Library Science and Related Areas, University of the Republic, Uruguay. She received her Ph.D. in Information Science from the University of Alcalá, Spain. She is an expert in information services for the citizens in the information society and has been in charge of research projects on user studies and human information behavior. The two latter projects are directly related to social inclusion and the digital gap and community information services for citizens in vulnerable situations. She is also a member of the National Researchers System of Uruguay. She has written various books and articles about these topics and has also participated in national and international events in Argentina, Brazil, Chile, England, Japan, México, and Spain.

Thomas Scheiding is an Assistant Professor of Economics and the Chair of the Business Administration Program at Cardinal Stritch University in Milwaukee, Wisconsin. His research interests are in the social studies of science in the 20th century. His focus specifically is on how the research infrastructure in a country and in a discipline is the result of contested negotiations between scholars, research administrators, and librarians. His future research interests remain centered on changes to the academic infrastructure in Mongolia and specifically on how the discipline of economics has changed in an environment of wider economic and social changes.

Borchuluun Yadamsuren is a user experience researcher at the School of Information Science and Learning Technologies of the University of Missouri. Her research focus is information behavior of different user groups in everyday life information seeking context, serendipitous information discovery, and scholarly communication. With her ongoing research in scholarly communication, she aims to explore what obstacles scholars in developing countries face in order to participate in the global scholarly communication process and what needs to be done to overcome these challenges.

Index